The Ethics of Kinship

The Ethics of Kinship

Ethnographic Inquiries

James D. Faubion

ROWMAN & LITTLEFIELD PUBLISHERS, INC.
Lanham • *Boulder* • *New York* • *Oxford*

ROWMAN & LITTLEFIELD PUBLISHERS, INC.

Published in the United States of America
by Rowman & Littlefield Publishers, Inc.
4720 Boston Way, Lanham, Maryland 20706
www.rowmanlittlefield.com

12 Hid's Copse Road
Cumnor Hill, Oxford OX2 9JJ, England

British Library Cataloguing in Publication Information Available

Library of Congress Cataloging-in-Publication Data

The ethics of kinship : ethnographic inquiries / [edited by] James D. Faubion.
    p. cm.
  Includes bibliographical references and index.
  ISBN 0-7425-0955-9 (cloth : alk. paper)—ISBN 0-7425-0956-7 (pbk. : alk. paper)
   1. Kinship. I. Faubion, James D., 1957–

GN487 .E86 2001
306.83—dc21

                                     00-054442

Printed in the United States of America

∞™ The paper used in this publication meets the minimum requirements of
American National Standard for Information Sciences—Permanence of Paper
for Printed Library Materials, ANSI/NISO Z39.48-1992.

For Professor Gail M. Kelly

On her retirement from the Department of Anthropology,

Reed College, Portland, Oregon, May 2000

Teacher, Scholar, Intellectual

Contents

Acknowledgments

This volume is appearing later than I had originally planned, and the responsibility for its delay is entirely my own. I would like to thank all the contributors for their patient tolerance of my distraction. The volume bears many of the marks of the Department of Anthropology at Rice University, where I have been teaching for more than seven years. I thank my students, graduate and undergraduate, for the ongoing inspiration and stimulation that they have provided me. I thank the chair, George Marcus, for his unflagging support and his critical readings. Thanks, too, to Lamia Karim, Kathryn Milun, and Paul Rabinow for their comments on my introduction. On behalf of all the contributors, I would especially like to thank Kath Weston, who revealed herself ex post facto to have undertaken to review the volume for Roman & Littlefield, and whose learned, generous, and acute scrutiny has been of great benefit to all the works that follow, mine included. I would also like to take this opportunity to thank the Rice University Center for the Study of Institutions and Values and Center for the Study of Cultures, for having offered financial support for the conference out of which the volume grew; and Carole Speranza, for having put up with it all.

Introduction

Toward an Anthropology of the Ethics of Kinship

James D. Faubion

Kinship once seemed the most exhaustively charted of anthropological territories. In the last two decades or so, it has proven at once more expansive and more complex than established cartographies had previously revealed it to be. What it has yielded has come in some measure through a methodological shift of attention. An older ecology was able to determine a rough but systematic correlation between modes of the organization of production and reproduction and modes of the terminological classification and effective extension of kin relations.[1] Its results continue to be the stuff of the standard anthropological textbook. A more recent turn toward interinstitutional analysis has, however, brought to light more intimate correlations, more intimate sensitivities and entanglements; the nation-state, the law, the church, the symbolic economies of gender and sexuality all might have their effects on kinship, which might have its effects on all of them in turn.[2] An older formalism was able to elaborate a typology of kinship systems and, after the publication of Claude Lévi-Strauss's *Elementary Structures of Kinship* (1969), to press increasingly for the theoretical primacy of alliance (in and through marriage) over filiation or descent. A more recent turn away from the semantics to the pragmatics of kinship systems, from the rules to the practices of relating as kin, however, has shown matters of form to be a poor guide at best to the more messy content of daily life.[3] People "fudge"—quite often with the blithe complicity of those around them. They make kin; they change kin; they forge and consecrate alliances, of greatly diverse sorts, in the very vocabulary of filiation and descent.[4] If the older anthropology of kinship is thus still with us, it has also had to endure the perturbations of an ever more unruly "supplement" (a term that I use, in its Derridean sense, to denote the

1

necessary and perhaps antithetical resolution of a primary, a hegemonic, an intellectually comfortable category).

The scholarship included in this volume further enriches that supplement—enlarging it, reflecting upon it, puzzling over it. In much shorter and more provisional form, most of the chapters were originally produced for a course on significant directions in anthropological thought since World War II, which I offered at Rice University in the fall semester of 1996. One-third of the course was devoted to kinship; toward the end of the course I asked those enrolled (1) to represent their own kinship system graphically in any way they thought most perspicacious, and (2) to offer a considered account of the picture they had drawn. Graphically, methodologically, and analytically, what they produced was provocative enough to inspire a conference the following year. Entitled Kinship and Cosmopolitanism, it brought John Borneman from Cornell to serve as keynote speaker, and Susan Ossman, now at the American University of Paris, to serve as discussant. Professors Borneman and Ossman have contributed their own papers to the volume (see chapters 1 and 7), as have several other of my students who were not part of the original cohort.[5] A few of those who chose to participate in the conference expressed—and perhaps would continue to express—concern that the autobiographical point of departure that I had imposed upon them could all too easily lead an unwitting, or in any event unwilling, exercise in "self-exoticization," and so, of self-colonization (see especially chapter 4 by Lamia Karim in this volume). Such, perhaps, are the current horizons of reception. Yet, I must hope that it is more than simply futile to point out that not one of the works flashes that pretty coin of "native authority" that so often has exoticism as its other side. Whether implicitly or—most often—explicitly, all begin instead by putting the self into anthropological question, proceeding from the inevitable singularity of the "I" to its status as a "subject," and from that status to the broader arenas in which any single subject is never more than one among many others. The self remains, but as a creature composed in part of what *is* always already not (exclusively) itself, always already somewhat the same as another, a subject that is always already intersubjective. Hence, exoticization must have its limits—one of them, in the alterity that each self has in common with every other. Current horizons of reception aside, the reflexive investigation of shared alterity does not and in fact cannot rest merely on the authority of the ethnographic "I/eye." It must also rest on the pragmatic or heuristic authority of those concepts that anthropology and its allied disciplines have fashioned to address the intersubjective domain itself, or at the very least on the authority of concepts that, whether imported or novel, are similarly intersubjective in their scope. The gaze of such investigation is consequently never omphalic. Its I's and its eyes are of necessity multiple and stereoscopic.

Kinship is in fact illustrative of the constitution of intersubjectivity, of organized alterity, in two respects. First, even when "descriptive" or "egocentric," the terms of kinship are very like those of offices, open to any number of individuals who happen (more often than not, as a matter of birth) to be qualified to occupy them. My mother may thus be unique, but mothers (and sons) are legion. Second, the terms of kinship are inherently linking terms; always and everywhere, they render the self in and through its relation to certain others (and vice versa). Mothers are thus who they are only because of their sons (or daughters); children are who they are only because of their mothers (or fathers). Yet such features as these hardly reveal all that is distinctive about kinship, semantically or pragmatically; much less do they reveal what seems to be exclusive to it. The works in this volume contribute to its more complete, and more precise, comprehension.

To begin with, however, it is better to turn to the tension, the apparent paradox, that animates virtually all of the pieces, if some more vividly than others. The tension at issue was by no means previously ignored, but it has become less bridled and more salient as supplemental research has increased. It has invited many phrasings, most of them familiar if not altogether adequate. So, for example, it has appeared in the guise of the tension between the putatively "natural" basis of kinship and the many obvious cases of its "invention,"[6] or between the putatively ascriptive and putatively permanent character of kinship relations and their frequent construction and reconstruction,[7] or between the putative "givenness" of kinship and its widespread susceptibility to refiguration.[8] Beneath all these guises lurks much the same, protean presence: a mode of organizing alterity that appears to rest on a biologically definite ground from which it nevertheless tends to float free; or to put it inversely: a framework of ostensibly conventional relationships, prohibitions, and obligations at least some of which are in fact so widespread, so profoundly compelling, and so little variable that they seem direct expressions of "human nature."

AFTER NATURALISM, AFTER SCHNEIDER

In *The Elementary Structures of Kinship*, Lévi-Strauss traces the dual face of kinship to the dual face of what he deems every kinship system's cardinal principle: the prohibition of incest between mothers and their sons, fathers and their daughters, and brothers and their sisters. The thesis that he defends construes that prohibition as the logical and functional equivalent of what Marcel Mauss had already identified as the cardinal principle of all systems of reciprocal exchange: the obligation to give to another an object one possesses as one's own. Correlatively, men emerge as the agents of the lineal groups to which they belong; women (in the logically simplest system, their sisters) are the objects, the gifts, that they dutifully pass between them from one generation to another. Lévi-Strauss's theoretical allegiances lie with cybernetics, not sociobiology. Yet, aiming to account for the universality at once of the incest taboo and of the horror that its violation inspires, he is unable to resist appealing to certain "facts of nature." For Lévi-Strauss:

> Women are a natural stimulant, and the only stimulant of which the satisfaction can be deferred, and consequently the only one for which, in the act of exchange, and through the awareness of reciprocity, the transformation from stimulant to sign can take place, and, defining by this fundamental process the transformation from nature to culture, assume the character of an institution. (1969: 62–63)

The bonds of "fraternity and paternity"—between brothers and their sisters, and between fathers and their daughters—are, moreover, further "facts of nature" that the incest taboo must specifically override (1969: 42). Should it fail, should "nature" not give way to culture, little would remain but Thomas Hobbes's war of all against all, the endless repetition of Sigmund Freud's parricidal primal scene, and the regression into jealously asocial or antisocial atomism.

Lévi-Strauss himself would come to regard his distinction between nature and culture as of more methodological than theoretical interest. Even so, the naturalism of the explanatory edifice of *The Elementary Structures* is inescapable, and it has had its share of detractors. Edmund Leach (1970: 111–13) and Jack Goody (1990: 341–54, 381, 390–91) cite evidence from the archives of ancient Egypt and Rome that suggests that the prohibition of sex and marriage between siblings is somewhat less than strictly universal. Leach raises further objections to Lévi-Strauss's reduction of the prohibition of incestuous sexual intercourse to the prohibition of endogamy (marriage within a given lineal group). In an essay that has inspired wide-ranging discussions among feminists and analysts of gender and sexuality, Gayle Rubin argues that the postulation of a heteroerotic "instinct" serves only to mask a cultural intervention at least as fundamental as the incest taboo, and to which the heteroerotic "traffic in women" owes at least as much of its anthropological ubiquity: the taboo against homosexual intercourse and homosexual marriage (1975; cf. also Pateman 1988). The latter prohibition is far from universal in its own right; but the historical, cross-cultural, and intracultural variability of erotic attraction ultimately lends even greater weight to the premises from which Rubin proceeds.[9]

Within anthropology, however, the most thoroughgoing and perhaps most uncompromising skeptic of the naturalization of kinship remains the late David Schneider. His most constructive conclusion in *A Critique of the Study of Kinship* (1984)—that whatever else they are, kinship systems are symbolic systems, the interpretation of which must derive not from the analyst's but from the natives' point of view—is also the least original. Indeed, it is as venerable as the work of Bronislaw Malinowski, with whom the natives' point of view had one of its earliest champions. Yet Schneider demonstrates that not merely Malinowski but virtually all those anthropologists who would follow him (or Émile Durkheim before him) in urging that the facts of kinship are not natural but instead sociocultural have, with an eerie consistency, fallen into naturalism, often quite in spite of themselves (1984: chaps. 11–14). Such slippage is manifest in the most standard of the discipline's translational practices: the glossing of the kinship terminologies of non-Western peoples into one or another of those inescapably biologistic terminologies long established in Europe. In Schneider's view, that practice is "but a particular instance of the more general characteristic of European culture toward . . . 'biologistic' ways of conceiving human character, human nature, and human behavior" (175). The founding anthropological presumption that kinship is a primordial, universal, and organizationally fundamental system is for its part little more than a technical generalization of that distinctively European bit of folk wisdom that would have "blood be thicker than water" (165–75). Not least because of his own fieldwork among the Yapese, Schneider "seriously doubts" that folk everywhere hold to the same wisdom, and so seriously doubts that kinship is either as primordial, as universal, or as organizationally fundamental as his European colleagues, lay or professional, would be inclined to believe (175).

It would not be entirely arbitrary to suggest that, at least in the United States, the anthropological study of kinship might be divided into "pre-Schneiderian" and "post-Schneiderian" periods. Though it runs the risk of attributing far too much influence to Schneider himself, the periodization roughly and readily marks the ascendance of several trends that coalesce in his *Critique*. The disciplinary decline of kinship, which began in the restless reflexivity of the late 1960s, is only one such trend. Schneider further doubts the theoretical integrity of politics, of economics, and of religion—which along with kinship comprise the other three canonical members of anthropology's indispensable institutional quartet (1984: e.g., 184). He is suspicious of the concept of the primitive, and of the evolutionism from which it derives (163–73). He is methodologically suspicious as well of functionalism, which he considers irremediably imprecise (182–83), and of formalism, whether structuralist or cognitivist, which he considers analytically imperious (154–55). He suggests that nothing short of a "general overhaul" of the discipline is in order (201), and though he demurs from defining its complete agenda, he is prepared to specify its categorical imperative:

> Anthropology . . . is the study of particular cultures. *The first task of anthropology,* **prerequisite to all others**, *is to understand and to formulate the symbols and meanings and their configurations that a particular culture consists of.* (196; typography follows the original)

From the middle 1980s to very near the present, anthropologists in the culturological mainstream have largely agreed.

Much of what has been added to the anthropological discussion of kinship has followed the symbological precedent that Schneider himself proclaimed in the *Critique*, but established well before it, in *American Kinship* (1968). Noteworthy examples include the essays collected in Jane Collier and Sylvia Yanagisako's *Gender and Kinship* (1987), Kath Weston's *Families We Choose* (1991), Marilyn Strathern's *After Nature* (1992), and John Borneman's *Belonging in the Two Berlins* (1992). Collier and Yanagisako propose a parallel and "unified" critique of the naturalization of gender and of kinship and join many of their fellow contributors in underscoring not only the cross-cultural but also the historical variability of the former, of the latter, and of the links between them (1987: 29–42). Weston explores the tensions and the possibilities that have come to those gays and lesbians who have had to resort to familiar categories of kinship and affinity in defining the intimate relations into which they have entered as well as those into which they have been born. Strathern addresses the semiotics of English middle-class kinship, but also those economic, political, and technological forces to which she attributes its disruption since the 1960s. Borneman investigates the contests and the concessions that animated both official and personal "emplotments" of being-in-relation in the divided Germanies.

If neither thematically nor methodologically all-encompassing, such examples at least hint at the topical arenas within which research on kinship now typically unfolds.[10] They also suggest that the "overhaul" that Schneider seems to have imagined has been less than complete; kinship—not even to mention politics, religion, and economics—is still with us, even if its theoretical reputation is somewhat diminished. Schneider himself predicted that he would be taken more lightly than he thought he deserved—a single, wry aside that would appear to lay the blame on disciplinary inertia (1984: 182). Other reasons may nevertheless be at play. Not least, his conclusions are almost entirely negative; they lead to very little beyond a renewed program of the most meticulous "emic" description, which would at last (or so it seems to have been supposed) leave a long anthropological century of error and misjudgment behind. Moreover, they owe virtually all their force to a philosophy of social-scientific description, conceptualization, and comparison, the soundness of which is far from self-evident. Schneider tellingly declares:

> I have spoken of the Doctrine of the Genealogical Unity of Mankind as *essential* to the study of kinship. It states that genealogical relations *are the same* in every culture. If they were not, cross-cultural comparison *would not be possible*. (174; my emphasis)

Several paragraphs later, he declares further that "insofar as the comparative study of kinship is a tenable or legitimate endeavor, it must be assumed that kinship is a *unitary phenomenon*" (177; my emphasis). This is a self-conscious rejection of the analytical propriety of the "polythetic class," which

Ludwig Wittgenstein illuminated in his analysis of games and (not irrelevantly) "family resemblances" and which Rodney Needham subsequently put forward for broad anthropological service.[11] Jointly, these declarations imply in no uncertain terms that Schneider holds his own discipline to the very same epistemological standards that prevail in the natural sciences, or at least those that prevail in the positivistic philosophy of the natural sciences, for which concepts lacking either referential precision or "essential generalizability" are "bad" concepts and are especially ill suited for disciplinary foundations.[12] Hence, he suspects the very concept of kinship itself and that vast majority of other concepts that have made their way into anthropology from the collective conscience of the European "folk." His suspicion is not entirely misplaced. The tension between naturalistic and sociological notions of kinship is sufficient in itself to render "kinship" categorically vague. The very same tension renders the notion of kinship far less general than that of, say, an electron or a chromosome, even if not perhaps so context-bound as the notion of, say, originality or Monicagate.

Is the father of symbolic anthropology actually a positivist? Surprisingly enough, he may well be. In any event, he is not a hermeneutician. His anthropology is an enterprise properly or ideally devoted to the accumulation of particular cases and the induction from them of universal types. In that respect at least, his methodology of concept formation aspires to natural scientific rigor. Hermeneuticians reject such aspirations in the name of the historicity—the inevitable contingency, specificity, and contextuality—of all human artifacts, all human inventions, kinship included. Among historical things—from actions to languages—exact equivalences and invariant unities are rarely, if ever, to be found. Comparing one historical thing to another, the hermeneutician rarely, if ever, has anything more than an always somewhat "vague" family resemblance to note. His or her enterprise does not stand or fall with the divining of the universal. It places its stakes rather with contextual diagnosis and pragmatic translation, in "thick description" and "interpretive understanding."[13]

INTERPRETING KINSHIP

Schneider's apparent opposition notwithstanding, a hermeneutical or interpretive engagement with kinship is a live possibility, and it is precisely the possibility that Collier and Yanagisako, Weston, Strathern, Borneman, and with Borneman, the other contributors to this volume, actively pursue. None of them accordingly aspires to define kinship, whether by appeal to genealogical relations or by appeal to other relations of putatively universal scope. They are not compelled, either, to banish kinship from the anthropological fold merely because it has vulgar origins. If Schneider has liberated contemporary researchers from the theoretical tyranny of biologism, he has also run the risk of begging the issue of the ostensible prevalence, and the ostensible symbolic and normative power, of "blood" (among the contributors, see especially Reddy and Bargach). The hermeneutical principle of charity alone would render it hasty, even irresponsible, to dismiss as a likely ethnocentric lapse what ethnographers within Europe and outside of it have, after all, long been consistently reporting: that human beings very often, and very widely, treat "blood ties" as evidential criteria of what looks to be eminently translatable as "kinship," even if not the only, or always the most decisive, criteria of it. Such ties, in short, still belong in the roving interpreter's translation manual, even in the absence of a clear grammatical function or rationale. As it stands, however, that manual—a thing of many authors—has already begun to indicate that blood ties are themselves an important but still partial symbolism of what sociological and anthropological fashion would now have us speak of as "identity."

Kinship and Care

Among post-Schneiderians, Borneman has equipped a hermeneutics of kinship with an especially generous reach. His characterizations remain preliminary and in need of further refinement, but they have much virtue, even so. On the one hand, they steer elegantly clear of naturalization, whether of a biologistic or any other sort. On the other hand, they allow for a due regard of the extant ethnographic record, whether functionalist or structuralist or social-psychological in its orientation. In *Belonging in the Two Berlins*, he is perhaps closest to the functionalists in approaching kinship as a response to a distinctive network of enduring human concerns (even if not every human being's concerns). His formulation is, however, intentionally imprecise. He proposes that we understand kinship as comprising more or less anything and everything that has to do with "households, partnerships, childcare, and self" (1992: 77). Borneman thus underscores a strong affinity between the symbolism of kinship and the organization of the domestic sphere, but he does not aim to derive the former from the latter. In a departure from the majority of functionalists (and quite a few structuralists as well), Borneman refrains from attributing special theoretical importance to "the family" or the mother–child bond, even though the social policies of the Germanies of his study might well have tempted him to do so. He is also careful to clarify that kinship is not the only semiotic grid of domesticity. Amid the cultural and social experimentation of postwar Berliners, as in our current Age of Alternatives, other idioms might take occasional precedence—those of "friendship" and "love" prominent among them. Nor should we forget other experiments, in certain utopian collectives of nineteenth-century France and the United States, in the early Soviet

Union, and in Israel, that have sought to put kinship under the erasure of a more embracing semiotics of communitas.[14]

Kinship—descent and filiation—was nevertheless the idiom to which each of the Germanies, if each in its own manner, gave pride of place in constructing and executing postwar "domestic policy." Whence comes such a privilege? Borneman discerns it neither in nature nor even in the "survival" of common custom; as with most other things German, kinship did not in fact weather World War II altogether intact. He points instead to the strength and variety of interests vested in another affinity: between kinship and the ideology of the nation. An imagined community indeed, but imagined in the ultimate analysis as a genealogical unity, the German nation emerged from the war twice split: into West and East; but further into an older generation whose political enthusiasms had become literally unspeakable and a younger generation whose loyalties were profoundly shaken and confused (Borneman 1992: 188–95). Kinship served both of the Germanies as a primary matrix in their separate attempts to articulate a national body, from one related citizen to another. It served both of them as well in preserving the vision of the future articulation of two bodies, two collateral citizenries, into one (79). It served them—so it now seems—quite well. That it did so, however, has implications that extend far outside of their recently fused borders. Borneman's treatment suggests that kinship is likely to be near the forefront of the collective imaginary wherever the collective imaginary is also national, and likely all the more so when it is actively nationalist.[15] In this volume (chapter 2), Denise Youngblood offers "cosmopolitan" Trinidad as corroboration; but one would hardly need to look far afield for many others.

Both Borneman and Youngblood take pains to remind us—though it would be difficult to forget—that kinship operates as a matrix at once of national inclusion and of national exclusivism. Borneman especially reminds us of yet another facet of its potential political utility: it is a matrix not merely of relationships but also of affect, of a distinctive sentiment or sense of "belonging." The planetary humanism of our spiritual virtuosos is a poor model. The sense of being kin, like the sense of being friends or the sense of being in love, is instead typically the more "effective," the more limited; the more determinate, the more particular its object. Whether or not it should be regarded as "primordial," as Edward Shils would have had it be (1957; cf. Geertz 1973: 255–310), it is certainly ubiquitous, and even in its nationalist extension, evidently quite humanly compelling (even if, once again, not equally compelling to every human being). So much is available through simple observation. Here, too, however, the facts want interpreting. Psychoanalysts from Freud to Žižek and Kristeva have taken up the challenge, but post-Schneiderians (and old-fashioned Durkheimians) might well hesitate to embrace their uniformly naturalistic resolutions.[16]

In the work he provides for this volume (chapter 1), Borneman turns his intuition toward another sort of resolution, though leaves it largely undeveloped. After reviewing the labyrinthine tactics that several persons of his acquaintance have had to devise in order to sidestep laws and policies that would have prevented them from being the families they sought to be, he extracts a lesson and delivers an indictment. The lesson: that a great many of those modern polities that portray themselves as being "pro-family" in fact consecrate families only of certain substantive kinds, and they leave the rest abject. The indictment: the same polities—and those anthropologists who have claimed to "discover" the essence of human culture and society in the difference between the sexes or heterosexual reproduction along with them—are guilty at once of thwarting the human capacity to invent and sustain new forms of relating and new modes of belonging together, and of depriving untold numbers of their citizens of the right fully to claim and to cultivate among the most abiding and urgent symptoms of the human condition. Specifying that symptom, Borneman calls upon Martin Heidegger:

> In *Being and Time* (1962), Heidegger based his existential analysis on Sorge (the thematic concept of care). He desubstantialized human experience and insisted that temporality is to be found not in a human essence or form but in the dialectic of coming to be, of having been, and of making present. *Dasein*, living/being in time, is defined not in a simple succession of discrete "nows" but in the temporal constitution of care. Humans, then, are not blind egos following deterministic sequences of events, of cultural paradigms and rules. They plot sequences of experiences in narratives organized around for whom and what they care. (p. 41–42)

"Care" does not—in *Being and Time*, at least—denote an "instinct." It does not even denote a particularly common human experience. As Borneman makes clear, it instead denotes the sine qua non of human "activity," the sentiment or sense without which human beings cannot even begin to escape the passivity of their everyday existence and get on with creating a genuinely meaningful life.

At first sight, the normative position that Borneman advocates might seem to be only a somewhat more abstract echo of the normativity of kinship itself. Whatever else, being-kin obliges us to care about and care for particular others, and obliges particular others to care for and care about us. Its entanglement with such obligations is dense and far-reaching and frequently visited in this volume (beyond Borneman, see Reddy, Carpenter, Babula, Peterson, Bargach, Deckha, and George). Yet, that Sorge is not an everyday affair is already enough to indicate that neither Heidegger's existentialism nor Borneman's appeal to it have what we typically think of as kinship ties as its inspiration. On the contrary: insofar as kinship is "given," is something we passively receive or—to use a more Heideggerian phraseology—something into which we are "thrown," it burdens us with inauthenticity and with "cares" that only distract us from a more authentic existential project. Borneman's acquaintances are hardly passive recipients of the kinship they would have with others; theirs are quite active quests for relationships voluntarily forged. Hence, the "displacement" that Borneman seeks to carry out: instead of the substantialism of either the biological difference between the sexes or the facts of heterosexual reproductive life, he would have us theoretically and normatively put caring first.

Yet, if one could hardly object to the spirit of this advocacy, one might still object to its letter. Perhaps Borneman's acquaintances do "care" in Heidegger's technical sense of the term. If so, however, what they must care about first and foremost is their own being. Heidegger's Sorge—which takes a good bit of existential reflection even to recognize as such—has the potentiality of being as its formal object. It is "about" the meaningfulness of one's own existence; it is about the meaningfulness that one's existence lacks when one is the mere recipient of the terms of one's life, when one has yet to embark upon a project of one's own devising (Heidegger 1962: 322–24). That one's project might involve the constitution of reciprocally caring affiliations with others—the mode of care that Borneman ultimately affirms—is merely one among myriad possibilities. Authentic existence would by no means require it. Much less would it require the establishment of kinship. But then we encounter a puzzle very similar to that which Schneider himself left us: If humans have no need of kinship, then why do so many of them cling to it so vigorously, even when fully aware of its contingency?

Kinship and Subjectivation

Heidegger, and Borneman after him, do in fact point to a possible solution to this puzzle, for both lead us to consider more generally the place that kinship occupies among all the other systems that weigh upon the self—the Maussian "me" (1968)—and upon its definition of itself. Kinship—as we provisionally think of it—resists conceptualization as a "status system," at least as Max Weber understood the latter. Kinship is not always constitutive of "estates"; and if its terms are very frequently indexes of differential status, they are rarely indexes of common "consumption patterns" or "styles of life" (cf. Weber 1946). Kinship and status appear rather to be systems of the same level or order. The terms of both are terms to which the self is "subject," and according to which it is a "subject" of one or another set of features or of one or another kind. The terms of kinship, however, have certain hallmarks, remarkable less individually than in sum. First, as I have already mentioned, they qualify the self as a subject *through its relation to others*. Correlatively, they *qualify others to identify the self through their relation to it*. Second, they are finitistic. Though rarely individualizing, they label the self *in its particularity*, and specifically, in the particularity of its relations to particular others. Third, whether given or "adopted," they are *normatively permanent*. Once ascribed, they presumptively remain with the self through the course of its life, and even in the aftermath of its death.[17] Finally, they are terms of *being*, not of doing. They can and of course often do come with scripts or rulebooks attached. Yet the normativity of kinship is just that: definitive not of being kin but rather of being a good or a bad kinsperson. (The prodigal son did not cease to be his father's son, however ungrateful a son he might have been.) In light of these hallmarks, it is hardly surprising that "blood" is so widespread a symbol of kinship, but hardly surprising, either, that it is in fact only one of many—from "milk" (in this volume, see Bargach [chapter 3]; cf. Delaney 1991: 157–58) and the sacral or legal "oath" to the formal, or informal, "christening" (see Borneman, Bargach, and Carpenter [chapters 1, 3, and 8, respectively]).

In his later writing, Michel Foucault had begun to devise an analytics that, with startling appropriateness, might encompass status systems and kinship systems alike. Both are instructively viewed as Foucauldean systems of "subjectivation [*assujetissement*]." In its technical usage, "subjectivation" has a double edge. On the one hand, it refers to all those processes through which individuals are labeled or made into subjects of one or another kind; it thus ranges over the domain of "subjection," or of what Louis Althusser called "interpellation" (Althusser 1971). On the other hand, it refers to all those processes through which individuals might make themselves into subjects of one or another kind; it thus also ranges over the domain of what Foucault characterized as "the relation of the self to itself," "the reflexive practice of freedom," or simply "ethics." The contrast should not be confused with Heidegger's contrast between inauthentic and authentic being; Foucault's analytics of subjectivation is not an existentialism. Nor should it be confused with an identity imposed versus an identity created out of whole cloth. Subjection is indeed imposed; but the reflexive practice of freedom is very far from being altogether free. Its resources come from a repertoire of "technologies of the self" that belong to or must be fabricated from a given collective repository. Its end—subjecthood—might be something of an "original." Yet it can never be so original as to surpass intersubjective understanding, never so original that it cannot publicly be counted as a subject, even if only to be disparaged. Nor again should the contrast be confused with one between those subjects that people are forced to be and those subjects they would like to be. For better or worse, human beings are quite capable of positively savoring their subjection; and quite capable as well of recoiling before the very idea of self-transformation. Subjection is rather the backdrop, the basic mode, of what might be thought of as a general human regime of subjectivation, which has had many and various modes, and just as many and as varied techniques at its disposal, from one place and time to another. Ethics emerges as a possibility within it insofar as the given techniques of subjection still leave room for the reflexive practice of freedom, for the deployment and exercise of techniques of self-transformation.

In its most familiar guises—in most of its anthropological guises—kinship appears to belong much more to the backdrop of subjection than to the open spaces of ethics. Where individualism or cosmopolitanism reigns, its terms tend not to dominate the definition of the self. Yet, as several of the contributors to this volume attest, even the individualist or the cosmopolitan might experience his or her being-kin as especially intransigent, and all the more so when its attendant obligations begin to nag (in this volume, see Reddy, Peterson, and Babula in chapters 5, 10, and 11, respectively). Schneider's warning against taking the universal constancy of the "grip" of kinship altogether for granted still deserves heeding. All the same, the bonds of being-in-relation seem to be unusually tight among many other peoples besides Europeans (as several of our contributors again attest), and even among many peoples for whom other things besides "blood" are thicker than water. If naturalism has proven seductive to so many theorists of kinship, this is in part because it seems to afford an explanation of just this peculiarity. The bonds at issue are quite so ubiquitous and quite so tight as they are—so naturalism would have it—because they are grounded in "instincts," or in such deep-set and ubiquitous psychobiological "needs" as the Malinowskian "need to reproduce" (viz. Malinowski 1939). Naturalism must be left behind; but if so, what might do better in its stead? A more rigorously sociological functionalism, perhaps, would do better. One might accordingly assert that there are certain conditions or activities vital to the survival of any society—the replacement of its constituent members, say, or the organization of child-rearing—that kinship serves to sustain; and that from the paramount sociological importance of what it does, the peculiar strength of its ties (and their attendant obligations) derives. Schneider worried about the circularity of such an explanation (see 1984: 138–39), but most of his worries are somewhat misplaced, at least from an interpretive perspective.[18] Even so, the explanation has the usual shortcomings. As Borneman would surely want to remind us, it is suspiciously heteronormative. It is also silent on the matter of why kinship—rather than the Fourierite commune, or any other conceivable alternative—should be so privileged and so widely dispersed a means of the organization of social reproduction. It barely begins to account for all the other functions that kinship might actually or conceivably fulfill. As Schneider rightly noted (1984: 139), it runs the risk of conflating what kinship does with what it is.

Back, then, to kinship as a system—or array of systems—of subjectivation, if perhaps many other things as well. Among interpreters, purists must refrain from defining its ultimate parameters at least until history is at an end. The more eclectic might turn to Françoise Héritier, whose recent effort at once to complete and to emend Lévi-Strauss's account of the prohibition of incest remains historically and semiotically sensitive, and heuristically provocative, even if its theoretical ambitions test interpretive propriety. Héritier is unabashedly the high theorist. She nevertheless succeeds in constructing a theory that preserves much of the past anthropology of kinship without sharing the most objectionable of its naturalistic biases. She departs from a common but by no means universal prohibition: that which forbids a man from marrying or having sexual intercourse with the sister or mother of his wife (1994: 23–24). Like prohibitions of sex or marriage between spiritual or adoptive kin, this one has no consanguineal rationale. It interdicts what Héritier deems "incest of a second type" (11). Differing from virtually all her predecessors, however, she demurs from deriving it "by extension" from the prohibition of sex among consanguines (which is itself very far from universal). She instead proposes the opposite: that the latter sort of prohibition has its inspiration in the former, the "second" sort.

Héritier proceeds to locate the source of that inspiration at the intersection of three (presumptively) universal preoccupations. One of these is a semiotic preoccupation with identity and difference. Another is an intellectual and affective preoccupation with the chemistry of combinations, of the "cumulation of the identical" (1994: 12) and the conjunction of the different. The last—the *prima materia* of the first (228)—is a preoccupation with the anatomical and physiological differences between the sexes. At their intersection, and only in the aftermath of "a profound interrogation of the sorting of bodies into those that are identical to the self and those that are different from the self, of attraction and repulsion," none but a single conclusion can emerge: "identity is non-productive"; "whether biological or social, reproduction requires difference" (365). The prohibition against sexual relations among (selected) consanguines thus has its semiotic sense, but only as a particular token of the more abstract prohibition against the "excessive" cumulation or intermingling of the same substances, the same fluids and humors in or between two or more sexed bodies. The semiotics of excess and of humors are of course variable. Héritier argues that the prohibition of secondary types of incest varies along with them—but only up to a point. The human tolerance for the cumulation of the identical finds its common limits in that possible impossibility, "the sexual union of the perfectly identical" (365).

Of course, many other systems of subjectivation reveal a preoccupation with sameness and otherness. Yet, as Héritier's treatment surely suggests, kinship permits of further useful comparison with far fewer of them than might be expected. Like nationality, race and caste evoke the ideology of a vast genealogical unity that is at once more restrictive and more abstract than the ideologies—whether genealogical or legal or spiritual—that provide the rationales for the operative and affective unities, the collective "bodies," of kinship. Of more or less straightforwardly comparable bodies, I can think of only one: the body of the elect as it is conceived in the Abrahamic religions, and especially as it is conceived first in the Gospel of Matthew and—read literally—the Book of Revelation.[19] The author of the Gospel—or perhaps Jesus himself—could hardly have recognized the ratio between the two more lucidly; in Matthew, though with echoes in many other biblical verses, kinship and election are binary opposites, and such structurally precise opposites that the terms of the former serve also as terms for the latter. In Matthew, the "few who are chosen" (the Book of Revelation sets their number at 144,000) must leave all their mundane kin behind. They will find another father; they will be brothers and sisters in his spirit. Like kinship, election thus renders the subject through its relation to others and in its particularity. Whether given (as Augustine and other predestinarians would understand it to be) or "earned," it is indelible, and it is an inscription at the very heart of one's being. It is a chrism that endows its bearer with many burdens. Yet it also endows him or her with an entirely inalienable, entirely indefeasible stigma, which has its experiential or epistemic manifestation in resolute, unshakable faith. The elect are saints. Whatever might be said about the vast remainder of mankind, they at least have an appointed purpose. They have the certain promise of storied lives and afterlives.

The elect themselves would surely avow that the inescapability of their condition, a stigma so absolute that it demands nothing short of surrender, is the work and the will of their god. The anthropologist—professional infidel—must rather note that the normative permanence of merely mundane kinship and the normative permanence of election have at least one common source. The terms of both constitute a sort of cybernetic absolutism.[20] They fix a privileged few of the parameters of the self that, once fixed, are normatively as unnegotiable as (well . . .) nature itself. They thus effect a dramatic reduction of the cybernetic complexity of those parameters, and a relative reduction of the complexity of any others with which they intersect. They effect a far more dramatic reduction of complexity than could ever be achieved by such indefinite, abstract, potentially infinitistic systems of subjectivation as those of nationality or race or caste, or for that matter, of class or gender or sexuality. Perhaps needless to say, they impose far more cybernetic order than one could ever expect from such particularistic relations as friendship or romantic love, of which "complexity" is the very spice (or bane, as the case may be). They thus render the self uniquely "communicable"—to others, but also to itself. They promise no bowl of cherries, but they at least enable the self to launch itself—or to be launched—on whatever else might come to be of its identity and the course of its life in a condition falling at least somewhat short of a constant and full-blown identity crisis.

In *The Elementary Structures*, Lévi-Strauss himself already suggests a cybernetic—or more accurately, semiological—modeling of a limited number of kinship systems—those that at once proscribe marriage between certain categories of kin relations and prescribe marriage between certain others

(1969: xxiii–xxiv). Semiologically, such systems are indeed the most elegant we have (at least if Lévi-Strauss's analysis is approximately correct). They establish a normative baseline at which the complexity of the self is reduced to the complexity (that is to say, the uncertainty) of its subject-position, and at which the complexity of communication is reduced to the complexity of the reciprocal exchange of (representative) women between lineally constituted groups. All the remaining systems we know are indeed (more) complex; virtually without exception, they preserve a similar proscription (an incest taboo) but abandon any similar prescription. They leave life courses and alliances open to a greater number of options and motives, but they increase the uncertainties of both as a consequence.

To be sure, none of these extrapolations quite entails an explanation of the universal "horror of incest"—but then, judging from the number of instances of its violation, pace Lévi-Strauss and Héritier, no such explanation seems necessary.[21] They do, however, strongly suggest an explanation of the endurance of kinship in the face of all the other systems of subjectivation and sociality that human beings have so far managed to create (and an explanation of the distinctive alarm that incestuous or homosexual or other "dangerous" liaisons provoke in quite as many human beings as they continue to do). They suggest that, cybernetically, even complex systems of kinship are in fact less complex than any others that have come to be available to us. It accordingly suggests that, cybernetically (that is to say, both cognitively and affectively), kinship is still our most secure "safety net" (in this volume, see especially Carpenter and Babula in chapters 8 and 11; and cf. George in chapter 9). Rend it, retract it, destroy it, and we inevitably face greater uncertainty, greater subjective and social risk—unless, of course, we are lucky enough to be among the elect.

As virtually all of the contributors to this volume teach us, what would thus be rendered more uncertain is the story that the self could tell, at once about itself and about its place in its environment. Kinship is informatic; it is also poetic, or at least supplies among the most pervasive, and pervasively entrenched, of the various motifs and formulas of life-narration. To be sure, not everyone clings to them—much less assigns them poetic priority in the determination of either personal identity or a personal project. A system of subjectivation, after all, kinship can devolve into sheer oppression, and an oppression all the more severe when (as is virtually always the case) it is imbricated with class, or caste, or race, or nationality (see Karim, Youngblood, and George in chapters 4, 2, and 9, respectively). The family romance can turn unpalatably sour, even positively poison. The admonition "not to forget one's roots" can come to stand in the way of a broadening of both sociality and poetic horizons (see George in chapter 9; cf. Carpenter in chapter 8). Among its many other attributes, the body of kinship very often delimits the arena in which the self garners its primary legitimation; it is often a court of both first and last appeal in the trials of self validation. Yet the body can reject those members it deems unworthy or corrupt, leaving the outcast either to cope with the intolerabilities of exile or to search out more sympathetic judges. Some psychoanalysts may beg to differ, but there is no good anthropological reason to insist that the cartography of kinship alone maps the route to maturity or "healthy" adulthood.

Like all systems of subjectivation, kinship limits the possibilities of the self and of its relations to others. It also produces such possibilities. Precisely because of its cybernetic security, it permits the self to put itself at risk, to explore uncertain territories that might otherwise seem too perilous even to begin to traverse. Semiologically and cybernetically at least, one might agree with Lévi-Strauss that kinship "survives" because "it is so fundamental that any transformation . . . has been neither possible nor necessary" (1969: 62). Yet one might further observe that the very attributes of social "modernity" that preclude kinship from reigning organizationally supreme—those that theorists from Durkheim and Weber to Niklas Luhmann have treated under the rubric of "functional differentiation"—have also tended to reinforce its cybernetic and poetic attractions. The modern self has quite a number of territories it might begin to traverse, from religion and politics to business to art. As Luhmann has, however, persuasively argued, none of these territories has any claim to semiological sovereignty (Luhmann 1990: 431–32). Except by arbitrary fiat, none is any more organizationally definitive than any other—kinship (or "the domestic sphere") included. Each territory thus affords only a vantage on what the self itself might be. Yet with the possible exception of religion, kinship continues to have its relative securities to recommend it; and the recommendation may well be all the more forcible the more the self is not merely able but positively obliged to "make something of itself" in territories where identity is a thing to be won or lost (see Ossman and Carpenter in chapters 7 and 8, respectively). Hence, if the ardent individualist might sometimes find kinship nagging, even he or she might find it of peculiar modern comfort as well (see Babula in chapter 11 and Karim in chapter 4).

TOWARD AN ANTHROPOLOGY OF THE ETHICS OF KINSHIP

Especially in functionally differentiated social organizations—those in which virtually all human beings now live—there is, in principle if far more variably in fact, much to be made of life beyond kinship. Yet when the ethnographic record includes any note of the matter whatever, it suggests that in virtually every sort of social organization known to us, past or present, there has always been something to make of life within the parameters of kinship as well. Nowhere does it seem that kinship, as a system of subjectivation, has assumed the exclusive character of a system of subjection. Perhaps it has come close, and in its various interfusions with class or race or gender, closer still. Yet it seems always to have stopped short of sheer imprisonment, sheer slavery. It thus seems always to have left a bit of room—if greater room for some (usually adult heteronormative male) beings-in-relation than for others—for what Foucault would have us understand as ethics.

What Foucault would have us understand as ethics, however, requires further parsing. To reiterate, he would have us understand it as the domain neither of Heideggerean authenticity nor of the existentially "free project." In characterizing it instead as the domain of the relation of the self to itself, Foucault seeks first of all to restore the distinction between ethics and morality, which has largely been lost in contemporary philosophical discourse (and in more common parlance as well). Morality comprises all those codes and rules that establish right and wrong conduct, what must or must not, what ought and ought not to be done. Ethics, for Foucault, involves the self's assessment of its relation to such codes and rules, of their applicability and situational relevance. It further involves the self's assessment of its relation to the kind of subject it is or might be, of the applicability and relevance of one or another "role model" or characterological ideal. It is thus never a matter of simple subjectivation, but rather of the self's (1) "mode of subjectivation," of the manner in which it orients itself toward a given environment of norms, and (2) ethical "ends," of actual and possible kinds of ethical being.

These are two of the dimensions of the ethical orientation. Foucault identifies two others: (3) the "substance" of the self's ethical concern, that "material" that is the focus of ethical cultivation; and (4) the self's *askêsis*, the works or exercises it must perform, or the training it must undertake, in order to realize itself as a subject of a certain kind (Foucault 1985: 3–25; cf. Foucault 1997b and Rabinow 1997).

All this perhaps makes ethics seem a quite personal preoccupation, to be conducted alone and in private. Foucault nevertheless dwells at length on what might be thought of as ethical exchange. Nor is his attention arbitrary. Consider his remarks on the ancient Greek ethics of the care of the self:

> The care of the self is ethical in itself; but it implies complex relationships with others insofar as this *ethos* of freedom is also a way of caring for others. This is why it is important for a free man who conducts himself as he should to be able to govern his wife, his children, his household; it is also the art of governing. *Ethos* also implies a relationship with others insofar as the care of the self enables one to occupy his rightful position in the city, the community, or interpersonal relationships, whether as a magistrate or a friend. And the care of the self also implies a relationship with the other insofar as proper care of the self requires listening to the lessons of a master. One needs a guide, a counselor, a friend, someone who will be truthful with you. Thus, the problem of relationships with others is present throughout the development of the care of the self. (1997a: 287)

Most of these remarks reach little beyond the Greeks, or at least beyond antiquity. The last of them, however, is more wide ranging. It acknowledges that ethics, like language, must be taught. If the reflexive practice of freedom might sometimes occur in the remote isolation of a desert cave, its primal scene must nevertheless be a scene of instruction, a scene of pedagogy, of that interactive art that has as its overarching end the crafting of human beings into beings of artful ethical craft.

This, in turn, might seem to follow very much in the footsteps of Aristotle, whose *Nicomachean Ethics* could well be read as a handbook of sorts of ethical pedagogy. Yet Foucault's notion of ethical activity in fact diverges sharply from Aristotle's, as the latter's analysis of *phronêsis*, or "practical wisdom," reveals quite clearly. The cardinal intellectual virtue of the ethical actor, practical wisdom cannot, to Aristotle's mind, be a "science," for it deals with the variable, not the fixed and determinate. "Nor," he continues, "can it be the same as an 'art' (or 'craft,' *tekhnê*) . . . [and] not art, because practicing (*praxis*) and making (*poiêsis*) are different in kind. The end of making is distinct from it; the end of practice is not: practicing well is itself the end" (*NE* VIv3). Shortly before this, he will have declared that "all art deals with bringing something into existence; and to pursue an art means to study how to bring into existence a thing that may either exist or not exist, and the efficient cause (*arkhê*) of which *lies in the maker and not the thing made*" (*NE* VIiv4; my emphasis).

This argument has a number of striking implications. First, those various activities that constitute pedagogy would appear to fall on the side of poiêsis, not praxis, and so, strictly speaking, outside Aristotle's ethical ambit. The same must be said of those various activities to which Foucault refers as "practices of the self" or "techniques of the self" or "technologies of the self" (Foucault 1997c). Hence, they fall into a realm of activity that Aristotle conceives as prior to, or as not yet involving, "choice" (*proairesis*). Or perhaps not even that much can be said. Aristotle may instead have no room, ethical or "pre-ethical," for Foucault's practices and techniques and technologies of the self. Taking him strictly at his word, he at least has no room for them in the realm of "art," for all that is art manifests a causal fissure between maker and things made. For Aristotle, the "middle voice" of reflexive activity, of an agency in which the self is at once subject and its own object, doer and that to which something is done, has no poetic pitch.[22] Foucault restores its pitch, and restores much of the genuine complexity of ethical pedagogy in doing so. He is not the first: one might look back to Friedrich Nietzsche, or to Jean-Jacques Rousseau, or to Michel Montaigne. Matters of originality aside, though, the analytic reincorporation of reflexive poiêsis into the ethical domain is a crucial emendation of a long-standing omission.

Yet we must still give Aristotle his due. If he did not adequately discern the importance, or even the possibility, of ethical "autodidacticism" (a term I introduce advisedly, since ethical pedagogy can never be purely autodidactic, even at its most reflexive), he must still be given credit for discerning, or reiterating (see *NE* VIiv2: once again, matters of originality are irrelevant), the depth of the divide between making and doing, between creation and choice. It is regrettable that so few moderns have preserved this bit of his broader wisdom. Having discarded it, too many modern philosophers of the self find themselves oscillating uncomfortably between two equally unacceptable poles: one that would place both creation and choice under the transcendental influence of a quasi-demonic psyche (or culture, or society); and another that would release both into the Elysian expanses of sheer contingency—hence, I would suggest, the decidedly modern quarrel between "primordialists" and "constructivists" that continues to plague us, including those of us who take up the topic of kinship. That antagonists on both sides of this quarrel have claimed Foucault as an ally is, I think, indicative less of his ambiguity than of his belonging no more to one side than to the other. With Aristotle, he sees in poiêsis an activity neither passively determined nor deliberately willed. Or to put it more positively: for Aristotle as for Foucault, poiêsis is an activity in which the peculiar dynamics of thought interposes itself between reaction and action. For Foucault, the indeterminate house of mirrors that thus permits access is the house of the self in ethical formation.[23]

The allusion to the Lacanian image of the mirror is intentional but not meant to suggest affinity. Foucault could perhaps agree with some suitably diluted version of Aristotle's postulate that "the life of right conduct is pleasurable in itself" (*NE* 1viii10). He could at least agree that pleasure is an important epistemological index for ethical inquiry (cf. Rabinow 1997: xxxvii). But unlike Jacques Lacan, he is not a theorist of desire (or "libido"). He is rather a genealogist of "those practices by which individuals [have been] led to focus their attention on themselves, to decipher, recognize, and acknowledge themselves as subjects of desire, bringing into play between themselves and themselves a certain relationship that allows them to discover, in desire, the truth of their being" (Foucault 1985: 2). Nor is his analytics closed to other genealogies, other practices, other subjects. With its more generous scope, it provides a refreshing alternative to those automatic psychoanalyses that too many contemporary cryptologists of subjectivity deploy in transferring—usually with dubious empirical warrant—the deep structures of the Lacanian psyche onto the social plane, the plane of interaction. It also provides us with the opportunity to reconsider the whole dialectics of internalization and objectification through which socialization itself transpires. It is especially striking that Foucault places within something like Husserlian brackets the prevailing tenet that our earliest, our primary socialization, bestows upon us our subsequent health or pathology, our subsequent psychic fate. He invites us to consider the possibility that technologies of the self might not always serve as the instruments of the reiteration and reinforcement of the cathexes and traumas, the defenses and disguises of our childhoods, but sometimes also as the instruments of their revision. Those of us who take up the topic of kinship should, I think, consider such a possibility most seriously; our "data" come very close to demanding that we do so.

Ethical Tropics and the Tropics of Kinship

Such a possibility would not, however, exist were the ethical Imaginary simply a shadowy double of a given ethical Symbolic (and vice versa). It would not, in other words, exist were ethical poiêsis limited merely to mimesis, were its sole master-trope the trope of simile. Foucault, for his part, does not develop an ethical semiology, a maker's guide to ethical creation, but from the cases and commentaries he has left us, we can say something about what such a guide would have to include. No less than praxis does poiêsis require reasoning about means and ends, so it, too, must rest upon the logic of that intellectual capacity that Aristotle regards as the signature of practical wisdom: the capacity for deliberation. Yet as figuration, it must further rest upon a tropology, for which simile would be adequate only if the ethical life always and everywhere consisted in "living up to" a given exemplar or ideal. The Christian valorization of the *imitatio Christi* is an obvious case in point, but the case on which Foucault comments in *The Use of Pleasure* is not in tropological conformity with it. For the "practice-oriented" ethics of the classical Greek elite, an ethics that has its fulcrum in the *hiatus irrationalis* between the generality of precept and the particularity of situation, simile frequently cedes its place to irony, tragic or comic from one instance to the next. I have myself argued that metalepsis is the master-trope of one prominent current of self-(re)formation in contemporary Greece (Faubion 1993). Or we could alternatively visit the Hageners of Highland New Guinea, for whom self-formation proceeds in an open-ended synecdoche that Marilyn Strathern has deemed "cyborgic" (Strathern 1991). Throughout a good stretch of contemporary North America, we could encounter a strange people whose ethical individualism has its tropological summum in Walt Whitman's grand metaphor: "I am everything." At the risk of advocating a formalism that would run counter to Foucault's methodological nominalism,[24] I cannot help but propose that tropology might in fact constitute the framework for a comparative hermeneutics of ethical modes of subjectivation. The variety and scope of its figures, its tropoplogical substance, must of course remain questions of ethnographic research.

From tropology it is but a short step to life-narrative, and from that, another short step to the life-narratives of those distinctive modalities of being-in-relation that are kinship. Hence, we arrive again at the contributions to this volume, which for all their diversity demonstrate again and again that an ethics of kinship is altogether bound up with the reception, negotiation, and revision of stories about the self and an "elect" group of others, some living, some dead. The master-tropes of such stories are metonymy and synecdoche, tropes of parts and wholes, elements and totalities. The modes of subjectivation to which they are testament are quite diverse. For several of the contributors, the irremediable givenness of ascriptive kinship is a central motif (see Karim, Reddy, Carpenter, and Babula in chapters 4, 5, 8, and 11); for several others, the tension between relations ascribed and relations achieved (see Youngblood, Bargach, George, and Peterson in chapters 2, 3, 9, and 10); for others still, what stories might be told, and what lives-in-relation might be lived, were there only world enough and time (see Deckha, Ossman, and Borneman). We learn of the intertwining of kinship and memory, of kinship and "fate." We learn also of the ample room for practical invention that the parameters of kinship might allow, sometimes inhibited but sometimes served by their intersections with class or caste or race or gender or nationality. All the familiar genres find good use: comedy, tragedy, farce, drama, even a bit of magical realism here and there.

This to be sure, is not to say that kinship, any more than the rest of life, is art; only that it would be ethically much diminished without it. Trust the contributions that follow to spell out the details.

NOTES

1. The ethnohistory of native North America has proven particularly illuminating here. See, for example, Eggan 1937; 1955: 92–95; and 1966. More recently, see Godelier, Trautmann, and Fat 1998.

2. Jack Goody's *Development of the Family and Marriage in Europe* (1983) is seminal. See also Watt 1992; and note 10, below.

3. The turn attests among other things to the impact of Pierre Bourdieu's *Outline of a Theory of Practice* (Bourdieu 1977).

4. The "classic" terrain of anthropological attention to—and debates about—such inventiveness is that of aboriginal Australia. For a review, see Shapiro 1979. "Spiritual" kinship (godparenthood, for example) has also received sustained treatment, especially among ethnographers of southern Europe and Latin America. See Mintz and Wolf 1950; Lewis 1951; Hammel 1968; and Nutini and Bell 1980–1984. See also note 10, below.

5. I would like to take the opportunity here to thank Professor Betty Joseph of the Rice Department of English, who also served as a discussant during the conference.

6. "Spiritual" kinship is an obvious case in point (see note 4, above); adoption is another (see Modell 1994 and Bargach, chapter 3 in this volume).

7. See, for example, Weston 1991 and Borneman 1992. For a rather different case, see Weismantel 1995.

8. Marilyn Strathern's *After Nature* (1992) is a somewhat troubled address of the refigurative consequences of political–economic and biogenetic developments for everything from kinship to the discipline of anthropology itself. Cf. also Paul Rabinow's observations on the emergence of "biosociality" (1992).

9. The first volume of Michel Foucault's *History of Sexuality* (1978) is seminal. See also Greenberg 1988; Laqueur 1990; Herdt 1991a, 1991b; and Epple 1998.

10. More recent contributions to this growing constellation include the following: M. Stacey 1992; Edwards et al. 1993; Ginzburg and Rapp 1995; Holmgren 1995; Maynes et al. 1995; Mundy 1995; Yanagisako and Delaney 1995; Allan 1996; Palriwala and Risseeuw 1996; Smith 1996; Stivens 1996; Thompson and Tyagi 1996; Dube 1997; Franklin 1997; Pasternak, Ember, and Ember 1997; Francisconi 1998; Franklin and Ragoné, eds. 1998; Hansen and Garey 1998; Roces 1998; and Carsten 2000.

11. See Needham 1974 and Wittgenstein 1953. Schneider's stance here is all the more striking for simply being asserted, not defended.

12. For an accessible epitome of the positivist position, see Hempel 1974.

13. Hermeneutical or interpretive methodologies perhaps no longer need an introduction. I should in any case clarify that I am using "hermeneutics" and "interpretation" as they appear in the tradition stemming from Wilhelm Dilthey (1961) and Max Weber (1968) to Clifford Geertz (1973, 1983) and his interpretivist contemporaries (see Rabinow and Sullivan 1987). More specific philosophical loyalties or theories are not at issue here.

14. On Charles Fourier and his flock, see Beecher 1986. On the Oneida Community, see Hine 1974 and Hudson 1974. On Soviet communalism, see Bartlett 1990; and on the kibbutzim, see Spiro 1970 and Near 1992.

15. Kinship (or "the family") has, of course, also been at the forefront of the biopolitical imagination, which has given us the many modalities of the "welfare state."

16. Freud's foundational text is *Moses and Monotheism* (1957). After him, see Žižek 1989; and Kristeva 1993.

17. I must stress "normatively." The actual permanence of kinship ties (and the identities that accompany them) is another matter. Yet, even when more or less formal mechanisms of the transformation of kinship relations are in place, the transformation itself seems virtually universally to come at considerable cost. In ancient Greece, for example, a man might wed an *epiklêros*—a woman who, lacking brothers or any other suitable male collateral relatives, was due to receive her father's legacy. In exchange, the groom was obliged to renounce his former patrilineal ties and adopt those of his father-in-law. The children of such a union would thus belong not to their father's but to their maternal grandfather's natal line. Such unions did indeed occur—but meant a precipitous loss of status for the groom, and they seem only to have been something of a last resort for the man who could see no other means of acquiring wealth or securing an inheritance for the children he wished to sire (cf. Goody 1990; Cohen 1994). Modern Western folklore is of course well stocked with tales of comparable "reinterpellations," from *Paris Is Burning* to *Six Degrees of Separation*. But most of these tales offer accounts of an individual's flight from the intolerability of abuse or the abjection of poverty or degradation, and almost all come to a distinctly sad and cautionary end.

18. The issue for the interpreter cannot be whether an interpretation is "circular," because all interpretation is circular. The issue must rather be whether or not such circularity is "vicious"—that is, whether or not it is merely tautological.

19. The Jewish conception of election (at least as one finds it in the Old Testament) is "ethnically" restrictive. Its counterparts in the New Testament are not. Yet for all that commentators have made of the "universalism" of the Christian conception of church membership, election itself—the charisma of the inflowing of divine grace—was

clearly a condition of the few, not even potentially a condition available to all. It was precisely that which distinguished the saint from the common run of women and men.

20. I refer to cybernetics here, rather loosely, as any "theory of information," but in no sense intend it to be understood as the sociological and culturological theory of foundations that its early advocates championed it to be. On the contrary: as Luhmann (1990) and others have argued quite persuasively, "information"—as news or puzzle or evidence or fact—is only perceivable as such against the background of the taken-for-granted. Semiotics is thus the nest of cybernetics, and cybernetics the metrics of relative semiological or informational complexity. I share with Luhmann and, again, many others the presumption—which quite a lot of information supports—that human beings are profoundly averse, perhaps even incapable, of tolerating unlimited or even only indefinitely limited complexity of that sort.

21. Héritier, for her part, recognizes the commission of "acts of incest of all sorts" to be a "statistical and social verity. [But] that it is a common, ordinary, banal event is not true" (1994: 24–25)—hence her urging of an account of a "fantasm" that remains to her mind "a major motor of our social imaginary" (1994: 25). Cf. Hage's further development of her central theses (Hage 1997). I would not, however, want to exaggerate the disagreement between us. Héritier and Hage are primarily interested in the logical formalities of the various nomenclatures of kinship, and only derivatively with what people actually do with, or to, or against, the nomenclatures to which they are heir (and even less with what they "feel"). With both Héritier and Hage, moreover, I share the conviction that kinship profoundly informs the definition and trajectory of the self—formally and in practice.

22. I owe much of my understanding of the distinctive poetics of the middle voice to Stephen Tyler. See especially Tyler 1998.

23. The preceding five paragraphs appear with several added details in my more extended treatment of Foucault's analytics of subjectivation and ethics, "Toward an Anthropology of Ethics" (©2001 by The Regents of the University of California. Reprinted from *Representations*, No. 74).

24. Foucault's "nominalism" was in any event a methodological posture, not an ontological one (see my treatment in Faubion 1998). I largely share it; but on the other hand, generalizations that might run afoul of methodological nominalism are not always easily—and not always usefully—avoided.

BIBLIOGRAPHY

Allan, G. 1996. *Kinship and Friendship in Modern Britain*. Oxford: Oxford University Press.

Althusser, L. 1971. Ideology and Ideological State Apparatuses (Notes toward an Investigation). In *Lenin and Philosophy and Other Essays*. Trans. B. Brewster. New York: Monthly Review Press, pp. 170–77.

Bartlett, R., ed. 1990. *Land Commune and Peasant Community in Russia: Communal Forms in Imperial and Early Soviet Society*. Basingstoke: Macmillan Press.

Beecher, J. 1986. *Charles Fourier: The Visionary and His World*. Berkeley: University of California Press.

Borneman, J. 1992. *Belonging in the Two Berlins: Kin, State, Nation*. Cambridge: Cambridge University Press.

Bourdieu, P. 1977. *Outline of a Theory of Practice*. Trans. R. Nice. Cambridge: Cambridge University Press.

Carsten, J., ed. 2000. *Cultures of Relatedness: New Approaches to the Study of Kinship*. Cambridge: Cambridge University Press.

Cohen, D. 1994. *Law, Sexuality, and Society: The Enforcement of Morals in Classical Greece*. Cambridge: Cambridge University Press.

Collier, J. F., and S. J. Yanagisako, eds. 1987. *Gender and Kinship: Essays toward a Unified Analysis*. Stanford, Calif.: Stanford University Press.

Collier, J. F., and S. J. Yanagisako. 1987. Introduction. In *Gender and Kinship: Essays Toward a Unified Analysis*. Eds. J. F. Collier and S. J. Yanagisako. Stanford, Calif.: Stanford University Press, pp. 1–13.

Delany, C. 1991. *The Seed and the Soil: Gender and Cosmology in Turkish Village Society*. Berkeley: University of California Press.

Dilthey, W. 1961. *Pattern and Meaning in History: Thoughts on History and Society*. Ed. H. P. Rickman. New York: Harper and Row.

Dube, L., ed. 1997. *Women and Kinship: Comparative Perspectives on Gender in South and South-East Asia*. New York: United Nations University Press.

Edwards, J., et al. 1993. *Technologies of Procreation: Kinship in the Age of Assisted Conception*. Manchester, N.Y.: Manchester University Press.

Eggan, F. 1937. Historical Change in the Choctaw Kinship System. *American Anthropologist* 24: 34–52.

———. 1955. The Cheyenne and Arapaho Kinship System. In *Social Anthropology of the North American Tribes*. Second edition. Ed. F. Eggan. Chicago: University of Chicago Press, pp. 35–95.

———. 1966. *The American Indian: Perspectives for the Study of Social Change*. Chicago: Aldine.

Epple, C. 1998. Coming to Terms with Navaho *nádleehí*: A Critique of "*Berdache*," "Gay," "Alternative Gender" and "Two-Spirit." *American Ethnologist* 25 (2): 267–90.

Faubion, J. D. 1993. *Modern Greek Lessons: A Primer in Historical Constructivism*. Princeton: Princeton University Press.

———. 1998. Introduction. In M. Foucault, *Essential Works of Michel Foucault*, Vol. 2. *Aesthetics, Methodology, Epistemology*. Ed. J. D. Faubion. New York: Free Press, pp. xi–xxxv.

———. 2001. Toward an Anthropology of Ethics: Michel Foucault and the Pedagogies of Autopoiesis. *Representations* 74.

Foucault, M. 1978. *The History of Sexuality*. Vol. 1: *The Will to Know*. Trans. R. Hurley. New York: Random House.

———. 1985. *The History of Sexuality*. Vol. 2: *The Use of Pleasure*. Trans. R. Hurley. New York: Pantheon.

———. 1997a. The Ethics of the Concern of the Self as a Practice of Freedom. In *Essential Works of Michel Foucault*, Vol. 1: *Ethics: Subjectivity and Truth*. Ed. P. Rabinow. New York: New Press, pp. 281–301.

———. 1997b. On the Genealogy of Ethics: An Overview of Work in Progress. In *Essential Works of Michel Foucault*, Vol. 1: *Ethics: Subjectivity and Truth*. Ed. P. Rabinow. New York: New Press, pp. 253–80.

———. 1997c. Technologies of the Self. In *Essential Works of Michel Foucault*, Vol. 1. *Ethics: Subjectivity and Truth*. Ed. P. Rabinow. New York: New Press, pp. 223–51.

Francisconi, M. 1998. *Kinship, Capitalism, Change: The Informal Economy of the Navajo, 1868–1995.* New York: Garland Publishing.

Franklin, S. 1997. *Embodied Progress: A Cultural Account of Assisted Conception.* New York: Routledge.

Franklin, S., and H. Ragoné, eds. 1998. *Reproducing Reproduction: Kinship, Power, and Technological Innovation.* Philadelphia: University of Pennsylvania Press.

Freud, S. 1957. *Moses and Monotheism.* Trans. K. Jones. New York: Vintage.

Geertz, C. 1973. *The Interpretation of Cultures.* New York: Basic.

———. 1983. *Local Knowledge: Further Essays in Interpretive Anthropology.* New York: Basic.

Ginzburg, F., and R. Rapp, eds. 1995. *Conceiving the New World Order: The Global Politics of Reproduction.* Berkeley: University of California Press.

Godelier, M., T. Trautmann, and F. Fat, eds. 1998. *Transformations of Kinship.* Washington, D.C.: Smithsonian Institution Press.

Goody, J. 1983. *The Development of the Family and Marriage in Europe.* Cambridge: Cambridge University Press.

———. 1990. *The Oriental, the Ancient and the Primitive: Systems of Marriage and the Family in the Pre-Industrial Societies of Eurasia.* Cambridge: Cambridge University Press.

Greenberg, D. 1988. *The Construction of Homosexuality.* Chicago: University of Chicago Press.

Hage, P. 1997. Unthinkable Categories and the Fundamental Laws of Kinship. *American Ethnologist* 24 (3): 652–67.

Hammel, E. 1968. *Alternative Social Structures and Ritual Relations.* Englewood Cliffs, N.J.: Prentice-Hall.

Hansen, K., and A. Garey, eds. 1998. *Families in the U.S.: Kinship and Domestic Politics.* Philadelphia: Temple University Press.

Heidegger, M. 1962. *Being and Time.* Trans. J. Macquarrie and E. Robinson. New York: Harper and Row.

Hempel, C. 1974. Reasons and Covering Laws in Historical Explanation. In *The Philosophy of History.* Ed. P. Gardiner. Oxford: Oxford University Press, pp. 66–89.

Herdt, G. 1991a. Representations of Homosexuality in Traditional Societies: An Essay on Cultural Ontology and Historical Comparison, Part 1. *Journal of the History of Sexuality* 1 (3): 481–504.

———. 1991b. Representations of Homosexuality in Traditional Societies: An Essay on Cultural Ontology and Historical Comparison, Part 2. *Journal of the History of Sexuality* 1 (4): 603–32.

Héritier, F. 1994. *Les deux soeurs et leur mère: anthropologie de l'inceste.* Paris: Editions Odile Jacob.

Hine, R. V. 1974. Communitarianism. In *The Rise of Adventism: Religion and Society in Nineteenth-Century America.* Ed. E. S. Gaustad. New York: Harper and Row, pp. 70–78.

Holmgren, J. 1995. *Marriage, Kinship, and Power in Northern China.* Aldershot, U.K.: Variorum.

Hudson, W. S. 1974. A Time of Religious Ferment. In *The Rise of Adventism: Religion and Society in Nineteenth-Century America.* Ed. E. S. Gaustad. New York: Harper and Row, pp. 1–17.

Kristeva, J. 1993. *Nations without Nationalism.* Trans. L. S. Roudiez. New York: Columbia University Press.

Laqueur, W. 1990 *Making Sex: Body and Gender from the Greeks to Freud.* Cambridge, Mass.: Harvard University Press.

Leach, E. 1970. *Claude Lévi-Strauss.* Harmondsworth: Penguin.

Lévi-Strauss, C. 1969. *The Elementary Structures of Kinship.* Revised edition. Ed. R. Needham. Boston: Beacon.

Lewis, O. 1951. *Life in a Mexican Village: Tepoztlán Restudied.* Urbana: University of Illinois Press.

Luhmann, N. 1990. The Paradox of System Differentiation and the Evolution of Society. In *Differentiation Theory and Social Change: Comparative and Historical Perspectives.* Ed. J. C. Alexander and P. Colomy. New York: Columbia University Press, pp. 409–40.

Malinowski, B. 1939. Group and Individual in Functional Analysis. *American Journal of Sociology* 44: 938–64.

Mauss, M. 1968. A Category of the Human Spirit (1938). Trans. L. Krader. *Psychoanalytic Review* 55: 457–90.

Maynes, M. J., et al., eds. 1995. *Gender, Kinship, Power: An Interdisciplinary and Comparative History.* New York: Routledge.

Mintz, S. W., and E. R. Wolf. 1950. An Analysis of Ritual Co-Parenthood (*Compadrazgo*). *Southwestern Journal of Anthropology* 6 (4): 341–68.

Modell, J. 1994. *Kinship with Strangers: Adoption and Interpretations of Kinship in American Culture.* Berkeley: University of California Press.

Mundy, M. 1995. *Domestic Government: Kinship, Community and Polity in North Yemen.* London: I. B. Tauris.

Near, H. 1992. *The Kibbutz Movement: A History.* Oxford: Oxford University Press.

Needham, R. 1974. Remarks on the Analysis of Kinship and Marriage. In *Remarks and Inventions: Skeptical Essays about Kinship.* London: Tavistock, pp. 38–71.

Nutini, H. G., and B. Bell. 1980–1984. *Ritual Kinship.* 2 vols. Princeton: Princeton University Press.

Palriwala, R., and C. Risseeuw, eds. 1996. *Shifting Circles of Support: Contextualising Gender and Kinship in South Asia and Sub-Saharan Africa.* Walnut Creek, Calif.: AltaMira Press.

Pasternak, B., C. Ember, and M. Ember. 1997. *Sex, Gender, and Kinship: A Cross-Cultural Perspective.* Upper Saddle River, N.J.: Prentice Hall.

Pateman, C. 1988. *The Sexual Contract.* Oxford: Polity Press.

Rabinow, P. 1992. Artificiality and Enlightenment: From Sociobiology to Biosociality. In *Incorporations.* Ed. J. Carey and S. Kwinter. New York: Zone, pp. 234–52.

———. 1997. Introduction. In *Essential Works of Michel Foucault,* Vol. 1: *Ethics: Subjectivity and Truth.* Ed. P. Rabinow. New York: New Press, pp. xi–xlii.

Rabinow, P., and W. Sullivan, eds. 1987. *Interpretive Social Science: A Second Look.* Berkeley: University of California Press.

Roces, M. 1998. *Women, Power, and Kinship Politics: Female Power in Post-War Philippines.* Westport, Conn.: Praeger.

Rubin, G. 1975. The Traffic in Women: The "Political Economy" of Sex. In *Toward an Anthropology of Women.* Ed. R. R. Reiter. New York: Monthly Review Press, pp. 157–210.

Schneider, D. 1968. *American Kinship: A Cultural Account.* Englewood Cliffs, N.J.: Prentice-Hall.

———. 1984. *A Critique of the Study of Kinship.* Ann Arbor: University of Michigan Press.

Shapiro, W. 1979. *Social Organization in Aboriginal Australia.* New York: St. Martin's Press.

Shils, E. 1957. Primordial, Personal, Sacred, and Civil Ties. *British Journal of Sociology* 8: 130–145.

Smith, R. 1996. *The Matrifocal Family: Power, Pluralism, and Politics.* New York: Routledge.

Spiro, M. 1970. *Kibbutz: Venture in Utopia.* Schocken paperback edition. New York: Schocken Books.

Stacey, M., ed. 1992. *Changing Human Reproduction: Social Science Perspectives.* London: Sage.

Stivens, M. 1996. *Matriliny and Modernity: Sexual Politics and Social Change in Rural Malaysia.* St. Leonards, N.S.W.: Allen and Unwin.

Strathern, M. 1991. *Partial Connections.* Savage, Md.: Rowman & Littlefield.

———. 1992. *After Nature: English Kinship in the Late Twentieth Century.* Cambridge: Cambridge University Press.

Thompson, B., and S. Tyagi, eds. 1996. *Names We Call Home: Autobiography on Racial Identity.* New York: Routledge.

Tyler, S. 1998. Them Others—Voices without Mirrors. *Paideuma* 44: 31–50.

Watt, J. 1992. *The Making of Modern Marriage: Matrimonial Control and the Rise of Sentiment in Neuchâtel, 1550–1800.* Ithaca, N.Y.: Cornell University Press.

Weber, M. 1946. Class, Status, Party. In *From Max Weber: Essays in Sociology.* Ed. H. Gerth and C. W. Mills. New York: Oxford University Press, pp. 196–244.

———. 1968. *Economy and Society.* Ed. G. Roth and C. Wittich. Three volumes. New York: Bedminster Press.

Weismantel, M. 1995. Making Kin: Kinship Theory and Zumbagua Adoptions. *American Ethnologist* 22 (4): 685–709.

Weston, K. 1991. *Families We Choose: Lesbians, Gays, Kinship.* New York: Columbia University Press.

Wittgenstein, L. 1953. *Philosophical Investigations.* Trans. G. E. M. Anscombe. New York: Macmillan

Yanagisako, S. J., and J. F. Collier. 1987. Toward a Unified Analysis of Gender and Kinship. In *Gender and Kinship: Essays toward a Unified Analysis.* Ed. J. F. Collier and S. J. Yanagisako. Stanford, Calif.: Stanford University Press, pp. 14–50.

Yanagisako, S., and C. Delaney, eds. 1995. *Naturalizing Power: Essays in Feminist Cultural Analysis.* New York: Routledge.

Žižek, S. 1989. *The Sublime Object of Ideology.* London: Verso.

1

Caring and Being Cared For: Displacing Marriage, Kinship, Gender, and Sexuality

John Borneman

UNMAKING AFFILIATION

Since the inception of the discipline of ethnology, and later anthropology, in the late nineteenth century, a major goal of its practitioners has been to find sets of practices and institutions that would enable the universal translatability of culture, thus "grounding" the "human being" as object of knowledge. Early anthropologists were thoroughly influenced by the growing paradigm of sexuality, what Foucault (1978: 154–56) parodied as the new truth "worth dying for . . . that agency which appears to dominate us and that secret which seems to underlie all that we are." But they predicated the human instead in reproduction and subsumed sex into the institution of marriage. They claimed to have identified and then industriously named a wide variety of regulative forms comparable to the marital arrangements in their own countries of origin including primitive promiscuity, marriage by capture, marriage by purchase, marriage by right, group marriage, primitive marriage, communal marriage, levirate, ghost marriage, monogamy, polyandry, polygyny, sham marriage, and love marriage.

Within half a century, they shifted their focus to kinship and developed two paradigmatic schools—descent theory and alliance theory—the most forceful proponents being A. R. Radcliffe-Brown and Claude Lévi-Strauss, respectively. Descent theory was organized according to principles of consanguinity or shared substance, alliance theory on principles of affinity or marriage. Critiques of kinship theory accumulated—for its nonuniversality, overformalization, and lack of coherence as a domain—and in the early 1970s many anthropologists turned to gender, which was frequently combined, or sometimes subsumed, within an analysis of prestige, status, and power. This is not to say that each object of knowledge replaced in turn a prior one or that marriage ever lost its centrality in analysis. Rather, each successive generation of anthropologists subsumed the prior object into a new one by making it secondary to or derivative of other units of analysis without in fact calling into question the initial object of research. In other words, sexuality became derivative of marriage, marriage of kinship, kinship of gender, and gender of prestige and power.

Today, marriage, exalted as the right to found a family, has established itself as global ideology and is explicitly protected in the constitutions of most countries throughout the world. Though claiming human universality and inclusiveness, what is most at stake for its proponents is the social and legal recognition and protection of a particular form of sociation: heterosexual marriage and family. Marriage and the protection of families are often claimed as a universal human right, more basic to "life, liberty, and the pursuit of happiness" than other human needs, such as, for example, the need to eat, to work, or to love. Even the United Nations has approached this "right" with a special kind of reverence, designating 1975 International Women's Year, 1979 The Year of the Child, and 1994 The Year of the Family. Indeed, the Christian idea of the "sacrament of marriage," defined in terms of institutionalized procreative heterosexuality, is one of the few positive rights that has attained nearly universal consensus. Because of this world ideology, the connections of marriage and the family—the principles of descent and affinity—to the assertion of privilege, abjection, and exclusion are rarely seen and, therefore, rarely examined.

Simultaneous with and running parallel to the process of universalizing and standardizing the forms, protections, and privileges of "marriage and the family" has been an increased awareness of the diversity of forms of intimacy and sociality within and across social formations as well as over time. Anthropologists have made major contributions to both processes: universalizing "marriage and the family" as a translatable form and increasing the awareness of cultural diversity. But these contributions have inherent conceptual limitations. For one, depending on choice of paradigm and the ideological inclinations of the researcher, anthropologists have tended to assert the logical or temporal priority of power, gender, kinship, marriage, or sex, without rigorously justifying the violent hierarchies that result from such prioritizing. They have also nearly totally ignored what is foreclosed, abjected, or excluded in the production of this diversity, focusing instead on the coexistence of plural, hierarchized forms.[1]

My response to this paradigmatic history is threefold: (1) I maintain that power, gender, kinship, marriage, and sex are part of a chain of signifying practices with no particular term being prior or more grounded; (2) I critique the privileged status of particular practices or forms by paying more attention to variability and instability in "occasions of symbolization" where practices and forms are reiterated; and (3) I argue that anthropology's quest for a regulative ideal for humanity has involved the repression of care and the privileging of forms of communal reproduction; anthropology should instead privilege in analysis caring and being cared for as processes of non-coercive, voluntary affiliation.

I take up illustrations of the breakdown of anthropological and legal categories of sex, marriage, kinship, and gender that nonetheless suggest alternatives for conceptualizing human affiliation outside reproductive ideologies and practices. Anthropological articulation and legal recognition are of course separate processes, though symbiotically related in constructing human affiliation. As the study of humankind, the discipline of anthropology prides itself on providing discursive frames for conceptualizing, demarcating, or understanding human affiliations and identifications across social formations and over time. Law, in its goal of harmonizing the social with an official vision of itself, prides itself on the moral regulation, through prescription and prohibition, of discursive practices and their forms of affiliations and identifications.

I focus on two occasions of symbolization of the principles of descent and affinity, by which I mean temporally sequenced situations in which these principles are performed. At these occasions, participation—and anthropological articulation—appears initially as foreclosed, and yet legal recognition comes about. The examples are of legal cases of adoption and of marriage in contemporary Germany. I conclude that because anthropological formulations and descriptions of affiliation have the regulative effect of constituting what should be, the discipline of anthropology is, much like law, a moral science. Hence it has a responsibility not to further the particular goals and institutional arrangements of diverse social communities but to examine critically and support in its normative frameworks diverse projects of caring and being cared for.

CASE 1. AFFILIATION THROUGH ADOPTION: DESCENT REVISITED

In December 1995 in Berlin I visited a friend, Harald, who had just received a letter from the municipal authorities of Potsdam granting his petition to adopt a son. Harald is fifty-five, his son, Dieter, is thirty-five. They have been living together for the past twelve years, and we have been acquainted for the past ten. The key question posed by the civil court in the adoption concerned the nature of the relationship between the two men—a question that other lawyers told me the court was not allowed to ask: Was the relationship between Harald and his friend similar to that between a biological father and his son? The judge who initially received their petition sent a letter to Dieter's mother—his father is dead—asking her if she was willing to allow Harald to adopt her child. In German legal practice, the only firm restriction on adult adoption is the age of the "parent," who must be under sixty years; there is no age restriction on the person adopted. In this case, if the mother granted someone else the right to adopt her son, she would retain her *Abstammungsrecht* (legal relationship of descent) while sharing with Harald the various diffuse rights embodied in laws pertaining to *Verwandtschaftsrecht* (legal kinship relations). In her reply, the mother agreed to the request but also added a few asides about the relationship of her son to Harald. She wrote that Dieter was homosexual and that his relationship with Harald was "like a marriage."

After receiving the petition, the judge scheduled a hearing where, among other questions, he asked the two men to explain the mother's written asides. Surprised that she went out of her way to make any comments whatsoever, they explained that she simply did not know what she was talking about. She had seen Dieter merely two times in the last ten years. Nonetheless, the judge said he needed further clarification of the relationship between the two men and scheduled another hearing. Throughout the adoption process, Harald's lawyer told them not to worry. Although he had never argued such a case before, he was confident about the prospects for success.

Several months passed before the second hearing. In the meantime, I wrote a letter in support of the petition, stating that I am an expert on East German family law and family structure (which I am), and that Harald and his prospective son never had a sexual relationship with each other (which is an obvious lie). The lawyer held this letter in reserve, to use only if a negative decision was reached in the second hearing or if the hearing was inconclusive. As it turned out, on the date of the second hearing before the court, the first judge was on vacation. His replacement was a young man in his late twenties or early thirties, who, unlike the first judge, Dieter told me, wore no wedding ring.

The second judge began by saying he "had no problems" with homosexuality, and then he asked the prospective son about his mother's comment. Dieter answered, "My mother hasn't had anything to do with me since I was four. I've seen her only twice in the last decade. You can still ask her again, if you like. But it doesn't make any sense to compare my relationship with Harald to a marriage. I never really had a father, and the one I had abused me. Harald has always taken care of me. And besides, you know that I like boys." Not wanting to hear any details about this "liking boys," the judge swiftly replied, "That won't be necessary. That's all clear now."

The judge had before him the verdict from Dieter's 1990 trial: guilty of having sex with a minor; in fact, with several minors. For this crime Dieter had received a prison sentence of five and a half years. In Germany, where few persons convicted of crimes sit behind bars, this is a very severe sentence. Even convicted murderers rarely get more than five years. Sentences given in the first forty trials of East German border guards who shot to kill on the Berlin Wall were rarely over three and a half years, and most of these were suspended! But the prospective son's trial had taken place in 1990 and 1991 during the chaos of unification of the justice systems. And the East German judge at the time—whose appointment was being reviewed—was probably concerned that his Western colleagues would think him too lenient in punishing *Sittlichkeitsdelikten* (crimes of custom, or, as Hegel would say, of "ethical substance"). Leniency in this case might have reinforced the stereotype that East German judges were soft on domestic crime but tough on "political crime." All of this was taking place during a frenzy of investigative reporting in the former German Democratic Republic (GDR) by East and West German television and print media, as they competed for public attention and for control of the new open market of the East. They were especially alert for scandals concerning abuse of power, such as fraud or sexual abuse, or to uncover "crimes" that might illustrate excessive severity or laxity on the part of the GDR's justice system. A special investigative television show discovered Dieter's case, but since he sat in jail, they pursued Harald. A television crew even tracked Harald down in his workplace, where they entered his office and stuck a microphone in his face, confronting him with questions about the circumstances of Dieter's arrest. For Harald, who had secured a post-unity job as a *Beamte* (civil servant) in the Ministry of Culture, this confrontation proved particularly unsettling, as it threatened his job security at a time when most East Germans with similar qualifications were being fired.

The judge in the second hearing turned to Harald and asked him to describe his relationship with Dieter. Harald explained, first, he was prompted to pursue the adoption when he learned that he had developed a terminal cancer from an unusual tumor found behind his left eye. Then he said that he cared for Dieter like a son and friend and therefore wanted to leave his house and other property to him. Adoption was the only legal means by which he could do this. All of this is true. Then, with great difficulty, he lied, as he had to, and he denied ever having had sex with Dieter. He supported this with a claim that for nearly a decade he had had a sexual relationship with another man, who is no longer living; and, he asserted, that in any case there never had been any erotic interest between him and the adoptee. The judge sensed Harald's ambivalence in telling this story and repeatedly questioned him about details. Dieter's questioning went smoothly. He lied with conviction, reaffirming that since he liked boys, it was implausible that he would have a sexual relationship with Harald. The judge seemed immediately satisfied with his answers. Three weeks later, Harald and Dieter received the court-approved adoption papers in the mail.

What is the significance of this adoption? Neither the discrepancy between legal norms and actual practice—this is always the case with law and nothing new to anthropologists—nor the confusion of anthropological categories of sexuality, marriage, kinship, and gender—also nothing new to us—is our primary concern. The significance lies in how the legal interpretation of formal heterosexual kinship norms is changing to adjust to the actual needs of people to care and be cared for. I am focusing on legal recognition not because it is the only type of social recognition, but because the state and its law remain the most powerful institutional force in our contemporary world conferring rights and privileges. Very few people can afford to live outside this law.

The logic of the adoption was in fact set up by the legal categories of kinship—which are also enshrined in anthropological theories—to which any petition must appeal. But once the petition was granted and the adoption approved, the initial legal kinship logic had been effectively stretched out of recognizable shape. Descent and alliance, consanguinity and affinity, the two principles of kinship, were no longer structuring the decision. In fact, a new principle of kinship was at work: an extension of *Sorgerecht* (custody, literally as the right to take care of) to those usually excluded from its protection. Even though, strictly speaking, the domain of practices at stake was that of *Erbschaft* (inheritance law), the judge specifically appealed to the principles of Sorgerecht (custody law) and thereby made the right to inherit wealth effective through a right to care and be cared for.

Traditionally, adoption in German law and in the Western legal tradition establishes a legal relationship of parentage by descent. Whereas parentage used to mean, to put it crassly, the rights of parents, initially fathers, to reproduce their image and employ their children as they saw fit, parentage has been redefined over the course of this century. With respect to the assignment of custody after a divorce of the parents, mothers have obtained priority over fathers. And parental rights have been tilted toward protecting and entitling children and assigning duties to parents. Today, while parents can make practically no legal claims on their children (e.g., to care for them in old age, to repay their debts, to work for them), children's rights have been expanded in the areas of Sorgerecht and *Erziehungsrecht* (the right to be brought up/educated).

Although there is no specific domain of Verwandtschaftsrecht (the right of kinship relations), kinship rights permeate all legal domains as relations between specific categories of kin (such as husband and wife or parent and child) and relations analogous to them are protected, supported, or forbidden. Today, adoption of adult by adult to establish legal "descent" for reasons of inheritance alone is, I am told, accepted legal practice in Germany. Yet the judge in this case did not begin by applying an abstract principle of descent to enable Harald to pass on his inheritance to Dieter. Instead he began as if he had just read Lévi-Strauss's (1969) *The Elementary Structures of Kinship*, where reproduction of societies is linked to respect for the incest taboo as the social precondition for the principles of heterosexual descent and affinity. Above all, it appears as if the judge was concerned with whether

Harald and Dieter had respected the fundamental incest taboo—no sex between parent and child. As Lévi-Strauss (1969: 50) argued, the incest taboo, or the forbidding of sex between people of the same descent, creates the possibility for and necessity of affinity. Marriage, then, as the key institution of affinity, is conceptualized as the antithesis of the incest taboo and is what creates the possibility of broader forms of sociality through obligatory sex outside the primal family. In this legal case, however, according to the mother, Harald and Dieter were already living in a marital relationship, were already engaged in an affinal relationship, which meant one of obligatory sex, and were therefore already in violation of the incest taboo. Hence, according to this logic, the preconditions for legal descent were absent.

Harald and Dieter and the judge were caught in a number of gendered kinship analogies about relationships of prescribed and prohibited sex. If Harald and Dieter lived together in a relationship, as the mother asserted, "like a marriage," then by analogy with heterosexual kin relations, sex between them was a necessary if not compulsory effect. This was in fact the conclusion drawn from the analogy made by Dieter's mother. Of course, anyone familiar with the long-term sexual patterns of men who live together as couples knows that although the variance is great, two patterns are in fact quite common. Frequently, the very idea of incestuous sex, between father and son, is part of the erotic dynamic between the partners. Alternatively, many such relationships may involve erotic activity, but they are sustained over time precisely through sexual relationships with others outside the primary relationship. In neither pattern is the enforcement of the incest taboo for purposes of social reproduction relevant as a structuring device. Unlike hetero-sex, such homo-sex is not oriented to enclosure within the couple and to the reproduction of the couple along with its past. Instead homo-sex assumes sterility while maintaining an openness to the world and an orientation to the future.

The application of the principles of heteronormativity and the law to such actual patterns is not only confusing, it is nonsensical and an insult to those involved. By analogy the judge was being asked if it might be possible to turn an affinal relation "like in a marriage" into one of legal descent—Dieter becomes Harald's son. But the incest taboo—by setting up descent and affinity as counterconcepts, the former lacking sex, the latter requiring it— expressly forbids such a transformation. Anthropological theory and the law have been in widespread agreement that nature bestows on us the principle of descent while culture specifies the rules of affinity. In theory adults are to enjoy both principles simultaneously as privileged relationships with culturally specified—gendered, sexed, and age-graded—categories of persons as long as both principles are not realized with the same person.

What I have identified here, in the judge's decision to approve the adoption despite the fact that there is no clear separation of affinity and descent, is the subordination of the principle of descent to a relation of care. In their enactment of care for each other, Dieter and Harald are reinventing human sociality. Specifically, they are reinventing the principle of "descent," without any knowledge about how such a reinvention might proceed historically. Is it possible to represent their relation in the formalized logic of the standard anthropological kinship diagram? These kinship charts have been to anthropologists what maps are to cartographers, not merely a formal tool of representation but an icon, a Logos, of the discipline itself. In such diagrams, a male-gendered ego at the center is shown to unite, to rearrange, two groups. The male (Δ) and female (O) are represented as objects held together by three functions: descent (|), siblingship (—), and marriage (=). Within anthropology, this particular form of representation had the initial effect of encompassing marriage in a larger network of kinship relations that included both principles of affinity and consanguinity. Indeed, Radcliffe-Brown (1950: 51) tried to gloss the representation in such a way that not marriage but what he called the "elementary family"—a man and his wife and their child or children—would constitute "the first order" or "unit of structure" of a human group. Alternatively, Lévi-Strauss insisted that not kinship units but the relation between groups, regulated by preferential marriage and the incest taboo, set up the conditions for exchange and thus comprised the elementary structure of human organization. Whether prioritizing the elementary family or exchange between groups, both theorists repressed care. They subordinated what was human about kinship practice to its organizational form and to the means of reproduction. Lurking behind and prior to either families or groups are relations of care.

Dieter's mother thought through analogy: the relationship between the two men looked like a marriage: $\Delta=\Delta$. But since the = is supposed to join only opposite-sex signs, $\Delta=O$, such a relationship of affinity as between Harald and Dieter is anthropologically problematic—unless one of the partners becomes gendered as a woman, in other words, a transvestite. The mother's analogy with affinity was not supposed to be the primary issue for the court, for the judge was being asked to think through a relationship of descent: $\Delta | ^\Delta$. Descent between the two men was indeed imaginable and representable—but only after the judge first established respect for the incest taboo, the precondition of kinship, which keeps the principles of affinity and consanguinity separate. Respect for this precondition is a matter of not having sex with relatives by descent. This essential bit of information—denial of sex between the two men—had to be created as a public secret by the court, enlisting lawyers, mother, lovers, friends, and anthropologist in the complicity of falsifying an actual relationship so as to fit it into the classic anthropological kinship paradigm. Can anyone wonder why those foreclosed from participation in kinship—except on the condition they publicly lie about the relation of gender to sex—might lack a certain respect for its heteronormative principles and for those who assume they can innocently practice, enjoy, and enforce them?

The breakdown in the ability of the categories of sex, marriage, kinship, and gender to represent an affiliation based on the fundamental need of care presents anthropologists with the task of finding a way to re-present the relation between Harald and Dieter—to turn abjection into inclusion, absence into presence, negativity into positivity. For law, the task is to take what is either outside or, at best, the "exception" and bring it under the rule. But the judge had no discursive options to do this. The first enabling step, then, belongs not to law but to anthropology to create the possibility of representation and articulation, to describe empirically what is. Technically, anthropological theory offers an analogy for adult-adult adoption: the option of reclassifying a nonconsanguineous relation into one of descent by means of the term *categorical kin*. Indeed, the judge analogized by means of a similar logic. But much as the term *categorical kin* presupposes a false distinction between real (biological) and cultural (categorical), the judge was forced to reason by means of spurious comparisons. The relationship between Dieter and Harald resembled neither marriage nor parentage, while containing elements of both over time. Their relationship was based neither on a set of communitarian foreclosures and essential exclusions—of sex or blood—nor on filling a lack through the incorporation of gender difference into a new unity. Rather, they were asserting an elementary principle of human affiliation: the need to care and be cared for.

CASE 2. AFFILIATION THROUGH MARRIAGE: AFFINITY REVISITED

One evening in 1987, shortly after I completed my first period of fieldwork in East Berlin and had moved to the West, my best East German friend invited me to a party in the apartment of a lesbian couple in the East where his ex-wife, Bärbel, would be present. The Berlin Wall was still intact, so I had to get a visa at the border, exchange the compulsory twenty-five marks, and reappear at the border before midnight, which definitely put a damper on attending parties in the East. Bärbel, who works as a nurse, came with her Czech lover, Mirka, who works for the city's housing bureaucracy, and her lover's son, Martin, who was an unemployed artist. Ages may help to keep these people distinct; at that time Bärbel was about forty-two, Mirka fifty-three, and Martin thirty-four years old.

Martin, with whom I later made a film, was a young director in Prague before he was convicted of some black-market activity, the circumstances of which are still unclear to me and for which he served two years in prison. We went on talking about this and that, while the others in the room, who knew each other very well, reminisced about the past. Time flew, and the witching hour neared when I was due back at the border. Bärbel approached us, and Martin put his arm around her and said to me, "John, did you meet my wife?" It took me a while to get it—Martin was married to his mother's lover, Bärbel. Bärbel was married to her lover's son, Martin. Mirka was both the lover and mother-in-law of her son's wife. Thinking in terms of anthropological or legal kinship terminology obviously confused the actual relations these people had with each other. Yet the legal, theoretical, and pragmatic dimensions of kinship were the terrains on which they fought for what was at stake, which, again, was the right to care and be cared for.

Each personal history reveals different dimensions of the ambivalence within categories of kinship, gender, marriage, sexuality, and the law. My best friend told me that he had married Bärbel out of loneliness, out of flight from homosexual desire, and due to the strong "recommendation" of the local Communist Party boss that he normalize his domestic relations. For several years he led a normal heterosexual marriage, though without children. And then he began taking on a series of lovers with Bärbel's consent, one of whom, a black Cuban *Gastarbeiter* (immigrant laborer), actually lived with the couple for a year. Then Bärbel met Mirka, they fell in love, and Bärbel divorced my best friend.

Mirka had been married for twelve years before her husband found another woman and fled to Switzerland. After Soviet tanks squashed the Prague Spring in 1968, Czechoslovakia entered a period of political and cultural stagnation, and Mirka, like many Czechs desiring a change, found a way through relatives in Austria to move to West Berlin without having to give up her Czech citizenship. Mirka therefore retained the option of returning to Czechoslovakia, if things did not work out, and as a Czech citizen, she could easily obtain a day visa for East Berlin to visit her friends. It wasn't long before Mirka met Bärbel at a party in East Berlin, and they decided they wanted to live together. Bärbel had to move to the West. Her options to leave East Germany were marriage, bribing authorities, or applying for a visa with an uncertain period of imprisonment before being bought by the West Germans. Marriage was the least risky option. But whom to marry? East German authorities did not usually approve of marriages with West Germans. And such approvals, if they occurred, usually took several years. There was no such delay or likely penalty if an East German married a Czechoslovak citizen. The governments of Czechoslovakia and East Germany were close fraternal allies in the Soviet bloc, and marriage across those national borders was relatively easy. Hence, Mirka paid a Czech man to marry Bärbel. With that arrangement, Bärbel could also retain her East German citizenship after obtaining a Czechoslovak one.

Bärbel then moved to Prague to live with her new husband. Much to her surprise, he developed his own romantic designs on her, which she managed to fend off for the several months it took her to establish residency.

Then, as a Czech citizen, she easily obtained a Czechoslovak visa to travel to Austria. And from Austria, her East German citizenship automatically qualified her for West German citizenship, since the West German state had claimed as its citizens all of the people in East Germany. This enabled Bärbel to move to West Berlin, where she joined Mirka, and from there she divorced her Czech husband.

Living in West Berlin, Bärbel's citizenship was immediately revoked by East German authorities, and they denied her a visa to return or travel through the GDR for the next eight years. During this period of exile, any time Bärbel and Mirka went to visit relatives in Czechoslovakia, Mirka would drive or take the train through the GDR (four to six hours) while Bärbel would have to take the train first to West Germany before crossing its border with Czechoslovakia (about twelve hours). Over the years, their travel became more frequent as they took on some of the increasing responsibilities of caring for Mirka's aging mother and other relatives living in Bohemia, an hour's train ride south of Prague.

Mirka's son Martin, meanwhile, decided after his two years in prison that he wanted to leave Czechoslovakia. Hence he petitioned to marry the twice-divorced Bärbel and to establish a residence with her in West Berlin. One of the requirements of legal marriage in nearly all states is a common residence. The other requirement is that the partner must be of the opposite sex, that is, marriage is a heterosexual, cohabiting union. Beyond that, states vary in what other content—such as love or property or religion—is a necessary precondition for marriage. For the next eighteen months Martin and Bärbel fulfilled this residency requirement by living together in an apartment in West Berlin, which they also shared with Mirka. Martin and Bärbel cohabitated, in this case, not because they were married but because they both had caring relations with Mirka. One of the relationships in this household inverted the anthropological/legal gender–sex paradigm: lesbian lovers, mother-in-law–daughter-in-law sex. The other extended the mother-son bond well beyond the culturally expected age of parental care. As in the case of adoption, this occasion of symbolization again suggests the limited utility of the classical anthropological kinship paradigm either as a descriptive device or as a means for self-articulation.

Elsewhere I have demonstrated how kinship diagrams are usually employed to create a representation of permanence and continuity, a wholeness and completeness that constantly denies death as it reaffirms perpetual life in a series of equivalent heterosexual unions organized by marriage. In all of the relationships examined here, this sociologic obscures the empirical behavior. The kinship of Dieter and Harald had nothing to do with establishing permanence or denying death through heterosexual union—it acknowledged sterility—and it was not envisioned as the completion of halves—it was not based on lack. Likewise in the case of Martin and Bärbel, the "=" signifying marriage links not husband to wife but "son" to categorical "mother's lover." Its purpose was neither reproductive nor to establish the possibility of descent. Likewise in the case of Bärbel and Mirka, their sex, if translated into their actual kinship categories following the marriage of Martin and Bärbel, would be sex between "mother's lover" and "biological mother." Relations of affinity based on care alone, without recourse to the incest taboo and the separation of descent from affinity, are neither articulable nor representable in anthropological categories.

In what way, then, beyond the local affirmation of care, was the relation between Martin and Bärbel and Mirka significant? Its primary significance, I would argue, is that it radically rearranged social structure so as to invent alternative possibilities of affiliation. It did this not only by subverting categories of kinship and citizenship but by creating hardly imaginable possibilities of affiliation within a world structured as a "dual organization," divided as it was between World War I and World War II, between enemy camps of the "Free World" and the "Socialist bloc." The formal structure of the order was, then, not reproduced or reaffirmed but fundamentally challenged and reordered. In short, this particular triangulation extended the meanings of descent and affinity in new directions anticipated by neither law nor anthropology. Has it not precisely been one of the major historical contributions of anthropology to seek out and document such alternatives?

These details of kinship, marriage, gender, and sex may be particularly complex because of the way citizenship was defined by the "dual organization" of the blocs during the Cold War. But my example is not unique to this time or place. After that particular evening in East Berlin, I became acquainted with a much larger group of people, many, but not all, of them gay men and lesbians who used legal kinship relations, particularly relations of affinity or marriage, to construct relations of intimacy that were not related to the two legal requirements of common residence and heterosexual union. Marriage, then, much like adoption, is undergoing some fundamental changes in practice. As the legal tool of marriage is stretched to fit and made to serve the practical goals and situations of actual and diverse peoples, in particular to foreground the needs of caring, it undermines its traditional institutional purposes. That is, this occasion of symbolization does not serve to reiterate a series of traditional foreclosures and exclusions but imaginatively refigures the anthropological conceptualization and legal application of principles of affinity and descent in the practical domains of citizenship, inheritance, health care, parentage, and sex.

AFFILIATION AND DEATH

Two months after completing this text, on March 31, 1997, I received a formal *Traueranzeige* (announcement of death). It was addressed to "Prof.

Bornemann" and read: "My father, Dr. Phil. Horst Lohr, passed away on Friday, March 7, 1997. In quiet mourning/His son Detlev Lohr and Prinz. The funeral ceremony will take place at 2:00 P.M. on April 4, 1997, at the 'New Cemetery' in Potsdam." Included with the announcement was a letter, with two parts, the first signed by Horst: "My last greeting/Do well, my loves/It was beautiful—through you/It's a shame/Your Horst"; the second, unsigned but typed in the name of Detlev Lohr, his loyal *Freundinnen* (female friends), and Prinz: "He didn't want to go. We didn't want to let him go. His unquenchable curiosity was oriented to this side. He wanted to know everything, above all how it all hung together. He saw the world as a giant puppet theater, himself as puppeteer and educator to a literary ideal. He was not spared disappointments, which made him ill. The game is over. He enriched our lives. For that we are thankful."

At this point, I no longer feel obligated to hide their names: Horst is Harald, Detlev is Dieter. In fact, I feel I can best honor Horst at this point by naming him. All along I had encouraged him to fight on for legal recognition of his living kinship ties with Detlev, even though this struggle also cost him tremendous energy and time when he had so little of both left to give. A friend asked me if the announcement of death was written in order to foreground "His son Detlev" for legal purposes. Absolutely not, I replied. It was a confirmation of one of Horst's final accomplishments—to have worked through and against the legal system of the united Germany to bestow on his friend Detlev one last act of care: his name and the rights of descent. Detlev, at this final moment, undoubtedly felt proud to have established social and legal recognition of his relationship with Horst, even though that acknowledgment mandated reducing their complex relationship to the legal status of father and son. Horst's female friends, who were extremely active in caring for him throughout his ordeal with Detlev's trial and imprisonment, and then throughout his illness, acknowledged in their letter of mourning the reciprocity of the care and the unrepayable gift they received from Horst as he permitted them to accompany him into death (Russ 1998). Finally, the inscription of Prinz, Horst's and Detlev's loyal golden retriever, in both the announcement of death and the letter of mourning demonstrates that for Horst and his kin the human principle of care extends well beyond caring for people.

MAKING AFFILIATION

In *Being and Time* (1962), Heidegger based his existential analysis on *Sorge* (the thematic concept of care). He desubstantialized human experience and insisted that temporality is to be found not in a human essence or form but in the dialectic of coming to be, of having been, and of making present. *Dasein*, living/being in time, is defined not in a simple succession of discrete "nows" but in the temporal constitution of care. Humans, then, are not blind egos following deterministic sequences of events, of cultural paradigms and rules. They plot sequences of experiences in narratives organized around for whom and what they care.

For most of this century, anthropologists have repressed care and instead been concerned largely with finding human origins, cores, foundations, and essences. Similar to how Christians located this core in suffering, Marxists in production, and Liberals in individualism, anthropologists have tended to locate human essence in practices and forms of kinship, marriage, gender, and sex, each of which has been defined in terms of a substance outside of time. In fact, anthropology has worked within a Christian tradition that assumes the possibility of Being in "an eternity where everything is present at the same time" (Ricoeur 1984: 86). Anthropological visions have revolved around an image of eternal "cultures" engaged in production and reproduction.

In the last several decades, many anthropologists, particularly those working on issues of sex and gender, have questioned the possibility of finding the universal truth of sex, marriage, kinship, and gender. They have also unwittingly been documenting Heidegger's basic insight and bold thesis about the temporal constitution of care. Especially since the reception of Foucault in the 1980s—whose basic insight was that human subjectivity is the product of power/knowledge and technologies of the self—ethnographers have paid less attention to paradigms of the Normal and more to normalizing practices as well as to the forms of subjectivity and subjection that result from them.

I am committed to a kind of anthropological endeavor that questions the equation of conventionally accepted norms, such as descent and affinity, with a human core or foundation. I have focused on how these normative frameworks are institutionalized in marriage and kinship, produced in time by acts of exclusion, and how the excluded nonetheless find means to articulate their needs. This "how" question moves us from a paradigmatic explanation to a narrative one. Instead of trying to escape from time by eternalizing the human condition in a reproductive ideology that pretends to subsume and explain us, I have attempted to recapture aspects of the variability and novelty of the human project as it unfolds. Rather than search for the interiority of Being or the inner life of the native, I have examined the surface logic of life plots and the relation of improbable plots to the heteronormative trinity of birth, marriage, and death. The pursuit of improbable plots has the advantage of openness to the spontaneity of unpredictability and an orientation to the future; such plots tell us much less about the reproduction of past paradigms of kinship. In fact, the search for a more powerful past reality beneath the surface, such as a foundational core of gender or sex or marriage, will nearly always point backwards instead of to an emergent future.

Finally, I assert the priority of an ontological process—to care and to be cared for—as a fundamental human need and nascent right in the international system. Carol Gilligan began such a focus on the "ethic of care" in 1982, attaching it to a feminine voice as opposed to a masculine "ethic of right." Although it is true that historically in most parts of the world care has been gendered in specific feminine voices (above all as mother, sister, wife), Gilligan undoes Heidegger's contribution by resubstantializing care as a necessary transcultural feminine trait. To be sure, today the articulation of care and the acknowledgment of right are empirically distributed by gender, much as they are by class, race, and geography. But "care" and "right" are neither theoretically nor essentially opposed; any consideration of one ethic imbricates the other. Caring belongs to every human as both practice and right.[2]

In his recent work on a "moral anthropology," Tzvetan Todorov (1996: 103) carries this insight further, claiming that among the three "ordinary virtues"—dignity, care, and life of the mind—caring is the "morally superior act." Care is "unlike dignity, where the 'I' addresses itself to the same 'I,'" and it is "unlike life of the mind, where the 'I' addresses itself to more or less numerous 'they's' who remain anonymous and no longer part of a present and ongoing dialogue." In caring, "the 'I' addresses itself to one or several individual 'you's'—in other words, to particular human beings with whom there has been established a relationship of reciprocity, a possibility of a reversal of roles." Not only do ethnographic accounts provide ample documentation for the diversity of relations in which caring is expressed and of the power matrix in which these relations are assigned value, but jural personnel are increasingly interpreting kinship law in light of these diverse relations—and not in terms of putatively fixed and innocent identities of sexuality, marriage, kinship, and gender. This suggests that I am identifying a shift in the object of anthropological research, already well under way, away from either the institution of marriage or categories of kinship, sexual identities, gender inequality, or of power differentials generally, to a concern for the actual situations in which people experience the need to care and be cared for and to the political economies of their distribution (Borneman 1997b). The simplicity of my formulation may appear deceptive, but we must resist subordinating particular practices and forms to any analytical type or communitarian standard and leave the ways in which humans define care up to them.

NOTES

Much of the first part of this article is taken from John Borneman, "Caring and Being Cared For," *International Social Science Journal,* vol. 154 (1997) © *UNESCO.*

1. See also Borneman 1996. For additional critical and ethnographic research: on gender, see Collier and Yanagisako 1987 (especially the essay by Rapp, pp. 119–31), Errington 1990, Godelier 1986, Newton 1993, Ortner and Whitehead, eds. 1981, Rubin 1975; on kinship, see Needham 1971, Schneider 1972, Schneider and Gough 1961, Strathern 1992, Weiner 1992; on family forms, see Lewin 1993, Weston 1991; on global

influences refiguring reproduction, see Ginsburg and Rapp 1995; in the growing field of queer theory, primarily outside of anthropology, see Butler 1993, Fuss 1991, Sedgwick 1990, Warner 1993; on sexuality, see Herdt 1987, Lancaster 1992, Rubin 1984; on ethnographic research on sexuality, see Herdt and Stoller 1990, Lewin and Leap 1996; on the influence of the AIDS pandemic and anthropology, see Bolton, ed. 1989.

2. Gilligan (1982) initially posits an opposition between a male ethic of justice concerned with equality and inequality versus a female ethic of care concerned with attachment and detachment. Her work, based on psychological research, has subsequently been productively taken up by other feminist scholars and criticized for essentializing gender; for a false universalism that ignores differences in race, class, and culture; for positing a false opposition of autonomy and care, as an ethic of justice encompassing care; and for lack of a critical perspective (see Clement 1996; the essays in Code, Mullett, and Overall 1988; Houston 1990; the essays in Larrabee 1993; Okin 1989; Tronto 1993). Indeed, no empirical relation between the category "women" and the ethic of care has been demonstrated. Moreover, Gilligan's own research was limited to the moral orientation of American, white, well-educated women. My own argument is that care and autonomy/justice are two necessary virtues in a moral theory, and two integral elements in the construction of kinship. Each is inadequate for analysis in itself, but both perform a critical function when used to interrogate each other's inadequacy. By suggesting that we replace *kinship* with *care* as a unit of analysis for forms of sociation, I am foregrounding the ethical dimension in the analysis of social practices often neglected in the focus on pragmatic institutional arrangements.

BIBLIOGRAPHY

Bolton, Ralph, ed. 1989. *The AIDS Pandemic: A Global Emergency.* New York: Gordon and Breach.

Borneman, John. 1996. Until Death Do Us Part: Marriage/Death in Anthropological Discourse. *American Ethnologist* 23 (2): 215–38.

———. 1997a. Caring and To Be Cared For: Displacing Marriage, Kinship, Gender, and Sexuality. *International Social Science Journal* 154 (December 1997): 573–84.

———. 1997b. *Settling Accounts: Violence, Justice, and Accountability in Postsocialist Europe.* Princeton: Princeton University Press.

Butler, Judith. 1993. *Bodies That Matter: On the Discursive Limits of "Sex."* New York: Routledge.

Clement, Grace. 1996. *Care, Autonomy, and Justice: Feminism and the Ethic of Care.* Boulder, Colo.: Westview.

Code, Lorraine, Sheila Mullett, and Christine Overall, eds. 1988. *Feminist Perspectives: Philosophical Essays on Method and Morals.* Toronto: University of Toronto Press.

Collier, Jane, and Sylvia Yanagisako, eds. 1987. *Gender and Kinship: Essays toward a Unified Analysis.* Stanford, Calif.: Stanford University Press.

Errington, Shelly. 1990. Recasting Sex, Gender, and Power: A Theoretical and Regional Overview. In *Power and Difference: Gender in Island Southeast Asia.* Ed. J. Atkinson and S. Errington. Stanford, Calif.: Stanford University Press, pp. 1–55.

Foucault, Michel. 1978. *The History of Sexuality.* Vol. 1. New York: Random House.

Fuss, Diana, ed. 1991. *Inside/Out.* New York: Routledge.

Gilligan, Carol. 1982. *In a Different Voice: Psychological Theory and Women's Development.* Cambridge: Harvard University Press.

Ginsburg, Faye, and Rayna Rapp, eds. 1995. *Conceiving the New World Order: The Global Politics of Reproduction.* Berkeley: University of California Press.

Godelier, Maurice. 1986. *The Making of Great Men: Male Domination and Power among the New Guinea Baruya.* Cambridge: Cambridge University Press.

Heidegger, Martin. 1962. *Being and Time.* Trans. J. Macquarrie and E. Robinson. New York: Harper and Row.

Herdt, Gilbert. 1987. *The Sambia: Ritual and Gender in New Guinea.* New York: Holt, Rinehart, and Winston.

Herdt, Gilbert, and Robert Stoller, eds. 1990. *Intimate Communications: Erotics and the Study of Culture.* New York: Columbia University Press.

Houston, Barbara. 1990. Caring and Exploitation. *Hypatia* 5 (Spring): 115–19.

Lancaster, Roger. 1992. *Life Is Hard: Machismo, Danger, and the Intimacy of Power in Nicaragua.* Berkeley: University of California Press.

Larrabee, Mary Jeanne, ed. 1993. *An Ethic of Care: Feminist and Interdisciplinary Perspectives.* New York: Routledge.

Lévi-Strauss, Claude. 1969. *The Elementary Structures of Kinship.* Rev. edition. Ed. Rodney Needham. Boston: Beacon.

Lewin, Ellen, 1993. *Lesbian Mothers: Accounts of Gender in American Culture.* Ithaca, N.Y.: Cornell University Press.

Lewin, Ellen, and William Leap, eds. 1996. *Out in the Field: Reflections of Lesbian and Gay Anthropologists.* Urbana: University of Illinois Press.

Needham, Rodney. 1971. Remarks on the Analysis of Kinship and Marriage. In *Rethinking Kinship and Marriage.* Ed. R. Needham. London: Tavistock.

Newton, Esther. 1993. *Cherry Grove, Fire Island: Sixty Years of America's First Gay and Lesbian Town.* Boston: Beacon.

Okin, Susan Moller. 1989. *Justice, Gender, and the Family.* New York: Basic.

Ortner, Sherry B., and Harriet Whitehead. 1981. Introduction: Accounting for Sexual Meanings. In *Sexual Meanings.* Ed. S. B. Ortner and H. Whitehead. Cambridge: Cambridge University Press, pp. 1–28.

Radcliffe-Brown, A. R. 1950. Introduction. In *African Systems of Kinship and Marriage.* Ed. A. R. Radcliffe-Brown and D. Forde. Oxford: Oxford University Press, pp. 1–77.

Rapp, Rayna. 1987. Toward a Nuclear Freeze? The Gender Politics of Euro-American Kinship Analysis. In *Gender and Kinship: Essays toward a Unified Analysis.* Ed. J. Collier and S. Yanagisako. Stanford, Calif.: Stanford University Press, pp. 119–31.

Ricoeur, Paul. 1984. *Time and Narrative.* Vol. 1. Chicago: University of Chicago Press.

Rubin, Gayle. 1975. The Traffic in Women. In *Toward an Anthropology of Women.* Ed. Rayna Reiter. New York: Monthly Review Press, pp. 157–210.

———. 1984. Thinking Sex: Notes for a Radical Theory of the Politics of Sexuality. In *Pleasure and Danger: Exploring Female Sexuality.* Ed. Carole Vance. Boston: Routledge and Kegan Paul, pp. 267–319.

Russ, Ann. 1998. Giving, Dying, and the Practice of Care in an AIDS Hospice. Ph.D. thesis. Ithaca, N.Y.: Cornell University Press.

Schneider, David. 1972. What Is Kinship All About? In *Kinship Studies in the Morgan Centennial Years.* Ed. P. Reining. Seattle: Anthropological Society of Washington, pp. 32–63.

Schneider, David, and Kathleen Gough. 1961. *Matrilineal Kinship.* Berkeley: University of California Press.

Sedgwick, Eve Kosofsky. 1990. *Epistemology of the Closet.* Berkeley: University of California Press.

Strathern, Marilyn. 1992. *Reproducing the Future: Anthropology, Kinship, and the New Reproductive Technologies.* New York: Routledge.

Todorov, Tzvetan. 1996. *Facing the Extreme: Moral Life in the Concentration Camps.* New York: Metropolitan Books.

Tronto, Joan. 1993. *Moral Boundaries: A Political Argument for an Ethic of Care.* New York: Routledge.

Warner, Michael, ed. 1993. *Fear of a Queer Planet: Queer Politics and Social Theory.* Minneapolis: University of Minnesota Press.

Weiner, Annette B. 1992. *Inalienable Possessions: The Paradox of Keeping-While-Giving.* Berkeley: University of California Press.

Weston, Kath. 1991. *Families We Choose: Lesbians, Gays, Kinship.* New York: Columbia University Press.

2

Rainbow Family, Rainbow Nation: Reflections on Relatives and Relational Dynamics in Trinidad

Denise Youngblood

The correlation of private issues and practices with public ideologies and paradigms in Trinidad is worthy of examination. In particular, how conceptions of intimacy within the domestic sphere have evolved over time and the role these understandings have played in constituting the Trinidadian social and cultural landscape should be emphasized. In so doing, I do not intend to postulate the conventional tension between private and public realms. Rather, I reflect upon the tandem functioning of the private or domestic domains of life, along with those of a public nature, in generating Trinidadian society and culture. Further, I critique the private–public distinction, as it has customarily been treated in kinship studies and literature, by relegating kinship exclusively to the private side of the divide. That is not to suggest that the private and public arenas are easily or consistently synchronized in Trinidadian society and culture. Instead, the space between the two realms acts as a kind of bridge, sometimes entirely conflating the two, so they are indistinguishable and seamlessly connected, and at other times, clearly indicating their points of affixation and disjuncture.

In the process of assessing these themes, I explore some of the contours of Trinidadian kinship through the lens of my own family's scenario, as a touchstone of the multiplicitous intersections of ethnicity, class, culture, nation, and other categories of being. These intersections are important to the discussion of the domestic sphere in Trinidad, because many previous studies of kinship in the Caribbean have treated only discrete categories of peoples, and have not emphasized the diversity found in this postcolonial, hybridized and creolized New World region.

Also central is the historical trajectory that indexes the social structure of Trinidad today. As such, I consider how class, ethnicity, and other status identifications shape the model of the family, as well as the texture of culture and society. Further, I outline how the ideology of cosmopolitanism in Trinidad relates to the production of both the family and the nation. In the Trinidadian sense, cosmopolitanism refers not only to the ethnic, religious, and cultural diversity of the population, or even to the processes of literal and symbolic creolization and hybridization that have taken place over time, but also to a totalizing vision of Trinidadian identity.

Finally, I question the idea of marriage and the family as the fulcrum of society. John Borneman has proposed that one approach family constructions as "a nexus of relationships and self-techniques always being constituted over time, rather than begin with the assumption that the family is a set of formal, already constituted relationships handed over from one generation to the next" (Borneman 1992: 77). In light of this statement, (1) I suggest that in Trinidad, the ties of alliance, specifically in the form of mixed marriages, are a form of integration, and they function as the grounds of contestation; (2) I propose that these particular kinds of kinship practices, in acting as a sort of bridge between various domains of everyday life, also reinforce the existing structure of power relations; (3) I argue that the totality of the cosmopolitan marriage and the family forecloses other possible articulations of being; and (4) I assert that these notions of marriage and the family naturalize social processes such as national identity formation.

CIRCULATING FAMILY STORIES

My family, in many senses, both literally and symbolically, can be described as *colorful*, something that has been jokingly referred to as a "rainbow family" because of its multinational, multicultural, and even multiethnic composition. In addition to this multifarious configuration, many family members live across national and cultural boundaries, and so are not often in the same country at the same time. Although both sides of my family have ended up scattered across the world, and despite our transient lifestyles, the circulation of stories about various family members has prevailed, especially at threshold moments such as births, deaths, and weddings. These stories and moments may reflect some of the ambient factors of kinship, such as the reproduction and termination of life, as well as marriage alliances. At the same time, they may also function as discourses and practices of contestation and integration within the social and cultural landscape. Accordingly, marriage is the centerpiece of my focus, and the stories that circulate regarding the marriages in my family serve as an entry point to examine family constructions in Trinidad.

Paternal Family

My father was one of nine children born to my paternal grandfather, Alfred R, and my paternal grandmother, Ruth-Mary H. My grandfather, Alfred R, was born in Trinidad in 1890. Apparently, his father, my great-grandfather, was a restless and rebellious soul who, in a fit of adventurous spirit, boarded a ship on the Indian coast and headed to the West Indies. He eventually landed in Trinidad, and, consistent with his propensity for unconventionality, he married a local Trinidadian woman of African descent. No other information is known about my mysterious great-grandmother. I can only hypothesize that her history is not unlike that of many other local African women in the region. My grandfather was one of their two sons.

My grandmother, Ruth-Mary H, was born on the island of Grenada in 1903. Her father, Reverend John Walter H, was a Presbyterian missionary who left Scotland for the West Indies in order to work in missionary service. He traveled throughout many of the islands, but in Grenada he met and married a wealthy Jewish woman, Deborah Z. The romantic version of the family folklore is that she converted to Christianity and that he was cured of his proselytizing ways.

When my grandmother was an adolescent, the family moved to Trinidad. It was there that my great-grandfather, John Walter H, met Alfred R. Impressed with Alfred R's ability to speak seven languages and philosophize eloquently, John Walter H orchestrated the marriage of his third daughter (my grandmother) to his new friend. I recall my grandmother bitterly confiding this story to me shortly before she died. She never quite recovered from being coerced into marriage with a man thirteen years her senior who was something of a drinker and a philanderer.

As for their children, I have an aunt who married a local Trinidadian magistrate from a family frequently lamented to be social parvenus. I also have an uncle who married a former Catholic nun from England. She decided to violate all the Catholic sacraments and scandalized the family by running off with another man. A second uncle married a French Canadian artist. They subsequently divorced, and she supposedly had an affair with a notorious Canadian politician.

Yet another uncle met and married a German student while attending university in Canada. Her family, admittedly sympathetic to World War II fascism, took at least ten years to recover from the horror of her marrying a "colored" man from the West Indies with a Jewish mother. The fourth uncle married a Spanish-Filipino nurse. By all accounts, they seem by far the most stable of all the marriages.

There is also one aunt who married a (perverse, obnoxious, and obese) cattle rancher in Australia. The youngest aunt married an Austrian engineer whom she eventually divorced. She now pursues her interest in professional golfing. My father's youngest brother shocked the family by marrying a former Brazilian actress twenty years his senior. They now live in a cabin in the Northwest Territories. All things considered, my parents' marriage in 1965 seems like a less colorful and somewhat tame interchange. Their story has little of the soap opera quality that pervades those of my father's other siblings.

Maternal Family

My mother was the eldest of seven children born to my maternal grandfather, Alejandro S, and my maternal grandmother, Daisie S. Alejandro S was born in Maracaibo, Venezuela, in 1910. He was the son of a wealthy Venezuelan, Fernando S. My great-grandfather, Fernando S, was proud that he could trace his heritage to the original conquistadors who had come from Queen Isabella's court in Spain.

As a result of this heritage, the S family possessed a great deal of "old money." Their wealth was later soundly invested in the oil industry that flourished in the Maracaibo region of Venezuela. Fernando S married a *mestiza* Venezuelan woman, Helena G. The surname of Helena G suggests ancestry other than that of *Latina* heritage, but I am not privy to any details that might clarify this seeming discrepancy. Most of the S wealth was left to my grandfather's elder brother, Esteban, who still lives in Maracaibo. As a young boy, my grandfather was sent to live with his Aunt Erena (Helena's sister) in Trinidad, not unlike many other Venezuelans who had migrated to Trinidad as far back as the nineteenth century.

Although Alejandro S traveled to Europe to be educated, when he returned it was not to his home in Venezuela but to Trinidad. There, he met and married my grandmother, Daisie S. Of my maternal grandmother I know very little; she is not the most forthcoming of speakers. Her father came from Benares in India to work as an indentured laborer in Trinidad. Her mother and her family immigrated to Trinidad to work as merchants, not unlike most other Arabs and Asians in the Caribbean region. I cannot remember ever being told her parents' first names.

In regard to their children, my mother and three of her brothers are in business together. Although all three brothers eventually married, it is not an exaggeration to say that they appear more committed to each other and their business interests than to anything else. They spend most of their lives on Boeing 747s, crossing the Atlantic between Trinidad and Europe. My mother's fourth brother, an engineer, and his family live in the United States, while my mother's sister and her husband live with my widowed grandmother. My aunt's husband has unfortunately gained the negative reputation among the family as being a "jack of all trades, and master of none." My mother's youngest brother died of pneumonia many years ago.

THE INTIMATE SPHERE

I began with a delineation of my family structure and dynamics because of its resonance with the history of the intimate sphere of Trinidad. In his discussion of kinship systems in the Caribbean, Raymond Smith states that "a creole kinship structure was established in the formative stages of Caribbean society" (1987: 167). In this model, the "domestic" sphere played a key economic, political, and status role such that "domesticity" itself became part of a unique social formation that was, and continues to be, Caribbean Creole society (Smith 1987). By way of explanation, "domesticity" seems to refer to the intimate relationships that evolve within family structures and systems and that extend to the larger societal realm.

The definition of the term *intimate* appears to have particular relevance in this regard. The word comes from the Latin *intimus* and refers to the innermost layer of an organism (OED 1992). Its definition follows:

> intimate (in-ti-mit) *adj.* 1. having a close acquaintanceship or association with another person. 2. (of knowledge) detailed and obtained from careful observation and experience. 3. having sexual relations with a person, especially outside of marriage. 4. most private and personal. *v.* to make known or announce, especially by hinting or implication.

From its definition, it would appear that *intimate* and its associated noun *intimacy* can be interpreted as: (1) a type of familiarity, its own etymological connection to "family" being sufficiently clear; (2) an affect-oriented type of knowing that links together knowledge with experience; (3) an emphasis upon the private rather than the public sphere; and (4) sexual or sensual relations, particularly those of the illicit variety. The verb form is also illustrative, because even though it entails the act of "making something known" explicitly, it is paradoxically an implicit and indirect explication. In this way, the intimate sphere of life and domestic relations in particular come to represent the intersections of the public and private realms.

Kinship studies have often taken private or personal experiences and presented them in rationalistic and objective terms, while utilizing essentialist language. As such, a dichotomy between the private and public domains has been instituted under the cover of academic descriptors, including "kinship patterns" and "social structure." The inflections of the term *intimate* offer a more complicated understanding of the intimate sphere and kinship relations.

Moreover, its nuances allude to the latticed relationship between the public and private realms, which, like the Latin form *intimus*, is often hidden within the interior. Indeed, as the very terms connote, "intimacy" and "intimate relationships," regardless of their effect in the public sphere, will never be explicitly expressed within the private domain.

Hence, to an extent, Trinidadian kinship practices and relations contribute to the interlacing of the public and private domains. Specific kinship practices, such as the ties of alliance in marriage, function as a transit of sorts, moving domestic relations, familial circles, and other aspects of the private sphere into the social, cultural, national, and other public realms of being. Yet as noted above, this transit is not a technology of publication; it is never wholly or completely public. In effect, the social mores toward marriage, and the cultural attitudes and practices that inform marriage, such as lateral alliances in the status hierarchy, belie an existing structure of power relations. Power, in Foucauldean terms, is often invisible, and its connection to the most intimate provinces of life cannot be expressed explicitly; it almost always is a matter of intimation.

CARIBBEAN KINSHIP STUDIES

In theoretical considerations of kinship patterns of the Caribbean, explanations tend to adopt a distinction between "domestic" (i.e., private) and "politico-jural" (i.e., public) domains, in addition to the "problem" of illegitimacy (Gopaul-McNicol 1993; Smith 1987). While these issues hold great significance, their broad applications to the Caribbean case are not always the most useful modes of inquiry, because they fail to address the diversity within the region. Similarly, binaries such as the public and private spheres do not account for the complexity and concurrence of these elements. For example, a substantial corpus of research on the subject of Caribbean kinship patterns since 1945 has tended to focus on the high proportion of "female headed households" in the "black lower classes" (Smith 1956; Braithwaite 1975; Freilich 1960, 1968; Rodman 1971; Senior 1991; Rheddock 1994, among others). The problem with this type of study is that it treats "the black lower class" and "black, female single mothers" as entities that can be defined and bounded hermetically for purposes of research (Smith 1987, 1988; Miller 1994; Young 1990). Within the social structure that prevails to date in Trinidad, it would certainly be erroneous to present "the black lower class individual" who suffers the deleterious effects of illegitimacy and single motherhood as a modal depiction of the Afro-Trinidadian.

Further, it should be noted that in studies that center on illegitimacy as well as in kinship studies generally, there is an implicit primacy placed on legitimate marriages and births as normative, if not desirable (Murdock 1949).

The general consensus by researchers shows that customarily, the so-called black lower classes of the Caribbean valued a Christian, monogamous family life and aspired to live that way (Smith 1987: 164). Circumstances and hardships were thought to have prevented them from actualizing this goal, thereby compelling them to "stretch their values" (Smith 1987: 164; Rodman 1971; Massiah 1986, 1988; Barrow 1986, 1988). Little consideration, however, was given to these governing factors, and so the "black lower class" became identified as aberrant.

I would add that the very category of "black lower class" is problematic, because in this kind of study, it becomes identified *as Caribbean*. In so doing, it obscures the variety of racial/ethnic/color categories in the region. In places such as the United States and the United Kingdom, mulattos and other mixed peoples who do not appear categorically "white" are deemed to be "black" (Gopaul-McNicol 1993).[1] As such, they may be contained within Caribbean classifications and they may be included in the overarching African diaspora. These representations, however, often do not coincide with the self-identifications held by persons of mixed ethnicity.

Additionally, if Indians, Chinese, and Middle Easterners are not pushed unceremoniously into the "white" or "black" category, they are simply ignored and not considered at all *as Caribbean* (Gopaul-McNicol 1993). By way of illustration, a notable body of work has been done on "traditional" Indian communities in Trinidad whose lifestyle, practices (including kinship patterns), and senses of identity supposedly parallel those of India (Klass 1961; Vervotec 1992; Nevadomsky 1982, 1983; see also Klass 1991 for alternative and updated accounts). This focus on cultural retention is often refuted by local political figures with nationalistic stances, as well as by academic critics. Both groups tend to emphasize the cultural syncretism and synthesis that seem emblematic of "New World" societies.

HISTORICAL CONTEXT

Historically, the social pecking order in Caribbean society was organized around the plantation household, with European plantation owners and their wives at the apex. While the original European population in the Caribbean encompassed mostly plantation owners, investors, and overseers, the increased immigration of upper-class European women made the type of family unit and social pecking order noted above possible. By the early eighteenth century, this resulted in a sizable local European population in place across the Caribbean (Brereton 1979). European women of lower social status who emigrated to the Caribbean as domestic or indentured workers were often able to move up in the power structure by marrying plantation owners (Smith 1987; Brereton 1979). Despite the seeming unevenness in hierarchical positioning, marriage functioned as a connective link between status equals, and it was aimed at the maintenance and reproduction of the existing power structure.

While these orthodox kinds of marriages are recorded as having occurred in a systematic fashion, it is clear that there were a number of extramarital unions and illegitimate children among the local European community itself (Smith 1987; Brereton 1979). Therefore, in the Caribbean, the domestic sphere included both legal marriage as well as nonlegal couplings. Not unlike Southern U.S. history, the Caribbean story is replete with voluminous accounts of European men married to European women but involved in nonlegal unions with African and mulatto women. Yet at the same time, as in the case of Southern U.S. history, it was not permissible for European women to indulge in sexual relations with African men, and marriage between the two was next to impossible (Smith 1987; Brereton 1979).

These social norms wove "a complex tapestry of genetic and social relations among various segments of society" that was capable of ordering sexual relations and generating sexual behavior among status equals and nonequals (Smith 1987: 168). Put another way, this tapestry of sexual relations was organized around the informal sexual practices and the legal marriages of local European men. Specifically, the upper European echelon of Caribbean society came to be associated with normative nuclear families formalized by legal marriage between status equals, despite the fact that the sexual practices of European men were frequently inconsistent with the idea of an exemplary Christian family life. Conversely, because nonlegal sexual unions between European men and non-European women were customary, deviant patterns of conjugal relations and asymmetrical dynamics of intimacy were considered commensurate with the lowest stratum of society (Smith 1987).

Interestingly, nonlegal unions, illegitimate children, and the like were not exclusively a New World phenomenon. These kinds of scenarios could also be found in Britain and other parts of Europe as well, and they were included in the uppermost strata of society. Indeed, they were considered part of the normal social structure (Smith 1987). Yet the image of illicit sexual relationships seems indelibly attributable to the Caribbean, the American South, and Latin America. Perhaps this is because the illicit aspect is not merely limited to the issues of illegitimacy. Indeed, it is amplified by the prohibitive attitude toward interethnic unions.

In Trinidad, however, because the colonial powers dispatched absentee jurisdiction, the degree of mixed marriages and liaisons was especially high. In addition, such marriages and liaisons tended not to contain within them the sense of illicitness that might be found on other islands in the Caribbean (Brereton 1979). As such, the practice of what was termed *miscegenation* became institutionalized in colonial Trinidad and issued in an increasingly creolized and hybridized population.[2]

With the cessation of slavery and African labor exploitation in 1838, Trinidad's cultural composition expanded as a result of the influx of Asian and Mediterranean indentured laborers. In addition, an increasing merchant class from places such as China and the Middle East proliferated over time. These waves of immigration resulted in further ethnic intermixing, despite the perception that certain communities, such as Indians and Middle Easterners, tended to be more insular in relation to the larger population.[3] The primary outcome of this increasingly diverse composition in Trinidad is that no single ordering system of domestic relations ever became dominant. Instead, the Trinidadian domestic sphere has come to include alternative and multiple forms of intimate unions that "mutually define each other and relate directly to the color/class hierarchy" (Smith 1987: 175).

Historically, this system embraced plural elements of interclass and interethnic relations. It extended from the uppermost European echelons to the bottom rung of African slaves, contrary to the representation of normative and nonnormative domestic relations in accordance with upper- and lower-class stratification, respectively. In contemporary society, this hierarchy has not disappeared; indeed, it continues to affect marriage and family structures and practices to date (Smith 1987). These alternative unions continue to operate as antagonistic correlates by disturbing, but not destroying, the family structure.

That is to say, the colonial upper classes as well as the subordinate classes were known to have indulged in family-making practices that could hardly be considered consistent with the norm of nuclear monogamy. As recorded above, this was not only true of Europeans at home, but also of the upper crust of expatriates in the Caribbean. Clearly, it applied across ethnic and class boundaries in the colonial enclaves as well. Because these practices were maintained in a system of relations that touched all segments of the population in the Caribbean, they augmented the centrality of marriage between status equals, while simultaneously maintaining the adjunct realm of asymmetrical sexual unions. In so doing, these practices coalesced, and a particular social structure was instituted in the Caribbean (Smith 1987).

SOCIAL FACTORS AND SOCIAL STRUCTURES

Many Caribbeanists present sweeping portraits of contemporary Caribbean society, with "a white upper class" inhabiting the most expensive residential areas and enjoying the most desirable accoutrements of life. Such portraits serve to document the fact that "ethnic differences are often reinforced by economics" (Gopaul-McNicol 1993: 35–36). They tend generally, however, to subsume economic class with ethnicity and often fail to articulate the interweaving of class and color. The two facets are so interconnected and interdependent that they would be almost impossible to separate "on the ground." Perhaps this is because the linkage between the two ascriptions is so deeply embedded that locals often have difficulty extricating the elements from one another (Gopaul-McNicol 1993: 35–36). Yet, despite the conflation of class and ethnicity, the two remain analytically distinct.

In the case of Trinidad, most of the major historians offer their findings on social structure in terms of clear ethnic/class fractions (Brereton 1981). The social structure is often portrayed as containing a European upper class, a light middle class, and an Indian/African under class (Birth 1997: 589). Though such a portrayal is insufficiently complex, it is clear that in contemporary Trinidad, ethnic origins and class are not divorced from each other or from other social, political, economic, and cultural considerations. To an extent, they work in tandem with each other, yet at the same time, they can be contradictory. This is exemplified by the fact that Trinidad is a predominantly middle-class society, with Africans and Indians sitting at both extremes of the sociopolitical and economic continuum. Europeans and other smaller groups may have a sound upper-middle level influence but in post-Independence Trinidad, this does not translate into political power or even a monopoly on business. Similarly, Syrians and other Middle Easterners hold substantial business influence but are outside the political arena.

Clearly, against Trinidad's multiethnic and largely middle-class backdrop, the usual "white"/"black" and rich/poor dichotomies used to describe Caribbean society are inapplicable. Instead, the prevailing social hierarchy in Trinidad is characterized by the interplay of factors such as wealth, illustrious education, notable family background, and favorable ethnic composition. These factors constitute the "symbolic capital" of the society and culture (Bourdieu 1984). Moreover, in Trinidad, wealth as a form of "symbolic capital" is relevant only in relation to the other constituents. Daniel Miller's research of consumption patterns illustrates the limits of a purely economic (i.e., Marxist) motive in understanding the social structure of Trinidad. He observes that trends such as the interior decor of homes and the proclivity for elaborate cake decoration seem to occur across economic categories in Trinidad (Miller 1994). He also indicates that the Trinidadian case contrasts with the kind of class-based antagonism that Bourdieu describes in his analysis of taste and preferences in France (Miller 1994; Bourdieu 1984).

Class-based antagonism, however, does indeed exist in Trinidad, although not exclusively on the basis of wealth. Wealth, as a source of currency and consumption, must be understood as a transient entity in Trinidad. This is because Trinidad has endured dramatic boom and bust cycles, which have transformed the elite power bases within the economic sector. Political changes as well as shifts in the commercial, business, and industrial arenas have contributed to further oscillations in the economic power bases. Status, then, cannot solely be established upon the basis of something so transitory as wealth. In contrast, education, family background, and ethnicity all withstand the forces of time and the fluctuations of economic cycles more durably. As a result, the correspondence between social status and distinctive properties entails the distribution of wealth in relation to the other nonmaterial constituents of "symbolic capital" (Bourdieu and Wacquant 1990). Stated differently, such "symbolic capital" as educational qualifications, family names, desirable ethnic identities, and wealth together represent the possession of real titles of symbolic power in the Trinidadian social hierarchy.[4]

STATUS CONSIDERATIONS AND THE TOTALITY OF MARRIAGE

Trinidad is characterized by an interrelational standard that reflects complex and even permissive attitudes to crossing social boundaries and to enduring restrictions (as distinct from prohibitions). Underlying this code is the matter of marriage, and in particular, that of intermarriage. While marriage, in the broadest sense, might be understood as a tie of alliance, intermarriage in Trinidad, across social boundaries (such as class and ethnicity) on the basis of "symbolic capital," functions as a mechanism for maintaining the existing power structure. Stated differently, such marriages help to maintain a dominant social network in Trinidad, consisting of individuals who possess "symbolic capital." My own family dynamics embody these trends, especially with regard to the difference in my parents' respective economic positions.

My mother came from an older, established, and wealthy family who claimed some aristocratic heritage. In a society that is defined, in large part, by whom one knows and how one is known, my mother's family retained their high social position even after large amounts of their investments had evaporated (see Oxaal 1982 for general explication of class in Trinidad). Since transformations in personal conditions do not usually result in changes in personal classifications, one who acquires a great deal of wealth without possessing other elements of "symbolic capital" would be considered *nouveau riche*. Consequently, they would find it difficult to elevate their social status, at least in the short run (Miller 1994: 272).

My father's family possessed very little wealth in comparison to my mother's, but they were well educated. Their lack of wealth was not an impediment to actualizing a rank in the upper tiers of Trinidadian society, because education is emphasized as a core value and the ladder of social mobility (Gopaul-McNicol 1993: 29–32). Although this quality suggests that social stratification was not static, social mobility was not, and is not, possible purely via wealth. It was, and is, somewhat like an education itself, "a slow, accretion process, something achieved as an aspect of personhood and not so easily lost" (Miller 1994: 272; Brereton 1993; Steedman 1986). Recall, for example, my maternal aunt's husband, whom I disparagingly referred to as "a jack of all trades, and master of none." Although he is a self-made man with a sizable disposable income, his lack of educational "mastery" is viewed negatively by other family members, and to this day, my aunt's marriage to him is considered to be "a bad match."

In Trinidadian terms, long-term conjugal relations involve the joining of status equals, economic disparities notwithstanding. Unlike my maternal aunt and her husband, my parents could be considered status equals, as each could count on some symbol of influence, be it education or being "known" (Birth 1997: 595; Smith 1987: 175). Similarly, the marriage of my paternal aunt into a family of parvenus was considered acceptable because her husband was a magistrate from a family of distinguished degree-holders. Their negative background was overshadowed by their educational eminence. While these cases echo the trend of marriage as an alliance between status equals, other elements in the narrative about my family indicate both hierarchical distinctions and the complexity of the social structure.

I recounted earlier the example of my paternal grandfather who had a proclivity for indulging in extramarital affairs. One woman, identified as a mistress of my grandfather, lived with her children in a small, dilapidated house that one could see from the back balcony of my grandparents' home, at the top of a hill in San Fernando. Apparently, my grandfather's philandering and other questionable tendencies did not prevent him from being my grandmother's status equal, in large part because of his intellectual distinction. As an adulterer, however, my grandfather is not so different from many heterosexual men in a society with a legacy of illicit sexual associations (Smith 1987; Miller 1994; Gopaul-McNicol 1993).

Certainly, it has been suggested that in contemporary society where landowners no longer interact with slaves or laborers, the whole system of illicit liaisons "shifted down one register" (Smith 1988: 189). Stated differently, intimate relationships marked by unequal power differentials did not disappear. Instead, they became more nuanced. So, if marriage is customarily and legally an affirmation of status symmetry, then infidelity might be an affirmation of asymmetrical relations. My grandfather, it would seem, was an exemplar of this trend as he continued his unofficial relationships, while the rest of the family dismissed his illicit partners as spurious and inferior.

As well as the problematic of symbolic equality within marriage, there are related contentions regarding marriage as a category. That is to say, marriage, a social invention, tends to be treated as a "given" in the human life course, in much the same way as are life and death (Borneman 1996: 216). The grounds for this approach seem to be what John Borneman designates as a symbolics of blood, forged by "a regime of power" that is founded upon both "inheriting blood by descent and mixing blood by marriage" (216). In this way, marriage is reformulated as natural, and it becomes a "common denominator for humanity" (219).

The hierarchical oppositions such as male and female within marriage are part and parcel of Derridean "violent hierarchies" that render the secondary category subordinate, but that are necessary to create a whole object (Borneman 1996: 219). It is a kind of equation of difference, in anthropological terms, where knowledge of the self is created through the other, and where that "other" is almost always located in the position of lesser value. Marriage, in this sense, is the totality to which these oppositions allude, and it is what enables the project of translation. The binarism of male/female and its associated dyads such as mind/body and aggressor/peacemaker reference this act of translation in marriage. It is a crossing of the boundaries in what Donna Haraway refers to as "the drama of touch across difference" (Haraway 1989: 149).

In terms of my family, it is clear that marriage as an act of translation occurred not only across asymmetrical male/female borders, but also across national, ethnic, and even professional boundaries. The case of my Indian great-grandfather, supposedly a Brahmin from an elite family in India, who traveled to the Caribbean and married an unknown woman of African ancestry, is particularly illustrative. *How and why did he transgress the prevailing proscription that discouraged such unions?*[5] As for my Jewish great-grandmother, it is clear that she was Christianized, creolized, *maybe even colonized.* In return, my Scottish great-grandfather relinquished his missionary efforts.

Both instances are emblematic of that dubious project of translation mentioned earlier. I label it dubious because I find it interesting that both my great-grandfathers capture somewhat rebelliously heroic roles in the stated dynamics, while my Jewish great-grandmother has to be converted to Christianity, and my African great-grandmother is entirely unknown and remains that way. Relating it to the discussion of class issues earlier, my Jewish great-grandmother is "reprogrammed" in a sense, in order to secure the right to marry her British, colonial, and Christian husband.[6] Likewise, my African great-grandmother remains unknown. These respective scenarios contrast with my mother's elite family, who retained their social status precisely because they were known. Marriage, therefore, functions as a type of transit. It interprets, corresponds, and ultimately renders the violent hierarchies into a semblance of totality, which rarely adds up to "wholeness" in actuality.[7]

COSMOPOLITANISM, CREOLIZATION, AND HYBRIDITY

In an essay on interethnic unions and transethnic kinship in Trinidad, Kevin Birth recounts an episode where an Indian grandfather hosts the wedding of his part-African granddaughter (Birth 1997). Birth notes that while the Indian grandfather considers his ethnically mixed granddaughter to be a full member of his family, interestingly, he bans a group of African men from the village from attending the wedding. In turn, the men interpret the grandfather's

behavior as being reflective of racist attitudes. They also perceive him as failing
to recognize the relational link between the two ethnic communities, provided
by the mixed ethnicity of the man's granddaughter (Birth 1997). That is to say,
the circumstances that Birth depicts are illustrative of the power-oriented complexities in Trinidad. The grandfather, in Birth's account, can embrace the notion of an ethnically mixed relative, because such an identity can be easily applied to his conception of Trinidadians as hybrid and creolized. Conversely, a
few random men of African ancestry, none of whom is properly identified in
Birth's account, fail to fit easily under the grandfather's mental rubric of personal identity, thus resulting in his discriminatory behavior.

In this way, the grandfather's seemingly contradictory behavior is not unlike
that of my own family. He cannot explicitly deny the African ancestry in his
granddaughter in much the same way that my family cannot abrogate the ancestry of my great-grandmother, or the existence of my grandfather's illegitimate children. Yet he denies the entry of the African men in much the same way
as my family ignores the existence of an African great-grandmother. Their similar actions reflect a kind of abstracted "disassociation" (Birth 1997: 589). The
"disassociation" functions to obliterate problematic kinship ties and to uphold
special notions of nationhood, which mixed offspring represent.

It should be noted that the standard taboos regarding interethnic marriages that prevail in the southern United States are not precisely in effect for
Trinidad. Most unlike the southern United States, where intermarriage is
discouraged and non-European ancestry among "white" Americans is often
denied or erased, intermarriage in Trinidad is encouraged. Primarily, this is
because intermarriage promotes a desirable hybrid identity. Second, this hybrid identity functions as the corporeal proof of a unified sense of identity
in Trinidad. Third, intermarriage acts as a point of mediation between
sociocultural distinctions. In Birth's account, the grandfather's rejection of
the African men at the wedding was, therefore, a direct repudiation of the
overriding telos of social and ethnic relations, as well as national identity.
Central to this telos is the notion of cosmopolitanism, which circulates in discourses and has been internalized by many people as well.

When I was in my freshman year of university in Canada, a fellow university
student asked me what Trinidad was like. Dutifully, I described the flora and
fauna, the political and economic scenario, and finally the history and how it
had contributed to Trinidad being "a cosmopolitan nation." My acquaintance
corrected me and said, "You mean it's a diverse nation." I did not respond immediately, because my assertion had been uttered automatically and its contradiction left me feeling a little mystified. In that moment, which gave me pause,
I was forced to rethink the matter entirely. *Was Trinidadian cosmopolitanism
different from that of other places? Were Trinidadians mere conspirants of cosmopolitanism in a world of other* real *cosmopolitans?* A host of like-minded
questions rushed through my mind in those few seconds, and finally, I re-

sponded, "No, I mean Trinidad is cosmopolitan." I do not recall exactly what transpired afterward, but the significance here lies in my certitude, *in that moment*, that Trinidad was indeed a cosmopolitan nation, not only because of its cultural diversity, but also because of its creole, hybrid, and other multiplicitous identifications, as well as its tenet of positive ethnic relations.

With time, and certainly as I examine my own family history, it is increasingly clear that the notion of cosmopolitanism, and the idea of harmony facilitated by the fusion of plural elements, are not necessarily a lived reality. Indeed, it is more of an ideology than anything else, much like the term *ideology*, which has itself become ideologized and essentialized (Geertz 1973: 194). The dismay that the African men feel when the Indian grandfather rejects them in Birth's aforementioned account, for instance, denotes how the ideology of cosmopolitanism often does not translate into practice (Birth 1997; see also Segal 1994 on cosmopolitanism in Trinidad). Also illustrative of this inconsistency is the suppression of my African great-grandmother in my family's narratives. Both examples suggest that Trinidadian cosmopolitanism, despite its principles of diversity and positive ethnic relations, remains an exclusive ideology, with genealogically suppressed aspects, primarily that of Africanness, being the element of exclusion.

On a broader scale, Katherine Verdery asks, in a discussion of nationalism, if there are differences in practices that make people "national" as opposed to "ethnic" (1994: 48). In Trinidad, it is apparent that "multiethnic" is to be understood as "national," irrespective of the presumable verities of practice. Further, the connection among cosmopolitanism, creolization, and hybridity is not to be understood as the latter two giving rise to the first through interethnic kinship practices. Ethnic, even multiethnic identities, do not develop into national identities per se. Rather, cosmopolitanism, creolization, and hybridity mutually define an ideology-orienting system that directly and indirectly influences senses of identity in Trinidad.[8]

FROM FAMILY TO NATION

It has been established that kinship is not a natural fact, but a social and cultural construction (Schneider 1984). Why, then, does a biologistic conception of kinship prove so tenacious? Some scholars have suggested that it is because the orthodox idea of the family serves as the foundation for society and social forms (Gilroy 1991). The tenacity of the biologistic conception of kinship, however, is more likely to be due to the mutual entanglement of discourses of naturalized origin, exemplified most profoundly by the interwoven discourses of kinship and nation.

John Borneman, for example, maintains that in the project of nation building, a process that entails the definition, regularization, institutionalization, and normalization of domestic practices also ensues. The state codifies and legalizes specific kinds of relations and selves (Borneman 1992; Foucault 1980, 1979). In some cases, the nation-state adopts roles previously held by kin in terms of providing security, education, careers, and even systems of punishment (Eriksen 1993: 108). Moreover, kinship terms such as "motherland" or "father of the nation" are often used in nationalist discourse so that the abstract community of citizens may be posited as members of a metaphoric kin group (Eriksen 1993: 108). Indeed, the very term *nation* is derived from the verb to *be born*, thereby demonstrating the symbolic naturalization of a system of organization (Verdery 1994: 50).

Hannah Arendt points to the religious nature of national constitutions (Arendt 1985, as explicated in Borneman 1992). The usage of the term *religious* indicates that a divine authority is supposed to delineate the disposition of the nation, and further, that the nation is legitimated by some eternal origin (Arendt 1985, as explicated in Borneman 1992). In this way, the legal basis for the existence of the nation is naturalized in much the same way as the family is. Both can evoke great sentiment. In addition, both appropriate meanings from cultural contexts that are important in people's everyday experiences and that contribute to unarticulated senses of "belonging" and being "at home" (Borneman 1992: 339). Indeed, the very inexpressibility of both kinship and nation testifies to the degree of naturalization that occurs. The naturalization process takes place through the folk grammar of *kith and kin* (Borneman 1992; Gilroy 1991). That is, nationhood is founded upon the soil of the nation's land, and it is founded through national ancestry—a task that necessitates the marital and procreative features of kinship.

In the case of Trinidad, there seems to be some connection between the naturalization of kinship and nation, and the internalization of the notion of cosmopolitanism. As I explained earlier, the idea of Trinidadian cosmopolitanism was so internalized for me that having it questioned rendered me literally speechless. In a sense, I became what Werner Stark refers to as "the ideological fool" who passionately believes what he or she advocates (Stark 1958 as cited in Geertz 1973: 196). Consequently, the ideological conundrum that I experienced indicates the naturalization of cosmopolitanism—in relation to interethnic kinship patterns and national identity.

Returning to the case of my family, the mythical invocation of identity through ethnicity, land, and nation, of which kin is considered the basis, can be brought to bear. My grandparents, parents, and uncles and aunts are Trinidadian, Grenadian, and Venezuelan. Further back, they recall parts of Asia, Europe, and Africa. Contemporarily, they have married people from a variety of nationalities and ethnicities. My cousins are nothing less than hybrids, and we ourselves are dispersed across the globe, transnationally and transculturally. In a discussion of roots, soil, purity, and nationhood, all this multiplicity may seem incongruous. Nevertheless, in a place like Trinidad, this cultural myriad is, in fact, central to the discussion.

By way of illustration, members of my paternal family are ancestrally part African due to my great-grandmother. In a sense, that is not an incorrect statement. Yet we, as a family, have chosen not to see ourselves as such. Family members who live in Trinidad view themselves as "brown," albeit in varying gradations of "brown" along the rainbow's continuum. They also think of themselves as Trinidadian, in a space where "brown" functions as a modal significator of a hybrid Trinidadian identity. My cousins in Canada (some of whom happen to have blond hair, blue eyes, light skin, and play hockey) classify themselves as Canadians of exotic origin. My very dark relatives do not view their darkness as evidence of "blackness" per se, but of their "rainbow nation" heritage, which is predicated upon creole and hybrid identities, in addition to a cosmopolitan ideology. These darker relatives may joke about their "throwback dark skin" in everyday conversation, but these discoursing descendants never name explicitly *her.* They never mention my African great-grandmother. *Who was the she to be named? All we know of her, all I know of her, is exactly* that.

Ronald Cohen explains that "once acquired by whatever process, an identity is passed down the generations for as long as the grouping has some viable significance to members and nonmembers" (Cohen 1978: 387). Perhaps the significance here does not lie in the facts of ancestry or its removal from the familial purview. Instead, it rests upon the discourses that prevail about my African great-grandmother, who married my Indian great-grandfather and produced a *dougla* son, and the son who then, in turn, married a Jewish-Scottish woman.[9] Meanwhile, however, the cases of genealogical suppression, like that of my great-grandmother, demonstrate how certain kinship issues and practices remain on the private side of the private–public divide, despite their inexorable connection.

Hence, in Trinidad, where descent-based criteria are derivatives of the ties of alliance, it is marriage that acts as a productive mechanism by framing creolization and hybridity and by creating the (false) totality of the family and the nation in the aforementioned project of translation.

MEMORY AND FORGETFULNESS, DISCOURSE AND SILENCE

Although official policy in Trinidad, through governmental apparatus such as the media, culture, and education, has been devoted to recording the contributions of Afro-Trinidadians, as my family history shows, individual Afro-Trinidadians are often surreptitiously omitted—and usually by family members. In effect, contributions—by blood or culture—to Trinidadian cosmopolitanism are celebrated, while African identities, or more specifically, "blackness," is viewed uncomfortably. Resultantly, traces are upheld and utilized to display a thriving cosmopolitanism, but the full-length stories are silenced. These kinds of family narratives are germane to the discussion of kinship in Trinidad, because while my African great-grandmother may be genetically related to me, I know nothing of her, including her name. She is, in effect, alienated from my circle of knowledge in a code of silence, presumably because (at least in part) she is of African ancestry. *Why was she, my great-grandmother, extradited from our family's collective memory?*

The most obvious rationale seems to suggest social forces such as racism. My paternal grandfather's social position in Trinidad is, however, unaffected by his part-African ancestry. In the United States, the one-drop (of "black" blood) rule persists, so that people with part-African ancestry are automatically classified as African American and, therefore, as inferior (Eriksen 1993: 83; Smedley 1993). In the Caribbean, where accommodation is made for more complex ethnic categories, a distinction between "black" and "brown" is made. "Brown," however, tends to be regarded as the more privileged classification (Eriksen 1993: 64). In Trinidad, where the demography is more diverse, "brown" includes interethnic mixtures. As the modal significator of cosmopolitanism, "brown" also constitutes a large portion of "symbolic capital." In the local version of racism and power relations, my "brown" grandfather is pivotal to the family narrative, while my "black" great-grandmother is marginalized.

The selective character of these familial stories points to what Jonathan Boyarin terms "a politics of memory" (Boyarin 1994: 2). By "politics of memory," Boyarin is not suggesting that memory is a sort of autonomous force that can dictate a political situation or a sphere of discourse. Certainly, in a discussion of my own family's kinship bonds and practices, I am not expressly referring to typical politics at all. At the same time, it seems apparent that there is an element of power at work in the form of status politics. This is illustrated by the fact that certain stories circulate within the family and particular memories are advanced, while other counterstories are quashed and contradictory memories are eschewed. Because these measures tend to be motivated by the rhetoric of the family, defended by the prevailing national ethos, and sustained by the centrality of *a specific kind of people*, it would seem that a "politics of memory" is indeed operating.[10]

Central to this form of politics is the matter of status considerations, and specifically, the accumulation of "symbolic capital." In this particular case, "symbolic capital" refers to desirable types of Trinidadian ethnicity and status that command power. Cosmopolitanism, as a form of hegemony and a variant of "symbolic capital" in Trinidad, exhibits a particular trajectory (Forte 1995: 44). It is primarily informed by an authoritative, "endlessly speaking us," made up of the brown upper and middle classes. Implicit within this trajectory, however, is "an unspoken, unspeakable presence," made up of the

African and lower-class substrates (Forte 1995: 44; Hall 1994: 398–99). In the case of the former, the hegemonic story endures and circulates, while in the case of the latter, silence abides.

At the institutional level, Trinidadian cosmopolitanism is extroverted in touristic paraphernalia, national tenets, and public slogans. Although such imageries and discourses may be viewed as part of a state-generated agenda, they function because of a high level of public consent and because they are the products of Trinidadian agencies and enterprises. The social, political, and corporate networks of Trinidad that constitute such establishments—that is, the "endlessly speaking us"—guide and influence the social life and interests of the citizenry. This paradigm is not unlike the American version where community bodies, such as churches and corporate institutions, command power and act as instruments of influence. Meanwhile, the underclass of substrates, whose genealogical features cannot easily be suppressed and who do not possess "symbolic capital," is silenced, marginalized, and never fully expressed.

These two trajectories are facilitated, to some extent, by what Boyarin describes as "embodied memory" (Boyarin 1994: 20–26). This he depicts as an analogy between memory and the body, which is bound through discourse in a kind of "genetic narrative" (22). In the case of my family, for instance, bodily manifestations of mixed identity such as skin color or hair texture bind us together. On a broader level, the family itself comes to embody the nation. That is, the nation works through the body and appeals to organic experiences to legitimate and naturalize itself (25). Like an organism that is hierarchically organized to sustain systemic functioning, the narratives and discourses of the rainbow family and nation are deployed for their own maintenance and reproduction.

On that account, my great-grandmother is intimated through implicit bodily symbols, yet never explicitly stipulated. In the narratives about our rainbow family, we may joke about "throwbacks," but *she* is never definitively part of the *we* that exists in multilayered forms of family, community, culture, or nation. Still, our omissions are not and cannot be ultimate absences, because the familial and national discourses are forged by the very existence of such ancestry. Thus, they require a strategic politics.

CONCLUSION

The fact of the matter is that nationalism thinks in terms of historical destinies, while racism dreams of eternal contaminations transmitted from the origins of time through an endless sequence of loathsome copulations. . . . The dreams of racism actually have their origins in the ideologies of class, rather than those of nation: above all in claims to divinity among rulers and to blue or white blood and breeding among aristocracies. . . . On the whole, racism manifests itself, not across national boundaries but within them. In

other words, they justify not so much foreign wars as domestic repression
and domination.

—Benedict Anderson, *Imagined Communities*

In examining the above theme, Paul Gilroy (1991) determines that for Anderson, racism is antithetical to nationalism because nations come into being
via language, rather than by accounts of biological difference or kinship. Becoming a citizen and acquiring citizenship, according to Anderson (1983), is
hence possible through a process of naturalization. Certainly, the analytical
usefulness of Anderson's efforts to demarcate mythic history, nationalism,
class, and subjugation, as well as his attention to the domestic locus of
racism, must be appreciated. To extrapolate, however, I propose that if
racism is located within national boundaries, it is likely that it can further be
identified within the domestic or intimate sphere of society.[11]

Although places such as Trinidad do not generally regard interethnic
unions as "loathsome copulations," but rather as "fortuitous combinations,"
totalizing tenets such as cosmopolitanism serve to maintain a regime of "violent hierarchies" within the family and repress the articulation of alternate
identities.[12] As well, these "fortuitous combinations," resulting from cultural
kinship practices in Trinidad, connote a kind of nationalism that is posited
upon ethnic intermixtures, class hierarchies, and status politics.[13]

It is no accident that my own familial memory was sufficiently sharp as to
trace our lineage back to the monarchical court of Spain in the fifteenth century, but was ineffectual in remembering much at all about a great-grandparent
who lived less than 150 years ago. The void in my memory and in our family's
narratives regarding my great-grandmother and my grandfather's illegitimate
offspring makes evident a form of exclusion that takes place in the intimate
sphere of the family, through descent lines and kinship practices, and that also
resonates on a national level.

Gilroy (1991) asserts that the discourses of nation and people are saturated
with racial connotations. I would add that they are suffused with other status accoutrements and the accumulation of "symbolic capital." Within the family, and
by extension, the nation, domestic repression has occurred and continues to
occur. In this way, kin relations produce both unified and disjointed dynamics.
In turn, these dynamics are reflected at the larger societal levels, not the least of
which is the nation. That is not to say that family practices serve to naturalize
social processes (Gilroy 1991: 43). Rather, the naturalization of kin relations and
the naturalization of the nation mutually reinforce one another and underscore
the intersection of the domestic and politico-jural domains of society.

Accordingly, practices of intermarriage and reproduction, along with
themes of ethnicity and status, act at once as the main social field of contestation and integration in Trinidad. Thus, the case of my family indicates that
kinship comprises a matrix for ethnicity, class, culture, nation, and other

categories of being. Conversely, ethnicity, class, culture, nation, and other such categories reinforce and reproduce the social and cultural landscape and influence kinship relations and practices. All of these identifications, to some extent, are mutually constitutive and naturalized referents that reflect the intersections of the public and private spheres as well as the inextricable element of power.

Kinship, as an object of knowledge, might be understood as a type of metaphoric "biopolitics" that theorizes about biological symbols such as blood while simultaneously and necessarily referencing the sociopolitical dimension. It is thus "a statement of power" (Haraway 1989: 100). Similarly, the omission of certain family members in the familial narrative is both a politics of memory and the construction of identity (Boyarin 1994: 23). Indeed, as has been delineated here, and as the act of writing illustrates, both memory and identity are the effects of intersubjective practices of signification that are ever re-created within contestable discourse.[14]

NOTES

1. It should be noted that I am specifically using the terms "white" and "black" because these identifications are used frequently in the studies discussed here. Also the color gradation is particularly applicable to the Caribbean context where ethnic origins are sometimes unclear or ambiguous.

2. As noted by Trinidadian historian Bridget Brereton, in the Caribbean, miscegenation was the rule rather than the exception (Brereton 1981: 114).

3. Until the early twentieth century, Indians were regarded as outside of the mainstream in Trinidad, and they appeared content to pursue their own way of life (Brereton 1979: 177). Generally, however, Indian immigrants arrived as individuals rather than as units, and so many were forced to marry across caste, religious, and even ethnic lines. Still, Indian-African unions were considered taboo due to imported caste and color values (Clarke 1993:133–34). The seeming coherence and continuity of traditions often noted in academic reports generally fail to address how Indian lifestyles were modified in Trinidad and fail to address the large degree of creolization that occurred in Indian and Middle Eastern populations, as a result of conversion to Christianity (Brereton 1979: 182).

4. "Symbolic capital," in turn, affords one the right to profit from recognition or what Bourdieu refers to as "distinction" (Bourdieu 1984: 114–38).

5. Unlike other parts of the Western Hemisphere, interethnic and interfaith unions in Trinidad were neither explicitly discouraged nor prevented a century ago (see Brereton 1979).

6. In deference to my great-grandmother, it should be noted that although she agreed to convert to Christianity and I have described her as "reprogrammed" because of that decision, in her own way, she maintained some semblance of her Jewish heritage by insisting on having three kitchens in her house—one regular, one for Passover, and one kosher kitchen.

7. In this manner, by creating some sense of a totality, marriage might be regarded as a subtle form of governmentality, by managing and maintaining certain familial, social, cultural, and national practices that underlie an existing power structure and hierarchy.

8. The terms *ideology* and *ideology-orienting system* are used to describe Trinidadian cosmopolitanism, in rough accord with Geertz, as a set of beliefs that members of a collectivity have at their disposal to interpret and to act (Geertz 1973).

9. *Dougla* is a colloquial term used in Trinidad to describe a person of mixed African and Indian ancestry.

10. Because ethnicity is pivotal to the discussion of kinship in this chapter, the term *politics of memory* also connotes a *racist* "politics of memory," even if what is criteria of belonging to a particular ethnic group is different from the U.S. equivalent.

11. The utility of Anderson's quotation in this chapter is largely to suggest that if racism exists within national boundaries, then it is plausible that it might also occur at the internal or domestic level of the nation-state, within the family and others. Nevertheless, I remain uneasy with the suggestion that racism occurs only within national boundaries and not across them. I concur with David Scott's statement that the whole problem of race and modern power has been inadequately dealt with, and as such, its relationship with the nation-state remains unclear (see Scott 1999: 119).

12. See Williams (1989: 433) for further explication of "fortuitous combinations" as this phrase relates to racism and nationhood. See also Derrida (1976) as explicated by Borneman (1996: 219) on "violent hierarchies" as this phrase relates to naturalized categories.

13. Trinidadians generally valorize ethnic and cultural creolization, as well as unions across and between ethnic and cultural lines. Attitudes that contradict this popular line of thinking, such as Indian-African union being regarded as "loathsome," are not well received by the public at large, who perceive such perspectives as evidence of undesirable racism. See Birth 1997 for an example to that effect.

14. In writing about gender and identity subversion, Judith Butler suggests that identities are assumed to be fixed in place through the artifice of binary oppositions. Butler argues against this line of reasoning and notes that identities occur through signifying practices, which themselves seek to conceal their own workings (Butler 1990). I have found Butler's analysis of identity and signification useful in thinking about the fluid, ambiguous, and contestatory nature of ethnic identity in Trinidad.

BIBLIOGRAPHY

Anderson, Benedict. 1983. *Imagined Communities.* London: Verso.

Barrow, C. 1986. Finding the Support: Strategies for Survival. *Social and Economic Studies* 35: 131–76.

———. 1988. Anthropology, the Family, and Women. In *Gender and Caribbean Development.* Ed. P. Mohammed and C. Shepherd. Mona: University of the West Indies, pp. 156–69.

Birth, Kevin. 1997. Most of Us Are Family Some of the Time. *American Ethnologist* 24 (3): 585–601.

Borneman, John. 1992. *Belonging in the Two Berlins: Kin, State, Nation.* Cambridge: Cambridge University Press.

———. 1996. Until Death Do Us Part: Marriage/Death in Anthropological Discourse. *American Ethnologist* 23 (2): 215–38.

Bourdieu, Pierre. 1977. *Outline of a Theory of Practice.* Trans. R. Nice. Cambridge: Cambridge University Press.

———. 1984. *Distinction: A Social Critique of the Judgement of Taste.* Trans. R. Nice. London: Routledge and Kegan Paul.

Bourdieu, Pierre, and Loïc J. D. Wacquant. 1990. *In Other Words: Essays towards a Reflexive Sociology.* Trans. M. Adamson. Stanford, Calif.: Stanford University Press.

Boyarin, Jonathan. 1994. Space, Time, and the Politics of Memory. In *Remapping Memory: The Politics of Time and Space.* Ed. J. Boyarin. Minneapolis: University of Minnesota Press, pp. 1–39.

Braithwaite, L. 1975. *Social Stratification in Trinidad.* Mona: University of the West Indies.

Brereton, Bridget. 1979. *Race Relations in Trinidad, 1870–1900.* Cambridge: Cambridge University Press.

———. 1981. *History of Modern Trinidad and Tobago, 1783–1962.* London: Heinemann.

———. 1993. Social Organization and Class, Racial, and Cultural Conflict in 19th Century Trinidad. In *Trinidadian Ethnicity.* Ed. K. Yelvington. Knoxville: University of Tennessee Press, pp. 33–35.

Butler, Judith. 1990. *Gender Trouble: Feminism and the Subversion of Identity.* New York: Routledge.

Clarke, Colin. 1993. Spatial Patterns and Social Interaction among East Indians and Creole Populations of Trinidad. In *Trinidadian Ethnicity.* Ed. K. Yelvington. Knoxville: University of Tennessee Press, pp. 133–34.

Cohen, Ronald. 1978. Ethnicity: Problems and Focus in Anthropology. *Annual Review of Anthropology* 7: 379–403.

Eriksen, Thomas Hylland. 1993. *Ethnicity and Nationalism: Anthropological Perspectives.* Boulder, Colo.: Pluto Press.

Forte, Maximillan. 1995. The Crisis of Creolization in Trinidad and Tobago. *International Third World Studies Journal and Review* 7: 42–49.

Foucault, Michel. 1979. *Discipline and Punish.* Trans. A. Sheridan. New York: Vintage.

———. 1980. Introduction. In *Herculine Barbin.* New York: Pantheon, pp. vii–xiv.

Freilich, M. 1960. Cultural Diversity among Trinidadian Peasants. Unpublished Ph.D. dissertation. University of Columbia.

———. 1968. Sex, Secrets, and Systems. In *The Family in the Caribbean.* Ed. S. Gerber. Rio Piedras: Institute of Caribbean Studies.

Geertz, Clifford. 1973. *The Interpretation of Cultures.* New York: Basic.

Gilroy, Paul. 1991. *There Ain't No Black in the Union Jack.* London: Hutchinson Press.

Gopaul-McNicol, Sharon Ann. 1993. *Working with West Indian Families.* New York: Guilford.

Hall, Stuart. 1994. Cultural Identity and Diaspora in Colonial Discourse and Post-Colonial Theory. In *Colonial Discourse and Post-Colonial Theory.* Ed. P. Williams and L. C. Chrisman. New York: Columbia University Press.

Haraway, Donna. 1989. *Primate Visions.* New York: Routledge, Chapman and Hall.

Klass, Morton. 1961. *East Indians in Trinidad*. New York: Columbia University Press.

———. 1991. *Singing with Sai Baba: The Politics of Revitalization in Trinidad*. Boulder, Colo.: Westview.

Massiah, Joycelin. 1986. Women in the Caribbean. *Social and Economic Studies* 35: 351.

———. 1988. Researching Women's Work: 1985 and Beyond. In *Gender and Caribbean Development*. Ed. P. Mohammed and C. Shepherd. Mona: University of the West Indies, pp. 206–31.

Miller, Daniel. 1994. *Modernity: An Ethnographic Approach*. Oxford: Berg Publishers.

Murdock, G. 1949. *Our Primitive Contemporaries*. New York: Macmillan.

Needham, Rodney. 1971. Remarks on the Analysis of Kinship and Marriage. In *Rethinking Kinship and Marriage*. Ed. R. Needham. London: Tavistock.

Nevadomsky, J. 1982. Social Change and East Indians in Rural Trinidad. *Social and Economic Studies* 21: 90–126.

———. 1983. Economic Organization, Social Mobility, and Changing Social Status among East Indians in Rural Trinidad. *Ethnology* 22: 43–79.

Oxaal, Ivar. 1982. *Black Intellectuals and the Dilemma of Race and Class in Trinidad*. Cambridge: Schenkman Publishers.

Oxford English Dictionary (OED). 1992. First edition. Ed. E. Ehrlich et al. Oxford: Oxford University Press.

Rheddock, R. 1994. *Women, Labor, and Politics in Trinidad and Tobago*. London: Zed.

Rodman, H. 1971. *Lower Class Families: The Culture of Poverty in Negro Trinidad*. New York: Oxford University Press.

Schneider, David. 1984. A Critique of Kinship. Ann Arbor: University of Michigan Press.

Scott, David. 1999. *Refashioning Futures: Criticisms on Postcoloniality*. Princeton: Princeton University Press.

Segal, Daniel. 1994. Nationalism and the Past in Post-Colonial Trinidad and Tobago. In *Remapping Memory: The Politics of Time and Space*. Ed. J. Boyarin. Minneapolis: University of Minnesota Press.

Senior, Olive. 1991. *Working Miracles: Women's Lives in the English Speaking Caribbean*. London: James Currey.

Smedley, Audrey. 1993. *Race in North America*. Boulder, Colo.: Westview.

Smith, Raymond. 1956. *The Negro Family in British Guiana: Family Structure and Social Status in the Villages*. London: Routledge and Kegan Paul.

———. 1988. Hierarchy and the Dual Marriage System in West Indian Society. In *Gender and Kinship: Essays toward a Unified Analysis*. Ed. J. F. Collier and S. J. Yanagisako. Stanford, Calif.: Stanford University Press, pp. 164–75.

———. 1988. *Kinship and Class in the West Indies*. Cambridge: Cambridge University Press.

Steedman, Carolyn. 1986. *Landscape for a Good Woman*. New Jersey: Rutgers University Press.

Verdery, Katherine. 1994. Ethnicity, Nationalism and Statemaking. In *The Anthropology of Ethnicity*. Ed. H. Vermeulen and C. Goves. Amsterdam: Het Spinhuis.

Vervotec, S. 1992. *Hindu Trinidad*. London: Macmillan.

Williams, Brackette. 1989. A Class Act: Anthropology and the Race to Nation across Ethnic Terrain. *Annual Review of Anthropology* 18: 401–44.

Young, V. 1990. Household Structure in a West Indian Society. *Social and Economic Studies* 39: 147–79.

3

Personalizing It: Adoption, Bastardy, Kinship, and Family

Jamila Bargach

THE SETTING

"So Jamila," said my sometimes sister–sometimes cousin, Salima, as we sat idly sipping our sweet-mint tea one beautiful early-autumn 1996 afternoon in the garden of our grandmother's old house, "we could do IT again."

My eyes . . . a petrified sob, hers . . . a frozen smile.

This IT, this is THE IT, unequivocally the famous IT so long hidden, so long murmured in curious ears, so long hushed up in midsentences, so long evoked to explain and excuse eccentricities and mischief, so long left unanswered by an intimidating command; so long known, felt, but incapable of being apprehended. This is the IT that, when it was to be finally born into the world of the clearly spoken, was to take so many versions; was to bear so many explanations; was to be interpreted, and reinterpreted, verging on the pathetic and the cynical; was to be intimidatingly subsumed into a course of fate that demanded no blasphemous explanations or excuses. Yet misapprehension continued, perhaps even more bewildering and painful than the one produced by silence and murmurs.

"So Jamila," continued my sometimes sister–sometimes cousin, despite the heaviness that suddenly descended on this beautiful early autumn afternoon, turning the mint tea's sweetness into a slow bitterness, "you know what I mean, we could do IT again, you could *rabi* Rita and take her to the states with you. . . ." And I crossed the river of language to become an orphan of words.

"You know I am only kidding," she says belatedly, considering what must have been a vexed and perplexed look on my face.

DEFINING THE IT—*RABI*

The IT that my sometimes sister–sometimes cousin is describing is my own customary adoption (*rabi*, Moroccan Arabic for informal adoption; the noun form is *trabi*) in my maternal aunt's family and her wish to have me adopt her daughter–my–sometimes daughter Rita. Between our mothers and our-selves lay a thirty-five-year space; even if there are similarities and overlaps, there is especially a divergence of latent and conspicuous reasons and ex-planations. These situated differences evoke social, economic, and political shifts, as well as shifts in identity whose strokes I am about to paint.

The portrayals, the scenarios, the narratives, and the incidents in my exercise of writing the self belong to my immediate and extended family. The periods in which these events took place portray social as well as personal changes, which themselves further paint those other strokes of historical permutations. Thus these events, by virtue of this historical nexus, belong to public knowledge and should not be construed as secrets. My own encounter with and understanding of these nuanced and context-sensitive changes, largely resisted in the con-tained and extremely protective world where I grew up, acquired their potency as a reality in the process of rethinking and articulating my fieldwork. All along, they have been solid points of attachments even while I have been rethinking, evaluating, and assessing them.

A VERNACULAR OF MOROCCAN ADOPTIONS

Formally, the practice of what is understood as adoption in the Euro-American context is strictly prohibited in Morocco.[1] Due to this legal interdiction, Jack Goody affirms that "Arabs forbid adoption" (1990: 380). Such a reading holds largely true when containing one's inquiry within the realm of orthodox legal-ity and jurisprudence. Removed from these structured and textually based sources, however, Moroccan culture and Moroccan social history offer ample evidence to the contrary. As a matter of fact, various styles of fosterage, ex-change, guardianships, and even adoptions were, and still are, practiced.

In Goody's earlier research, namely *The Development of the Family and Marriage in Europe*, brief reference is made to how, despite church prohi-bitions, for instance, the practice of adoption persisted in its customary forms in a tacit manner not directly in conflict with the religious–legal establish-ment. The customary adoptions endured also in late Imperial China (Waltner 1990) even while they were legally prohibited across surnames. So, too, whereas legally adoption is strictly forbidden in Morocco, various culturally sanctioned forms of adoption do exist.

The following is an initial typology of Moroccan practices of fosterage, guardianship, and "adoptions." There is a family or customary adoption by which I mean the gift of a child from one family to another. The scenarios may vary widely, but generally in this kind of adoption, a family with no child or one with only boys or only girls may solicit a brother or a cousin who may be willing to give a child. This exchange, often but not always between close kin (agnate or collateral), is an informal transaction that does not require a "legal" procedure.[2] The ties between adopted child and biological family are usually sustained; so for example, the last name would remain that of the biological family were the names of the families different. This might seem a simple relocation or a transfer of the guardianship of the child to a host family—uncle, aunt, grandmother, sister, or other relatives. Yet if this outwardly seems like a visit, it is from within an "interminable" visit that entails the inevitable development and entanglement of feelings of attachments, anger, love, and jealousy among children, siblings, and parents, just as if the ties were truly those between natural children and parents.[3]

The second form of adoption is an informal, word-of-mouth, or secret, adoption: a child is given by its mother, or someone *close* to her,[4] to a family, or an intermediary who then hands the baby to a family or another individual. This family then goes through the process—"fictive," that is—of having given natural birth to the child. The fictive aspect is the act of registering the child in the official civil registry as one's own; it is an administrative ruse that endows the child with a biological genealogy.[5] Generally, it is the adoptive parents who often "dupe"—although they can sometimes bribe or plead with—the civil register official by presenting fake birth documents so that the official may proceed with the registration so as to have this child be officially theirs through the artifice of the name. Through such a process (considered a counterfeit and a criminal activity by the legal apparatus in place) they circumvent an unyielding and uncompromising system of descent rules. Interestingly, this sort of extralegal secret adoption, where there is an erasure of the natal identity, is the enactment of the Euro-American understanding of adoption. But while in the Euro-American context, such a procedure takes place within the accepted and legitimizing frame of legality, in Morocco it is falsely legitimized and justified through and by an administrative procedure, but within a larger legal corpus that denies its existence, or even further, considers it a criminal activity. Given, then, that this sort of adoption is illegal, once it takes place (i.e., it is normalized and is subsumed into a context of natural reproduction), its very existence is automatically canceled out. The authenticity (the naturalness of the bond, that is) can be called into question by the adopted persons or extended family members in bitter cases over inheritance, but even in the midst of such questioning or family rivalry, once a secret adoption goes into effect, it discursively negates itself by falling into the course of normality. It becomes, hence, an elusive practice caught between the status of being (practiced) and nonbeing (prohibited).

The third form of "adoption" is legal guardianship of a minor. This is called taking tutelage, or *kafala,* and within kafala there are two genres. One is called *kafala itifâqiya,* a kafala of agreement, whereby parents or a mother give their *legal* or natural child to a family or an individual after drafting a binding legal contract;[6] in other words, this kafala takes place between two private parties mediated by a legal contract. The second kafala is effected when an abandoned child, technically considered a ward of the state, is taken into kafala by a family, once again, after drafting a legally binding document. In this case, the contract is between the state and a private party. My sister wanted me, in effect, to do a kafala of agreement by which Rita would become my "daughter." But the other form of kafala, as a bureaucratic procedure, has since the 1960s been the subject of debate until a relevant law was finally ratified in the parliament in 1993.

LEGAL VISIBILITY OR THE MOVE TOWARD ACKNOWLEDGING THE EXISTENCE OF A PROBLEM

On 10 September 1993 the Moroccan parliament finally passed a pending bill concerning abandoned children and systematizing the process of kafala for abandoned children. This was one of many that were long awaiting approval in the parliament. After being approved, it became law. The promulgation of a law is hardly an extraordinary achievement in itself: every issue of the *Moroccan Official Bulletin* invariably has a section with new or revised laws. The law concerning abandoned children is, however, considered nothing short of a milestone: an open recognition of the existence of a category labeled "Abandoned Children" in the fold of Moroccan society, a society in which the stigma of "illegitimacy and bastardy" is extremely potent, to put it mildly. For such a topic to become a matter of public debate, even momentarily, draws attention to itself given that questions regarding this social segment have been usually buried under silence.

Abandoned children were never, however, entirely absent from the "consciousness" of the state; their visibility was a necessity within selected pockets of those administrative apparatuses that address some of their concerns. Indeed, prior to the birth of the 1993 decree and law, administrative circulars regulated the procedure concerning the kafala of abandoned children. These functioned within the three ministries that took part, directly or indirectly, in the regularization and officialization of the kafala contract.

Unlike a circular, a law is published in the *Moroccan Official Bulletin* and is therefore widely offered to public view.[7] By passing the 1993 bill, the parliament not only made the public statement that there are indeed abandoned children in Morocco, but also acknowledged the existence of the crisis that had engendered them in the first place.[8] Such children are evidence of clearly shifting patterns of attachment and family dynamics that are almost the antithesis of those values of love, selflessness, and sacrifice that are considered to be timeless and have long been brandished as inviolable both by the state and by the cultural imaginary. The passage of the 1993 law amounted to the formal recognition of the reality of a social fissure to which academics and responsible educators had been adamantly calling attention since the 1960s (e.g., Belarbi 1989; Etienne 1979; Radi 1977; Zkik 1994; Chekroun and Boudoudou 1986). This law is, consequently, remarkable not only because it implies official admission of the existence of a social category where there had formally been none, but also because it endowed this category with a legal visibility that it had formerly altogether lacked.

Yet placed in a larger legal, administrative, and social context the law remains a rather tentative step. First of all, it is quite limited as a legal idea. Within the rigid and hierarchized set of rules, a law must be supplemented by a decree of application (*décret d'application-laiha tanfidiya*) that explains it and turns it into an applicable "reality." Seven years after its publication in the *Moroccan Official Bulletin*, the law concerning abandoned children still lacks a decree. Without a decree of application, a law remains a closed box without a key, while the intent of having the box is the ability to open it!

Second, as a legislative text, it is replete with flaws. The latter can be located at different levels—that of organization, unity, applicability, or even formulation. So, for example, in the law's first section (*Dispositions Générales*), an abandoned child can be anyone under eighteen years old who falls into one of the following categories:

- having parents incapable of ensuring protection and education due to major forces outside of their control;
- being an orphan and not having any legal means of subsistence;
- having parents who are not assuming their moral responsibility to guide their children toward the right path.

The social, cultural, religious, and judicial implications of openly and straightforwardly recognizing the existence of abandoned children might have been genuinely radical. Yet the legislators diluted their significance by blurring the linguistic boundary between an abandoned and an orphaned child. Playing *with and on* this possibility of meaning cast more legitimacy on a reality that exposes the increasing disparity between actual social practices and the long-standing norms of social propriety and other idealized notions of social cohesion.

The definition of "abandoned" is clearly broad, thus purposefully ambiguous, if not elusive. At the very least, it is less contained or circumscribed than open to further interpretations. The criteria for judging are lacking. What is this "right path," for instance? What are the reasons for setting the limit of age at eighteen years when the minimum legal age for marriage is fifteen for girls? In other words, there are serious discrepancies between this law and existing family law. In addition to many subsidiary, more or less rhetorical concerns, the most important question that the text invites is: Are all the children enumerated in these three clusters to be taken up for kafala? Of course the law does not address this question. In effect, it cannot answer this question because it is a law and not a decree; "practical" details are usually addressed in the latter. The situation of having a ratified law without its decree, however familiar, has placed all individuals who work for and with abandoned children in a precarious situation: neither are they totally free to follow the preexisting procedures of kafala, nor can they totally ignore the 1993 law. For the social worker, it is a continual dilemma and involves an awkward process of negotiation, and sometimes confrontation, between families wishing to take kafala and the administration that mediates this process.

Ambiguities abound at all levels of this law, but the section of the statute describing the content of the file forms perhaps its most controversial aspect. First of all, the legislature has called for the creation of a "family commission" that is to study the requests presented to it, and decisions to grant or deny kafala are consequently to be based on its recommendations. Who is to sit in this family commission, how it is to proceed with the evaluations, and what criteria it is to utilize are, however, questions that are not clarified by this law. In other words, the law simply calls for the creation of a family commission (in itself a potentially good idea) without introducing any of those basic procedural rules that should be technically and unquestionably covered. More important, this new legislation has made it imperative that for the family commission to consider the requests it receives, the files include a court order clearly testifying that the infant or child has been legally abandoned. To have this court order be issued implies taking the abandoning party to court. Prior to this edict, a generic certificate signed (or thumbed) by the mother was sufficient; in the aftermath of the new law, however, if a woman delivers in the hospital and declares her intention to relinquish the infant, the hospital authorities are forced to notify the police. The police then write a report, and a court case is launched against the mother. The mother must go to the court as an offender and be judged on two counts: adultery and intention to abandon an infant. Of course the man who impregnated her neither appears in these legislative texts nor partakes in the ensuing punishment when it does indeed take place.

In defense of these edicts, social workers and several lawyers explained that the strict requirements have a noble intention. They aim at giving a sense of *security* to the family assuming the kafala; biological mother, parents, or related relative(s) will not appear one day claiming their child back and being able to do so as the right of blood supersedes that of the old edicts of the kafala laws. By having a legally certified court order testifying the child to be a ward of the state and granting its tutelage to a family, the state's law nullifies any potential claim that could use blood relation as grounds for claiming the child back. The child was *only* given for kafala when it had no blood relation to assume the responsibilities incumbent on blood. Such a presupposition is at best problematic, if not genuinely suspicious: Can a court order erase the natural, biological ties when they are known?[9] Can it inhibit extended family members from holding this truth as a time bomb over the adoptive parents, or the adopted person in the event that the latter does not know? Socially, such legal security is preceded by the natural bond between natural parents and their children. This is reinforced by a general distrust of the judicial system. In the words of one judge, "The institution of law is detached—divorced from reality" (Judge Abdouni, personal communication, Rabat July 1997). In addition, the resolute and overemphatic tone of this specific edict makes it seem as though it is trying too hard to alter an assumption and a status that are taken to be unquestionably natural and that, through other genealogy laws, only make evident the primacy, potency, and sanctity of blood as inalienable relation. A continuation of this same problematic edict of judging the mother for abandoning is the Moroccan Penal Code (section 459) that stipulates that it is a punishable crime to abandon a child. The system, therefore, is making single mothers look for other solutions than handing the baby to a shelter or a hospital. The consequences of this law will be fully evident only in the long run, but very recently two cases of traffic in babies, one in Casablanca and one in Ceuta,[10] have come to light. In addition, a rise in infanticide and hazardous abortions may be only a few of several further consequences. Such intransigence (at least on paper) points to the staunch belief of the lawmakers in their infallible hold on *the one* truth. In its own turn, however, such a belief finds its legitimization in the remote folds of a benchmark episode in the history of Islam's jurisprudence.

THE DISTANT ROOTS OF A DISTINCTION

A classic of the nineteenth-century intellectual tradition, Robertson Smith's *Marriage and Kinship in Early Arabia* (1885) surveys kinship and marriage laws as a means of studying systems of tribal organization. The general criticism directed against this study coalesces around what Jack Goody has labeled as its "speculative propositions and imagined reconstruction" (1990: 363). These imagined reconstructions are a continuing subject of debate among other scholars, such as Patricia Crone (1987), who has entirely dismissed the idea that fictive ties (adoption, patronage, and the inclusion of emancipated slaves) were equal in value to those bonds created by blood in pre-Muslim Arabia. I am not presenting the adoption practices that Robertson Smith describes, concomitant with these other laws of protection, as a historical and unequivocal reality, but as a starting proposition for later historical debates once again as voiced by Crone or Goody. Utilizing early Arab genealogists, Robertson Smith writes:

> As regards freedmen, indeed, the only point that concerns us here is that they were often adopted by their patrons. . . . The right of adoption, however, was not limited to the legitimization of the offspring of a free tribesman by a slave girl. Mohammed, for example, adopted his freedman Zaid, a lad of pure Arab blood who had become a slave through the fortune of war. Here, then, a man is incorporated by adoption into a group of alien blood, but we learn that to preserve the doctrine of tribal homogeneity it was often feigned that the adopted son was veritably and for all effects of the blood of his new father. . . . As there was no difference between an adopted and real son before Islam, emancipated slaves appear in the genealogical lists without any note of explanation, just as if they had been pure Arabs. (52–53)

Beyond Robertson Smith, one should note that the being of a tribe depended on its size, which in its turn depended on socioeconomic and demographic conditions. As the number of individuals in each clan increased, the clan automatically acquired more power and prestige. Adoption of adult males was seen therefore as an effective means of acquiring the human capital not only ready to fight and defend the clan, but also to add to its general prestige by adding to its sheer number. As mentioned by Robertson Smith, the act of adoption entailed bonds very similar to those of biological descent: lineage, inheritance, payment of ransom, and marriage prohibition. In other words, the distinction between the biological and the adopted was utterly void, or so it was constructed later. Many Muslim historians and jurisconsults have highlighted this custom of a total assimilation as a part of the unnaturalness and barbarous traditions of pre-Muslim Arabia. Plain adoption countered the natural flow of things first by creating, then encouraging, perpetuating, and believing in fiction and lies: a nonblood relation truly equals the sanctity of a blood bond. From the official point of view, this simply cannot hold.

The episode of Zaid ibnu Harita, formally known as Zaid ibnu Mohammed, invoked by leading Muslim scholars and jurisconsults for centuries, constitutes the backbone of the construction of what a Muslim family is *not*. Fatima Mernissi writes:

> The most significant example of women's irresistible power over the Prophet is probably his sudden (and *scandalous, by his own people's standards*) passion for Zainab bint Jahsh, the wife of his adopted son Zaid. In Muhammad's Arabia, the link created by adoption was considered identical to blood-ties. Moreover, Zainab was the Prophet's own cousin, and the Prophet himself had arranged her marriage with his adopted son. (1987: 56; my emphasis)

On one of the Prophet's visits, Zainab hurriedly opened the door while not totally covered, not wanting to let the prophet wait. Upon seeing her, the

Prophet hastily left, declining her invitation to enter and wait for Zaid. When Zainab reported the incident of the Prophet's hasty leaving to her husband, the latter went to his adopted father saying that he was ready to divorce Zainab if the Prophet wanted to marry her. The Prophet declined Zaid's offer. A revelation came, however, in which a divine sanction was given to his marriage with Zainab bint Jahsh.

> Allah has not assigned unto any man two hearts within his body, nor hath he made your wives whom ye declare (to be your mothers) your mothers, nor hath he made those whom ye claim (to be your sons) your sons. This is but a saying of your mouths. But Allah sayeth the truth and He showeth the way. Proclaim their real parentage. That will be more equitable in the sight of Allah. And if ye know not their fathers, then (they are) your brethren in the faith, and your clients. And there is no sin for you in the mistakes that ye make unintentionally, but what your hearts purpose (that will be a sin for you). Allah is Forgiving, Merciful. (Quran, Surat 33 [Al-Ahzab]: 4–5)

In Quranic commentary the consensus is that this verse draws attention to the very unnaturalness of certain givens:[11] a woman cannot be a mother and a wife to a man; a man cannot have two hearts; and a man cannot be a father if he is not so naturally. Sonhood is the product only of a biological tie and not a set of binding words. God utters only words of truth and does not punish mistakes committed unintentionally, but rather one's sinful intentions, the religious scholars (*fuqaha*) argue. In the aftermath of the prophet's divine revelation,[12] creating bonds of sonhood and parenthood through the fiction of adoption were no longer allowed, or, once again, so it was construed later.

The prophet then married Zainab, the newly divorced wife of Zaid, a fellow Muslim, no longer an adopted son. The marriage, previously considered incestuous, constituted the symbol of a final break with the pre-Islamic tradition of open adoption. According to Gertrude Stern, following this verse,

> the circulation of the Tradition[13] shows that the people had accepted the ordinance in the Qur'an as a religious sanction of Muhammad's marriage. It must be remembered that a wider issue than the marriage of Muhammad to his adopted son's wife was *possibly* also in question. The ordinance was probably part of Muhammad's policy to abolish the practice of regarding adopted relatives in the same light as blood relatives. (1939: 105)

What Stern characterizes as a possible probability has indeed become an accepted reality, as later jurisprudence clearly shows. An adopted relationship cannot be or assume the function of a natural relationship. The prophet indeed did not marry his ex-daughter-in-law, but a divorcee of a fellow Muslim and his own paternal (patrilateral) cousin. These verses, in conjunction with the historical context in which they were revealed, shaped the ideal of what a Muslim family was: a unit based on the dual criteria of marriage and blood, whereby these became the only sanctioned means through which to acquire a *nasab* (lineage). Verging between a loose and sometimes faithful relationship, it is these edicts that now structure the contemporary Moroccan Personal Status Code.

CONTEMPORARY MOROCCAN PERSONAL STATUS LAW (*MOUDAWANA*)

In the aftermath of Morocco's independence in 1956, the judicial–religious body was reinterpreted and rearticulated to produce the "modern" Moroccan Moudawana. Through the matrix of its rules and symbols, the Moudawana drew the image of its ideal family where adoption (*at-tabani* in classical Arabic) appears only as a prohibited practice and a negated activity. The text clearly stipulates that "adoption does not have any judicial value and does not engender any lineal consequences" (Moudawana, stipulation 83). Kafala, on the other hand, does not at all appear in this text, which is the cardinal legal codification of the family and of the rights of succession and inheritance. The concept of kafala finds its root in Morocco's *Law of Contracts and Obligations.*

Etymologically, the word *kafala* has two distinct meanings in classical Arabic: to guarantee (*daman*) and to take care of (*kafl*). In the former sense, the word *kafala* has been mainly employed in the realm of commerce and business transactions. Legal kafala stands close to the Western establishment of a surety bond; kafala in this context is analyzed in great detail by fuqaha in order to determine and set its correct parameters given that Islam strictly forbids usury. Moroccan legislation has also adopted the concept of kafala in its commerce or business sense to be part of *The Law of Contracts and Obligations.* But the meaning of kafala as implying a "partial" adoption, bestowing a gift and taking-charge-of, is derived from Quranic example: "*And her lord accepted her with full acceptance and vouchsafed to her a goodly growth; and made Zachariah her guardian*" (*kafalaha Zachariah,* Surat Al Imran: 37). The broad semantic scope of kafala permits it further to be used to suggest the combination of all these attitudes and behaviors toward a minor. Unlike the Euro-American understanding of adoption, kafala does not automatically imply the living of the person taken into kafala with those who offer the kafala. It is a bond of protection or guardianship, but such guardianship may be financial, moral, physical, or any of these in combination. Such details are usually drafted in the contract (*iltizam*) that binds the adopting party. These distinctions remain in essence legal and, in any particular social context, might only be evoked for strategic reasons.

The fact that the legal concept of kafala finds its root and general currency in *The Law of Contracts and Obligations* necessarily invites a number of questions, among them that of its basic nature. In its capacity as a gift and as "taking-care-of," it fulfills (perhaps creates) the terms of the relationship between donor and minor. The fuqaha clearly see kafala as a commercial transaction even while it is inscribed in a rather humane domain. One is indeed buying a place in paradise by engaging herself to the physical upkeep of an orphan or a foundling. It is therefore similar to a business transaction. The Moroccan legislature, like those of many other Arab-Muslim countries (except Tunisia), has chosen this concept for the act of "adoption," since it is a contract and an obligation toward the self. The question then is: If there are so many possible legal relations, what is the specific kind of relation, and what kind of moral authority (that is, theoretically and legally) is there, between the *kafeel* and the minor? Such behavior is supposed to be directed by the Islamic code of charity. Yet this frame sometimes fails to satisfy adopting parents, who express their wish to exercise full parental presence and agency. By stressing the kafala in its transaction/business aspect, the Moudawana restricts the space of the engagement to physical needs (food, clothing, medical care) and moral needs (education), but refuses to extend it to the space of the name.[14]

REMEMBERING

My sister was not precisely concerned about the name, but only about education. My mother and her mother probably had a different agenda and one that I can only extrapolate from fragments of stories. There is no definitive story about what occurred thirty-five years ago, and as I have come to believe, neither should there be. The stories I was told varied from those who told it all and those who resisted the telling. Both spoke rivers even when they remained silent. I do not have a definitive story, and the "eye/I" (Kondo 1990) of the anthropologist understands the construction but also the necessity of a story, she understands why my biological mother (whom I always call "Aunt") needed to protect herself from the unspoken blame of having forsaken her offspring, and she understands why my mother (my biological aunt and whom I always call "Mother") needed to be able to own me in an unfettered way as her legitimate and fully fledged daughter. She understands why my biological father (whom I call "Uncle") needed to openly accuse the women and denounce their conspiracies, and why my father (my biological aunt's husband whom I always call "Father") needed to welcome me as being almost as "real" as his own "real" sons; why my biological siblings (especially the older ones) needed to reminisce about this event and to construct it as a dramatic denouement and an additional skeleton in the closet of the family secrets; why my biological cousins (whom I have always called brothers) needed to stubbornly retreat into their silence and occasional indifference; why my extended biological father's family of Rabat needed to give me sidelong glances in family gatherings with the never failing comment that "even if she was brought up as one of them she is still one of us, she looks exactly like her father;" why my father's extended family from Fez needed almost always to say, "She is now one of us, she only has theirs as a name, for she acts exactly like her [adoptive] father;" or yet why in my mother's family (since both of my mothers were sisters) the *nasab*—the lineage—was not an issue, was collapsed, denied relevance, or delegated to having no importance. I was then in the uterine space, the distinction between the mothers being inconsequential. The somewhat preferential treatment I received from my own maternal grandmother may have been due to my being an insatiable listener and a perpetually curious child, though it might have been also an atonement of guilt, given she was the engineer of this transaction. But then again, this might be my own overreading of the situation, for she used to say, it is always the mothers who count; men are instrumental and sometimes almost incidental.

My sometimes cousin–sometimes sister and I, sitting in our grandmother's house, were almost like a mirror, reflecting a faded black-and-white picture of our own mothers. This reflection was, however, different: it included several actors (the husbands) who did not actively participate in our mothers' time, and it did not include the fundamental actor (the grandmother) as it did during our mothers' time. The explanations, the reasoning, even the inception of what unfolded between us reflected a different cosmology. Our manners, our values, and even our way of speaking were not those of the past. The difference was indeed nothing short of dramatic, a story in its own right.

STRADDLING GENERATIONS, CHANGING VALUES

Despite the many perspectives of what took place in Salé in the summer of 1963 through 1965, there is one point on which all agree: my maternal grandmother, Hajja Zineb, played a decisive role. She was a woman of weight and respect in the extended family. She epitomized what are now largely construed as nostalgic values and norms: selflessness, generosity, and wisdom. Her words run as unyielding verdicts. When the two sisters sat that one day after the death of my mother's own daughter, Umnia (her name means "the consecration of a wish," which ironically was not fulfilled), my aunt, in her first month of pregnancy, had agreed to give her sister her second daughter, Halima, as their own mother, the rule of law, sat between them as an arbitrator. My mother was very happy and resolved to find solace in this daughter. She took Halima with her, but Halima was almost three years old; she knew everything. After about a month, Halima could not get used to living with her aunt, and was becoming sickly because she was crying all the time.

So my mother decided to return her, as the specter of death was still too close and real to her. Her sister and she (living in different towns) decided to meet in Salé, in their own mother's house. My mother returned Halima to my aunt, and once again, as they both sat with their mother, Hajja Zineb made my aunt promise she would give the fruit of the current pregnancy to her sister if the baby happened to be a girl. A few months later, it was summer vacation, and all the sisters, cousins, and extended family met in the ancestral house owned and run by the grand matriarch, the two sisters included. I was born to my aunt in August of one summer and taken by my mother the next August.

Emotional capital was at stake in this pseudo-exchange; my mother wanted to have a daughter, a confidante, an ally, given that she had two sons with my father. The image associated with a daughter is that of a "cover" (*ghta*) for the parents, but more significantly for the mother. This image is quite potent, as the proverb that uses it is still widespread and commonly evoked; a daughter is a cover for her parents (*lbant ghta lil walidin*). She indeed protects the intimacy and is supposed to be an unfailing source of emotional and even material support. The rhetoric employed by my grandmother must have underscored this aspect. My aunt already had three daughters; she could part with one. My grandmother was the one speaking, speaking from experience and authority, and must have placed the emphasis on my mother's possible and continuing fate as a lone and overpowered female in her household. This concern for domestic service and emotional capital is of paramount importance in arousing the sentimentalism of advanced age—weakness and dependency are often the winning cards whose potency as arguments rarely fail.

The male point of view is missing here. I have never been able to get that side of the story; I am a woman now, and I can only have access to what my gender-circumscribed space of rumor would allow me. Having said this, however, it has been possible to reconstruct matters from my uncle (my biological father), given his own bitter and repeated criticisms of everything, as the true anarchist he was fond of proclaiming himself to be. Interjected comments here and there only made sense in my twenties once I realized the ambiguity of the situation, particularly during family get-togethers in the ancestral house of my grandmother, where I stayed when my father was sick and my mother took care of him. I felt excluded from common jokes and the internal knowledge of my cousins-siblings. Moments of awkwardness and uneasiness were more the rule than the exception. My uncle did not agree with the fact I was given to his sister-in-law, but neither could he offend his mother-in-law nor find fault with the exemplary *wasat* (environment) where I was brought up. His authority in this context could not have any weight, for this was the bosom of women and their togetherness. This illustrates what a number of women expressed: "Never be fooled by the men; the baby is your flesh; it belongs to you; it is a part of you because it is born out of you . . . the men seem to be incidental . . . a father may only come afterwards."

My sometimes cousin–sometimes sister and her husband spoke at length about Rita to my husband and me. I do, as a matter of fact, show her preferential treatment, and their suggestion was not entirely unfounded. The conversation among us, however, remained largely female, within a female space. The male views were secondary to whatever female decisions might be made. Still, the very presence of our husbands bespoke of the contemporary, as did the reasons put forward for what was being offered us. My aunt acted out of respect for her mother, and what she did is almost always characterized as a gesture of generosity, love, and perhaps even of sacrifice for the sake of her own sister. My own sometimes cousin–sometimes sister's act would also have been sacrificial, but not for the sake of my own possibly lonely demise. It would rather have been done for the sake of her own daughter. The sealing of my own fate as belonging to two families was largely decided by the rule of my grandmother; my aunt could only comply. My sometimes cousin–sometimes sister, however, sought to create and write a distinct fate for her daughter, a desire inspired of her husband's and her own concern for the educational future of their daughter given the rather grim educational landscape in Morocco.

While for the older pair of sisters, the overriding importance of emotional capital was not even put to question, for us it was not even worth questioning. For both of us, the importance lay in the process of education, formal and domestic. If, for our mothers, concerns over fate, love, and blood were central, they were superseded in our present rhetoric and ordering of priorities by the future of the little girl; that was, beyond doubt, *the* question. The transaction and exchange here, once more, only confirmed the emphasis on the child rather than the parents, a solid middle-class emphasis.

Despite my fondness of Rita and the wonderful potential she might have and could further develop, I decided not to take her kafala. My decision was based on a number of facts. First, it is not that I could not give her the education her own parents wanted for her, but because being reminded of the value of an education, no matter how illuminating, could never appease a six-year-old if, in tantrums or fits of tears and despair, she should ask about her own mother, father, grandmother, sisters, and brother. For me, even such an educational utopia, no matter how much both my husband and I cared for her, could never be enough of an incentive to uproot her from her family. Second, and perhaps more important, my decision was made due to the catalytic field research in shelters of abandoned children where I came face-to-face with a stark reality of a different face. Unlike Rita's potentially better formal education, the lot of abandoned children is essentially one of almost instinctual survival; Rita has a family she calls her own; abandoned children are not only deprived of a sustaining love and attention, but live in a state of marginality and nothingness. Despite the incremental legal changes in the status of abandoned children, the cultural stigma of being a bastard has not been eroded and persists in surviving through diffuse and subtle ways. Of these ways, I'd simply highlight how by its mere totalitarian normativity, the sanctified biological family makes all other potential family formations deviant, often denigrated, abject entities.

AN ALL-IN-ONE: LOOKING AT THE FAMILY

Whether it is procreation, economic reproduction or a process of socialization, in other words all the functions which maintain the permanence of its economic, social and ideological reproduction, the family fulfilled its role against all odds. . . . being part of a family, either biological or adoptive, a person could live normally without needing to develop any relation with other institutions, but the inverse was *unthinkable*. By its multifunctional character, the family could influence its own destiny. (Radi 1977: 1–2; my emphasis)

In this excerpt, Abdelwahad Radi, a Moroccan sociologist, describes historically the sustaining and generative mechanism of the Moroccan family up to the institutionalization of the centralized postcolonial nation-state and its diverse ideological and repressive apparatus. This inclusive system of reproduction—biological, economic, and symbolic—is the matrix through which to reconstruct the profile of Moroccan family in a historiography that has paid it little attention. Moroccan historiography is replete with "grand narratives" of feuds, wars, and changes in ruling dynasties, but includes little on those areas constitutive of everyday life. While in the previous section I briefly introduced the constitution of the family from a religious–legal perspective, in this section, I intend to give an equally brief historical bird's-eye view of the family. Through such an exercise, my intention is to locate those niches of continuity and change within the discourse on the family, especially as they pertain to the conception of the role of the children.

The word for family in Moroccan Arabic is *'aila,* which Mohamed Chekroun, another Moroccan sociologist, defines as "the household" without identifying its nature, whether extended or nuclear. This word comes from the verb *a`âla,* that is, "to take-charge-of [take kafala in its largest sense] of all those who constitute one's household" (1987: 60). He further elaborates that a family is "the one household which constitutes at the same time a productive unit, a unit for owning, and a unit of reproduction (biological, economic, and symbolic). Such a unit is under the custody of the leader-patriarch of the family [who] oversees all productions and transfers within the family" (63). The family is the omnipresent and many-faceted institution through which all processes have to flow: it is the one institution where all interests are supposed to converge. Neither symbolic or economic reproduction nor the continuity of the family household is possible, however, without elemental biological procreation. Without children to sustain and perpetuate this sum of reproductions, everything will simply come to a halt. The primacy of procreation is indubitable: the children become therefore *the first capital* into which all the *other capital*—economic, emotional, and cultural—is funneled and invested. Having offspring was all but absolute for the being and the functioning of the family, especially considering that no other alternative means of continuity was legally possible other than the levirate, for instance.

The family is thus the pillar and the constant on and through which all ties, institutions, functions, and relationships were constructed, maintained, reproduced, severed, or destroyed. Mohammed Ennaji[15] writes that the sense of empowerment "in yesterday's Morocco [could only be derived from] one's entourage: from the family, slaves, rural followers, clients and allies" (1999: 25). It is a power intimately woven in the fabric of the household if not dependent on it. The family had the many-faceted capacity of being "all-in-one," and thus the very idea of a family without children could not stand; it is rather a nonfamily, or better yet, an antifamily.

Generally then, all efforts were mustered in order not to fall into this antifamily. Thus childless families and even families with children sought and took care of orphaned or forsaken children, for the "abandoned child" is, in historical terms, a recent category. Historically, these were the possibilities available for absorbing the children in the larger 'aila, especially in their capacity as a workforce and possibly to be claimed as one's own in light of the high rate of infant mortality. Today's abandoned and street children are *the flesh and blood crisis of contemporary Moroccan society*. Families, as previously understood through such an institution, are no longer able to accommodate this surplus of children. Thus, these children become the embodiment of a crisis that neither philosophical, historical, sociological, nor economic models of change or modernization can truly accommodate. Or even when an explanation is given, it cannot address the humane and ethical quandary the children pose. With the continuing escalation of this social phenomenon, heated polemics concerning whose responsibility it is also continue to rage, mainly through written Moroccan media. Such an issue is generally characterized as being a dreadful topic and the sign of the decadence of the times. Although recently an institution (*Darna*) has been created in order to attempt to somehow reintegrate these children in the social mainstream, it only treats the tip of the iceberg.[16]

Older street children or abandoned babies waiting in shelters for a family are the surplus bodies in a society whose beliefs and structures have undergone massive mutation in less than a century. The often-recalled values of charity and support are not believed to be able to address the magnitude of the social problem, given that these acts are believed to benefit only a small number of individuals and not address the ill at its root. These children are the costly price in an emerging system where ties are increasingly embedded in a sense of committed responsibility tied exclusively to blood, decreasingly to other forms of social responsibility and cohesion, and to the professionalization of caring systems, especially through various civil society actors. These are the norms that are now believed to form the nexus of what is held as middle-class values.

In the words of Abdallah Saaf, a law professor, "the truth is that the values of these middle classes dominate the entire society from top to bottom. They represent the aspiration of society as a whole" (1990: 142). The diffusion of middle-class values is a phenomenon that other Moroccan and foreign scholars alike have commented upon (Belarbi 1991; Kapchan 1996; Ossman 1994; Al-Khamlichi 1987). With this homogenization—only blood relations entailing responsibility—the institution of the family as a bounded biological unit becomes exceedingly valuable. Even though the meaning of 'aila technically encompasses nonbiologically related individuals in a single living unit, with this noted emphasis on blood, the other nonblood relations or potential relations become inconsequential and are thus dismissed. The sphere of responsibility is thus prescriptively confined to the radius of immediate biological kin. This results in a conservatism mostly manifest in the creed that enforces how one's emotions *should and had better* be invested in one's own flesh and blood. Further evidence of this restriction is suggested by the fertility rate,[17] which has sharply decreased in the last decade. The parents' argument now stresses the quality of the children and not their quantity. The better quality of education and care one invests in one's children, the better one is likely to prepare autonomous and responsible individuals. This view is flagrantly contra older wisdom, in which a large number of children forming one 'aila was construed and interpreted as an act of strength, power, richness, and unfailing security for the future.

When not in the bosom of this family, either idealized or real, bastardy, as in *uld lhram*, acquires its sense of the profane. It is a concept that is heavily infused by all that is held to be the ultimate taboo; it is the other spectrum of the normal and the normative. The potency of bastardy lies precisely in its being the recipient of a *sum total* of dishonoring practices. Illegitimacy is constructed as the result of a chain of events that goes against the grain of social norms, starting with sexual nonconformism and ending up in social anathema and obloquy. Illegitimacy and bastardy are more a social than a moral quandary and are interpreted and seen by focusing on two distinct phenomena, that of naming and a reading of a number of customs, beliefs, and opinions. Taking the kafala of abandoned children, who are often assumed to be bastards, is a decision that has to fight and question these beliefs and the fear and stigma that actively inform them.

NAMES, A RITUAL OF THE MODERN NATION-STATE

Foundlings are given an arbitrary first name as a matter of routine. Their visibility is primarily an administrative necessity, for only after they have a last name—arbitrary choice of the civil register servant—can they be taken into kafala. Following Michael Herzfeld, I argue that "nation-state bureaucracy [as an institution] is directly analogous to the ritual system of a religion. Both are founded on the principle of identity" (Herzfeld 1992: 10). Civil register and official naming procedures are indeed a ritual that entails a long process of waiting, preparation, undergoing a test before the final initiation, and reaggregation in the social–official body by acquiring a fixed name, printed on an identity card.

In her article about family relations, Hildred Geertz discusses the variegated naming of Moroccan culture and society and singles out how outside these bureaucratic criteria

> patronymic association and the name cluster are products of Moroccan procedures for identifying and sorting persons according to their most important affiliation. The patronymic association is a complex Moroccan cultural concept that, like an unspecialized, all-purpose tool, can be adapted to many special situations. (1979: 351)

This complexity has to do with the identification *with and by* the patronymic name, the common norm of identifying individuals in the American context, for instance, but intermittently employing other ways of identification; the context largely shapes the choice. Yet many choices are predicated on being firmly embedded in a network that allows such associations. When an adopted person, especially an adult who knows about his or her situation, is given a last name, this is more an identification than a means of establishing or claiming an identity through lineage, a genealogical tree, or the web of relations established through these. It is a name and will remain a name only, an empty shell that cannot establish the other intricate means of identification and belonging.

Although Morocco's "progress and modernization" are usually and overtly indexed through the proverbial economic, health, and educational realms, the normalization and homogenization of naming is an additional, if not widely proclaimed, index, by the view of those working in the civil register that is an integral part of the Ministry of Interior. Prior to this normalization/homogenization, the concept of a single last surname could not be farther from the norm. When the French colonized Morocco, they brought their own system of civil registry in order, first, to keep count of their soldiers, the early settlers, and later their own offspring. The civil register was officially recognized as a part of the colonial administrative machine as early as 1915. This system, as an extension of the system in France, was used to register births, marriages, and deaths so that the colonial state might know at any given time the number of its colonizing nationals (*les pieds noir*). In France itself, enlisting men in the army, for instance, was done through the civil registry (Decroux 1950). The 1950s witnessed the birth of the natives' registration, but those who registered were mostly the urban elite. By 1959 the skeleton of the system was in place, but because it was a system still in its initial stages, it lacked trained officials and necessary expertise; decisions were made on the spot without any legal idea informing them. Despite the drives that the state organized, and still organizes, to have all individuals—from urban and rural, mountains and plains—register, it is a procedure that people have only reluctantly accepted because of the skepticism surrounding the question of *why* it is being done, since it is a procedure that was strongly identified with the French's goal of "knowing it all and controlling it all."

In its early stages, the civil register bureau suffered, generally from lack of proper services, lack of interest, and lack of funds. It was seen as an institution of an inferior order. But such status gave way to the understanding that registering a name is of capital importance, that it has to do with the security of the state. By 1975 the civil register bureau was incorporated within the Ministry of Interior. This date coincides with a noteworthy event in Morocco's recent history. In 1975, the king called for the Green March to annex the Southern Sahara, still under the colonial rule of Spain. It followed two failed coups, after which a decision was made to be careful as to whom to recruit in the Moroccan army, that is, to inquire into the *nasab* (the genealogy and the place of origin) of the soldiers, since one conspiracy theory at the time had it that one of these coups was ethnically motivated (Waterbury 1972; Marais 1972). The Ministry of Interior is considered the spine and essential instrument of state control, security, and internal intelligence (Rousset 1970). The status of the citizens—the registering of births, the regulation of names, the systematization of naming, the inscription of deaths—suddenly became a matter of national security for the state.

The civil register law distinguishes between three categories of infants to be registered: "normal," foundling, and natural children. They all need to be registered within one month of birth. All are entitled to a civil birth certificate, but the difference lies in what is actually written on the certificate. An infant brought to a center is given a name as a matter of routine either by the police, a social worker, or an individual working in the center.[18] A last name is chosen for the child by the civil registry officer directly out of a compendium of last names written and compiled by the official historian of the kingdom, Abdelwahab Belmansour, in the early 1970s. As for the natural infant brought in by his or her own mother, it is possible to give the newborn the mother's last name provided her own male family members do not object to it. While for a "normal" child, the first name of the father figures preeminently in the birth certificate, in the case of a foundling or a natural child, none is written. Refusing to write a fictive first name on the birth certificate constitutes the knot of conflict between the civil register legislators and the children's defenders, individuals and various nongovernment organizations. The civil register officials consider giving a fictive patronymic name to a foundling or a natural child a significant step beyond what used to take place. Not only were such children formerly threatened with total anonymity, as they would have two subsequent first names as their total name; "child of adultery" was also clearly written on their birth certificate—an everlasting brand. At least now there is a sense of hovering ambiguity, as some officials say in justification of the edict.

As Herzfeld (1992) argues, even if it is not consciously recognized, the notion of blood suffuses modern bureaucratic nation-state formations. The Moroccan civil register and its rigid restrictions are an eloquent example. The latest laws, which call for a systematization of names and the order in which names are to appear in official papers,[19] have met with resistance and have been subject to heated polemics in the written media. Concern over the naming or not of abandoned and natural children was not—as usual, in keeping with the unspoken laws of silence concerning them as a marginal social segment—ever mentioned in the public media. The claimed sense of "hovering ambiguity" disappears every time a natural or illegitimate child, or his or her custodians, hands a birth certificate over for hospital shots, for school registration, for a request of an identity card, for passing an entry exam to a school, for requesting the necessary documents to get married, for getting a job, for carrying out all those necessary rituals of survival in a modern theocracy. And as Chekroun puts it, "This is translated for each one of us as an obligation to 'register.' . . . There is the first registration of civil register, but afterwards we need to register in many guises, otherwise we face exclusion. . . . These many registrations define partial identities: school, health, insurance, salary, water and electricity" (1996: 63). Although a legal institution is ideally neutral, objective, and impersonal, in fact it re-creates, reinforces, and shapes the cultural parameters of what is acceptable and what is not. While some concerned parents who took the kafala, committed social workers, and a variety of associations are advocating a right for a fictive first name for the father on the birth certificate, the civil registry advocates its right to report with truth and accuracy. Civil register regulations and laws constitute and reinforce the edifice of the normative family as a unit built on the dual criteria of marriage and blood. A name can establish social citizenship and the barest cultural visibility, but it cannot pretend to establish anything more.

Questions concerning abandoned children's last names are mainly found in legal literature (Amal 1977; Chafi 1991; Bennis 1996). Abandoned children are mostly discussed as "problems" that upset the "natural" order of things and that require having a handy, perhaps quick-fix solution devised for them. Even in such supposedly impartial literature, a decrying of the state of immorality never fails to surface and perhaps a passing comment on the actual or possible psychological ramifications of this or that law on the children themselves.[20]

In his *Court Cases of the Civil Register,* Bennis writes that in the court it is "difficult to get to the truth sometimes when an individual takes the kafala of a foundling, and then this changes into a situation of plain adoption because of the ignorance of the law or because it is done on purpose" (1996: 95). The sense of ambiguity hovers forever over the identity of the secretly adopted person. The fate and destiny of a natural and illegal child are precarious and remain vulnerable to many whims and possibly abrupt changes. In a context in which origin, ethnicity, and social hierarchy may be, and often are, implicit in a name and its associations, what name a natural child, a child taken into kafala, or a child growing up in an orphanage has may not be important after all, as it is only an index lacking any implication of connectedness (Geertz 1979) or points of attachments (Rosen 1979). Foundling, illegal, and natural children's names are the mimicking of an identity, a form with no content because there is no nasab, that is, no lineage to tie the intricate knot. In the case of a secret adoption, these names are established, but they remain essentially a fiction, and it is a fragile fiction threatened both from the inside and the outside, legally, emotionally, and socially. It is predicated on the collusion of all, so that the adopted may not be told about his "real" identity, that is "no identity." An adopted person is one who has to contend with a state of anonymity and live in a perpetual state of fear, one in which the entire edifice of the belief in relatedness could be annihilated, could collapse into anonymity and nothingness, with no ritual to absolve it.

BASTARDY THROUGH CULTURAL LENSES

The aberration against bastardy finds eloquent expression in a number of cultural beliefs. The state legislation regarding last names, social indifference, the strong anathema and obloquy conveyed in calling someone a bastard, *uld l-hram,* as a real insult and not metaphorical one, all reflect and reinforce the unspoken assumption that abandoned children—and they are only abandoned because they are bastards—are polluting and dangerous, because they have the potential of disturbing the normal and accepted. Many support these ideas by relying on religious sources. Thus, adoption is often and generally stigmatized, because it is seen as a desperate last resort, almost a debased form of parenting. A stronger stigmatization, however, hovers over abandoned children themselves, who are "abject" and somehow polluting because they are polluted and profane. The stereotype of adoptees who kill is the culmination of the sum of stigmata believed to be inherent to being a "bastard." They are the profane who pollute what is held to be the most sacred: food, house and home, and the sense of unity and togetherness these symbolize. Such beliefs find clear articulation in a bit of folk wisdom: "Shouts of bastards introduce chaos to one's home and their urine will pollute it." By religious and social standards, such a view is not only uncouth but unfounded and totally erroneous. Bureaucratically and culturally, it is downplayed, if not veiled, through various other ploys and rhetoric.

There is, however, bitter criticism and resistance to this sort of totalizing popular-folk opinion. Mohammed Ben M'ajouz (1994), for instance, argues that the belief that Islam somehow sanctions this callousness, abhorrence and apathy toward abandoned children is due to a misunderstanding of one of the prophet's sayings.[21] Another form of resistance to the stigmatization of the bastard, not a textual one, but voiced by an older woman of my acquaintance, stems from a sense of belief in the sanctity of birth, regardless of its legal status. Haja Faqira, an older midwife in the region of Oujda, furiously answered me when I asked her reaction to the above saying with the declaration that "these children are *born the true Muslim among the odious atheists and infidels,* who are these people to decide they are dirty or not, who are they?" To answer Haja Faqira's question is to point to the social–cultural "whole" for creating this monster, but then even within this whole—and she is one of its voices—there are countervailing currents where such a monolithic representation is strongly decried.

"Bastard" is the pinnacle of insults. It is the profane in all its sense of the dangerous, the disruptive, and the polluting. Through lullabies, similes of endearment, and concepts of love, the sacred revolves around and is located in the domestic and contained world of the house. Fear of the bastard is precisely fear of what social norms consider to be unnatural and to have the potential of bringing chaos to this contained domestic world: abject, transgressive pollution and a possible disruption of the normal, causing chaos.

FINAL ACT

Unlike one adoptee who describes growing up as being an "amputee" (quoted in Nelkin and Lindee 1995), in cases of customary adoption such as my own, the truth is generally known. I have, however, chosen to construct my own truth later, especially after the catalytic volunteering in the abandoned children shelters where knowing about biological relations, fictive relations, and ones we choose to create is always subjected to imagination and negotiation, for being a bastard is a heavy cross to bear. But knowing does not cancel out painful questioning, considering that this questioning is constantly fueled by social commentaries from the benign to sometimes the intentionally evil. This questioning takes the painful form of accusations once one gets to the threshold of becoming the cover, that is, the threshold at which one begins to return the protection and the nurturing one received. I am not willing to subject Rita to these same questionings. Moreover, I feel that Rita already has her share of love, attention, and warmth. When I decide to take the kafala of an infant, it will be one of those whom I have changed and held in my arms as a volunteer in the orphanages. I am deeply convinced that they are the ones in need. Far from me is the pretension of claiming a pioneering activity, but like a number of families and individuals who took the legal kafala of an abandoned child, I want to be part of those who have opted for a love of the will; be part of those who are convinced there is a rich nature in alternative conceptions of family; be part of those who make and partake in the slow change of an emerging understanding and enactment of self and family; be part of those who have consciously and willingly walked a difficult path in order to debunk social hypocrisy and stop the perpetuation of a system that brands its victims.

NOTES

I wish to wholeheartedly thank my mentor and adviser James D. Faubion, who has encouraged again and again this project from its very beginning and has commented on the many different drafts of my doctoral dissertation. I would also like to thank my colleague and friend Lamia Karim, who read a shorter version of this chapter in absentia during the conference that gave birth to this collected edition.

1. This legislation applies to the rest of the Muslim world, with the exception of Tunisia where Personal Status Law, *The Magalla,* has divorced itself from the Muslim Shari'a in many respects.

2. It does not require a legal procedure unless the adopting party wants to secure a part of the inheritance to the adopted person, in which case the adopting party "writes" this person down as a partial inheritor.

3. Such customary adoption would be close to what some activists in America are calling for today, namely open adoption, where one's biological ties are sustained even if one grows up adopted.

4. A *close person* in this context is quite problematic, for it may be a person located at two contrary ends of the spectrum. *Close* may be a brother, a mother, or a boss (who could be the father) who pressures the young mother to relinquish the baby because of social stigma and fear. In this case, *close* means exercising a "negative" power. *Close* also may be a person who really loves the new mother and is genuinely concerned about her welfare; the attention is mostly directed to the mother and not the fear/stigma component. A certain complicity and understanding between the new mother and her mother, a sister, a cousin, or even a friend who may have gone through similar conditions assure that this baby is placed in as "nice" an environment as possible. But most of these can only be judged on individual cases.

5. There are equally ritual celebrations, namely the `aqiqa, or naming ceremony, which enters into a different religious–cultural context of endowing the child with a name and appropriating him or her as one's natural child.

6. I am italicizing legal here because the distinction between a legal, a natural, a foundling, an orphan, and an abandoned child is extremely important legally.

7. It is rather ironic and sad to say that even if such a law is published in the *Moroccan Official Bulletin,* it does not necessarily receive a wide public audience. Moroccan buying power is very limited, and Morocco has a high illiteracy rate.

8. This includes "taboo" practices of illicit sexuality, "unnaturalness," and abandoning a weak and fragile newborn, all of which are considered by the Moroccan penal code to be crimes punishable for up to a year imprisonment.

9. The American controversy over the erasure of the natal parents in the birth certificate in favor of the adopting parents has not stopped some adopted persons from searching for their natural parents. The controversy over the sealed records is inscribed largely within this rhetoric.

10. There have been so far two cases that made the national news regarding "baby trade." The first one came to light in the end of 1993 when a Spanish couple who owns a restaurant in Ceuta would "buy" babies through the intermediary of its employees and "resell" them to Andalusian couples looking to adopt. Although this case was not tried in Morocco, given that Ceuta is a Spanish enclave, it brought attention to this most abject traffic (*Opinion,* 3 January 1994). The second case occurred in Casablanca, where it came under investigation at the beginning of 1995. One woman, Rkia Nidir, through the intermediary of other midwives, would get infants of single mothers and "prostitutes" and would then sell them to women and couples looking to adopt. She would introduce herself as the mother of the infant in question to the adopting party. She has been sentenced to five years in prison, and her collaborators have been, likewise, sentenced to different prison terms (*Opinion,* 24 July 1995).

11. Quranic commentary is a self-standing discipline called *'ilm a-tafsîr.* The texts I have consulted are the most canonized ones such as Tabari, ninth century; Al-Zamakhchari, twelfth century; Baydawi, thirteenth century; and Ibn-Kathir, fourteenth century.

12. In Islamic scholastic tradition, there is a discipline called *asbab al-nuzul,* occasions for revelation, which situates the historical circumstances for each revelation. These reconstructions have been equally a subject for debate and evaluation.

13. The term *Tradition,* as employed by Stern here, stands for comments and views that were gathered and appended as books contextualizing events that occurred in the life of the prophet. There is a very elaborate scholastic tradition in the study of Islam. One of these, for instance, is *isnad,* which Fazlur Rahman describes as the "Apostolic tradition subsequently compiled in a series of works, six of which came to be accepted as the authoritative second source of the content of Islam besides the Quran" (1966: 43).

14. I am thankful to Dr. Jean-Joseph Goux of Rice University for this comment.

15. Slavery, akin to family, is not a topic that solicited historical attention as a "grand narrative." In light of an absence of direct documentation, Mohammed Ennaji, for instance, utilizes legal edicts and personal correspondences in order to study slavery in Morocco.

16. Dr. Najat Mjid, M.D., founded with the help of a number of associations, individuals, and the city of Casablanca (l'Heure Joyeuse, Terre des Hommes, and the prefecture of Ben Msik) in April 1997 a house called *Bayti*—house in classical Arabic. This house is open to street children, but it is not a coercive structure or one that, akin to correction houses, tries to immediately put the children, in a classroom envi-

ronment or force them to become "mainstream." Dr. Mjid put forth enormous effort in creating this unit. It is of course only a first step, and so it only offers about forty beds, while there are between two-thousand to three-thousand street children in Casablanca alone, according to different sources. The problem relating to Bayti is that it has been publicized to such a degree that it has become the only example cited every time street children are mentioned; Bayti was co-opted by the media and instead of being just an example, it became *the* institution. Another center located in Tangier, but not publicized at all, is called *Darna*, and it opened in March 1994 (*our house* in Moroccan). This is mostly an after-school center for children from poor families who cannot go to their homes because their parents are still in the workplace.

17. The following statistic is part of a long-term study carried out within the Ministry of Health. I am only giving total numbers, although they are organized by rural and urban areas.

Number of Births per Woman by Year

	1979–1980	*1987*	*1992*	*1995*
Total	5.9	4.8	4.2	3.6

Preferences in Terms of Timing for Procreation by Year

	1992	*1995*
Pct. of women who want to limit the number of births	49	49
Pct. of women who want to put more time between births	24	26
Pct. of women who want to have children immediately	18	17

18. A foundling or, sometimes, child may be registered through the attorney general, who would have already received a police report if the deadline is passed, so as to authorize the agent to register this infant or child. The newborn may also be registered by the social worker in whose institution the baby was born, or it may have been delivered after the police brought it there.

19. Naming, as a state institution, is a hotly debated issue among many different actors. Systematizing/nationalizing names within the diverse ethnic, regional, and linguistic groups has proven, and still proves, to be a serious issue of contention, exemplified by the new laws excluding a variety of names because they are believed not to be Moroccan. They are Moroccan-Berber and Moroccan-Jewish but not Arab. This sort of ambiguity has arisen because of the readings and views advanced by Belmansour, the kingdom's official historian, who comes from a strongly urban, elite family and who has received an urban and Arabic education.

20. It is almost a rule to find a moralistic and moralizing judgment in all of these writings no matter how bureaucratically prescriptive they are, or are supposed to be.

21. In a long footnote in his *Akham al-usra fi al-shari'a al-islamya wifqa mudawanat al-ahwal al-shakhsiya*, Ben Ma'jouz explains that "Islam does not want to

have the offspring bear the responsibility of the action of the parents." He argues that "this misunderstanding finds its genesis in the semantic misinterpretation of a hadith that says 'son of fornication does not enter paradise,' but this sentence structure of *son-of-fornication* is akin to the sentence *son-of-the-road, ibnu sabil,* which stands for he who travels. The sentence structure of son-of . . . means to be addicted to doing such an activity" (1994: 15 n. 6). In other words, the structure of "son-of" means to be accustomed to something as in being "addicted to fornication" and not the outcome of an illegal union. Ben M'ajouz further dismisses the truth of the belief that there is a prophet's saying that the offspring of adultery will be burned. In terms of Tradition, religious exegesis, its truth is indeed questionable.

BIBLIOGRAPHY

Al-Khamlichi, Ahmed. 1987. *Widjhat Nazar.* Dar-al-Bayda: Matba'at al-najah al jadida.
Amal, Jalal. 1977. Ba'du al-jawanib al-qanuniya li ri'ayati a-tifl fi al-maghrib. *Al-majala al-maghribya lil qanun, wa a-siyasa, wa al-iqtisad* (5): 9–49.
Belarbi, Aicha. 1989. Identité et crise d'identification chez les enfants marocains. *Signes du Présent* (5): 77–76.
———. 1991. *Enfance au Quotidien.* Casablanca: Editions le Fennec.
Belmansour, Abdelwahab. 1997. *Kashaf asma' al-usar al-maghribiya.* Second edition. Rabat: n.p.
Ben Ma'jouz, Mohammed. 1994. *Akham al-usra fi al-shari'a al-islamya wifqa mudawanat al-ahwal al-shakhsiya.* Dar-al-Bayda: Matba'at al-najah al-jadida.
Bennis, Khaled. 1996. *Da'awi al-hala al-madaniya* [Court Cases of the Civil Register]. Damascus: Matba'at al-kitab al-arabi.
Chafi, Mohammed. 1991. Al-ism al-aili li tifl ghayr a-shar'i bil-maghrib. *Al-majala al-maghribiya lil iqtisad wa al-qanun al muqaran* (16): 175–82.
Chekroun, Mohamed. 1987. Nidham al-qaraba wa al'aila fi al-mudjtama' al-maghribi. *Majalat kuliyat al-adab wa al-'ulum al-insaniya* (13): 59–89.
———. 1996. *Famille, Etat et Transformations Socio-culturelles au Maroc.* Casablanca: Editions OKAD.
Chekroun, Mohamed, and Mohamed Boudoudou. 1986. Définitions sociale de l'enfance et de l'enfant: Conditions sociales de production de la légitimité social de la mise au travail des enfants au Maroc. *Bulletin Economique et Social du Maroc* (157): 99–123.
Crone, Patricia. 1987. *Roman, Provincial and Islamic Law.* Cambridge: Cambridge University Press.
Decroux, Paul. 1950. L'Etat civil au Maroc. *Hesperis* (38): 237–88.
Ennaji, Mohammed. 1999. *Serving the Master: Slavery and Society in Nineteenth-Century Morocco.* Trans. S. Graebner. New York: St. Martin's Press.
Etienne, Bruno. 1970. Quelques réflexions sur l'enfant marocain entre la tradition et la modernité. In proceedings of *L'enfant, l'education et le changement social.* 28 Mai au 2 Juin 1979. L'Ecole Normale Supérieur, Université Mohammed V.
Gager, Kristin Elizabeth. 1996. *Blood Ties and Fictive Ties: Adoption and Family Life in Early Modern France.* Princeton: Princeton University Press.

Geertz, Hildred. 1979. The Meanings of Family Ties. In *Meaning and Order in Moroccan Society.* Ed. C. Geertz, H. Geertz, and L. Rosen. Cambridge: Cambridge University Press, pp. 315–506.

Goody, Jack. 1983. *The Development of the Family and Marriage in Europe.* New York: Cambridge University Press.

———. 1990. *The Oriental, the Ancient, and the Primitive: Systems of Marriage and the Family in the Pre-Industrial Societies of Eurasia.* New York: Cambridge University Press.

Herzfeld, Michael. 1992. *The Social Production of Indifference: Exploring the Roots of Western Bureaucracy.* New York: Berg Press.

Kapchan, Deborah. 1996. *Gender on the Market: Moroccan Women and the Revoicing of Tradition.* Pittsburgh: University of Pennsylvania Press.

Kondo, Dorinne. 1990. *Crafting Selves: Power, Gender, and Discourses of Identity in a Japanese Workplace.* Chicago: University of Chicago Press.

Marais, Octave. 1972. Berbers and the Moroccan Political System after the Coup. In *Arabs and Berbers: From Tribe to Nation in North Africa.* Ed. E. Gellner and P. Micaud. London: Lexington Books, pp. 397–423.

Mernissi, Fatima. 1987. *Beyond the Veil: Male-Female Dynamics in Modern Muslim Society.* Bloomington: Indiana University Press.

———. 1996. *Women's Rebellion and Islamic Memory.* Atlantic Highlands, N.J.: Zed Books.

Nelkin, Dorothy, and Susan Lindee. 1995. *The DNA Mystique: The Genes as Cultural Icons.* New York: Ferman Press.

Ossman, Susan. 1994. *Picturing Casablanca: Portraits of Power in a Modern City.* Berkeley: University of California Press.

Pickthall, Marmaduke. 1930. *Translation of the Holy Quran.* New York: Alfred A. Knopf.

Radi, Abdelwahad. 1977. L'adaptation de la famille au changement social dans le Maroc urbain. *Bulletin Economique et Social du Maroc* (135): 1–36.

Rahman, Fazlur. 1966. *Islam.* New York: Holt, Rinehart, and Winston.

Rosen, Lawrence. 1979. Social Identity and Points of Attachment: Approaches to Social Organization. In *Meaning and Order in Moroccan Society.* Ed. C. Geertz, H. Geertz, and L. Rosen. Cambridge: Cambridge University Press, pp. 19–122.

Rousset, Michel. 1970. Le role du ministère de l'interieur et sa place au sein de l'administration marocaine. In *Pouvoir et Administration au Maghrib.* Paris: Editions du Centre National de la Recherche Scientifique.

Saaf, Abdallah. 1990. The State and the Middle Classes in Morocco. In *The Moroccan State in Historical Perspective (1850–1985).* Ed. A. Doumou. Dakar, Senegal: CODERSIA.

Smith, W. Robertson. [1885] 1990. *Kinship and Marriage in Early Arabia.* London: Darf.

Stern, Gertrude. 1939. *Marriage in Early Islam.* London: Royal Asiatic Society.

Waltner, Ann. 1990. *Getting an Heir: Adoption and the Construction of Kinship in Late Imperial China.* Honolulu: University of Hawaii Press.

Waterbury, John. 1972. Le coup manqué. In *Arabs and Berbers: From Tribe to Nation in North Africa.* Ed. E. Gellner and P. Micaud. London: Lexington Books.

Zkik, Said. 1994. *La répression de l'abandon en droit marocain.* Rabat: Mohammed Vth University.

4

A Kinship of One's Own

Lamia Karim

When two Bangladeshis meet it is customary for them to ask, "Which village are you from (*Apnar desher bari kothai*)?" If the village happens to be the same, or even within geographic proximity, the next response is invariably, "You are almost like kin." Among Bangladeshis one of the fundamentals of social relationship is based on some putative or given kinship codes. Strangely enough, this address—*Apnar desher bari kothai*—so rooted to the identity of Bangladeshis, so deeply held by most people that it is the first act of curiosity toward others, is absent from the self-constructions of my family members. The identity the family has constructed for itself is indexed differently from origins densely rooted in village-based kin ties. In order to make sense of how this came to be I have to tell you a history of a family of women.[1] I would like to insert a voice of caution here. My family's history should not be taken as a template of kin relations among middle-class Muslim Bangladeshis. It should be read as one possible way in which women who found themselves caught in different structures of discrimination and patriarchal subordination sought to create moments of liberation in their lives. The results of these moments were often unanticipated.

STORIES WE TELL

My family, my mother says, has an illustrious history of female accomplishments. She holds up a faded picture in front of my eyes. In the picture there are five generations of women: my great-great-great-grandmother, who knew Arabic, Persian, Urdu, and Bengali and had completed the Hajj twice; her only daughter; one of her two granddaughters, several great-

grandchildren, and a couple of great-great-grandchildren. Five generations of women. In the picture my grandmother is still very young; she was not yet married. Although all the older women have their heads covered with the edges of their silk saris, none of the women wears a burqa, the traditional head-to-toe covering for Muslim women. The women face the camera with strong and determined faces. Their eyes are not averted or downcast.

Dhaka, 1970: My Grandmother's Story

I got married along with my immediate elder sister. She was four years my senior. I was maybe ten at the time of my marriage. On the day of my wedding, nobody told me what all the fuss was about. Nobody bothered to explain to me why I was dressed in a red silk sari, why someone had stuck heavy gold earrings onto my ears, which were ringing with pain. My sister and I had to sit still while everyone else ran around the house. With all the wedding festivities going on, nobody had remembered to feed us. I kept falling asleep, both from hunger and the lateness of the hour, and my sister kept on waking me up.

Massachusetts, 1980

Outside my window the New England snow falls. I am trying to work on some problems for my economics test tomorrow, but my mind wanders. My mother has written to me again. Her letters never inquire about certain aspects of my life: my dreams and aspirations, my achievements and failures. Her letters remind me, again and again, that my duty is to return home next summer and get married to a Bangladeshi man of her choice. And according to her, if he gave his permission, I could return to the United States to continue my education. I knew nothing of the marriage plans that my mother had made immediately upon my departure for the United States. My mother writes, "education can always happen at a later date. I got married and then went abroad. Now, you must return and get married." As bait, she offers a gold-embroidered sari she has bought for my wedding.

On July 15, 1980, my mother, my immediate elder sister, several maternal aunts, and my grandmother came to see me off at Dhaka Airport. I was leaving for America for my undergraduate studies. Although I had received a four-year scholarship to a prestigious American college, my relatives seemed dismayed at my departure. The contrast between my departure and that of a male cousin who had left two years earlier on a similar scholarship was striking. As I trudged the distance between the red and blue British Airways plane and the tarmac, dressed in my sari and heavy gold jewelry, the refrain I heard over and over again was that I was female, nineteen, and unmarried. In the judgment of my family, my departure for America was "not the proper thing to do." On my part, I was glad to be leaving my country of birth and my "home"—places that had come to signify "lack"—for America, which signified possibility in imaginative contrast. America, at that moment in my life, symbolized a place where opportunities were in excess of what I could expect as a middle-class woman coming from the postcolonial state of Bangladesh. There are layers of paradoxes and irony captured at the moment of my departure, but none looms as large, for me, as the apparent repudiation of my family's grand narrative of progressive attitudes toward women. These lofty tales of female accomplishments are called into question at key moments in the lived experiences of women in my family. To what extent have these monumentalized narratives of individually accomplished women *in the past* normalized the perpetuation of a sexist culture in the *present*?

The historical narrative that my family constructs for itself maintains that the education of women and a recognition of women's autonomy have long been two of its defining principles. The family therefore claims for itself a unique and peculiarly progressive spirit within an Islamic patriarchal culture. Although this claim appears at first glance to be supported by the achievements of a few women, it is at odd variance with the lives of other women in the family. How is it that a family that boasts so many independent women, arranged my grandmother's marriage at the age of ten? How could the family that prides itself on high-achieving women put *so many obstacles* in the educational aspirations and self-making desires of women in my generation? How is it that the same family that boasts of an aunt who became a published poet in Calcutta in the 1930s (no small feat for a Bengali Muslim woman in undivided Bengal) and who had elected to remain single in that era seems to place a greater premium on the prospect of my marriage than that of my education? Why is it that my mother, who appears to exemplify the family's narrative of high-achieving independent women—she had lived on her own in Calcutta and Dhaka both as a graduate student and as an assistant professor during and after the partition riots of 1947, and subsequently, traveled for further studies abroad—was hostile to my own educational aspirations? Tension straddled the normative or given values of the Bengali Muslim society within which my family operated, and the progressive values of female education and autonomy that my family putatively celebrated. The normative community values and the performative responses of my family intersect in complex and intricate ways to make or unmake the possibilities of "specific kinds of selves" (Borneman 1992: 30) for female subjects in specific configurations of kinship. The self constitutes itself through what Michel Foucault has called "techniques"—these are practices deployed on the self to remake oneself. I do not suggest that individuals ever possess the agency for infinite "self-making." I do suggest, however, that institutions and structures do not possess the capacity to perpetually control "self-making," and that women in my family adopted different techniques of self-realizations in response to the politics of the state and social structures they operated within.

Against the background of the circulating mythologies of my family, I show how kinship as a generative structure of possibilities and impossibilities of self-making operated and continued to operate within women's lives. I will analyze the life trajectories of three generations of women in my family (my maternal grandmother, my mother, and me) and the changing forms of kinship structures from colonial to postcolonial to transnational times. These life trajectories are closely intertwined with the role of the state, both colonial and postcolonial, in matters of education and employment and in the creation of a middle class that was anchored to the state bureaucracy for the production and maintenance of itself.

Pierre Bourdieu has argued that kinship is a set of open-ended relations that are employed by individuals seeking to satisfy their symbolic and material interests (1977: 38). Kinship operates through what he calls "practical relations" (i.e., fictive relationships that people adopt at their convenience to increase their self-making possibilities), and these "practical relationships" lie outside the anthropological grids of kinship terminology and alliance theories constructed on consanguineal and affinal ties. Jonathan Borneman makes an argument similar to Bourdieu's, although he is more influenced by David Schneider's work on kinship. Borneman defines kinship as "the structuring of belonging patterns to realize specific kinds of everyday relations" (1992: 30), and he sees kinship as the "desires of specific kinds of selves, and of specific kinds of relationships" (75). Following these two authors, I argue that kinship, as a structure of patterns of belonging, *is always in excess* of moral and jural obligations and consanguineal and affinal ties. I argue that kinship practices are about the production and maintenance of a specific sense of self within particular social formations. When traditional kinship systems are insufficient in the production of oneself in a changed context (in fact, they may even hinder the production of oneself), alternate forms of social relations may emerge to facilitate the remaking of oneself.

Over the last twenty-five years, my family, which was originally rooted in precolonial Bengal, has become a multinational family. My widowed mother lives in Dhaka, my eldest sister lives in Hawaii with her Anglo-American husband, my immediate elder sister lives in Ohio, and I reside in Texas. Beyond my immediate family, each of my aunts and uncles has at least one member living outside Bangladesh; in some cases, the entire family has migrated abroad. This is not atypical for many middle-class Bangladeshis.[2] In an age of transnational migrations, what kinds of social ties hold the family together when family members are dispersed globally? With specific reference to my extended family, I have a tentative argument. I argue that the transition of an individual from a local to a national to a transnational subject necessitates forms of relations that are beyond traditional kinship structures.

It can be argued that my project, or any project similar to mine, risks accepting personal narratives "as uncontestable evidence" (Scott 1993: 339). The "evidence of experience," in this case, the experiences of individual women, risks becoming an untroubled and fundamental category of knowledge. Feminist historian Joan Scott argues that the writer of histories of difference must examine how difference is produced in the first place: "how difference is established, how it operates, how and in what ways it constitutes subjects who see and act in this world" (400). The challenge then is not to simply narrate experiences of some women in my family, but to analyze how the normative and performative codes—the given and the made codes—operated within colonial and postcolonial contexts to construct different female subjectivities at different points in time.

STATUS STRATIFICATIONS AMONG BENGALI MUSLIMS

The first census of Bengal taken by the British colonial administration in 1872 revealed a large number of Muslim inhabitants. According to the census, the majority of the Muslims of Bengal were rural, belonging either to the agricultural sector as tillers of land or to the lower sectors of the economy as weavers, barbers, tailors, and so forth. The census also revealed that Bengali Muslims were seriously underrepresented in higher education, with only a small Muslim elite in the urban centers. The majority of the urban elite was comprised of the Hindu *bhadrolok,* or the gentry, and was made up of Brahmans, Kayasthas, and Baidyas. Sustained opportunities for higher education for Muslims in Bengal were introduced as late as 1871, when the British passed a resolution to rectify the lack of modern education for Bengali Muslims. An editorial published in 1899 in the *Muslim Chronicle* asserted that "the whole educational policy of the Government of Bengal was formed in 1854, yet the subject of Muslim education was taken up almost twenty years later" (S. Ahmed 1996: 9). The failure of the colonial government to secure higher education for Muslims in Bengal seriously handicapped Muslims in terms of employment opportunities within colonial India. Bengali Hindus had adopted Western education much earlier. By the early 1800s they occupied a central role in the colonial administration. For example, in 1875 the total number of college graduates in Bengal presidency was only 5.4 percent for Muslims compared to 93.9 percent for Hindus (R. Ahmed 1981: 135). Until the year 1854, Muslims were still found in their local *madrassahs* and *maktabs,* religious institutions dedicated to Quranic knowledge, and not in government or missionary schools. The madrassah/maktab education emphasized the Mughal court languages of Persian, Arabic, and Urdu, and theological instruction—knowledge systems that had lost their value under British rule in India. Such education helped only to eliminate a majority of

Muslim graduates from applying for jobs in the colonial bureaucracy, jobs that required a more secular and modernist training. In 1837 the British replaced Persian with English as the official language of the courts, which further shrank the value of madrassah trained scholars.

The Resolution of 1871 officially targeted Bengali Muslims for secular education and training, and it broadened access to higher education and employment opportunities for them. It had a two-pronged approach to the education for Muslims. In the first instance, incentives were set in place to encourage college education for Muslims: scholarships were provided, the court languages of Arabic, Persian, and Urdu were added to the syllabi of government schools, separate Muslim hostels were created so Hindu and Muslim students would not come into conflict over dietary and religious practices, and Muslim educational officers were appointed to oversee the facilitation of Muslim higher education. In the second instance, secular courses were added to make the education and training of Muslim graduates at par with the rest of the graduates of Bengal (R. Ahmed 1981: 140–41). This Resolution of 1871 created some social and economic mobility for the Bengali Muslims, and it constructed a small Bengali Muslim middle class anchored to the colonial state for the maintenance of its new status in culture. This middle class was comprised of "intermediate tenure holders, partly a creation of the Permanent Settlement Act (1793), and a few government servants, teachers, and a few others in similar professions" (R. Ahmed 1981: 26).

Although the Resolution of 1871 was for education of the Muslim masses, Muslim elites were the ones who lobbied against higher education for Muslim masses, claiming that the highborn (*ashraf* Muslims) and lowborn (*atraf* Muslims) should not intermingle.[3] A report published by a Madrassah Committee appointed by the government of Bengal in 1871 claimed that "respectable Muslim families of Bengal were not ready to admit children from the lower-class families into the Madrassah Institution, and they wanted to retain it exclusively for the education of the upper classes" (R. Ahmed 1981: 21). Despite this attitude, the social structure of Muslims was more flexible than the Hindu caste structure of colonial Bengal.[4] This flexibility enabled middle-class Muslims to improve their status by marrying the daughters of ashraf families whose fortunes had declined after the Permanent Settlement Act of 1793.[5] These social relations were based on affinal alliances between an emergent class defined by educational credentials and employment opportunities in a colonial bureaucracy, on the one hand, and an older elite that had retained symbolic power and cultural capital, on the other.

Where does my family fit into this grid of colonial self-constructions? My paternal great-grandfather was a beneficiary of the pro-Muslim reforms in higher education. In 1893 he graduated from Calcutta University, the first Bengali Muslim college graduate in his district of West Bengal. He later became the divisional inspector of schools in North Bengal. The title of khan bahadur was conferred upon him by the British because of his commitment to education. His father was an officer in the colonial bureaucracy, and his older brother was a teacher of Persian and Arabic at the local madrassah. Since my great-grandfather was not from a landowning class, education was the only way for members of his class—the emergent Bengali Muslim middle class—to enter into the colonial bureaucracy. His family belonged to the rural ashraf class, and it was because of his educational achievements that he was able to form an alliance with a family of a higher ashraf status than his own.[6] My maternal great-grandmother's father worked with the colonial bureaucracy in Bihar. The fact that her great-grandmother knew the court languages of Mughal India suggests to me that she was probably descended from the ruling Muslim elite of Bengal. Her skin was very fair, and this was cited as evidence of her Middle-Eastern origins. My great-grandmother was one of two sisters who were raised in the city of Patna in Bihar. While my great-grandmother married an educationist in the colonial administration, the other sister married into an illustrious zamindari (landlord) family of Bengal. My great-grandmother's niece married a senior railway officer who was posted in Mumbai. These kinds of cross-regional alliances (between Bihar and Bengal, or Mumbai and Bengal) took place largely because the crop of educated Muslims was so small that Muslim men seeking to improve their status by marrying into ashraf families could form these alliances easily. By the turn of the century, higher education for Muslims had made some of the educated members of the family disperse around the landscape of colonial India.

A FAMILY OF WOMEN AND THE MYSTIQUE OF KINSHIP

Grandmother

The family's narrative is constructed around the performative acts of two visible women: one who performed the Hajj thrice and the other who became a published poet. The narrative renders invisible the rest of the women in the family and constructs a mythical world in which all women supposedly occupy the same subject position. My family's narrative, like all family histories, deletes what it finds shameful, objectionable, or contradictory to the image it wants to portray. I agree that in colonial India my family probably had a comparatively more progressive attitude toward women. This may have been due to the influence of the woman-centric ideology of the Brahmo Samaj as well as the centrality placed on the Indian woman in the nationalist debates of the twentieth century.[7] My family effectively exchanged one form of patriarchy, in this case, Islamic patriarchy where women were expected to remain in purdah and were educated only on the Quran, for a new kind of nationalist patriarchy where women were allowed a more liberal education but still remained within male domination.

Under this new patriarchy, educated women were expected to have modest aspirations. At a more fundamental level, educated women were expected to observe bodily modesty; they would not, for example, be allowed to pursue careers in athletics, performance arts, or politics, where the female body is on display. The female body was redeemed from the worst excesses of the purdah, but it was still covered and constrained by a pervasive and discriminatory ethic of modesty. Women were expected to discipline their minds of sensual thoughts and to control their bodies in public—in speech, attire, and manners. The nationalist patriarchy of colonial times—the era of the "new woman" in India—began to break down for my family in 1947. With the formation of Pakistan, which took Islam as its national symbol and central metaphor, my family had to adjust to a national ideology that restricted opportunities for educated women. The Islam-centric ideology of the military dictatorship of Bangladesh similarly restricted women's options in public life.[8] But more important, the asymmetrical female-to-male ratio in my family meant that more women married out of the family and had to adopt the norms of their affinal families. By the time I grew up in the postcolonial nation-states of Pakistan and Bangladesh, my family had internalized conservative mores and had abandoned any semblance of "progressive" attitudes toward women's education.

My great-grandfather became a widower when my grandmother was a young child. Of his five daughters, only one was married by the time he lost his wife. My great-grandmother suffered from prolonged illness before her death, a condition at least in part brought on by frequent childbirths. Because of her ill health, her widowed mother and widowed great-grandmother (the woman who knew four languages and had performed the Hajj thrice) came from Patna to her house in Bengal to look after her and her young children. My grandmother's father remained a widower although he had a number of very young children to raise. It is customary among widowed Bengali Muslim men to remarry, and the alliance is usually between the widower and a female member (such as a younger sister-in-law) of his late wife's family. In my mother's family it was not customary for men to divorce or take a second wife. While I cannot speculate as to why my great-grandfather didn't remarry, family lore claims that it was because of his great love and respect for his wife. By narrating this story the family also maintains certain lofty behavioral codes that supposedly set them apart from the Bengali Muslim community.

In the early 1900s the person who defined the household was my great-great-great-grandmother. She was said to be a pious person, and under her tutelage my grandmother read the Quran at the age of seven.[9] At the time of my grandmother's wedding, her great-grandmother left their house to live with another great-grandchild in Mumbai. The reason for the great-grandmother leaving the house had to do with the breakdown in a marriage proposal that her grandchild from Mumbai (also called Mumbai Aunt) had brought in. Mumbai Aunt had wanted my grandmother's immediate elder sister to marry her husband's brother. By the time Mumbai Aunt made the proposal, my great-grandfather had already arranged for his daughter's marriage elsewhere. My great-grandfather was unwilling to break his promise to satisfy the wishes of Mumbai Aunt, a kin member. Mumbai Aunt's failure to bring someone from her natal family to strengthen her position in her affinal family and, consequently, her loss of face in her affinal family apparently made her so angry that she forced her widowed great-grandmother and grandmother to leave with her for Mumbai. She also broke all ties with my great-grandfather's family. It is this branch of the family that has more symbolic and material capital, and although we never had any close social or kin ties with them—we were the poorer half of the family—my family always spoke of them as "relatives," and their political and social activities were followed and discussed with keen interest.

My great-great-great-grandmother's leaving probably marked the passing of Muslim traditions in the family, and their replacement with a secular ideology more closely identified with the ideals of Bengali nationalism of the 1920s. This nationalism privileged the language and culture of the educated upper class of Bengali Hindus over religion and regionalism. Following the adoption of a secular ideology with respect to daily life, the family effectively lost the urge to organize the extended kin group around religious ceremonies (i.e., religion was not a socially shared thematic). They did not replace this loss with any other core organizing principle, which effectively meant fewer occasions for the family to collectively gather and cohere.

Along with the new nationalism that had entered the *andarmahal,* another key conjunctive factor in the making of kinship and self-making for women in the family had to do with the gender asymmetry in the family (table 4.1). Table 4.2 shows that there were fourteen girls and only seven boys. My grandmother's brother married late, and his sons were much younger than the rest. The family, in order to maintain internal coherence, opted for a self-imposed restriction on matrilateral parallel-cousin and cross-cousin marriages,[10] which over time became normalized as a taboo. The absence of male siblings rendered it impossible. It is also significant to point out that the family adopted and practiced a kinship prohibition of Bengali Hindus. Among Bengali Muslims, residence is patrilocal and descent is patrilineal. This gender asymmetry meant that the family lost more members than it gained. Women marrying out had to adopt the ways of their affinal families, and women's roles in their affinal families did not necessarily correspond to the ones practiced in my great-grandfather's house. My father often teased my mother that her family had "Hindani hal-chaal," that is, they behaved liked Hindus. While it was said in jest, there was always an underlying tension in the statement because of my mother's more superior attitude toward her family.

Table 4.1   Gender Asymmetry

Great-great-great-grandmother	one daughter
Great-great-grandmother	two daughters
Great-grandmother (died very young)	five daughters, and one son

Table 4.2   My Grandmother's Family

First sister	four daughters, two sons
Second sister	no offspring
Third sister	four daughters, two sons
Fourth sister (my grandmother)	six daughters
Fifth sister	three sons
[Brother	one daughter, nine sons]*

*Discussion to follow

My grandmother's eldest sister, as the oldest child, had elected to live with her husband in her father's house. In the absence of a mother, she effectively became the head of household. This is not a normative practice in Bengali Muslim families. It is, in fact, customary for a woman to leave her father's residence after marriage. However, because Muslim women inherit property from their parents, daughters maintain ties with their natal families even after marriage. At key moments in life, such as the birth of a first child, daughters customarily return to their father's residence.

Inside our family's *andarmahal* or *zenana*—the private sphere of women—women did not observe the purdah. When female family members went out in public, they wore burqas, but under those burqas they wore all the bodily adornments that had come to symbolize the "new woman" in Bengal—blouse, petticoat, shoes, and brooches to hold their saris. The adoption of such codes was seen as a form of *distinction* by the family; it was a way of differentiating themselves from the less-educated Muslims in their town. The town the family lived in had a high number of Brahmos, the Hindu Reform Movement of Raja Rammohan Roy. My great-grandfather, because of his education, maintained close relations with the Brahmo community in town. The older daughters often visited the homes of Brahmo women and through that association were exposed to ideas extolling the virtues of the "new Indian woman"—an educated woman who upheld traditional female values within a new ethic of modesty. The second daughter, because of her literary interests, subscribed to women's magazines where contemporary social issues affecting the education and welfare of women were discussed.

The great-aunt who was the head of household had views that were quite radical for her times. For example, she liked to go for picnics (these outings could only take place at night because of the purdah that the women had to observe in town.) Her second daughter lived in a women's dormitory in Calcutta while attending college. A female relative, appalled that an unmarried woman lived alone in Calcutta, remarked to my great-aunt that now no self-respecting Muslim man would marry her daughter. In response she is supposed to have said that if no Muslim married her daughter, then her daughter could find a Hindu or a Christian, and failing that, she could remain unmarried! Such unconventional opinions were made possible by the fact that my great-aunt had never left her father's house and that, as the eldest child, she held a powerful position that enabled her to have stronger views of women's education.

Given the family's social position and a great-great-grandmother who had performed the Hajj, one would have expected the family to emulate the ways of ashraf Muslims: speak in Urdu at home, emphasize Quranic education and observe purdah for women, and follow Muslim endogamy rules. Contrary to such expectations, the women in the family adopted a self-making technique that mimicked the constructions of educated upper-class Hindus of their town. The Muslim elite (the urban Urdu-speaking ashrafs) of Bengal were a closed status group. My grandmother's family, which had entered the middle class through education and not through ancestral wealth, probably found the non-orthodox Hindu bhadrolok class of professional people—the Brahmo Samaj identified people—to be more willing to accept them as social equals than the Muslim elite. Status in their town was determined by the Hindu bhadrolok class, and belonging to that class meant adopting the behavior of upper-crust Hindus. Moreover it is possible that a family defined by women probably saw more self-realization possibilities within the ideational framework of the Brahmo Samaj that encouraged women's education and advocated a more public role for women than were encouraged for Muslim women of elite status. In addition to that, it was a fictive kin who helped materialize many of these ideas concerning women's education and new role in society into my great-grandfather's house. A young male Congress worker who was a friend of my great-aunt's husband was adopted by her and her sisters as their *dada,* or brother. He was affectionately called *Kolkatar Dada* (brother from Calcutta) by them, and *Kolkatar Mama* (uncle from Calcutta) by their children, and eventually *Kolkatar Nana* (grandfather from Calcutta) by the grandchildren. This "practical relationship" was cultivated by the women in the family to realize some of the social capital they had lost in not having an elder male brother in a culture that valued men more highly than women.

Among Bengali Muslims, the mother's brother *mama* (*ma* stands for mother in Bengali, *mama* stands for double mother) is the most important male figure after the father in the family. Many important decisions, including marriage and property distribution, are decided only after consultation with the mama. Although my great-grandparents' youngest child was a son, he did not take on the role of mother's brother. Influenced by Gandhian ideology, Kolkatar Mama had left his orthodox Hindu family to work for a casteless society. Later he became an impassioned champion in the nationalist struggle of the Indian Congress Party. Although he lived in Calcutta, his po-litical work took him all over Bengal, which made it possible for him to stay in touch with all his adopted sisters who were married and scattered throughout Bengal. He also became the local guardian for my mother and her cousins when it was time for them to attend college in Calcutta. Kolkatar Mama introduced my mother and her cousins to Calcutta; he took them to movies and plays and occasionally to the zoo or the parks. After the partition of India, Kolkatar Mama remained in India. Fictive brother and sisters could only meet after the independence of Bangladesh in 1972.

My grandmother's second sister (the poet) became one of the women who came to dominate the family's narrative of women achievers. There is no doubt that she was, from all accounts, a remarkable woman for her times. She had studied up to grade six in a missionary school. Social pressures forced her to leave school, and she continued with her studies at home. She was the first woman in the family to play a public role, and in the 1930s she became a published poet in Calcutta. It was no small accomplishment in those times for a woman, especially for a Bengali Muslim woman, to take up her pen and write. She was well regarded by many of the literary luminaries of her day; she even had letters from Rabindranath Tagore encouraging her to continue writing. The family narrative was that she had remained single because of her commitment to literature. It was only after her death that I heard on national television that she had once been married. I then found out that she was mar-ried against her will to a man many years her senior. What is so remarkable about the story is that as a young teenager she had refused to accept the mar-riage as emotionally binding on her, because she was in love with her matri-lateral parallel cousin. Her marriage to her parallel cousin could not take place because his family wanted an alliance with a wealthy family. She had stood up not only to her father and all the older relatives, but also against the social expectations of her time, and she refused to consummate a marriage she considered loveless. This sad and yet exhilarating story is cleansed from the family's collective narrative, and her voice is disciplined as the spinster aunt who never had any sensual desires because she was committed to a loftier ideal, writing poetry. In other words, the ethic of modesty that pre-vailed in my family disallowed women from having any sensual desires out-side the normative structure of marriage and family.

Turning to my grandmother, how does one reconcile her child marriage with the narrative of the great-aunt who became a poet? My great-grandfather had enrolled my grandmother and her immediate elder sister in a missionary school run by nuns. After a month of school, their maternal aunt (the older sister of their mother who was married into the zamindari family) arrived at their family home. She used to spend a lot of time in their house because her widowed mother lived there. Upon finding out that they were in school, she immediately told her brother-in-law that it was socially inappropriate to educate his daughters in a missionary school where they could be influenced by Western ideas. The story goes that she threw such a tantrum that my grandmother and her sister were brought home in the middle of the school day in a covered palanquin. The missionary nuns came to plead with their father to allow them to return to school, but it was the aunt who decided the fate of their education. After I started school and learned English, my grandmother once asked me in an embarrassed manner if I could tell her the meaning of some English rhymes she knew. More than half a century later, my grandmother still remembered the rhymes she had learned from the missionary nuns in a dusty town in Bengal!

Whenever my mother or my aunts overheard my grandmother telling us the story of her wedding, they would ask her not to talk about those days. My mother and aunts considered the early marriage of their mother an embarrassment, something they did not want to acknowledge. As a child I first heard that my grandmother was married off at the age of seven; as an adult I was told that she was married at the age of ten. I cannot determine at what age she was married other than to say she was married very young. It was a secret to be kept in the family, because it did not correspond with the narratives the family told about itself. I was told that the early marriage of my grandmother was engineered by her maternal aunt, who was married to a zamindari family. This aunt, who was said to be extremely arrogant of her social status, would often tell my great-grandfather that because his daughters were dark-complexioned they would have difficulties in getting married and that he should not educate them but marry them off as soon as possible. This color prejudice is derived from the Bengali Muslim's desire for high ashraf identification—Middle Eastern, Arabic, or Persian roots. This attitude has become so normalized in culture that one of the first questions that a potential groom's family asks is "Meye forsha toh?" (Is the girl light-complexioned?). The more troubling aspect of this form of discrimination toward darker complexioned women is that these women have a very difficult time getting married, their dowries have to be much bigger, and even after marriage, they have to endure slights and taunts from their husbands and in-laws.

My grandmother was married to a family that had less education and cultural capital than her own. At the age of ten (or seven), my grandmother married and left home with her husband for his ancestral home. However, she did not sever ties with her father's home. She came back, year after year, to spend the holidays with her daughters in her father's home. My grandmother remembered that her older female relatives never allowed her to spend time with her father, or to get to know him better. My grandmother, married into a family of modest means, became the "poor" sister, the one who was the least financially well off among all her sisters. In addition to that, she had six daughters to marry off, which put her in an unenviable position in a culture that devalues women. If the family is poor, the situation gets more complicated. Too many daughters mean a huge financial burden for the family. Parents with daughters to marry off face another stigma from relatives with male children. They are seen as people who are always looking for potential sons-in-law for their daughters. This socially ascribed stigma, along with a fall in my grandmother's status, prevented my mother and her siblings from forming close relations with the rest of their matrilateral cousins. From conversations overheard as a child, I knew that my grandmother and her daughters were not treated well by the rest of the family; growing up they did not possess the symbols that made them sought after as kin. Growing up, I often heard my aunts grumble about how their mother had never received her share of property or household goods. I think this desire was partially due to the fact that they felt they were entitled to a higher social status than they were accorded.

My Mother

My maternal grandfather was the youngest of four children. His father had moved from his village to the provincial town of Bogra and had later married and settled there as a lawyer. His mother had died when my maternal grandfather was quite young. Growing up in a motherless home with an autocratic and conservative father, my maternal grandfather never formed close ties with his siblings. My grandfather was a graduate of Calcutta Presidency College. After graduation he joined the Bengal Civil Service. His postings took him throughout the provinces of Bengal and Assam, and he took his family with him. As a result, my grandmother was not compelled to live with her husband's family, which was more conservative and less culturally cultivated than her father's family. Certain conjunctive factors such as the absence of any in-laws, and the fact that my grandfather worked in a job that required frequent transfers, allowed my grandmother to maintain family ties selectively. After the death of their father, my grandfather and his two brothers chose to live independently, and family visits became more rare because my grandfather's eldest brother, for whatever reasons, did not take on the role as head of the family.

My grandfather was a cosmopolitan man (by cosmopolitan I refer to attitudes that did not correspond to local norms), and although he was not a man of wealth and affluence, he valued a secular identity, education, music, and sports. He had wanted to become a doctor, but because of financial constraints, he had to abandon his educational plans and take up a job with the colonial bureaucracy. Although the family did not have money, it was he who encouraged his daughters to pursue music in addition to their academic interests. My mother was given a violin and an organ as a child. Once these instruments broke, there was not enough money to replace them (by this time there were many more children in the family as well), and my mother abandoned her musical interests.

My grandparents had six daughters and no sons. My mother, as the eldest child, was raised in the role of the eldest son, who traditionally took care of the parents in their old age. It was the need to ensure social security for themselves in their old age that made my grandparents emphasize my mother's education more than the education of the other children. The support of her parents made it possible for my mother to pursue her education. Her family operated within a social space that allowed them to selectively maintain kinship ties. My mother's paternal grandfather's death when she was seven made certain educational choices easier for her and the family. My grandfather wanted his first-born child to be a doctor, a decision my grandmother vehemently opposed. For my grandmother a medical career meant close association with male doctors and patients, and given her more traditional beliefs, education for women could not be allowed to go to such an excess. Why was it that my grandmother and her oldest sister differed so dramatically in their attitudes toward the education of their daughters? Although sisters, these two women occupied different positions because of differential statuses. My great-aunt, as the oldest daughter of the educationist Khan Bahadur father, wielded more status and power in the family. My grandmother, as the wife of a junior officer, was under greater social pressure to observe social norms carefully. In the case of my mother's higher education, my grandmother's wishes prevailed, and my mother transferred from Calcutta Medical College to Calcutta University. When I asked my mother what were her own desires, what was it that *she* wanted, she looked perplexed. She replied, "What do you mean, my wishes? I did what my parents asked me to do." For a woman of my mother's generation, higher education was the only available means to fulfill personal desires—a place of her own before she was forced by convention to get married and bear children, and then, if her husband willed, renew her educational and professional interests. My grandmother, who was married off as a child, mentioned many times that she had wanted to educate all her daughters, not because she wanted them to work and earn a living, which would be improper given the social class to which they belonged, but because she did not want them to marry early. This did not prevent my grandmother from expecting her eldest daughter to take on the role of a son. For my grandmother and mother, higher education was not seen as a way of confronting the limits of patriarchy or of questioning the restrictions placed on women's role in public life. It was a way to have a room or socially sanctioned freedom of their own before they had to marry and bear children. Education became a strategy of coping with the patriarchal structures they found themselves in, and not necessarily as a tool with which to fight patriarchy. Gayatri Spivak cites Kalpana Bardhan in an essay that makes this point forcefully.

> Female conservatism . . . is often explained in terms of false consciousness (or cognitive dissonance, a euphemism for underdeveloped psyche). . . . However, female conservatism develops logically out of women's strategies of influence and survival within patrilocal, patriarchal structures. They are . . . the product of resourceful behavior under extremely disadvantageous circumstances. (Spivak 1993: 89)

My grandparents married within the same region, and at the time of the partition of India in 1947, we did not lose any significant kin. In contrast to that, my parents had a cross-regional marriage. My father was from East Bengal, and my mother is from North Bengal. In 1951 when they got married it was very rare for interregional marriages to occur, partly because of linguistic differences between the two regions.[11] My mother mentioned that she could understand the dialect used by my paternal grandfather only 50 percent of the time and that she failed to understand my paternal grandmother almost 100 percent of the time. Since my mother lived in the city and not in the ancestral home of my father, she did not have the social pressure to learn her in-laws' dialect. Her refusal to learn the manners of her affinal home did not endear her to her newly acquired kin group. Given such little interest on my mother's part to become part of her affinal family, one wonders why she married my father in the first place. According to my mother, what facilitated my parents' marriage was education. My father wanted an educated wife, and at that time, there were very few Bengali Muslim women with an advanced education. My mother had a master's degree in economics from Calcutta University, and at the time of her marriage she was an assistant professor of economics in a women's college in Dhaka.

Most Bengali Muslim women of my mother's generation did not go beyond high school. After marriage, however, many middle-class women did return to school to complete their college education. While education created opportunities for women like my mother, it also created new burdens. Among my mother's contemporaries, educated Muslim women often had to marry cross-regionally, because most Muslim families did not consider educated women to be suitable wives for their sons. Educated women had far fewer choices in terms of possible marital alliances. This is true for women of my generation as well. Women indexed as independent and Western-educated, especially those women who have been educated abroad (most of these women do not opt for arranged marriages in any case), find it difficult to find mates within their own community, because few families are willing to accept them as brides. Attitudes toward Western-educated men are very different. These men symbolize affluence and prestige regardless of what they actually do. Such men become the most desirable bachelors, and the same families who would not take a Western-educated woman into their home would happily marry their daughter to a man who lives in the West. One explanation of this demonization of independent women is the prevailing myth that such women will not care for their parents-in-law in their old age. Being "modern" in this context means the abdication of all traditional ties and responsibilities. It is not surprising that many of these women who are indexed as "Western" chose to marry out of the community.

My paternal grandparents had seven sons and two daughters. My paternal grandfather was a schoolteacher and retired as a subinspector for schools.

He married a woman from his own village, and they had seven sons and one daughter. My paternal grandfather was educated within the madrassah education of Bengal, but in order to improve his sons' chances at a better life, he encouraged them (my father was sixth in line) to pursue a Western-style education instead of a religious education. As a general rule, women's education was not encouraged in his family. My paternal grandfather worked in a town fifteen miles from his village, and his wife and children lived in the ancestral village home. He visited them on weekends and maintained a close relationship with his extended family members. He brought his family to the town only after it was time for his eldest son to attend school. Thus, the need of a good education in a colonial state facilitated the move for the family from the rural to the urban center. Although a man of modest means, my paternal grandfather supported his widowed sister and her eight children as well as the children of his other sister while they attended school. Since his sisters lived in the village where there were no good schools, they sent their sons (but not the daughters) to live with their brother while they attended school. As the mother's brother, *mama*, it was his kin duty to do so.

The position of women also differed between the two families. Women in my father's family played a less powerful role compared to my mother's family; women who joined the family through marriage had no role in family affairs. Women in my mother's family were more conscious of their social and economic rights because of education and because of the role that certain older women had played in the family. As a general rule, men in my mother's family did not divorce their wives if they did not give birth to sons; dowry was also not practiced in the family. This is not to be taken to mean that other forms of sexist oppression did not exist in the family—they did—but the issue I want to highlight is that women did enjoy a certain status in the family. At the time of my mother's marriage, her family had negotiated the terms of the marriage contract. According to the contract, my mother retained the right to divorce my father.[12] After her marriage, my mother found out that my father's family had removed that clause from the contract without notifying her family. Against my father's wishes, my mother got a court affidavit to add that clause back into the contract. This gesture, along with many such gestures, was read as the behavior of a disobedient wife by my father and his kin group. My parents' marriage was conflict-ridden, and my father, who was a man of uncontrollable rage, often threatened her: "I'll divorce you." I have asked my mother again and again, why did you choose to stay in the relationship if it was so painful? Why, when you had a government job with a good income and free housing, did you live with a man who apparently abused you? My mother tried to answer by saying, "Your father's family did not respect women." Finally she confessed, "I had five unmarried sisters. If I got divorced, nobody would marry them." It is difficult to say if circumstances were different, that is, if she did not have five unmarried sisters, whether she would have left her husband. What I can say is that writing the clause into the marriage contract did not mean the acceptance of such values by her.

My mother left on her own to pursue an advanced degree from Columbia University, an act that did not endear her to her newly acquired kin group. My mother says that the main reason for her going to America was to get an advanced degree that would secure for her a good job. My maternal grandfather retired soon after my mother's marriage. He died ten years later, leaving four unmarried daughters. In the absence of a brother, my mother took on the role of elder brother. My mother chose to perform the role of eldest son/oldest brother to her mother and siblings over that of her duties to her husband and his relatives. This was the reason of the conflict between my parents. In large part what enabled her to make this decision was her education and the government job that she held. In addition to that, my mother gave birth to three daughters in a culture where male children are valued over female children. For us children, gender played the definitive role in our self-constructions as young girls. My father and my uncles were not interested in us, because we were girls, and there was no effort made on their part to regulate our education.

In fact, my father was actively hostile toward the idea of his daughters getting an English and science-oriented education. In the middle-class background I come from, parents try their utmost to send their sons and daughters to English-language schools and privilege a science education over liberal arts. Knowledge of English and mastery of science subjects allow students to get better paying jobs and also prepare them to travel to Western countries (the United States primarily) for higher education. My father, a well-known scholar in Bangladesh, worked hard to prevent us from getting an education that would improve our life choices. This was a result of my father's acrimonious relationship with his wife, whose independence posed frequent challenges to my father's authority. My mother's ability to resist my father's wishes was a consequence of her education. He saw the cultivation of an English and science-oriented education as producing daughters who would become independent women. When I was a child I often heard my father say, "Girls should stay at home and learn *ranna-banna* cooking." As the youngest in a family of three daughters, I learned early on that my only escape route to a better life lay in education and a knowledge of the English language. I had no desire to live out my life as a woman in Bangladesh. So, when my father refused to send my middle sister and me to a school where we could get an English education and training that would prepare us to compete in a global society, I spent hours and hours poring over dog-eared copies of old sociology books to learn English.

With the partition of India in 1947, my parents' generation further broke with traditional kinship ties. As mentioned earlier, my mother's family was urbanized from the time of her grandfather. My father's family became urbanized with his generation. With the creation of an independent Pakistan for Muslims, both sides of the family saw their future not in the villages or small towns of Bengal, but in the capital city of Dhaka. Some of the policies of the postcolonial state of Pakistan further accelerated the making of the Bengali Muslim professional middle class and thus the tying up of this class with a new set of social relationships. Educated graduates were recruited for high-ranking bureaucratic jobs with the Pakistani Civil Service. During British India, there were perhaps fifteen to twenty Bengali Muslim Indian Civil Service officers (one of the highest ranking administrative posts in the colonial government for natives).

Immediately following the partition of 1947, the Pakistani Civil Service had a large percentage of its new recruits from East Pakistan. Many young graduates, like my parents, went overseas for advanced professional training. Some members of my parents' kin were posted to the former West Pakistan (now Pakistan), where they continue to live, and the family has, of course, lost touch with them. The state also solidified this emergent bureaucratic middle-class through property relations, by selling land to government employees at very low rates and by providing them with low-interest loans to build homes. Increasingly, people who wanted to belong to this emergent middle class sold their ancestral homes to buy property in the city. With that transfer of property there were fewer incentives to cultivate older forms of kin relations. My father and his brothers sold their ancestral home after their father's death in 1954 and moved to Dhaka where they could make their futures. This migration to the city of a postcolonial state required new social ties that were based on educational credentials—scientific knowledge— which further removed the family from village-based kin networks. In the post-1947 phase, the future of the educated class lay in the city and not in the villages, because state policies did not target the villages for growth and development.

My mother came to Bangladesh (former East Pakistan) in 1948, and because she had a master's degree from Calcutta University, she immediately got a government job as an assistant professor in a women's college. Soon after her marriage, she appeared in a competitive scholarship examination held for all graduates of Pakistan. In this exam, she came first in order of merit. Her result enabled her to win a fellowship from the Pakistani government to go to Columbia University for higher education. Although my mother had academically outperformed most of the male graduates of her time, a powerful career as a diplomat or as an education secretary was not an option that she could pursue in a state that defined a woman's position as subordinate to a man's. My mother always said that she was very happy with her professional life. But as the gendered subject of the state, she could not opt for a career choice in excess of the will of the state.

IN SEARCH OF FRIENDSHIP AS A WAY OF LIFE

Letters from my mother remain unopened on my desk. Somewhere in my past a great-aunt had stood up to tradition and resisted family and social pressures to get her married. My choice too has been made. I stop replying to her letters.

My mother's return to the former East Pakistan after obtaining her degree in contrast with my permanent migration to America speaks to the historical transformations in the postcolonial politics of the emergence of Bangladesh as an independent nation-state as well as to its effects on personal and kin ties.

In 1975, four years after the independence of Bangladesh, the military overthrew the civilian government. The military rulers remained in power until 1990. During military rule, the middle class (the class I belong to) was increasingly marginalized by the military, both professionally and academically. In many instances, government bureaucrats were replaced by military personnel and subordinated to military authority. The military rulers were not interested in building civil society but in consolidating their power by forging links with the Islamic political parties, parties that had aligned with the Pakistani army against the independence struggle of Bangladesh in 1971. It is not surprising that the military bypassed the middle class, because it was precisely this class of people that directly challenged its legitimacy. The middle-class intellectual elites had given ideological shape and momentum to the independence struggle of 1971, and they considered it their right to define the Bangladeshi nation-state in its postindependence phase. The military rulers, many of whom were expatriate officers from Pakistan and had not participated in the freedom struggle of 1971, correctly identified the middle-class elites as a threat and sought to neutralize their power and influence in society. In its efforts to factionalize political loyalties, the military allowed the politicization of the higher education system, which became the recruiting ground for young students into one political party or another.

The education system effectively broke down, so that in the mid-1980s a three-year bachelor's degree, to use one example, took almost seven years to complete. This breakdown literally meant that social mobility for the middle class was virtually nonexistent. This was a critical factor in the decision by many professional people to migrate from Bangladesh permanently. Around this time, many members of my extended family, uncles who had bureaucratic jobs with the state, left for jobs outside the country; their children also opted for the life in the diaspora. The effect of this migration on my family was felt in the fewer number of people at family gatherings. As a result, events such as marriages, births, and deaths that brought the family together as a unit were rendered unsustainable in the new environment of the United States, where most of us now live. This dispersion of my extended family has resulted in members marrying outside the community. These new affinal ties do not create new kin groups, because of cultural differences and geographical distance, but also because most members of this generation see their futures in the West. There is little interest in cultivating ties with people residing in Bangladesh. The secular beliefs of my family have further loosened kin ties, because persons marrying outside Islam are not forced to become part of an Islamic identity, and thus the possibility of a coherence around a unifying belief structure is further corroded.

My mother and I have had very different experiences in America. For my mother, America was a place she came to get a degree; it was not a place in which to make a home. My mother's inability to make friends in the United States speaks in part to the patriarchal structure she operated within—all social interactions were filtered through my father. Her relationship with the homeland was also different; close kin ties and a good job awaited her. For me, America symbolized a place that had to accommodate me, albeit temporarily, while I crafted a self other than the one my mother envisioned. Unlike my mother, I no longer saw an economic or social future for myself in Bangladesh. Some of these personal choices, in turn, reflected my diasporic urge to remake myself into a subject who transcended kinship ties and was not bound by local and national habits and prejudices—a cosmopolitan subject. By making these claims it may appear that I am rewriting myself as a volitional subject possessing full agency. My refusal to operate within the new patriarchy of my family—the educated woman who is subordinated to men—had situated me within a context where I had no option but to remake myself, often consciously, selfishly, and deliberately. I had to create another mythical home, a place forever outside the restrictive boundaries of my family and the postcolonial nation-state of Bangladesh. My marriage to a person from outside of Bangladesh, then, made that invention of "another home, another place" a material possibility. In leaving home, I was faced with the necessity to remake and reevaluate my kin relations, a function that I now, perhaps for lack of a better term, call *cosmopolitan.*

Since all three daughters have left Bangladesh, and none of us has affinal ties there, it has put my mother in a difficult position. In the absence of adequate health care or pension benefits for older people, children in South Asia have functioned as social security for their parents in their old age. As more and more children of professional middle-class families leave Bangladesh for employment opportunities abroad, the lives of the older generation are placed in jeopardy, because neither the state nor the private sector has stepped in to provide the needed services for them. An informal survey of my mother's middle-class neighborhood in Dhaka shows that almost each and every household has one or more members of the family who have migrated abroad. Her relatives—the diasporans—come for brief visits to the country. As their children marry outside the community, those visits diminish in number.

At the time of my marriage to a Punjabi Indian, my mother mentioned that she would prefer I marry a Bengali Hindu from India rather than a Punjabi. She mentioned that the cultural differences between us, Bengali and Punjabi, would be too great to bridge. I realize now that she was, at some level, anxious about the continuation of kinship relations. Bengali Hindus would, in many ways, replicate the kinship characteristics of middle-class Bengali Muslims. My mother never brought up any serious objection to the marriage on religious grounds.

My mother-in-law used to say: I would tell my son that he could play with Muslims, but Beta you must not eat in Muslim homes. They are not clean, they do not follow our dietary laws. . . . But Ammi, he would say, they make such good kebabs.

My former marriage was a union outside both of our respective communities and did not result in a wider kin group (I am Bengali of Muslim heritage, and he is Indian-Punjabi and part Hindu and part Sikh); in fact, it reduced the number of kin members who accepted us and with whom we could interact. Given the cross-religion marriage (Muslim and Sikh-Hindu), it was difficult to establish kin contact with my new in-laws, who were refugees from West Punjab and had lost significant members of their extended clan during the Hindu-Muslim-Sikh partition riots of 1947. For them, religious as well as ethnic identity mattered. Not only was their son expected to marry a Sikh or a Hindu, but more specifically, someone from the Punjab or northern India. While they could accept friendship with Muslims, they also had unspoken restrictions on connubiality and commensalism.

My mother's family was urbanized from my great-grandfather's time, and several of her cousins had married Western women whom they met as students abroad. On the contrary, my former husband's family came in contact with the West only in his generation—in 1981 when he came to the United States to pursue higher education. Most members of his family still lived in the provincial towns of northern India, and only part of his family had moved to the urban center of Delhi and settled there. The cosmopolitan attitudes toward marriage that I had taken for granted were absent in his family, and it complicated the problems that we had after our marriage. For my former parents-in-law one of the most pressing and embarrassing issues was how to face their kin, how to tell them that their son, the successful immigrant of whom they were so proud, had brought home a Muslim wife. In order to protect me from their slights, so to speak, my parents-in-law insisted that I not meet these relatives. They were, of course, protecting themselves, and by not allowing me to make any contact with the kin group, they were, in effect, writing off the marriage as fiction, as an aberration.

Sons, unlike daughters, are seen in many South Asian families as investments, and dowries are common practice especially among north Indian
households.[13] For the son who becomes the nonresident Indian (NRI), the
obligations to the natal family are high and restrictive. By investing in their
son's education, my in-laws, like others of their generation, had effectively
tried to provide for their own security in old age, as well as maintain status
among their peers after retirement. Marriage outside the community, and on
top of that, outside the faith, imperiled them in understandable ways. What
if the new wife, who had no linguistic knowledge or cultural understanding,
now insisted that the son break with tradition, not only his affective ties but
also his financial duties and obligations to his family?

*My mother-in-law said to me several times, I am a fortunate woman be-
cause I do not have a daughter, because if I had a daughter she would have
to have at least five sets of gold ornaments and a hundred silk saris before
she could leave our house. I do not have to worry about that; I do not have
to worry about what my daughter-in-law thinks.*

My crossover marriage, in this case, became the site where national and
religious identities came in conflict. The state, at that moment, became the
ideologically identified Hindu state, and the unspoken connubial laws between Hindus and Muslims became the defining parameters of the legality of
the relationship. My former father-in-law, who was a senior officer with the
Indian military, felt that a Muslim daughter-in-law from Bangladesh might
mar his career advancement within the Indian army. His suggestion was that
I not tell people that I was from Bangladesh or that I was Muslim! Effectively,
I was to enter their house as someone without history or voice, a woman
whose history he could rewrite. In order to visit him at the hill station where
he was posted, I had to get clearance from the Indian Defense Ministry. I also
had to get permission from the local immigration officer in town. While the
defense department gave me clearance during my first visit, the immigration
officer kept on giving me one excuse after another. Often, while I waited in
his office, I had to listen to his conversations that were peppered with references to how Muslims were dirty, how they produced too many babies, how
they were getting too may benefits in India, how Muslims in India had a
much better deal than Hindus in Pakistan, and so on. Finally, I left India
without ever getting my visa extended. In my next visit to India, I was pulled
over by the immigration authorities at Delhi Airport. Someone had posted
the following message in their computer: "The holder of this passport is ab-
sconding the law and must be remanded into police custody upon appre-
hension." The local police officer as the symbol of the state reified the
Indian state as a Hindu state and my marriage as outside the bounds of the
social imaginary.

TOWARD VIRTUAL KINSHIP

The fluidity of structures in America and the apparent ease with which friendships are made and unmade make it appear possible that an invented family can replace a consanguineal family. My desire to practice these "new kinds of relationships," pressed against the inability of traditional kin structures to accommodate them, resulted in consanguineal ties being replaced with friendship or fictive kinship, or a kinship of one's own. Soon after my marriage, I met an American family that had unofficially adopted my former husband as their "Indian son." Their son and my former husband were roommates in college together, and the family genuinely extended the hospitality of their home to him, and then later to me. Between the years of 1984 (when we got married) and 1988 (the year we separated), we were frequent dinner guests at their home. Summer vacations were often spent in their New England cottage by the lake, and holidays such as Christmas, Thanksgiving, New Year's, and the Fourth of July were celebrated as one year-long tradition of family reunions. We were counseled on marriage, investments, education, and professional aspirations and introduced everywhere as "our Indian son, and his wife." I was, of course, the appendage—the woman brought in from the outside—who could be replaced if the need arose. I had thought that membership in a family by choice was almost as good as membership by consanguineal ties, but after our divorce the fiction of an invented family—a family of choice—remained a fiction, and nothing more. These fictive kinship ties produce a fluidity that is necessary for the production of a cosmopolitan subject, because friendship in this mobile culture is both functional and temporal. A romantic alliance, outside of one's kin networks and culture, has no enduring structure to stand on once the romance is over. The cosmopolitan subject requires kinship only to the extent that it makes certain self-realizing ambitions possible.

In my family, all these transnational dispersions and relocations have resulted in a new form of communication among my cousins in the United States. These days we stay in touch electronically through e-mail and home pages set up by different people. Cyberspace gives us the fictional notion of being in contact; in reality it gives us a new mode of modified distance from each other's lives, *a virtual kinship*. It is a new making of kinship without its cares, without its reciprocities, without its anchored meanings. Our life trajectories, tied up with *specific desires* to succeed in a new culture as professional immigrants, produce certain indifferences toward kinship. Thus, the death of an aunt becomes a sigh; births and weddings, smiles; and an occasional divorce, a shrug. Interest in such events flags, because they have become inadequate mechanisms for the production of ourselves as members of new social formations that lie outside the traditional kinship structures that governed the lives of my grandparents and parents. This is not to suggest that kinship has been effectively erased in the family, but that, pressed against emergent needs and desires, its role in our lives has shifted to a marginal position.

NOTES

I am grateful to my mother for sharing some of her stories with me. I remain solely responsible for the interpretation of those stories. I also wish to thank James Faubion, Betty Joseph, Apollo Amoko, an anonymous reviewer of this chapter, and the commentators at the conference on Kinship and Cosmopolitanism at Rice University, March 1997.

1. This chapter is about my mother's family. Family here is used to refer to my mother's matriline.

2. I do not address the effects of global capital and migrations on the lives of rural Bangladeshis, especially among the young men who have left their rural homes to seek their fortunes in the oil fields of the Middle East, or in the burgeoning markets of the Asian tigers, or on the streets of New York or Bonn. Most of these men are single. Many of them will not return home because of work permit restrictions and financial constraints, and a significant number of them will establish new affinal relations in the countries to which they have migrated. These transnational migrations pose compelling questions for the ethnographer of kinship, questions that are not addressed here.

3. The Muslims of Bengal broadly classified themselves into *ashraf* (highborn and *atraf* (lowborn) Muslims, but within this twofold stratification there were gradations of statuses. Contrary to the principles of Islamic doctrine, Muslims in Bengal practiced class and caste distinctions, and interestingly enough, they divided themselves into a fourfold ashraf group stratification, namely, (1) Syeds, (2) Sheikhs, (3) Mughals, and (4) Pathans. This stratification mimicked the fourfold stratification of the Hindu caste system. All four ashraf status groups were considered noble. The classes of the Syeds and Sheikhs were said to be descended from the Prophet Muhammad and they belonged to a higher social rank than the Mughals and Pathans, who were said to be descended from the Muslim rulers of India. Although this classificatory system was flexible and allowed for social mobility, entry into the highest status group—the Urdu-speaking ashraf Muslims—was restricted. Such ashraf Muslims considered themselves to be racially superior to the local converts (the atrafs); they claimed to be of Middle-Eastern origin and traced their genealogy to the Prophet Muhammad or to the Mughal and Afghan conquerors of India. Given this context, it is not surprising that the ashraf, or upper-class Muslims, did not want to associate themselves with the local converts.

4. One of the former viceroys of India, Warren Hastings, established the Calcutta Madrassah for Muslims in 1781, but it was restricted to "highborn" Muslims. Not only were high-status Muslims against the education of the masses, so were the upper-class Hindus. When the first girls' school was established in Calcutta by a colonial officer, D. Bethune (c. 1840–1850), there was a lot of opposition from Hindus. One of the conditions of the Bethune School was that no Muslim girl would be allowed to enroll. Later, when Bethune College was established, the same opposition was raised by the Hindu *bhadrolok* community that Muslim and Hindu girls should not study to-

gether, but this time these objections were overridden, and Muslim girls were allowed to enroll in the college but not the school. The Maharaja of Natore in Rājshāhi District (now in Bangladesh) established a school in memory of his mother, but no Muslim girls were allowed to study at this school. According to my mother, this is why my grandmother and her sister studied at the missionary school in Rājshāhi District.

5. The Permanent Settlement Act of 1793 enacted by Lord Cornwallis effectively changed the land ownership pattern in Bengal. Prior to this act, zamindars in Bengal were the agents of the government and had hereditary claim to the lands, and rarely were they dispossessed of their lands. They leased out their lands to local people, and in turn they paid the government a rate that was annually decided through arbitration between the government and the zamindars. The British changed this system into a fixed rate of taxation that did not take into account the effects of any natural calamities on local crop production. Failure to pay the revenues resulted in the loss of one's property. With the enactment of this system, many of the traditional Muslim zamindari families became dispossessed of their lands, and a new class of land speculators from Calcutta, many of them Hindu traders who had made fortunes through trade with the East India Company, became the new landlords in Bengal. See Guha 1982.

6. See R. Ahmed 1981, pp. 133–59. He writes that within the ashraf classification there were three status groups. The highest status group was the urban Urdu-speaking ashrafs who observed endogamous marriages. The second status group was the Urdu- and Bengali-speaking ashrafs. This group had married locally with Bengalis but still maintained their foreign ancestry, so to speak, through linguistic differentiation. The lowest-status group was the Bengali-speaking rural ashrafs, who were small landholders and had attained ashraf status through education, and not through any genealogical association.

7. See Chatterjee 1993. The Brahmo Samaj Movement is associated with the Hindu reform ideas of Raja Rammohan Roy in the late 1820s. It advocated, among other changes, the eradication of Hindu women's oppression through the abolition of widow immolation, Kulin Brahman polygamy (a custom among high-caste Bengali Brahman men to marry multiple times), the legalization of Hindu widow remarriage (advocated by reformer Ishwarchandra Vidyasagar), property rights for widows, and the abolition of child marriage. The Brahmo Samaj also advocated the education of women and a more public role for Indian women. In the 1870s the Brahmo Samaj fought to abolish child marriage and sought to increase the age of sexual intercourse for Hindu girls from ten to twelve years of age.

8. As part of the Islamization efforts of military dictator General Mohammed Ershad (in power between 1982–1990), women were prohibited for a short time from entering the police service. This decision was reversed after strong opposition from women's groups. Women were officially allowed into the police force under assassinated military dictator General Ziaur Rahman, who was in power between 1976–1982.

9. "Reading the Quran" refers to the ability to pronounce the sounds of the Arabic alphabet and does not mean that the person understands the Arabic language. This oral culture of the Quran is highly valued among Bengali Muslims. Prospective in-laws/matchmakers tested young girls on their ability to recite the Quran.

10. Cross-cousins are those whose parent is of the opposite sex to the linking parent of an individual (Ego). A matrilineal cross-cousin is a mother's brother's child. A patrilineal cross-cousin is a father's sister's child. Parallel cousins are those whose parent is of the same sex as the linking parent of an individual (Ego). A matrilineal

parallel cousin is a mother's sister's child. A patrilineal parallel cousin is a father's brother's child.

11. These linguistic differences have been partially erased among the educated elites after the creation of Bangladesh. The Bangladeshi state nationalized the usage of literary Bengali as its national language in 1972 and homogenized some of the regional differences in spoken Bengali.

12. According to the Hanafi School of interpretation of the *sharia,* which is followed by the majority of Muslims in Bengal, Muslim women are allowed certain marital rights, such as the right to divorce the husband, as long as these terms are written into the marriage contract. In Pakistan the Family Laws Ordinance (1961) undertook some reforms to curb polygamy and to offer women some legal protection. The husband could take a second wife only after informing his first wife and the arbitration board; he could obtain a divorce only after notifying his wife and the arbitration board. A man could not divorce his wife through verbal repudiation: by saying *talak, talak, talak* (I divorce you) thrice in front of another male witness. The wife's right to divorce was ensured by requiring a standard contract for all marriages. This law still exists on the books in Bangladesh but is not applied in most cases.

The three conditions of the marriage contract that were agreed upon by my father were: (1) As long as my wife is alive and I am officially wedded to her, I will not take a second wife; (2) If my wife chooses to do so, she can dissolve the marriage bond; (3) If I have to live apart from my wife for any reason, I will provide her with a monthly maintenance fee.

13. As a general rule, dowry was not practiced in my mother's family.

BIBLIOGRAPHY

Ahmed, Rafiuddin. 1981. *The Bengal Muslims, 1871–1906.* New Delhi: Oxford University Press.

Ahmed, Sufia. 1996. *Muslim Community in Bengal, 1884–1912.* Dhaka: University Press Limited.

Borneman, John. 1992. *Belonging in the Two Berlins: Kin, State, Nation.* Cambridge: Cambridge University Press.

Bourdieu, Pierre. 1977. *Outline of a Theory of Practice.* Trans. R. Nice. Cambridge: Cambridge University Press.

Chatterjee, Partha. 1993. The Nation and Its Women. In *The Nation and Its Fragments.* Princeton: Princeton University Press, pp. 116–34.

Fruzzetti, Lina, and Akos Ostor. 1984. *Kinship and Ritual in Bengal.* New Delhi: South Asian Publishers, Pvt. Ltd., pp. 202–9.

Guha, Ranajit. 1982. *A Rule of Property for Bengal: An Essay on the Idea of Permanent Settlement.* New Delhi: Orient Longman.

Hara, Tadahiko. 1967. Poribar and Kinship in Muslim Rural Village in East Pakistan. Ph.D. dissertation, Australian National University, Australia.

Scott, Joan W. 1993. From the Evidence of Experience. In *Gay and Lesbian Studies Reader.* Ed. H. Abelove, M. A. Barale, and D. M. Halperin. New York: Routledge.

Spivak, Gayatri. 1993. Woman in Difference. In *Outside in the Teaching Machine.* New York: Routledge, pp. 77–95.

5

Kousi Oda Ponnu
(*Kousi's Daughter*)

Deepa S. Reddy

> Between these two cliffs, which preserve the distance between my gaze and its object, time . . . has begun to pile up rubble. Sharp edges have been blunted and whole sections have collapsed: periods and places collide, are juxtaposed or inverted like strata displaced by the tremors on the crust of [a] planet. . . . Events without any apparent connection, and originating from incongruous periods and places, slide one over the other and suddenly crystallize into a sort of edifice.
>
> —Claude Lévi-Strauss, *Tristes Tropiques*

ONE

pretensions

Years I have spent wishing for a family of friends. The greatest achievement was to be fast friends with your mother, your father, your cousins, I thought, turning the stark reality of your blood bond into a relationship on equal footing, of ideas, emotions, feelings.

Mata-pita-guru-daivam, my mother teaches me—mother-father-teacher-god, always in that order, leaving no room for my imagined family of friends. And yet I know she wishes it, too. She reads to me from *Little Women,* my head on her lap, slipping on the cool folds of her georgette sari or leaning on her blouse that does not match. But perhaps she prefers *Are You My Mother?* by P. D. Eastman, a story of a newly hatched chick that sets out in search of its mother, asking a kitten, a dog, and even a plane "Are you my mother?" only to have all doubts removed in a moment of instant recognition at the end when the mother bird flies back with a worm in her beak—there is something in this story of the perfect harmony of a blood relationship that is appealing, comforting, touching. "Are you my mother?" she mimics the shrill voice of a young child, and laughs.

Years later, I am standing at my cousin Shekhar's wedding when a man I could swear I have never seen before approaches. "Kousi oda ponnu thane?" he asks. ("You are Kousi's daughter, aren't you?") He must have met me as a child, at somebody else's wedding, quite possibly. He promises to phone later to give me the addresses of relatives in San Antonio whom I can contact when I return. Here was a moment of instant recognition, and I am embedded in a dense network of relationships, given a place, a function, a set of responsibilities. I am a little bewildered, but moved nonetheless by this most natural gesture of acceptance and inclusion.

"Hey, Shekhar!" I approach my cousin as he steps off the *medai* (platform/stage) with his new wife. He is garlanded, wearing a silk dhoti, *poonal* across his chest, and *vibhuti* and *kunkumam* on his forehead. "*Yenna, Shekhar, nalla Brahmana-payyan madiri irukkiye.*" ["What, Shekhar, you look just like a nice Brahmin boy!"] Shekhar's face breaks into a mischievous grin, but before he can respond, someone nearby interjects sharply in English: "What are you saying? He is not *like* a nice Brahmin boy, he *is* a nice Brahmin boy! What are you saying?" I bite my lip to suppress a smile and think of ways and means to duck.

I am used to asserting the constructedness and metaphoricity of words and relationships and things. And yet it is impossible to ignore that kinship asserts its presence as though it is part of the natural order of the world: it has, within its own cultural constructedness, a certain taken-for-granted quality; it has, in spite of its own fluidity, levels of meaning that are assumed, relationships taken as given, configurations of intimacy that carry the confidence of the formulaic. It is impossible to understand kinship as a system of relationships that is always in flux, forever in the process of being constituted, without recognizing that there is *also* this element of the given, the already constituted and the already understood, at its very core. My purpose in this chapter is not to reinstate biology as the irrefutable "natural" force behind kinship, but to bring the argument of the social constructedness of things full circle: to ask, that is, how our socially produced worlds come to be *naturalized* or experienced as real and given at particular moments, and as complete fictions and facades at others. My purpose is to explore kinship from such shifting points of view.[2]

Of course, even as I spell out my perspective, thus attempting to cast kinship neatly in one mold or another, I must be prepared for the inevitable: for the neatness to fall apart, the tidiness to give way, for the mold to chip and crack in places. The stories and events that make up the material have a life of their own, despite my efforts to contain them with my voice and my pen. It is, for one, a life that belongs to many other people: my mother, my father, my sister, husband, parents-in-law, cousins, and still others. And then it is a life that is, like any other, structured by social beliefs; fashioned from tradition and custom; filled with affections, devotions, resentments, hearty agreements, and passionate contraries: in short, it is a life that is shaped by too many unruly forces and counterforces that each clamor for attention and make writing a very messy business indeed. Can I fit all that and more into an argument about kinship? And then if there were room for it all, would I want to, could I even afford to take on such a task? You would concur, I believe, that there is no completely comfortable place for me to sit or stand to tell this tale of kinship. There are no soft cushions here, no soporific lettuce leaves[3]—in short, no cool outsides to step into to draw sharp breaths of fresh air, no planned routes of escape.

My writing, then, becomes a game of drawing lines, between telling and not telling, risking and not risking; lines that at once create a new order and a new chaos, that simultaneously establish and dismantle my authority as storyteller, as they mark the reach and limits of my voice. My writing, then, becomes my intervention into this narrative of kinship.

Lakshman-rekha, Or the story of Sita's Abduction

The deer that appears in the forest is really the demon Maricha. "*O Lakshmana, O Sita*," he cries, mimicking Rama's voice, as he lies wounded by Rama's arrow. But before Lakshmana leaves in search of his brother, he draws a line outside the hut, the famous *Lakshman-rekha*. "Stay behind this line," he tells Sita. "Stay behind this line and no harm will befall you."

In the garb of a sage, there is Ravana, King of Lanka, demon of demons. "Some food, Sitamma, some water," he begs. Sita pauses for a brief moment before the line that Lakshmana has drawn, remembering Lakshmana's warning. But then he is only a sage, she reasons; what harm could possibly come from giving a sage food and drink? And in a split second it is all over. When Lakshmana returns, he finds food spilled over the line and knows at once what has happened.

TWO

closeness

nandavanathil or-andi
avan nal-aaru madamai kuyavanaai vendi
kondu vandaan oru thondi
adai kuthadi kuthadi potudaithandi

My mother sings. *Amma, Adu yenna paattu* (what song is that)? *Thatha paaduvar* (Thatha used to sing it). What does it mean? There was once a potter. For ten months he prayed to god and was given a pot. He danced and danced with the pot, round and round, until he dropped it and it broke. . . . Why ten months? Because a baby grows in the mother's stomach for ten months.

Kousi oda ponnu. There I am. The daughter of Kausalya and Sankaran, who are married at Tilak Mahal Bungalow in the village of Kallidaikurichi in Tirunelveli District, Tamil Nadu, in September of 1971. My mother is twenty-six, old by any standard to be getting married, but accomplished. The only one of ten children to hold a postgraduate degree, she also does what few women from such places even consider an option: she works as a lecturer at Holy Cross College in Trichy *before* getting married. My mother may be married even later if not for her own intervention. "Your grandfather," she says, "was not really interested in settling my wedding." I never understand why Thatha bears such anger toward her, but I think it has something to do with her going against his wishes and studying botany instead of medicine. My father says he felt sorry for her. And after a few letters are exchanged between a young accountant working with a British oil company in Assam and the talented daughter of a prominent banker of Kallidaikurichi, a marriage proposal comes from my father's older brother in Tirunelveli. I am born a little over a year later.

The romance ends quickly, and in its place the inescapable reality of my parents' affinal ties, the bitter aftertaste of cruel words spilled carelessly over the floor and flung in terrible desperation against the walls, leave behind an entangled mess of loyalties, affections, sentiments. At first there are the gifts, small tokens of regret, gestures of goodwill, but those, too, stop coming, suddenly, predictably. They are in my jewelry box now: a gold band, once decorated in green and red enamel paint, but smooth now after years of use, and a pair of *jhimikis*, bell-shaped earrings studded with stones and decorated with bunches of tiny dangling pearls. My mother-in-law says, "These are nice, Deepa," looking at my earrings. "Did your father buy them for you?" "No, Amma," I reply, brushing aside rancid memories and inventing for myself sublime moments of affection when mothers give their daughters precious mementos of beautiful pasts. Feeling self-conscious and silly and rather overly determined to allow myself this moment of romantic indulgence, I reply, "No Amma, my mother gave them to me—Appa bought them for her soon after they were married."

My mother learns cooking in that first year of her marriage from her mother-in-law, who comes to stay with them in Digboi. "I did not know anything!" she tells me, her mouth curving into that usual expression of regret. "Your Pati taught me everything I know." The daughter of a private banker, lessee of *adheenam* (privately owned) lands and grains procurement agent in Kallidaikurichi, never learned to cook. Instead, she set her sights on education, and on working *before* getting married. Determined not to allow me to slip into this disadvantaged position of privilege, my mother makes me cut cu-

cumber for lunch salads, teaches me to chop off the ends, sprinkle them with salt, and rub them against the cut surfaces to remove the bitterness that is concentrated there. Then she tells me to slice them into thin, thin slices. She makes me watch as chapatis are being prepared for the afternoon meal, as *dosas* are being poured at suppertime. Visiting her sister's family in Bombay, my mother remarks on how well my cousin Uma cuts vegetables, how deft she is and how neat is her work. I know, however, that my mother does not care. She does not care about neat houses and decorated tables, beautiful saris and thinly sliced cucumbers. Or perhaps I should say that she stops caring.

Some years after I am born, my mother cuts her hair so it falls only to her shoulders. I see her in old photographs, the color almost completely faded, wearing sleeveless blouses with pale printed saris, sitting beside her colleagues in the school where she teaches in the evenings. At home she makes fresh bread and pours over cookbooks for new recipes for cakes and Swiss rolls. Then we go to Tirunelveli, to my uncle's home, and news reaches my grandfather ten villages away that his daughter has cut her hair so it falls only to her shoulders, and then news reaches us that he is angry, so angry, he does not want her to visit him as planned. I do not remember my mother's exact reaction, but somewhere between her father's anger and her husband's uninterested tolerance of her fancies, somewhere between the curious glances of strangers and the cruel silence of family, my mother's already mild interest in hair, makeup, cooking, and decorating all vanishes in a single puff, a wave of a wand, leaving me to learn the role of an Indian wife from a woman who performs it only as a matter of course. So, really, I know that my mother does not care about neat houses and decorated tables, beautiful saris and thinly sliced cucumbers. She reads to me from books of fairy tales and from the philosophy of Schopenhauer, filling the opening pages of our dictionary with quotations and marking out the meanings of unknown words. She spends many hours every day teaching me Carnatic music in the tradition of her father and grandfathers and slaps me hard when I write the word *english* without capitalizing the "e." She is determined that I will marry only an oldest son so I will not have to suffer the indignities of submitting my will to that of some domineering sister-in-law (there are only a few requirements she says: he must be brahmin, must not smoke or drink, and must be vegetarian. And he must be the oldest son. "From one direction Anna manni, from another direction Jaya manni—we don't want that," she says, in caustic tones).

"Deepa" . . . my mother whispers to me early one morning in Tirunelveli before the news of her short hair has reached my grandfather, "I'm pregnant." That is my mother. No fussing with words, no fiddling with myths of how babies come into the world, just the plain fact conveyed as if she were talking to a close friend, a confidante: "I'm pregnant." I am barely awake, and so I nod and go straight back to sleep, hardly registering the news or my mother's apparent happiness, while she lies beside me, stroking my hair perhaps, or slowly sipping a tumbler of coffee. But the crows are loud outside, and soon I have to wake up. My cousins and I play for long hours on the terrace, and at the old water pump, the sun beating down on us, slowly burning to bronze the brown of our skin.

By the time my sister is born one May morning in 1979, my mother's hair is long again. Appa's older brother and wife are preparing to move into the house next door to ours. Appa has arranged it for them so the family can be closer, but his decision is carried out much against my mother's wishes. My mother's hair is long again, but thinning, beginning to gray, and she selects blouses to wear with her chiffon and georgette saris so carelessly, they hardly ever match. Her sister, who is always impeccably dressed, who still wears the glass bangles that filled her arms at the time of her first pregnancy, is amazed. "Yen, Gashi, you have such beautiful saris, why do you wear them like this?" Gowri Chitti, the older of my mother's two younger sisters, calls my mother "Gashi," a name given to her by an infant niece who mispronounces "Kousi" as "Gashi." The three then unmarried youngest sisters are delighted with Uma's baby talk, and the name sticks, conveying a closeness and friendship that is masked by the formal term for older sister, *Akka*. Gowri Chitti packs all my mother's saris in a suitcase and takes them to the cloth shop, where she selects matching blouse pieces for each sari. Then she has my mother measured and all the blouses sewn. The two sisters spend their time playing dress-up, that time in Vellore, wearing each other's saris and makeup and bangles. Of course, as with any other children's game, the charm wears off soon enough, and my mother's blouses are all mismatched again.

"Amma, can I call you Gashi also?" I ask, though I need not—the answer is predictable enough: "Yes, if you like." My mother never does mind such breaches. But I cannot, and neither can my sister. The intimacy is overwhelming. Instead, we call her *amma, ammi, ma*, and even *maamsam*, preserving at all times a distant familiarity, and a familiar distance.

So I am surprised, very surprised, when Gowri Chitti loses her temper at my mother one evening in Madras, when she has come to visit with her husband and son because my mother is alone with us, my father being away in Nigeria. It happens suddenly, almost at the exact moment that the monsoon bursts over the city. My mother stands in a corner of the kitchen, by the sink, and cries as Chitti's tirade continues. There is no food at home; Chitti is in a rage because there is no food at home. There is nothing prepared for her family; her son and her husband are going hungry. Would she do this if Gashi came to her home in Vellore? Would she neglect to feed Gashi's husband and the two girls? My aunt's sharp movements as she moves around the kitchen are accompanied by the sound of her glass bangles hitting against each other. Outside, in the bustling streets of Madras's Pondy Bazaar, there are an abundance of restaurants and eateries, but the absence of food at home expresses, above all, a certain lack of caring that is unexpected, even unthinkable, for it is a break in cultural and emotional communication, a loss of language.

My mother stands by the kitchen sink and cries as the tirade continues. (She cries softly, I think, and that is unusual. My mother never cries softly. She never gives in and sobs to herself like this. There is always a loud argument, a big fight, with all the demons climbing out of the dark shadows of her mind and sitting there—just like that—in a ring in the middle of the room. I strain my eyes to see them. Always a fight to the death, when something in my mother and something else in my father dies a violent and terrible death.)

On the back of an old photograph of my mother in a cotton sari, two long plaits, and girl guide tie are these lines in her familiar handwriting:

Born in 1945.
Did M.Sc. in Holy Cross, Trichi.
Married to Sankarji in Sept., 1971.
Made her husband's life
A fountain of perennial happiness thereafter!!

It is as if she has proved herself, proved something to herself, by getting a master's degree and working before her marriage. So now my mother proceeds to ask my father's permission for everything she does as a matter of ritual course. She knows the role of an Indian, a Brahmin, a Hindu wife, and she tries to play it faithfully, but as the sharp edges of her conservative Brahminism cut deep into her hopes and dreams and ambitions of independence, as the role of the fourth daughter-in-law in her husband's household interferes persistently with her status as an educated woman from a prominent Kallidaikurichi family, my mother begins to break. "Don't answer them," my father counsels her, before visits to his older brothers' homes. "Don't answer, just keep quiet." What he does not add is this: "because I cannot defend you, because they are my older brothers and sisters-in-law, and we are a family, we must be close like a family; they can taunt, but you must not respond because *it is not right,* I do not know how to defend you against my own brothers who have brought me up." But with my mother it is always a fight—she has a flair for the dramatic—always a gruesome fight to the bitter end.

"Your thatha was a very important person in the village"; she would tell us stories about him in the night. He owned four houses and the first car in Kallidaikurichi. Rajaji used to visit him, and Ariyakudi came to *his* house to teach Pati (my grandmother) music.[4] When we visit I notice the photograph of Rajaji hanging above a doorway; I see that the police have bought the property he owned beside Tilak Mahal Bungalow in Kallidaikurichi, and they let my youngest aunt use the telephone when she needs it because she is Kolathu Iyer's daughter. Thatha's phone number is the number of the police station. The post office sets up shop in the now unused garage. "Do you know where the word *Kallidaikurichi* comes from?" Appa is in a joking mood. My sister and I giggle in anticipation of his response; "No, where?" "There were two boys standing under a tree. Suddenly one of them saw a crow sitting above them on a branch. He said to the other boy, '*hai da—kall edu ya* (*hey, you, get a stone*)!' But before they throw the stone the crow says 'kurrrr' and drops on the boy's head. '*Chi*' says the boy in disgust when he realizes there is bird dropping in his hair." Kalledu-kurrrr-chi—that is how the name *Kallidaikurichi* came into being. My mother glances at him from the corner of her eye and bites her lip to suppress a smile.

(There are paddy fields now where my father's village once was; only the small Shiva temple is left standing, tended to by a single priest in the mornings and evenings. I drink in the air and the vast stretches of paddy green; the breeze mixes the sound of temple bells with burning camphor and incense. But my father's descriptions of what was once a village called Chirumazhanji are always unreal; the village remains—like R. K. Narayan's fictional Malgudi—a place of the imagination inhabited by scores of amusing characters, including a little boy who, asked to fetch a flask of buttermilk for his teacher, drinks half and fills the flask with water to disguise his mischief. "Folktales," my sister calls Appa's stories even when she is only six or seven years old. And as Appa tells of the path he walked to go to school, the mango tree he climbed to steal ripe fruit, the tangerines he ate at midnight once, I try hard to visualize this place that he describes, but the streets and buildings and orchards that appear in my mind are suspiciously similar to those I know in Kallidaikurichi. The Chirumazhanji of my mind's invention is a fictional town that I can never place amid the vast stretches of paddy green, next to the small Shiva temple, tended to by a single priest in the mornings and evenings. We never visit the town of my father's later childhood, Vallivor. Somewhere in the distance is the outline of another *gopuram*: it is Sastankoil, temple of Sasta, who is our "*kuladaivam*," or family deity. Appa's grandfathers or great-grandfathers are supposed to have contributed substantially toward the building of the shrine. My mind places the figure of my paternal grandfather, a poor middle-aged brahmin man with *vibhuti* streaked across his forehead in the traditional Iyer caste marking, outside Sastankoil, the sun beating down on him, serving buttermilk from a clay pot to workers from the fields. My paternal grandfather dies when Appa is only ten, leaving his younger sons and all his grandchildren few memories of himself. We visit Sastankoil now as though we are making a pilgrimage to the ancient source of our heritage; we bring new spouses here, maybe also new children, and as with all pilgrimages, we do not come frequently, for the place is quite far away. In the end, my sister and I trace our descent through our mother, from the place we visit not as reluctant pilgrims but as schoolchildren on holiday, from the grandfather who takes us on a tour to see the famous temples of the South, storing large ripe guavas in his aluminum carrying case and rationing them out, lest we get sick by eating them all at once. We gather together the bits and pieces of our history and heritage from the many rooms at Tilak Mahal Bungalow in Kallidaikurichi.)

After my father has left, my mother buys a bottle of Horlicks. "Oh god, Amma, why did you buy Horlicks?" My sister and I simply detest drinking Horlicks mixed with warm milk. "Don't worry, it's not for you, it's for Thatha." "*Yedduku, Gashi,*" my youngest aunt interrupts our celebrations, complaining, "Appa will not drink all this. *Ellam waste aahum.*" My mother is silent. Or at least I imagine she is. For my part, I am now crushed over this ten-rupee bottle of Horlicks because my mother's hesitant gesture has not been understood, will not reach her father for what it is meant to be. "Your father," she will tell us about her husband, "does not know how to express himself. He cannot show his affections very clearly." And yet my mother, for all her talents and demonstrations, always gets it all wrong. In Bombay, Atthai asks, pointing to us, "*Ivvalukku yenna pudikkyum?*" [What do they like (to eat)?"] and my mother replies—without hesitation—"*Poruccha-kurambu.*" Kapila and I suffer through three or four more meals of this mixed vegetable curry with coconut and dal that we have had practically every day for as long as we can remember before pulling my mother aside in that small flat, overcrowded and overpowering in its dark dankness, begging her to please suggest something else for the next meal. It is a great joke with us, of course, that Amma does not know how much we hate the dish, how tired we are of eating it, a great joke because it is such a perfect example of how she always gets it all wrong, upside down, mixed up. (And what does Amma tell Atthai? "Porr-chomb!" stressing the syllables with comic exaggeration: we are tickled pink with the memory.)

In Toronto my mother gradually grows obsessed with prayer, with ritual, the washing of the hands and feet, reciting just so many lines of prayer every morning and just so many more in the evenings. In Toronto I stay away from home on Saturday evenings, inventing some pretext or other of school work, preparatory meetings for presentations and seminars, later and later still just to avoid the hours of chanting Sanskrit verse like automatons. There is a deepening obsession with being brahmin, the twice-born, the purest of the pure, and obsession ushers in a kind of madness. My mother knows the roles of a Brahmin, a Hindu, an Indian wife, and tries to play them faithfully, and then when her dreams clash with her own expectations of what it means to be a Brahmin, an Indian, a Hindu wife, clash again with her daughters' interpretations, grate painfully against each other, it is a gruesome fight to the bitter end.

Madness, says my sister, in a moment of uncharacteristic bitterness and uncontrolled anger, runs in our family. And unfortunately that means us, too.

Really, I know that my mother does not care about neat houses and decorated tables, beautiful saris and thinly sliced cucumbers. Spending time in the kitchen is a colossal waste of time for her when there are books to be read, music to be learned. She never cares much for the unexplained affection of a favorite dish prepared on a birthday or some special occasion, or for the expressiveness of a meal cooked in anticipation of somebody's visit, somebody else's tiredness or hunger. She does not sit by us and fill our plates as we empty them, but tells us to finish up faster and clean the table. "You must not be fussy about food," she says. "You must be able to eat *anything*," and indeed that is just what we do, as a matter of necessity and ritual course. Sometimes my mother reads to us while we are eating, while we are playing with our food, making mountains of rice and rivers and lakes of yogurt. My mother's affections are contained in the books she reads to us and the music she teaches us, a single-minded and solitary preoccupation with knowledge and learning. And then when we are too old to be read to and too far away or too busy to spend hours singing, there is a break, a cut, *a loss of language.* How to speak now, and what to say?

Sometimes, my mother makes me put my hand on her belly, as I would when she was carrying my sister. This is where you were, she says, holding my hand in place, as if keeping it there for longer and longer still would deepen the natural bond between us. At other times she is angry because I am being rebellious and disrespectful: "*Patthu masama unna thookkinen, marakkade*" ["I carried you around for ten months, don't forget"], she says resentfully. But we have done away with cultural formulae, and opted instead for a kind of universal friendship, a relationship based in the objective exchange of ideas, in the open sharing of emotions. And when that does not work, neither then does the last-ditch attempt to retrieve the relationship by invoking a kind of biological guilt. How to speak now, and what to say?

I do not write about my mother, or even about myself. I write about the innumerable details that make a relationship that began, as my mother might say, with the ten months I was inside her belly: a relationship that begins as a biological tie and a cultural given, already understood and already planned according to certain prescribed cultural formulae, with only marginal allowances for deviations or unpredictable eventualities. But deviations and unexpected eventualities have an odd way of taking over, of exceeding by far their marginality with dogged determination, and suddenly I realize they are all I have to write with.

Reading this, my mother will say, "Deepa, always remembers all petty details"; she keeps track of little silly things: the thinly sliced cucumbers, the porccha kurambu, and my mother's mismatched sari blouses. Yes, I am interested in such details. But that is because if I began with a statement such as "My mother and I have not spoken for three years now, and counting"—if I began with that kind of bold, almost brutal statement of fact—I would not know what to say next, where to go with that thought, except into long, involved sentimental–emotional rationalizing explanations, and that is far too draining a prospect to consider. Also, it would hardly be fair to begin with a statement like that one, to enlarge the last three years of our lives to a daunting size, emphasizing the shock value they hold. And there is shock value, isn't there, in the sharp cracking of that uncrackable maternal bond, in the undoing of a relationship that began, as my mother might say, with the ten months I was inside her belly? No, I would rather focus on cucumbers and sari blouses for the quiet solace of their banality.

THREE

marriage

So finally, Deepa, you will be part of our family

When the news is out that Shrikanth and I intend to be married, I go to visit his aunt whom I have known well for some years before. "So finally, Deepa," she says to me, putting her arm around me, "you will be part of our family." It is a happy moment, of course, but I cannot help but feel just the slightest twinge because I have to realize at last that there is no such thing as fictive kin. I do not intend an absolute generalization of course, but mean only to say that kinship does on some level describe and circumscribe a set of *formal* relationships, and for as long as you say "She is *like* my own daughter" or "He is *like* a brother to me," the relationship remains—like the language used—a simile, a stand-in: always a comparison, and never the real thing.

I wonder, what is it that prompts my cousin, many years my senior, who knew me first as a baby in Assam and then very briefly as a teenager, determined *not* to study computer science, to attend my wedding specifically because she knows my mother will likely not be there? What is it that urges Malathi Akka to make the long journey from Trichy to Bangalore with her two sons and husband though she is ill with cancer, urges her brothers to take it upon themselves to talk to Kousi Chitti in Toronto, tell her, entreat her to go to India because her daughter is to be married? To explain all this by merely invoking the obligatory duties of kinship would be to reduce my cousin's actions to something far less than they were. To explain all this by invoking simultaneously many levels of closeness, obligation, affection, loyalty, and duty would be more accurate, more acceptable. But then do I begin with the story my mother tells me of how she falls down a staircase in Kallidaikurichi, and how Chandra Periamma (Malathi Akka's mother), who loves her younger sister deeply, rushes to her side in a panic and uses the cloth of her new silk sari to bind the wound on my mother's forehead? Perhaps I should start instead with the many hours Malathi Akka spends sewing little frocks for me, with her friendship with my father, who drives her and her husband from Digboi to Shillong for their honeymoon. I have little assurance, however, that once

I tell all these stories and analyze them in great detail, I will have established the exact nature of my cousin's closeness, obligations, affections, and loyalties. I think I shall have to take the easy way out: *not* by suggesting that Malathi Akka comes to my wedding merely because she is a relative, but by pointing out simply that my closest friends send wedding cards to us in Bangalore that summer because they are in Calcutta and Madras and Benaras taking care of their mothers and fathers, making sure *their* children are spending enough time with uncles, aunts, and grandparents.

A friend here in Houston, hearing that my mother has no plans to come to my wedding, is confident that she will come around. "She is mother, she will come," he says with remarkable certainty. Mark the words. *She is mother*— not "your" mother, not "Deepa's" mother, but just *mother*, the culturally specific figure of the nurturing, sacrificing woman whose bond to her children is so strong, nothing can surpass it. Indeed, my mother does come in the end. But she comes to play exactly that role of the nurturing, sacrificing woman whose bond to her children is so strong, nothing can surpass it: she performs this role, too, as a matter of ritual course. A Hindu couple must always participate in ceremonies and rituals together; in rituals and ceremonies they are an integral unit. For as long as my mother stands beside my father as he chants the lines that the priests dictate, helping him pour milk into our hands or ghee into the fire, no questions are asked, no eyebrows are raised. And even in the artificial togetherness of these fleeting moments there is a level of comfort for each of us, of the kind that comes from sinking into a predetermined role as one might sink into the familiar cushions of an old chair, of the kind that comes from disregarding one's tutored tendencies toward skepticism, disbelief, and criticism, and finding underneath it all a place, a function, a set of responsibilities, but above all, a place.

All that closeness is gone now, says my mother, thinking of her fall down the Kallidaikurichi staircase, and the way Chandra Periamma rushes to her side in a panic, tearing a piece of her new silk wedding sari to bind my mother's wound. Is closeness only measured in such moments? A year after I am married, Chandra Periamma and Swaminathan Periappa visit Bangalore and make it a point to meet my in-laws. Then, while visiting family in Calgary later in the year, they phone me on my birthday. I am amazed that they have even remembered the date and thank them also for their invitations to my in-laws in Bangalore. "That was so very good of you," I tell them, fumbling for the right words to convey my gratitude. "Nanna so enjoyed meeting you." My Uncle replies simply, "But that is what we *do*, isn't it?" And in so *doing*, my uncles and aunts who hardly know me except as "Kousi oda ponnu" soften the harsh brahmin orthodoxy that prevents my mother from accepting my marriage, draw me closer and closer still by their most natural gestures of acceptance and inclusion.

May 25—12:30 P.M.

This is my formal arrival into my husband's home. I am still in my wedding sari, looking somewhat more disheveled than I did before the car ride from the *mandapam* and holding a framed photograph of the goddess Lakshmi in my right hand. For the first time in the ceremony, I am asked to move in front of my husband and enter the house before him. As I cross the threshold, I must kick the vessel of rice and jaggery placed there so the contents spill out onto the floor. My gesture is symbolic of the prosperity that I will bring to my new home. Then I am taken with my husband into the puja room, where I place the picture of Lakshmi, light the lamps, and pause for a moment of prayer. The photographer, suddenly realizing the significance of this moment, asks us to hold that pose so he may capture it for our wedding albums.

The next day, I arrive with my husband at his home for the *sambandhi chappaadu*, the traditional lunch given by the groom's family. It is well after eleven in the morning. Shrikanth's aunt approaches us at the gate. *"Idu eppidi?"* ("How can this be?") she teases in Tamil. "Should a daughter-in-law arrive so late or should she come early and make coffee for all of us?" My father beside me is laughing heartily, wondering perhaps, if I know how to make good coffee at all.

Perhaps I should have been more careful in picking out my first gift to my new mother-in-law, but I was thinking rather too practically. I thought a set of six knives and a wooden block to hold them would be a perfect present, useful, and not too large or small for a first gift. The knives I remember using in Madras stayed sharp for the first week; after that my sister and I literally had to saw vegetables into pieces. My gift is appreciated, no doubt, but I am teased to no end about it. You see, I had forgotten completely that knives are not given as gifts to anybody, because they are such sharp unfriendly instruments. But if that problem is easily overcome by paying me a token one rupee, the image of a daughter-in-law arriving at her new home wielding *six* knives and a block of wood to boot is far too amusing to be quickly banished. I am suddenly transformed, in this room full of new faces, to a Kali-like figure with six arms, each holding one shiny new American steak knife.

Come, come, now, interjects another aunt, don't scare her. But really, I am scared already, unsure of how to stand and where to sit, who to talk to and what to say. I do not know the role I am supposed to play. Suddenly I realize the pointlessness of thinly sliced cucumbers arranged in attractive spirals on glass plates with carrots, perhaps, or tomatoes for color. The cauliflower is tougher here, the sugar not quite as sweet, the chilies not hot enough. I am used to canned beans and ten-minute dinners; I lack the basic culinary tools of expression that my mother, too, fumbled for many years ago. And when my mother-in-law is away, I do not know how to sit by Nanna and fill his plate as he eats; in my awkwardness and uncertainty, I am more inclined to wish that the meal be over quickly so I can clear the table. Amma says quite matter-of-factly when we praise her meals, "I don't like cooking. But somebody has to do it, no?" A sense of an ordained place in the world. The place I always held as "Kousi oda ponnu" is elsewhere. Here, now, I am someone's wife and someone's daughter-in-law (in Telugu, kodalu; pointing to the kitchen where chicken curry is being prepared, I ask, "Am I *kodalu pilla* or *kodi pilla* [daughter-in-law child or chicken child]"? making my husband's aunt laugh and pinch my cheek gently). I have lost my frame of reference; I am out of context. It is not that Amma and Nanna have any expectations of me, not that the role of "kodalu" hangs like iron ropes around my neck. Had that been the case I would likely be telling a story of restrictions and resentments, not of cauliflower and diffidence. In fact, had there been a set of clearly defined expectations, a predetermined list of duties to perform; had Amma sat back and waited for coffee in the morning, *rasam* and *koora* (curry) in the afternoon, and dosas at night, I would have known to pinpoint my place in and through these things; I would have known to say *this* defines my role as daughter-in-law here, *this* is my place. Instead, Amma keeps me away from the kitchen: "You will have plenty of this to do when you go back to the States," she says. "Why do you want to do it here also?" When the *doing* is not merely a matter of practice, habit, and ritual course, it becomes even more a matter of communication, of shaping and reaffirming the bonds of kinship. I apologize to Amma, when she returns from a trip to the village, for using up all her oil and wasting milk and for cooking rather badly. It's okay, she says, you did something. Who else would have been here to do even this much for Nanna? Slowly, but very slowly, I am drawn into another frame, and uncertainty gives way to something already constituted, already understood.

FOUR

distancing

A few weeks after the wedding, sitting on the sofa in my in-laws' home, I am reading a letter published in the *Deccan Herald* newspaper. A woman has found, tucked in the lining of her old trunk that carried her saris and dowry to her husband's home, a folded hundred rupee note. After wondering for a few moments how the note could have been so carelessly left in the trunk, she concludes that it was not carelessly forgotten there at all, but was probably hidden deliberately by her own mother: a wedding gift, money for an emergency, money to pay for a train ticket should she ever need or wish to return home. The woman wonders how her mother could have had so much money, and she thinks of the years she must have secretly saved to give her daughter this most precious of gifts. "As it happens I did not need it," she writes, "but I am so grateful for the thoughtfulness and care it represents. How many other daughters might have needed this money desperately?" "Thank you," says the woman, "for celebrating my marriage, *and* letting me know that I could still come home if I needed to."[5]

Reading this letter, I feel distinctly lucky to be born in a place and time where such distances between a woman's natal and affinal families are not so insurmountable and marriage does not necessarily mean leaving your parents' home for good. Today nobody objects when my cousin's wife stays with her parents, who happen to be in the same city, moving back and forth as and when she is needed in each place. And yet, we think of the arrangement as temporary: it has to be, because she is married now. And yet, there is distance: stories in magazines and newspapers and in the case histories maintained by women's groups of young wives who turn to their families for help and are told to return, at once or after a decent interval, to their husbands' homes; the implicit understanding that after my wedding, I will stay with my in-laws, even if my husband has returned to Houston; Amma's warning that staying too long with your wife's family will reduce your esteem in their eyes.

When Kapila and I play games in Thatha's home on our visits to Kallidaikurichi, we are careful to keep a safe distance from the room at the end of the passageway. It is a small room, we can see, and the wooden doors have metal bars, letting in the sunshine and the noises of our games. Inside there is a woman, Indumati Periamma, the fourth daughter of Kolathu Iyer and Seethalakshmi. I remember her in a blue sari and black blouse, her hair loose, sitting still mostly. We are curious, but we dare not approach, because we think, we believe, we have been told that she is mad. Sometimes she sings, and we listen because it is strange to hear her and because she sings well. She had the same esteemed teachers that Pati did, and my mother. In Thatha's front office, there is a photograph of her, taken on the day of her wedding. She is tall and elegant, with very striking features and a gaze that penetrates.

Amma tells us that she has a son in Coimbatore, where her husband is, and we learn from overheard conversations that she was beaten sometimes by a drunken husband, and then given shock treatment repeatedly by her in-laws because they believed her to be mad. Chitti always closes the door to the dining hall before bringing Indu Periamma out to bathe and feed her. At night, we are put to bed first before she is allowed to come out of her room. We learn from overheard conversations that Thatha is urging her to go home to her family because that is where she should be. She has a son who is twelve to take care of. Sometimes when we visit Kallidaikurichi the room is empty, and sometimes Periamma is there. My mother asks her once, *"Akka yaaru theriyarada"* ["Akka, do you know who I am"]? and she replies abruptly, "O!—[but of course]—Kousi." My mother does not tell us anything more.

In early 1985, she disappears suddenly. My mother tells us she ran away from her husband's home in Coimbatore. The most comforting conclusion available is that she must by now be dead.

Kinship is its own mythology, and in the particular world that it imagines here, my aunt's story is whispered, put into parentheses, because it is out of place within the narratives of kinship—not out of the ordinary, just terribly out of place. This story of my aunt slips and falls into the gaps of kinship; it disappears into the distances created and legitimized by the mythology of kinship; it crashes silently into the darkened depths below. Oddly enough, it would take a narrative as far removed from my aunt's life in Kallidaikurichi and Coimbatore as *One Flew Over the Cuckoo's Nest* to provide us a means to understand something of what must have happened to her. "They gave her shock treatment, Deepa," my mother tells me at the most unexpected moments, her voice edged with acid anger, like when I am passing her in the hall or getting ready to take a bath. *They gave her shock treatment.* I never know how to respond.

On our family tree, my aunt's name is followed by a black dot that indicates she is no longer alive, but she is there still with her husband and son, just like the rest of us, *as if* her family was like any other on the tree. My mother is angry because her sister is labeled as "mad" and then that her treatment is drastic and brutal, but she too accepts, in her most practical moments, that her sister must return to Coimbatore: there is, after all, no life for a married woman in her father's home. "It is sad to have a daughter," says my mother. "Why," I interrupt [I have had enough of this], "because you would rather have had a son?" But my mother continues as though she has not heard me: ". . . because she will have to leave home someday, and she will suffer." She leans toward me and runs her fingers through my hair. My Indu Periamma is trapped not merely by a cultural practice that we call "virilocality" but by the very *givenness* of the practice, its unquestioned status, its assumed nature. Along with the hundred rupee note tucked away into the lining of an old trunk, my aunt's story is a secret closely guarded by the mythology of kinship, in the one case because it represents an unthinkable possibility, and in the other because the unthinkable happens. Like the hundred rupee note, my aunt's story tells of certain cultural practices taken as given, and in so doing exposes a yellow-white underbelly that this particular mythology has no tools to accept or language to describe.

No language, that is, other than that of yearning. Margaret Trawick describes the process of "seeking mother" (in Tamil, *ammavai thedi*) as a "natural activity . . . a formula" in which all women, no matter how old or how far away, participate (Trawick 1990: 166). The power of the metaphor lies, however, in the unattainability of its end: had my grandmother been alive, I suspect that my aunt would still have been told, like she was by her sisters, to return to her husband and son after an interval. The given closeness of a biological tie is ultimately superseded by the given distance of kinship.

The fluidity of kinship practices? Why, it would take two generations from my grandfather's time, many social movements and political agitations, and shifts of global economies for the encoded message of the hidden hundred rupee note to give way to other, more direct interventions.

Reading the letter in the *Deccan Herald* and sifting through scattered memories of my missing aunt, I suddenly understand a phone call I receive from a much older cousin in Bombay. I think he is calling to speak to my father-in-law, but he tells me he wants to find out how I am and to say that if I need anything—*anything at all*—I should not hesitate to let him know. I am a little startled by his insistence, a little shaken by his reading of me as just another Indian woman to get married, who is no less unlikely, for all her education and independence, to face harassment, or the burden of her own uncertainty: in my mother's words, to *suffer*. I turn red as I speak to him, though I know no one else can hear us, but I am deeply touched.

Indeed, there is this distance, and amid all the talk of marriage as a grand ritual of kinship, family, alliance, and togetherness there must also be talk of marriage as a *gendered* ritual of distancing and displacement.[6] Kinship measures and maintains distance just as much as it measures and maintains closeness. My husband's aunt says, "We were so afraid that you would not talk to us, that you would sit there"—she points to a corner—"and not mix with us." And that would have been the ultimate failure of kinship, wouldn't it?—a breach of a most intimate kind, if distancing from my natal family did not occur, or if distance was imposed where there was the expectation of closeness. Of course marriage marks a *formal* moment of distancing, an accepted moment, so my cousin from Bombay can phone sometime after my father has left the country to fill this gap that my parents might otherwise have filled, as if to say there is this distance, we know it and we accept it, but it need not be so vast. His is an intervention that checks the seemingly unstoppable flow of this kinship narrative, prevents it from writing itself further and from growing large and self-satisfied with its own dominance. My cousin's intervention is an intervention that insists—however haltingly—on the need for another kind of ending to this story.[7]

Can I admit now, after all I have said, that I am glad to be distanced from my family's Brahminism? Even though all I have done is exchange one caste for another, I am grateful to escape wearing the traditional brahmin nine-yard sari at my wedding. I have seen my cousins wear it at their weddings: it does not need a petticoat, and so you have to stand in only your undergarments in front of so many women while they tie it around you. It is embarrassing, and then the sari looks bulky. I would not know how to hold myself in it. So I am glad to escape this Brahminism into which I am born; it hangs around me in awkward drapes that I have never learned to hold. "*Akka*, what is your *gotra*?"[8] Shrikanth's cousin asks me soon after we are married. "Bharadhwaja," I reply, and my husband jokes, nudging me: "Yeah, the Brahmins took all the nice gotras for themselves and left us with names like 'Kanagala'!" The utter seriousness of it all eludes us for the moment; the arbitrariness of caste distinctions in modern Indian society dissolves easily in the laughter of our privilege. So I can poke fun at my cousin Shekhar, telling him he looks *like* a good Brahmin boy because he is wearing the right clothes, only to be reprimanded by an older man who overhears me (he is not *like* a good Brahmin boy, he *is* a good Brahmin boy!). The tensions remain in the world outside these large brooding things, but at home they are the stuff good jokes are made from. We even laugh gleefully at the orthodox brahmin woman who, discovering that my father is brahmin and my husband is not, looks me up and down with a gaze that burns me to the ground, sizes me up perhaps as one of "those" women.[9] "The price of meat has gone up now because all the Brahmins have started eating it," quips my mother-in-law (who is herself vegetarian), and as I imagine my mother's expression turning from horror at the joke to despair at the state of affairs in the world, I am grateful to be able to escape this past, with all its convoluted justifications of itself, by laughing at it so openly.

I am not, however, just speaking of marriage. It has taken years of *unlearning* these very established codes and markings that guide my affections, that temper my sentiments, to accommodate the gulf between my mother and me. It has taken years of conscientious unlearning of affections, loyalties, and obligations to submit myself to this distance with indifference, or, at the very least, with poise.

To many in my family, this would be a stunning admission, an unimaginable acceptance of a profound failure and a profound loss of nothing less than *Mother*. It strikes me, as I imagine their reactions, that I have said too much already. I have wound myself tightly into the very corner I wanted to avoid. To escape it, I will have to get into long rationalizing emotional–sentimental explanations to which there is no beginning and no logical end. And rather than becoming mired in all that, I shall have to do as I normally would when some well-meaning friend asks too many close questions, or when I, not knowing how to draw the line or where to place it, volunteer too much information. Before it is too late, I shall have to retreat into the pretense of kinship, with all of its always–already understood elements circumventing the need for further explanation.

FIVE

formulae

My mother says sometimes that I will marry her brother's son, my cross-cousin, and Raji Chitti teases me about the idea. When the time comes, so also does the proposal, but nobody is disappointed or angry that I turn it down flatly. The proposal is from a different time and place, I think, but my father is simply relieved not to have to reinforce his ties to his wife's family in this drastic manner. I meet Shekhar a year later in Austin. He shows me photographs of himself and his buddies taken after Black Sabbath concerts, when they are still not completely drunk. The more anti-Christ, the better, he informs me, speaking also of how much he has reformed himself.

So I do not marry my biological cross-cousin, though my marriage creates the same relationship between my husband and me: by the names I must call my in-laws, his aunts and uncles, I realize my father has become his mother's brother, and my mother his father's sister. My husband and I are cousins in terminology, whichever way you look at it; our marriage creates a grand new network of formal kinship ties. But my father and my father-in-law address each other not as *bava* (brother-in-law) but as "Mr. Bhaskara Reddi" and "Mr. Sankaran." There is an awkwardness, perhaps, about how to bridge this gap between communities, traditions, and languages. The common denominator—put in place by default—is English. So although this is an Indian wedding that joins together two Indian families in a tight knot of kinship ties, with each loop and thread clearly defined and named, a certain inevitable awkwardness creeps in and translates everything into a foreign tongue.

Shrikanth's younger brother and some of his cousins are instructed to call me "*vadina*," or older sister-in-law. The word sounds funny and strange and alien, and nobody seems to care for its formality, especially because I am younger than any of them. Of course, my own age is not supposed to matter; what does matter is that I have married the eldest son in the family, and am, by that relationship alone, the eldest daughter-in-law. Nanna impresses on me the importance of this role. "You are the oldest daughter-in-law," he tells me, "you have great responsibility." But I know already that the name and the accompanying expectations are things from another time and place. The affections they express and the relationships they structure belong to a time and place where the closeness of friendship has not yet replaced the closeness of kinship ties. So it takes conscious effort to use the old names, deliberate actions, like the time I tell my cousin's two-year-old son that I am not "Aunty" but "Chitti"; not some distant family friend, but his mother's younger sister. And when my brother-in-law Arvind puts aside the knowledge that he is a month my senior and calls me "vadina" ("Deepa," he says, and then after a pause ". . . vadina") it is a conscious effort to tap into the feelings and emotions conveyed by the name. The names evoke kinship: particular kinds of relationships with particular kinds of cultural expectations, loyalties, and affections spread thick and even on them (cf. Trawick 1990: 151–55). But we have done away with cultural formulae and opted instead for a kind of universal friendship based in the objective exchange of ideas, in the open sharing of emotions. We are all related, we know, cousins of the same age group and with similar education. But there is nothing always–already constituted or presumed or given about our relationships;

there are no more encoded inequalities. Our relatedness means only that now we can begin to get to know each other as friends. "Do you call your brother 'Anna' [older brother]?" I ask a friend. "No!" he replies, "the guy doesn't deserve it!" No longer is there any self-evident justification for this handed-down system of ordering inequalities. The names have become like titles, I suppose: one has to work to earn them.

("Amma, can I call you Gashi also?" I ask, though I need not—the answer is predictable enough: "Yes, if you like." My mother never does mind such breaches. But I cannot, and neither can my sister. The intimacy is overwhelming. Instead, we call her *amma, ammi, ma*, and even *maamsam*, preserving at all times a distant familiarity, and a familiar distance.)

And yet, the names constitute a point of reference to which we frequently return. When I meet Malathi Akka after many years of living in Canada I address her simply as "Malathi"—I am not thinking—and there is instantly a certain stiffness in the air, a measure of aloofness. I do not know her well enough to call her by her first name. "Akka" reintroduces a point of reference, provides an irrevocable link to a small village near Tirunelveli called Kallidaikurichi, and to a vast extended family that lives all over India and all over the globe. "Akka" softens the moment, gives us a common background, skirts the need for a deliberately and meticulously constructed friendship.

I wonder sometimes if my mother realizes that I have indeed married an oldest son, as she always wanted. I think that more likely she has forgotten this requirement in favor of other things, just as she forgets tunes to songs she once set. I remember the songs, each and every one, in Tamil, English, and sometimes also in Hindi, but when I sing them my mother hardly recognizes the tunes she once set, and then when I tell her, she seems indifferent. So I don't imagine she has even noticed that I am married to an oldest son, though I remember and want to show off to her as if I have won some coveted prize at school, because this is what she always said she wanted. Could she have predicted, however, the shift that would take place, that would steadily lessen the importance of these roles and privilege instead authority resting on such things as education and experience? I think perhaps that she could. My mother searches for that authority in all that she does, strives for it in the hours she spends poring through *Small Is Beautiful* and *The ABCs of Relativity*, and ensures that her daughters will have it also by teaching us English before our mother tongue Tamil. And yet, sitting in the cool of our living room in Nigeria, the woman who insists on working *before* getting married and who then educates her daughters so they can do the same does not see the world changing around her. And when she finally does, it is such a shock that she must wrap herself in her nine-yard sari for protection.

But I do not write about my mother, nor even about myself. I write about the words and things we use to define our worlds, and about how these grow old, leaving us to rethink and redefine our links to one another. It is meant to be about the inability of one woman to do just this, for while her longings and aspirations are rooted in one time, her beliefs and convictions are fading into another. And then my mother's story within this larger tale of kinship is meant to be *about* a system of ordering gender and other inequalities that my mother rejects with every breath and yet willingly upholds because it is the only source of her self. The contradiction that shapes my mother's life dissipates in my own:

traditions,
named and renamed—
translated
and trans-located

fold one upon the other
like pleats in a sari
which rustles, whispers
as I walk.

—from "Id-entity" by
Lakshmi Gopinathan Nayar

SIX

pretensions

Years I have spent wishing for a family of friends. The greatest achievement was to be fast friends with your mother, your father, your cousins, I thought, turning the stark reality of your blood bond into a relationship on equal footing, of ideas, emotions, feelings.

"Does Amma ever talk about me?" I ask my sister in a moment of weakness. "Yes," she replies, "sometimes. But then she talks about you as if you were a small child again, you know, the way you used to say you were not hungry—'yenakkupaschikallaima'"—Kapila imitates my baby talk as she has heard our mother repeat it. It strikes me now after all these pages that I have done much the same thing: I have said my piece with childhood memories, randomly assembled things from a distant past, collapsing my adult years with my mother in Toronto to a paragraph here, a few lines there. There is a break, a cut, a loss of language, and I retreat into a pretense of kinship because that is what is most easily understood, most easily communicable. The "family" is a rhetorical device that requires no translation, or any further explanation of my motives or intentions or choices.

"It is not right," says my father with an increasing sense of exasperation, when he realizes that I will not be convinced to marry someone of his choice, "what will happen to the family?" And I reply, cruelly, "What family?" But I know that once my anger has passed, I, too, am a willing participant in

this pretense; I too am shaped by this "family" that does not exist. I remember that my father is so happy, so very satisfied and pleased, when my mother finally announces her intention to attend my wedding. My father, who has sworn not even to print invitations, then ceremoniously presents me with one: "Kausalya and Ramachandran Sankaran cordially invite you to attend the wedding of their daughter. . . ." The invitation has been printed only for distribution to my father's colleagues and friends in Nigeria. Now we go around in the drenching humid heat of Madras handing the cards to family, friends, and relatives. I remember at the wedding the great pleasure Appa takes in performing the ceremonies with his wife by his side, his broad smile when my husband and I touch our heads to the floor to ask my parents' blessing moments after we are married. A Hindu couple must always participate in ceremonies and rituals together; in rituals and ceremonies they are an integral unit. For as long as my mother stands beside my father as he chants the lines that the priests dictate, helping him pour milk into our hands or ghee into the fire, no questions are asked, no eyebrows are raised. So this ceremony is the ultimate pretense, for it relies almost wholly on the rhetoric of the family; it puts the "family" on display for a brief but glamorous moment of triumph over unfulfilled desire and longing.[10] And after the ceremony, my mother leaves quickly for Canada and disappears into a resentful silence.

She is long gone, she is light-years away, and still, in spite of it all, she is my link to my past, my explanation of myself. When I am seven and a half or eight years old, my mother decides it is time for me to begin learning music. I don't remember how it all begins, but I do recall the long afternoons spent in practice: my mother's perseverance and her unusual techniques, how she makes me figure the *svaras* (notes) for each line of a song, forcing me to learn the piece not merely by repetition but also by understanding. The room fills with her irritation and my annoyance, her frustration and my restlessness, until the air is so hot and so thick that we can hardly bear to continue. It will take nearly ten years for me to discover that this music is our only form of communication, our language of kinship, if you will. It defines a kind of closeness for us at moments when the world that creeps in through workplace politics, peer pressure, television sets, and open windows creates too many dilemmas, too many strong disagreements. And so, when someone asks me where I learned music, and I reply that my mother taught me, it is that *particular* closeness that I describe. "She would make me sing that whole song over and over and over," I say, with much-delayed gratitude, resurrecting the image of the middle-class *mother* who spends hours with her children every day after school, helping them with homework and teaching them everything she knows. The image is not by any means a fiction—my mother *was* in many ways that *mother*—but from here onward the narrative of kinship enters, takes over, and writes itself.

("Seeta devi," my mother calls me sometimes, perhaps when I am wearing a sari on some special occasion, with my hair pulled back, a *bottu* on my forehead. "Seeta de—vi," extending the vowel to express affection; she touches my temples and pushes her knuckles against the sides of her head to ward off harmful forces from me. My mother places me in a familiar cultural category in an attempt to interpret me, not pausing to see if in fact I fit there. And now when I remember her out loud to people who want to know where I learned to sing, I place her, too, in a familiar cultural category, exorcising from my mind all that does not fit. Then I look over to the figure I have just introduced, and ask what song I should sing.)

Ever so often someone will ask me, "Do you think you might return to India someday?" and I always reply, "Yes, eventually"—and if the person demands more information, "because my family is there." It is so simple, you see, to invent that closeness and those responsibilities, and then to rely on tidy images of happy homes and happy families for the profound comfort of knowing you have a place within them. It is so easy because then everything is self-evident. My answer explains my sense of belonging without paradox or contradiction. Would I reveal instead that my parents are not even in India, that my mother cannot return now more than ever to the suffocating closeness of her husband's family after knowing what opportunities for work and education a North American city affords? Would I then tell of my father's resignation, and the awful dilemma of having to choose between one family in Toronto and another in India? If I did that, I would also have to draw my in-laws into the picture and explain how I have grown attached to them and why, tell of how their presence in Bangalore has deepened and strengthened my roots in India. Would I explain all this and so much more, in so many ways, in so many words? No, that is too much. I choose instead the simplest route: using merely the rhetoric of family, I offer an understanding of my belonging and identification without going into the mess of my family history, my cultural education, my personal commitments. Quite conveniently, I leave out the complexities and inexplicable details, like the deep sigh of relief that escapes me, even surprises me, when I land in Bombay's Sahar International Airport, in spite of the heat and humidity and politics and inefficiency and all the little details that make daily life so difficult and so tiring. And, as I have said before, my answer is accepted readily because it explains itself.

There is more to the rhetoric of family than just this, however, for all my inventions cannot exist without a semblance of truth at their core: somewhere, in the midst of all the ambivalences and ambiguities is indeed the very matrix of caring relationships and attachments, the tightly woven threads of interdependencies that are the heart of my pretense. The line between the imagined and the real begins to blur, and somewhere in between what is always–already given and what is always–already fluid is the force of this rhetorical device that draws me closer and closer still in most natural gestures of acceptance and inclusion. And though sometimes I resist, with all the strength I can muster, mostly I give in.

Like the woman who grows so large with all the stories she keeps inside her that one day, finding herself in a deserted old house, she tells all her tales to the walls, and they each collapse for they are now too heavy to stand upright. When the fourth wall falls, the woman looks down and sees she is thin again. Then she goes home.[11]

SEVEN

lines

I began with some lines written by Lévi-Strauss long after his return from travels in Brazil. Since the passage can apply specifically to the process of ethnographic analysis and, more broadly, to any other act of writing from memory, it blurs the lines between genres and styles, allows me to incorporate elements of analysis into autobiography, aspects of autobiography into an essay on kinship, privileging neither mode of thinking nor writing.

Then suddenly the categories I have set up collide, forcing me to define a hierarchy. I begin to insist that I write *in fact* about things larger than the individual events or people I describe: that, therefore, I write *more* about the complicity of kinship with overarching structures of power and inequality, *more* about kinship in an age of cosmopolitanism, than about myself, my mother, or my family. My insistence, however, serves to undermine itself by its own apparent arbitrariness: it is a diversion and an abrupt full stop; it is the line drawn in mythical sand, the ultimate *lakshman rekha*, and the excuse that allows me to escape for a time the unstoppable cascade of the autobiographical narrative. For when I am ready again to continue with the telling, it is too late to pick up where I leave off.

I want to produce a "resolutely social" tale that explores the ways in which the personal is always–already political. I am intent on dragging the intimate stuff of everyday life out of its assigned realm in personal narrative and pushing it into the limelight of political processes, where it rightly belongs. Indeed, I write not merely about the rule that permits cross-cousin marriage or the logic behind my mother's sister being my "Periamma" and her brother my "Mama." I write about caste, gender, and patriarchy; the inevitable chain of events that takes my father from a village outside Tirunelveli to Madras, Calcutta, Assam, Nigeria, Canada, and *back* to Madras in an endless search for education, jobs, opportunities for his children, and his own happiness in "family life." Any story of kinship in contemporary society is, no doubt, a national story, a transnational story, a cosmopolitan story that inhabits a world far larger than itself. But the act of inserting the family—*my* family—into these larger frames is also a way of explaining why this particular autobiography should be interesting; it is a way of locating the *relevance* of these stories to the study of kinship. To that end, I need the voice of an analyst, an ethnographer, a writer of academic prose well before I need the voice of "Kousi oda ponnu." This separation of voices and the relative privileging of one over the other usher in also a level of discomfort: there is a sense in which I am marginal in my own narrative. My insistence that I write about *more* than anecdotes and personal impressions constructs my academic authority. It indicates that these are not the muffled mutterings of a confession, the aimless wanderings of a collector in a curiosity shop, or the choice tidbits offered by a native informant—an awkward effort, I will admit, and somewhat contrived, but my words are the product of my discomfort. And rather than allow autobiography to become the tool, material, and "evidence" of a look at kinship, I would prefer to stretch its boundaries to their own natural breaking points, and only at the last moment, to preempt any questions about what the point of it all could be, take recourse to another kind of authority, and explain my game of lines. I want it to be known that there is indeed a point and an argument in all the details that I present, but even more, that autobiography carries its own authority because *it is itself the argument* (cf. Kondo 1990: 24–25).

"Things are not supposed to turn out this way," I imagine my mother thinking sometimes. I am supposed to marry her brother's son or someone else of my parents' choosing; she is supposed to dress me in beautiful clothes in the days before the wedding, when the house is buzzing with activity and friends and relatives are visiting. She is supposed to finish an education degree in Toronto and teach school there or in India. But the narratives we write for ourselves or that we are written into collide at every turn with the forces of unpredictability, with the armies of indeterminacy, making the task of staying on a preset course a dream, a desire, a profound longing. I am left with nothing but a suitcase full of knickknacks, details with no apparent connection, nor any large consequence, that I turn around on my palm realizing they are all I have to write with. And as I try to place them on paper, with all their gaps and inconsistencies and jagged edges, the impressions of a master narrative become visible, though it is clearer or more smudged in places. I find refuge in it sometimes; at other times it is suffocating, oppressive, and then I distance myself from it or challenge its edicts. But undo it completely I cannot: like a child in my mother's belly, sometimes kicking, sometimes quiet, I know it is the only source of my self.

NOTES

I would like to thank James Faubion, George Marcus, and Julie Taylor for going through several successive drafts of this chapter and for all the comments and encouragement along the way. Thanks also to my husband Shrikanth, who was a friend well before he became family, for helping me through many knots and blocks, as always. This is for Amma, of course, though she may never read it.

1. Sacred thread worn around the right shoulder and torso by brahmin men.

2. David Schneider writes that social kinship could never be freed of physical kinship, which is its "defining feature," "the very essence of what [is] deemed to be its significance: biology, procreation, conception, gestation, parturition, seen either as "the real thing" or the folk theory of it." "Robbed of its grounding in biology," he continues, "kinship is nothing" (1984: 111–12). Yanagisako and Collier further point out, "Although it is apparent that heterosexual intercourse, pregnancy, and parturition are involved in human reproduction, it is also apparent that producing humans entails more than this" (1987: 31). I take as my starting point the very "folk" conceptions of biological reproduction that Schneider argues are *contained* in kinship theory, and I try to move into those other "nonbiological"/social domains that contribute to the production of adult human beings. The motion is not, however, unidirectional: "folk" beliefs resurface from time to time, sometimes disrupting the logics of our constructed social worlds, which we frequently experience as "natural," making the two domains experientially impossible to separate.

I draw in part from Marilyn Strathern's argument on the supposed "primordiality" of kin relations that define, in turn, ideas about what is and is not "natural" in family life (1992). I also respond, again only in part, to John Borneman's suggestion that "we approach family constructions as a nexus of relationships and self-techniques always being constituted over time, rather than begin with the assumption that the family is a set of formal, already-constituted relationships handed on from one generation to the next (1992: 77). This chapter is, however, less a criticism of Borneman's suggestion and others like it than a further probing from an Indian context, as I believe that Indian kinship—even in an age of transnationalism and cosmopolitanism—requires a somewhat different framework to be properly understood than those frameworks we might apply to North American/European worlds.

3. The phrase is borrowed from Beatrix Potter's *The Tale of the Flopsy Bunnies* ([1909] 1987), and from a line that my mother and I especially enjoyed: "It is said that the effect of eating too many lettuce leaves is 'soporific.' *I* have never felt sleepy after eating lettuces; but then *I* am not a rabbit."

4. "Rajaji" is Chakravarti Rajagopalachari: freedom fighter, statesman, and poet, he was the first Indian governor general of India. Ariyakudi Ramanuja Iyengar was a singer and composer, well known in south Indian classical music circles and a good friend of my grandfather. Thatha was widely recognized as an ardent devotee of Ariyakudi's music, as he would travel frequently to attend his concerts and go as far as to fix wedding dates only after determining Ariyakudi's availability. My mother was always proud of this heritage.

5. See Trawick 1990: 163–69, for an analysis of "the break in mother–daughter continuity" and its inherent dilemmas as these are expressed in (Tamil) myths and ritual practices.

6. Jack Goody, following the arguments of the Indian theorist Irawati Karve, suggests also that since cross-cousin marriages are common in south India, and since the preference for such alliances is strong—enough to be built into kinship terminology—the degree of a woman's alienation to marriage is proportionately less: "In the North," writes Goody, where cross-cousin marriages are not permitted, "a wife is a stranger, in the

South a kinswoman" (1990: 263). I have no doubt that there is some truth in this deduction, even when it applies to non-cross-cousin marriages such as my own: the terminology, I would also argue, creates a particular kind of closeness between my natal and affinal families. It is also true, however, that while there might be "no terminological distinction between parent-in-law and parent's siblings of the opposite sex" (267), there *is* a very clear terminological distinction between daughter (or niece) and daughter-in-law. In Tamil, marriage transforms *ponnu* into *naattu-ponnu*; in Telugu, *kuuthuru* becomes *kodalu*. As a niece visiting my maternal uncle's (mama's) home, I am much like a daughter. But I reenter on marriage, ceremoniously cross the threshold, perhaps with a photograph of the goddess Lakshmi in my right hand. The faces and surroundings may be familiar, but the role and the expectations that come with marriage are not. I deal more with names and kinship terminology in a following section.

7. An anthropologist might note that my cousin's gesture makes explicit the role of the "older brother" in Indian society who is charged with the protection of his sister even after marriage. In north India, this brother–sister relationship is formalized in the ceremony of "Rakshabandhan," where a woman ties a *rakhi* or a small string ornament, onto her brother's right wrist asking for *raksha*, or protection (Goody 1990: 222–25). The woman's brother also has a crucial role to play in many south Indian weddings, as does her maternal uncle, in giving gifts to the groom, even in inviting him to marry his sister. These many elements construct what Trawick calls "structurally enjoined sentiments" (1990: 154): in my vocabulary, the "given" aspects of kinship, the culturally specified affections. It is painfully obvious, however, especially given the many occurrences of dowry deaths all over India, that the brother's symbolic role as protector may remain merely symbolic when other considerations (such as family honor and marital harmony) are placed before those of the woman's own comfort. (Threats to her physical safety are rarely perceived, as a result.) My cousin's intervention must be read in this context, as it emphasizes—however haltingly—the need for the symbolic narrative to assert itself in reality.

8. A *gotra* is a designation of ancestry. Belonging to Bharadhwaja gotra, for instance, means that your family is supposed to have descended from the sage Bharadhwaja. Marriage between two people of the same gotra is forbidden, as it is akin to marrying a brother or sister. A woman takes her husband's gotra on marriage, of course. (The punch line of the joke told here lies in a perceived difference in the sounds of the gotra names, a difference that is accentuated in enunciation for its comic effect.)

9. It is interesting, though completely predictable, that I bear the ultimate "blame" for my marriage in this brahmin woman's eyes. Not even my husband bears as much responsibility in the matter as I do, for while men are allowed some "character flaws," women certainly are not. There are no categories through which to understand my actions save those of "looseness" and immorality. The story is long and familiar, of course.

10. Cf. Trawick 1990: 152. "It is possible to see kinship not as a static form upheld by regnant or shared principles, but as a web maintained by unrelieved tensions, an architecture of conflicting desires, its symmetry a symmetry of imbalance, its cyclicity that of a hunter following his own tracks."

11. This is a Tamil story, retold in Ramanujan 1989: 248–49.

12. The quoted phrase is from Carolyn Steedman 1986: 6.

BIBLIOGRAPHY

Borneman, John. 1992. *Belonging in the Two Berlins: Kin, State, Nation*. Cambridge: Cambridge University Press.

Goody, Jack. 1990. *The Oriental, the Ancient and the Primitive*. Cambridge: Cambridge University Press.

Kondo, Dorrine. 1990. *Crafting Selves: Power, Gender and Discourses of Identity in a Japanese Workplace*. Chicago: University of Chicago Press.

Potter, Beatrix. [1909] 1987. *The Tale of the Flopsy Bunnies*. London: Frederic Warren.

Ramanujan, A. K. 1989. Telling Tales. *Dædalus* 118 (4): 239–61.

Schneider, David. 1984. *A Critique of the Study of Kinship*. Ann Arbor: University of Michigan Press.

Steedman, Carolyn. 1986. *Landscape for a Good Woman*. New Brunswick, N.J.: Rutgers University Press.

Strathern, Marilyn. 1992. *After Nature: English Kinship in the Late Twentieth Century*. Cambridge: Cambridge University Press.

Trawick, Margaret. 1990. *Notes on Love in a Tamil Family*. Berkeley: University of California Press.

Yanagisako, Sylvia J., and Jane F. Collier. 1987. Toward a Unified Analysis of Gender and Kinship. In *Gender and Kinship: Essays toward a Unified Analysis*. Ed. J. F. Collier and S. J. Yanagisako. Stanford, Calif.: Stanford University Press, 14–50.

6

The Ethics of Affect:
The Public Politics of Intimacy
in the Bloomsbury Group
and *Sammy and Rosie Get Laid*

Nityanand Deckha

Identity formations and practices are increasingly prevalent in the ongoing articulations of "politics" in the West. In their invention of languages of cohesive group identification, affiliation, and allegiance, identity practices exert pressure on Western nation-states to continually expand and redefine the terms of the more conventional code of belonging, that of citizenship. One significant example of such politics resonant particularly in Australia, Britain, Canada, and the United States is multiculturalism. In this regard, anthropologist James Holston (1996) argues that the internationalization of capital and labor and the related everyday realities of a multicultural metropolis should enable us to rethink of citizenship beyond the bounds of the nation-state. I would take Holston further to suggest that metropolitan dwellers, in their involvement in various practices of identity, exercise agency by establishing new kinds of alliances of support, networking, and senses of belonging.

My interest in the relationship between multiculturalism and the agency of "new citizens" of the West stems from my upbringing in officially multicultural Canada and my engagement in Toronto, Montreal, and Houston in various migrant South Asian cultural practices, themselves interwoven with questions of race, gender, sexuality, and postcolonialism. Multiculturalism, like other registers for identity politics, provided a point of departure for these practices. However, as I learned from preliminary ethnographic research on oppositional subjectivity among South Asian Americans, migrant identity politics lacks linkages to older radical practices and social movements to which it may share kinship. Moreover, similar to Holston, I felt that the specificities of place, social space, and everyday life that anchored diverse hyphenated identity practices of South Asian Canadians/Americans and British Asians were inadequately addressed.[1]

One of the better efforts in migrant filmmaking that situates identity practices is Stephen Frears and Hanif Kureishi's film, *Sammy and Rosie Get Laid* (1988). Later I will discuss the film more fully; I will now only mention what caught and kept my attention. *Sammy and Rosie*, beyond its montage-like staging of stylized Asian and Black British radicalism in a London caught in the jaw of Thatcherism, throws in the figure of Virginia Woolf on two occasions. Woolf and the circle of friends she belonged to, the Bloomsbury Group, are well known for their artistic, literary, and political interventions during the early decades of the twentieth century. Could Kureishi and Frears be hinting at a shared kinship between the aesthetic politics of the Bloomsbury Group and the identity politics of the characters of *Sammy and Rosie*, politicized Asian and Black Londoners? Could this movie better historicize migrant identity politics and make a greater claim to its importance to British public culture? Could the Bloomsbury Group have anything to say to late-twentieth-century hyphenated metropolitans? These are the kinds of questions I ask as I juxtapose the practices of the Bloomsbury Group with those portrayed in *Sammy and Rosie*.

If we look at the memoirs of the Bloomsbury circle[2] against Kureishi and Frears's film, we quickly observe that they share a concern for a politics of the private sphere, anchored by the physical and social space of the house. The house, I argue, mediates an *ethics of affect*, whereby aesthetic, erotic, and political enjoyment are interwoven in the making of identities. By "aesthetics," I refer to what we perceive with our *senses*, which is roughly similar to a notion of "feeling." As such, I contend that aesthetics can be used to describe feelings toward houses, philosophies of life, the city, the organization of space, and the family, to name some major motifs. These motifs have required me to take the literary, the cinematic, the architectural, and the historical and weave them into a prelude of what we may call the anthropology of spatialized feeling, feelings invoked and elicited through spatial structures, here predominantly represented by the house. Of course, neither the return to Bloomsbury nor the showcasing of *Sammy and Rosie* are original in and of themselves.[3] What remains striking, however, is how we can forge ties between the two, by which the pivotal concerns of kinship, such as family, marriage, and for our concerns, enactments of agency and solidarity, are points plotted on a grid of ethical acts.

I present my material in four movements. First is a brief description of my usage of the term *house*. The second movement, the largest, examines the feelings of some of the key Bloomsbury figures, such as Virginia Woolf, Lytton Strachey, and Vanessa Bell, about their houses, and it provides a sociology of the families. Blood and marriage relationships organize Bloomsbury socialization. Nonetheless, I argue that the shift from their parental houses in

London's West End to new living arrangements among friends, lovers, and siblings in the more easterly Bloomsbury district articulates the displacement of kin in fomenting a particular way of life, love, and livelihood that the Bloomsbury Group professed.

In the third movement, I follow these discontinuous lines into Thatcherite London and its provocative presentation in *Sammy and Rosie Get Laid*. I argue that, if Bloomsbury accomplishes the displacement of kin around a notion of old friends (cf. Clive Bell 1957), *Sammy and Rosie* does so by the difficulties of solidarity across racial, gender, sexual, and class lines and the parochialism of contemporary identity politics, migrant or not. The fourth movement, a tentative tracing of a trajectory of a British urban ethics, finds in philistinism a common enemy for both Bloomsbury and its legacies in some of the characters of *Sammy and Rosie*. For both, a discourse of kinship has been transformed, through the house's spatiality and temporality, by which questions of forming connections with others, the everyday, and with London are explored.

THE HOUSE IN ANTHROPOLOGY

In using the term *house*, I point to a specific category of not only experiencing the everyday, as *home* may suggest, but a political economy of property and planning. I am wary of the tendency of cultural studies discourses on the home to overlook the materiality of the house as an architectural structure within a particular civic townscape. To elaborate this point, I reproduce some of Marilyn Strathern's citation of Osbert Lancaster's commentary on the home:

> On closer investigation one is able to isolate the proper application of the word "home" still further, and properly confine it to the inside of ones house. . . . [The] word implies a sphere over which the individual has control; hence its enormous popularity *in a land of rugged individualists*. And whereas the appearance of the interior of one's house is the outcome of one's own personal tastes, prejudices and bank balance, the outside in ninety-nine cases out of a hundred is the expression of the views on architecture of speculative builder, luxury flat magnate, or even occasionally an eighteenth-century country gentleman. (Lancaster 1953: 9; cited in Strathern 1992: 32)

Strathern highlights "in a land of rugged individualists" to demonstrate how a notion of Englishness is being deployed through the trope of the house, and attaches it to her description of the spatialized elaboration of the middle class in the nineteenth century. This bears out in historian Donald Olsen's remark of the construction boom in the early nineteenth century whereby the London house becomes an archetype (1986: 1).

Hence, on one hand, the house is a culturally relevant category to English life. On the other, following Claude Lévi-Strauss, the house represents ancient (European Middle Ages), Native North American (of Kwakiutl societies), and contemporary social organization for which none of the usual metonyms of society—clans, lineages, families (Lévi-Strauss 1991: 435)—seem to suffice. In this way, anthropological attention to the house means an expansion of the bounds of kinship discourse, as it means a refusal to folding back onto the home's interiority for its own sake. Such an effort is under way in *About the House* (1995). Authors Janet Carsten and Stephen Hugh-Jones extend the work of Lévi-Strauss (e.g., 1987, 1991) by arguing for a language of the dwelling that is not only situated in kinship relations, but refigures questions of the organization and design of space, the scripting of memory and history, and the everyday ordering practices of bodies and psyches. In brief, in their plea for making houses new objects for analysis, they seek to forge an intersection between architecture and anthropology, one supplementing the other: anthropology offering the significance of the house's ontology; architecture suggesting the influence of domestic aesthetics, the latter which is at the forefront of Bloomsburyite praxis, to which I now move.

COLONIAL KIN, VICTORIAN VALUES:
SITUATING THE RADICALISM OF THE BLOOMSBURY GROUP

In explaining the East End, London artist Mark Gertler's ambivalent relationship to Bloomsbury, and the English avant-garde of the early twentieth century, Janet Wolff provides a snapshot of the then-contemporary cultural political stage. She writes:

> First, there was a strongly conservative streak in what was ostensibly the most avant-garde tendency in England, namely the Bloomsbury circle. Second, the more radically modernist work was (is) produced from the apparently conservative inclination to work from a given social situation. . . . It is worth adding too, that the connection between aesthetic, social and political values is more complex. . . . It is clear, for example, that members of the Bloomsbury group were far more progressive politically and in terms of sexual politics than Gertler, [Wyndham] Lewis, and others. (1996: 50–55)

To what extent is the "strongly conservative streak" of Bloomsbury commensurable with their "more progressive" political and sexual practices? In framing my response, two axes of investigation are helpful. One is the rhetoric of philistinism that floats over the last decades of the nineteenth century. Another is the imperial careers of many of Bloomsbury Group's families. I argue that kinship relations and philistine worldviews are linked objects in the acts of rebellion of Old Bloomsbury, the early pre–World War I period of the group. Furthermore, using the figure of the house, we grasp the material context in which Bloomsburyite relationships flourished and by which an ethics was fashioned. In this way, we can situate how conservatism and radicalism are copresent among the Bloomsbury set, and the consequences for maintaining an ethical position.

I begin with Lytton Strachey's account of his family home from 1884 to 1907, 69 Lancaster Gate, in Bayswater, and then proceed to Virginia Woolf's memoir of her Kensington house, 22 Hyde Park Gate. Both pieces were written for the Memoir Club, the gathering of the Bloomsbury circle from its formation in 1920 to the 1940s. Members took turns in contributing pieces to be read out during the meetings. I then contrast these with the centrality of the Stephens's first house in the Bloomsbury district of London, 46 Gordon Square, in shaping the group's ontology. With this juxtaposition, I demonstrate not only the particular social origins of key Bloomsburyites, but also significantly, how the notion of a "room of one's own" fixes an understanding of individuality that shapes their sexual, aesthetic, and political transgressions.

Describing badly designed Lancaster Gate, Lytton recalls its narrow dark passage of ochre walls and the magenta and indigo tiles, how the seemingly endless staircase threaded a house that "contained seven layers of human habitation" (Strachey 1971: 18). The rooms "that looked onto the street (one on each floor) were tolerable; all the rest were very small and very dark. There was not a scrap of garden, not even a courtyard" (19). Lytton remembers how his four sisters shared the "miserable little young ladies' room"; only his father had a sitting room to himself. He remarks that his mother "had no room of her own," so that her writing table, scattered with household papers and personal correspondence, "stood out obvious and unashamed among the largest dinner parties" (24). However, it is the drawing room for which Lytton provides the thickest description and through which he reads his family history and the Victorian society into which he was born:

> The gigantic door, with its flowing portière of pale green silk, swung and shut behind one. One stepped forward in the direction of the three distant windows covered by their pale green limitless curtains, one looked about, one of the countless groups of persons disintegrated, flowed towards one, one sat and spoke and listened: one was reading the riddle of the Victorian Age. I only mean to say that the Lancaster Gate drawing-room was, in its general nature, the concentrated product of an epoch; for certainly it was too full of individuality and peculiarity to be typical of anything. . . . No doubt a contributing cause of our dowdiness was that we were only precariously well off. What had happened was that a great tradition— the aristocratic tradition of the eighteenth century—had reached a very advanced stage of decomposition. My father and my mother belonged by birth to the old English world of country-house gentlefolk—a world of wealth and breeding, a world in which such things as footmen, silver, and wine were the necessary appurtenances of civilized life. But their own world was different: it was the

middle-class professional world of the Victorians, in which the old forms still lingered, but debased and enfeebled, in which Morris wallpapers had taken the place of Adam panelling, in which the swarming retinue had been reduced to a boy in livery, in which the spoons and forks were bought at the Army and Navy Stores. And then, introducing yet another element into the mixture, there was the peculiar disintegrating force of the Strachey character. The solid bourgeois qualities were interpenetrated by intellectualism and eccentricity. (Strachey 1971: 20, 24, 25)

Strachey unwittingly creates an image of the educated upper middle class forced to retreat to coding prestige through the recast meanings of certain things: silverware, wallpaper, servants. In an increasingly urbanized England, organized by surfeit and neglect, the house emerges as the epitome of changing notions of individuality, sociality, and cosmopolitanism. It materializes the politics of the personal as it demands a connection beyond oneself. An indexical relationship is formed between certain objects and drawing-room culture that suggests a self-understanding of what it is to be English to someone as wellborn as Lytton.

Intriguingly, Virginia Woolf's memory of her home at Hyde Park Gate continues mapping the transformation of their class position through the shifts in how interior spaces were inhabited. She recalls:

It was a house of innumerable small oddly shaped rooms built to accommodate not one family but three. . . . There were chests of heavy family plate. There were hoards of china and glass. Eleven people aged between eight and sixty lived there, and were waited upon by seven servants. . . . The place seemed tangled and matted with emotion. I could write the history of every mark and scratch in my room, I wrote later. The walls and the rooms had in sober truth been built to our shape. We had permeated the whole vast fabric—it has since been made into a hotel—with our family history. (1985: 182, 183)

My room in that very tall house was at the back. When Stella married, Vanessa and I were promoted to separate bed sitting rooms; that marked the fact that we had become, she at eighteen, I at fifteen, young ladies. My room, the old night nursery, was a long narrow room, with two windows; the fireside half was the living half; the washstand half was the sleeping half. . . . In the living half was my wicker chair, and Stella's writing table made after her design with crossed legs, and stained green and decorated by her with a pattern of brown leaves (at that time staining and enamelling and amateur furniture decorating were much the rage). On it stood open my Greek lexicon; some Greek play or other; many little bottles of ink, pens innumerable; and probably hidden under blotting paper, sheets of foolscap covered with private writing in a hand so small and twisted as to be a family joke. (1985: 122)

With this inventory of the furniture of daily life, Virginia deploys the figure of the writing table and bottles of ink to richly evoke what Lytton had described as the seeping of intellectuality among the British bourgeoisie.

In their textured snapshots of their respective pasts, Lytton and Virginia confirm N. G. Annan's notion of the "intellectual aristocracy," formed through the "persistent endogamy" of middle classes during the nineteenth century. As he describes:

> Members of these intellectual families became the new professional civil servants at a time when government had become too complicated and technical to be handled by the ruling class and their dependents. They joined the Indian and Colonial services; or they became school inspectors or took posts in the museums or were appointed secretaries of philanthropic societies; or they edited or wrote for the periodicals or entered publishing houses. . . . Thus they gradually spread over the length and breadth of English intellectual life criticising the assumptions of the ruling class above them and forming the opinions of the upper middle class to which they belonged. (1955: 244)

Annan's discussion is invaluable for our purposes, for he allows us to situate the self-understandings of Lytton and Virginia with the ascendance of professional families during the expansion of the British Empire. He also shows how private members of the English bourgeoisie could enter public discourse as an intelligentsia. An abridged version of Lytton's patriline includes Sir Henry Strachey (1736–1810), Lytton's paternal great-grandfather, one-time secretary to Lord Clive and Edward Strachey (1774–1832), his paternal grandfather, freelance writer, judge, secretary to the Resident at Poona,[4] as well as a gentleman scholar of Persian and Sanskrit. Also active in the British administration of India were Lytton's uncle (FB) Sir John Strachey (1823–1907), known for his work on expanding the rail network and introducing the metric system in India; and his own father, Richard Strachey (1817–1908), who was a general in the British Indian army (Holroyd 1967: 4–16).[5]

The family of Virginia and Vanessa is not dissimilar to Lytton's, but it is more literary. Their father, Sir Leslie Stephen, was a Cambridge fellow, literary critic and historian, and the founding editor of the *Dictionary of National Biography*. Their uncle (FB) Sir James Fitzjames Stephen (1829–1894) was a judge of the High Court and a prolific journalist. However, their paternal great-grandfather and grandfather reveal their links to the middle-class English church reformist and missionary group, the Clapham sect. This relationship was solidified by marriage to daughters of prominent Clapham evangelicals, one a Venn, the other a Wilberforce. Their great-grandfather, James Stephen (1758–1832), married the former and was a prolific pamphleteer and an eventual member of Parliament (Bell 1972: 1–9). Their grandfather, also James Stephen (1789–1859), married the latter and became an undersecretary in the Colonial Office and drafted, Annan tells us, "the bill to free the slaves in the British colonies" (1955: 274).

English descent is bilateral, and matrilineal genealogies would provide a richer sense of how Annan's notion of the aristocracy of intellect is being formed through kinship. For example, Lytton's mother, Jane Maria, was a Grant from the Scottish Grants of Rothiemarchus, a rather military family. Her father, Lytton's maternal grandfather, was Sir John Peter Grant (1807–1893), who served as a governor, first in India and later in Jamaica. Indeed, the Indian connection becomes all the more significant if we consider that Lady Strachey was born on an East India Company merchant ship, and that her brother, Bartle, was a major in the Indian army and the father of yet another Bloomsbury member, Duncan Grant.

It was Lytton's mother, Duncan's aunt (FS), who rescued Duncan from the army class at St. Paul's, a respected public school, persuading her brother and sister-in-law that Duncan should instead pursue art (Holroyd 1967: 261).[6] While Duncan was enrolled at Westminster School of Art, he lived in the Strachey family home at Lancaster Gate. His further artistic education in France, curiously enough, was financed by a stipend given by another of his father's sisters, Lady Frances Elinor Colville (271). While studying art, Duncan had an affair with John Maynard Keynes, the famous economist and fellow student at Cambridge with Lytton and Thoby Stephen, the brother of Virginia and Vanessa. Unbeknownst to Lytton, he fell in love with Duncan. Yet, if the homosexuality of this triangle is noteworthy, more remarkable was the fact that Duncan and Lytton were first cousins.

No such transgression marked the matrilineage of Vanessa and her siblings, except for the incestuous sexuality of their half brothers, George and Gerald Duckworth, sons of their mother's first husband, Herbert Duckworth, a publisher. Moreover, the operation of India in the fashioning of daily life— remarkable later, it seems, only in the shawls they procured—is given presence by the seven Pattle sisters, of which Maria (1818–1892) Jackson was the middle and maternal grandmother. The second, Julia Margaret Cameron (1815–1879), became a famous Victorian portrait photographer, whose "photographs of Horschel, Lowell, Darwin, Tennyson, Browning and Meredith" (Spalding 1983: 46) were rehung on freshly painted white walls at 46 Gordon Square. The sixth, Virginia (1827–1910), linked the family most ostensibly with aristocracy through her marriage to Charles Somers-Cocks, Third Earl Somers.

As Virginia suggests, her aunt's ambitions didn't end with being Countess Somers:. "Aunt Virginia, it is plain, put her own daughters, my mother's first cousins [MMZDs], through tortures . . . in order to marry one to the Duke of Bedford, the other to Lord Henry Somerset" (1985: 88). Nonetheless, Virginia, Woolf that is, continues: "The beauty of our great aunts had allied us in the middle of the nineteenth century with, I think I am right in saying, two dukes and quite a number of earls and countesses. They naturally showed no particular wish to remember the connection" (169).

Maria Jackson married John Jackson, a Calcutta doctor, and had three children, all daughters: Adeline Maria (1837–1881), Mary Louisa (1840–1917), and Julia (1846–1895). All three married scholars. Adeline wed Henry Halford Vaughan, professor of history at Oxford. Mary, closest to the Stephen women, married Herbert William Fisher, the tutor to the then prince of Wales; and of course, their mother, Julia, married Leslie Stephen (see Annan 1955: 274; for extended discussion, cf. Stephen 1977). The Vaughans and the Fishers, that is, the families of Virginia and Vanessa's mother's sisters, figure prominently in Virginia's memoirs (e.g., Woolf 1985), not only as close relations, but in the case of cousin Florence's (MZD) husband, Fred Maitland, as their father's biographer, and cousin William's (MZS) wife, Cecilia Warre-Cornish, who was the aunt [FS] of Bloomsbury member and Memoir Club leader Molly (née Warre-Cornish) MacCarthy.

If the kin relations of Virginia and Lytton, Vanessa and Duncan convey the formidable role work and life in India and other British colonies played in the rise and extension of the upper middle class in Britain, the gradual extinguishing of empire in the twentieth century is discernible in Lytton and Virginia's use of domestic icons to represent the formation of a national intellectual culture. In fact, Virginia's interjection of a brief obituary for Hyde Park Gate, the family house made into a hotel, marks the moment when it shall no longer serve as a synecdoche of English kinship. Lancaster Gate faces a similar fate.[7] Yet, if the future death of both dwellings captures the closing of an era, for Virginia and her siblings, it is the death of their father in early 1904 that makes them leave Hyde Park Gate forever.

All Virginia can ask in her letters of the time as she recovers from mental strain in the southern English countryside is a room of her own. She exclaims, "I long for a large room to myself, with books and nothing else, where I can shut myself up, and see no one. . . . This would be possible at Gordon Square: and nowhere else."[8] Gordon Square is among the other squares built in the late eighteenth century in Bloomsbury district. According to Andrew Byrne, the first of the squares to be built, Bedford, set the standard for "refinement and elegance" for the rest of the Georgian period in London domestic architecture (1990: 9).

All the Bloomsbury squares, such as Tavistock, or Fitzroy—to which Virginia and Adrian moved after Vanessa's marriage to Clive in 1907—or Brunswick, where at number thirty-eight, they shared a house with Duncan Grant, Maynard Keynes, and later Leonard Woolf, "suffered from being built in fits and starts." Nevertheless, Byrne continues, they were all built "at a time when architectural effect depended more on the treatment of complete estates rather than on the design of a street or a group of houses. Lavish fitting out of the interior was also a priority when the influence of Robert Adam was at its height" (1990: 9). Yet all the architectural splendor seemed unknown in the world of the young Stephens, at least in that of Vanessa, who recalls in her memoirs:

> My first memory of Bloomsbury as a district is of a remote, melancholy, foggy, square-ridden quarter and of myself in evening dress in a hansom cab being

trotted through square after square in a nightmarish attempt to find No. 24 Bedford Square. I was going to dine with the Protheros, Fanny Prothero an impish monkey faced little Irish lady, said never to have been seen without a hat—and her husband, dull and pussy like, who collected Adam mantelpieces and filled the house with them; perhaps they are still there. They were thought eccentric for living in Bloomsbury at least by our friends who all inhabited Kensington or Bayswater, or possibly Chelsea, Westminster or Mayfair. My Kensington cabman did not know the way and I was very late. In spite of this first rather dream-like and agitating vision I cannot have been repelled by Bloomsbury. For in 1904, after my father's death . . . we resisted strong pressure put upon us by family and old friends to live as they did in one of the recognized districts and insisted on inspecting houses in Bloomsbury. (Cited in Spalding 1983: 43)[9]

Here, in the geography of London housing that maps the terrain of a certain moral imagination and order with the interior design of Robert Adam as its hallmark, we also have the gesture of rebellion: to live in one of the city's "unrecognized" districts. Vanessa's inability to refuse Bloomsbury reflects Virginia's careful comparison of 46 Gordon Square with 22 Hyde Park Gate:

To begin with it was astonishing to stand at the drawing room window and look into all those trees. The light and the air after the rich red gloom of Hyde Park Gate were a revelation. Things one had never seen in the darkness there—Watts pictures, Dutch cabinets, blue china—shone out for the first time in the drawing room at Gordon Square. . . . But what was even more exhilarating was the extraordinary increase of space. At Hyde Park Gate one had only a bedroom in which to read or see one's friends. Here Vanessa and I each had a sitting room; there was the large double drawing room; and a study on the ground floor.[10] To make it all newer and fresher, the house had been completely done up. Needless to say the Watts-Venetian tradition of red plush and black paint had been reversed; we had entered the Sargent-Furse era;[11] white and green chintzes were everywhere; and instead of Morris wall-papers with their intricate patterns we decorated our walls with washes of plain distemper. (1985: 184, 185)

Vanessa chiefly did the elaborate decorations. Having sold a great deal of the family furniture to Harrods, space and freedom from clutter became the key motifs in arranging the living spaces at Gordon Square. She bought a new sofa and desk for Virginia and "resurrected some Indian shawls ([that were] probably left over from Little Holland House days as they were often worn by [our] great aunts)" (Woolf 1985: 46).

I have given lengthy accounts of three Bloomsburyites' memories of dwelling, decoration, and design. They themselves have narrated their own social positions and coded sentiment and space, taste, and time, through the houses in which they lived. Moreover, 46 Gordon Square held the Thursday evening "at homes" where the Stephen women and Thoby's friends from

Cambridge began to socialize in the autumn of 1904. If Thoby was the hinge who initiated the shift of an intellectual circle from Cambridge to Blooms-bury that survived his death at twenty-six in 1906, it was aesthetics that trans-formed homosocial collegiality into an intellectual and sexual culture fash-ioned through everyday experience.

As Virginia continues: "We were full of experiments and reforms. We were going to do without table napkins. . . . we were going to paint; to write; to have coffee after dinner instead of tea at nine o'clock. Everything was going to be new; everything was going to be different. Everything was on trial" (1985: 185). This domestic aestheticism, elaborated during those "astonish-ingly abstract" Thursday night talks on art, literature, and philosophy, was "the germ from which sprang all that has since come to be called—in news-papers and in novels, in Germany, in France—even, I dare say, in Turkey and Timbuktu—by the name of Bloomsbury" (185).

This revisionist project, I contend, begins in the form of (the) dwelling, as the space of being, and of being itself. It starts as private interests formed around the domestic sphere of the upper-middle-class intellectual family that it seeks to exceed in order to achieve public presence. As such, it is the Vic-torian house(hold) that becomes the first object of attack in representing what we can call the "philistinism"—the gross indifference to aesthetic or in-tellectual pursuits—of the social milieu in which many of the Bloomsbury Group were raised.

For Matthew Arnold, the philistines are roughly, but not exclusively, the middle class, who "not only do not pursue sweetness and light, but who pre-fer to them that sort of machinery of business, chapels, and tea meetings" ([1869] 1994: 68).[12] With this statement, Arnold makes an aesthetic judgment on British public life, precisely the arena that became central for the Blooms-bury circle. For Old Bloomsbury, participating in unraveling British intellec-tual and artistic apathy involved maintaining an emphasis of a domestic aes-thetic as well as for the visual artists Vanessa Bell, Duncan Grant, and Roger Fry, a development of techniques, styles, and forms of art that rejected the austerity of prevailing ideas of "proper" art, taste, and style. This, as Vanessa suggested in a letter to Roger, was "especially important in England where it seems one can never get away from this fatal prettiness. Can't we paint stuffs etc. which won't be gay and pretty?"[13]

The point of departure for their campaign countering philistinism was the exhibition Roger organized called "Manet and the Post-Impressionists," the latter term coined by Fry (Collins 1984: 1). Held at London's Grafton Gal-leries over the winter of 1910, the exhibition included works by Cézanne, Van Gogh, Matisse, and Picasso that shocked the sensibilities of the British viewing public. Commenting on the Grafton affair, Virginia, during a period of flirtatious rapport with her brother-in-law, Clive, writes to her friend, Vio-let: "Now that Clive is in the vain of aesthetic opinion, I hear a great deal about pictures. I don't think them so good as books. But why all the Duchesses are insulted by the post-Impressionists, a modest sample set of painters . . . I can[']t conceive."[14]

During the following February, Roger, Vanessa, and Duncan exhibited collectively for the first time at the Alpine Club Gallery in London. This was organized by the Friday Club, Vanessa's society of artists that had been regularly meeting at Gordon Square for six years. Their artistic collegiality led to the participation in creating patronage networks for working artists like themselves, a common theme in what David Morgan (1982) has called the "friendship work" in Bloomsbury social relations. The earliest and strongest was the Omega Workshop that ran from 1913 to 1919 in Bloomsbury and where Roger, Vanessa, Duncan, and others for a time, applied art techniques in decorating and designing upholstery, wood furniture, linen, and carpets. Key to the short-lived success of Omega was the use of craftspeople to actually execute the designs in the more applied arts. The pivotal role of the house in the Bloomsbury imagination was demonstrated by Omega's securing of the *Daily Mail*'s commission to design the sitting room of their Ideal Home exhibition in 1913. Successful commissions for decorating West End houses soon followed (Collins 1984: 87–89). More than painting the walls, they "could produce, besides mosaic floors and stained glass corridors, marquetrized and painted furniture, sofas, painted cushions, and rugs" (89).

Although their artistic philosophy, of an art liberated from "morality, illustration, and the faithful depiction of the world of appearances," moved them away from the dominant impulses of nineteenth-century British art, Janet Wolff insists that they were not influenced by the continental avant-garde, "not only in 1909, but throughout their painting careers" (1996: 53). Wolff's reaction seems to my eye to be somewhat of an overstatement. Yet she is right in pointing to the conservatism of their artistic practices, if by "conservatism" we mean a development of the aesthetic that challenges British artistic representational languages, but works within the vernacular of the upper-middle-class intimate sphere. The drawing rooms, the walls, murals, and portraits that feature so heavily in the work of Omega make spatial what Patrick Wright has called "Deep England":

> To be a subject of Deep England . . . one must have grown up in the midst of ancestral continuities and have experienced that kindling of consciousness which the national landscape and cultural tradition prepare for the dawning national spirit. . . . The approved and dominant images of Deep England are pastoral and green, but there is also something "green" about everyday life, whatever the situation in which it is lived. Deep England makes its appeal at the level of everyday life. In doing so it has the possibility of securing the self-understanding of the upper middle-class while at the same time speaking more inclusively in connection with all everyday life, where it finds a more general resonance. (1985: 85, 87)

From Lancaster Gate and Hyde Park Gate to Gordon Square, houses reveal the sensuality of Deep England across particular spatial arrangements and temporal narratives. By this process, the familiar objects of a certain imperial affluence, such as silverware, china, and servants, trigger what architectural historian Dolores Hayden calls place memories (1995: 46). The place memories of cluttered and cramped Victorian houses or of freshly painted and spacious Edwardian rooms are signs in the everyday, class-marked social practices of Deep England, whereby seemingly private feeling takes on the significance of a larger, national discourse of heritage.

Moreover, other seemingly private memorabilia, such as the Indian shawls and the photographs of the Victorian portraitist Julia Cameron, one of Virginia and Vanessa's great-aunts, are symbols of enjoyment in the nodes in the public culture of late British imperialism. Enjoyment, Slavoj Žižek argues, may be constituted as excess (1989: 52); it is also, significantly, "only possible on the basis of a certain non-knowledge, ignorance" (68). Keeping with this vein, the Bloomsbury Group's enjoyment must ignore the knowledge of its relations of property, class, and nationality, as it must invoke the structure of feeling of deep England without naming it. That is, they must overlook the social conditions that have enabled them to move from being private citizens to public figures.

Nonetheless, the Bloomsbury Group makes an appeal to the ethical in their sexual and gender politics, their undoing of British philistinism, their pacifism and eventual anti-imperialism, however they vary from one member to another. Moreover, what we cannot forget is that their identities as writers, painters, decorators, polemicists, and critics—an intelligentsia working outside academia—are informed by a consciousness "of the drone of daily life," as Virginia writes in a letter to her sister from her Sussex cottage.[15]

This consciousness is evinced in Bloomsbury's preoccupation with the house as a symbol of a materialist politics of the everyday. Hence, it is the house that fixes their curious blend of conservatism and radicalism, and their ventures in fashioning a way of life and work that recalls the private traditions of their birth as it refuses the public philistinism of the day. In this way, Raymond Williams is right to describe them as a civilizing fraction of the English upper classes that for "all its continuing general orthodoxy . . . appears now much more often as a beleagu[e]red [rather] than as an expanding position" (1980: 165).

Leonard Woolf dramatically captures this sense of beleagueredness by describing the Bloomsbury Group as "that class stratum or strata which . . . are now practically extinct; they were almost destroyed by the 1914 war and were finally wiped away in the 1939 war" (L. Woolf 1964: 79). If Leonard sounds the death knell of the spirit of Old Bloomsbury, Virginia keeps the burial ritual at bay when she closes her memoir of the group with: "Old Bloomsbury still survives. If you seek a proof—look around" (V. Woolf 1985: 207). This haunting closure parallels her ghostly cathected image in the montage and narrative of the film *Sammy and Rosie Get Laid,* to which I now turn.

PERFORMING POLITICS IN THE AGE OF THATCHER: MIGRANT IDENTITY AND MULTICULTURAL SOLIDARITY IN *SAMMY AND ROSIE GET LAID*

All the traits that organized Old Bloomsbury—strong aestheticism and intellectualism, the recharting of sexual organizations through the house, scorn for bourgeois jealousy, shifting representations of privacy and publicity—run through *Sammy and Rosie.* Intriguingly, in her commentary on the film, deconstructionist Gayatri Spivak picks up on Williams's discussion of the beleaguered subjectivity of the Bloomsbury Group to argue that the "old British ideological subject of radicalism" (1993: 245)—which Bloomsbury represented at the turn of the century—is figured in the film by Rosie. Whatever we may think of the film, Spivak's suggestion encouraged me to wonder whether the film's screenwriter, Hanif Kureishi, born in London to a migrant Pakistani father and English mother, imagines himself not similarly placed and thus pays homage to his critical aesthetic and erotic forebears. Moreover, since I want to maintain that such a genealogy should emphasize the significance of the house in defining the "ethics of living in London" that *Sammy and Rosie* animate, I keep issues of the (private) household and (public) housing central to my reading. I would argue that this animation is neither accidental nor forced. Rather it is an attempt by Kureishi to historicize, however discontinuously, the radical identity politics of Thatcherite London.

The film begins with the arrival of Rafi, a Pakistani government minister whose life is endangered, in London to see the son, Sammy, and the lover, Alice, whom he abandoned many years ago. Sammy, an accountant, lives with Rosie, a social worker, in a multiracial inner-city London neighborhood. There has been a police shooting of a black woman, causing a rebellion to break out in the streets.

As Rafi tries to reacquaint himself with his son and Rosie, Rosie's friends, Rani and Vinia, track down a dossier on Rafi that has been prepared by a local activist group. The file documents reports of killings and torture that Rafi sanctioned while a high-ranking minister in the Pakistani government. This disclosure precipitates the further fraying of an already unraveling common-law marriage between Sammy and Rosie. They turn to other amorous possibilities—Sammy with Anna, the American journalist, and Rosie, with Danny/Victoria, a squatter/housing activist who befriends Rafi, and to whom Rafi turns to for shelter after being rejected by Alice and haunted by his bloody past.

However, the most evocative scene is near the end of the film, when all the major characters gather to witness the eviction and destruction of the squatter settlement being bulldozed for redevelopment. Here the raw realities of the effects of Thatcherite social policy are set in motion—the displacement of a community in the name of development, the exchange of the social democratic principles of the vulnerable citizen's right to housing for capitalism's need to traffic in speculative real estate. With the ironic melding of the melancholic overtones of a paean to the nation, "I Vow to Thee My Country," and the heroic and proud pronouncements of Maggie Thatcher, Kureishi and Frears present an emotional scenario in which the inner city actor is truly beleaguered, caught in the vortex of a nation of decline. However, if this scene brings all the major and minor plots together for the viewer, it is only temporary. For, in the last scene we are left scrambling for meaning in the face of Rafi's suicide and Sammy and Rosie's shared mourning.

The demolished squatter community is foreshadowed in the opening sequence of the film, with Thatcher reminding a crowd of supporters to enjoy themselves this weekend, but come Monday, "we have a big job to do in some of those inner cities." Thatcher mimics the sovereign exerting demands on her citizen–subjects. Her political philosophy, Iain Chambers argues, evoked "Victorian values [that recall] not the liberal aristocrat but the sober virtues and rational order of a middle class whose personal capacities were realized in a moral relationship to the market and to domesticity" (1993: 155). I return to the issue of the middle class and morality later, but, already, from the film's beginning, Thatcher's persona provides a bracketing of the film as a period piece, in which a different antagonism is operating in Britain. If earlier it was a division "between rich and poor or North and South," with Thatcherism, Wright suggests, it is "between the grand if not always aura-laden symbolism of Empire and War on one hand and the bureaucratic imagery of the welfare state on the other" (1985: 183).

It is the projection of the latter whose effect is marked by the squatters. As inner-city dwellers occupying invaluable private property in the heart of London, and regardless of the collectivized spirit of the squatter-housing activist community, they must be cleared off. This portrays the brutality and encouraged anonymity of Thatcherite London, where the inadequacies of urban housing, including the mismatch of council housing and its governing notion of the needy family, are rampant (Elliott 1986: 48). *Sammy and Rosie* presents the community that the eviscerated welfare state wants to vanquish, in an image of England that prefers the nostalgia of the green and bucolic, here represented by Alice's nineteenth-century suburban house—the "country" in Danny/Victoria's unknowing yet telling words.

The theme of the house circulates through the three principal sexual (re)encounters in the film. For example, housing activism and the politics of property in central London are focused by the relationship between Danny/Victoria and Rosie. The intimate sphere of the suburban upper middle class is evoked by Alice's house, and her delayed sexual tryst with Rafi. Sammy's philandering with Anna (and Rosie's scorn for monogamy) points to how the gentrified, inner-city house he shares with Rosie may be perfect for multicultural, multisexual parties, but strains to reproduce marital bliss. Mediating both dire socioeconomic realities and changing sexual relationships is Sammy and Rosie's house. During one night, it stands unscathed in the middle of a neighborhood revolt. On another, its living room and kitchen are party areas for "the usual social deviants: communists, lesbians, blacks, and Victoria."

Yet, one of the most interesting encounters in Sammy and Rosie's house is Rosie's study. There, hung low on a red wall in the nineteenth-century style of postage-stamp display, is a portrait of a middle-aged Virginia Woolf. In a remarkable scene, Rafi is awakened from a bad dream with the noise of the riot outside, only to see the portrait superimposed between the window and the white, fake lace curtain. The portrait, foreshadowing an impending ethical dilemma, is "aflame." Rafi looks at the picture, and Virginia's gaze hits him, in a glance rich with what her sister Vanessa once called "the pathos of her position." To read Virginia's glance as evoking the end of civilized culture seems greatly to miss the mark. Rather, in Virginia's and Rafi's interocular communication I saw the residual ethical appeal of the Bloomsbury Group, communicating a practice amid crisis that traverses the colonial and imperial, the urban, the cosmopolitan, the Londoner, and the postcolonial. As Rafi stares, it is as if the pathos vanishes, replaced by a glare through which beleagueredness itself becomes an ethical stance. In this way, the position of a Londoner for whom Rafi's self-declared image of the city as the center of Western civilization and of the English nation as "hot buttered toast and cunty fingers" is effectively dislocated.

Both the Bloomsbury Group and the diasporans and postcolonials of *Sammy and Rosie* imagine London as the center of an ethical universe, but with varying trajectories of different beginnings and ends. Broadly, they are linked to each other by the long history of British colonization in the Indian subcontinent. The Bloomsbury circle is the first generation of the colonizers to oppose imperialism, while the characters of *Sammy and Rosie* represent the second generation of the ex-colonized living as migrants in the former seat of empire. Yet, both groups also share the need to order a set of aesthetic and political practices in protest of the philistinism of the middle classes. The members of the Bloomsbury circle accomplish this through radicalizing a conservative aestheticism. The elite postcolonial, such as Rafi, does so by claiming solidarity with his or her lower-class migrant compatriots who have migrated and live in Britain, such as the taxi driver to whom Rafi says nonchalantly, "Like you, it's the middle class I hate."

Yet, such solidarity is contrived, for, as Raymond Williams argues of Bloomsbury, and I of Rafi, the crux of the ethical dilemma is not one of solidarity with the Other, but *conscience*. As Williams elaborates, Bloomsbury related "to a lower class *as a matter of conscience:* not in solidarity or in affiliation, but as an extension of what are still felt as personal or small-group obligations, at once against the cruelty and stupidity of the system and towards its otherwise relatively helpless victims" (1980: 155). In *Sammy and Rosie*, it is Rafi's conscience that Rosie and her friends, Rani and Vinia, appeal to, as does the figure of the lower-class, migrant Pakistani taxi driver, who serves as both guide and ghost, a phantasmatic embodiment of one of the tortured victims of Rafi's administration in Pakistan.

That Rafi, in the end, sees suicide as the only ethical response and commits suicide in Rosie's study in the last moments of the film alludes to how suicide slithers through the ethos of the Bloomsbury Group. Is it ridiculous to suggest that suicide unites Virginia and Rafi, a shared response to insufferable life conditions?[16] In any case, if for Virginia and Rafi, suicide is a matter of conscience, I agree with Spivak that, for Sammy and Rosie, it is a question not just of sufficient love, but of *interracial solidarity* (1993: 253).

Solidarity may also be the source of Alice's gesture of wearing an Indian shawl to the party, another Bloomsbury household object that becomes transformed. When I described to a friend how the shawl coded an imperial connection between Bloomsbury and *Sammy and Rosie*, and between Alice and Rosie's London Asian and African Caribbean friends, I thought his first reading of it as solidarity was far-fetched. However, in the scene before Rafi commits suicide, around the dining table, where Rani, Vinia, and their lesbian friends are gathered, Alice is shown to have become part of a female, multiracial, multisexual, inner-city community, displacing her own "Deep Englishness."

Earlier I critiqued Bloomsbury's complicity with the upper-middle-class narratives of Deep England. Simultaneously, however, we must note the critique of the upper-class postcolonial Pakistani position that refuses any accountability, which reacts against the West as it confirms its moral superiority. In this way, the communication between Virginia and Rafi, staged in a female social worker's study, British but of a lower-class origin than either Rafi or Virginia, assumes a shared position that is distinct from the identity politics of the film's other moral nexus, the South Asian–Black British lesbian couple, Rani and Vinia.

Rani and Vinia are self-styled feminist lesbians, antiracists, and activists; in the couple, Rani is assertive and dominant, flirting and pursuing another woman at Rosie's party. She then tries to reenchant a very hurt Vinia, as she talks to an amicable Alice, who says of her cohort: "Loyalty and honesty were the most important things to us, not attraction." Later in the film, when Rafi swears in Punjabi upon seeing Rani and Vinia in bed together, Rani gives it back. As such, Rani and Vinia are positioned as the erotic-political conscience of the film by their Asian–Black lesbianism and their antagonism to elite postcoloniality. In fact, Rani gives voice to this politics when she confronts Rosie's accommodating response to Rafi's visit to London as "Typical of your class and background. Your politics are just surface. This is liberalism gone mad."

Indeed, in their exploration of private desires and public politics, it is almost as if Frears and Kureishi are pitting liberalism and philistinism against each other, where the liberal is invariably white and the philistine is the dogmatic, moralizing, yet ahistorical migrant identity practitioner of color. For it is the migrant identitarian in the film—Rani—who rejects the heterodox play of notions of class, race, gender, ethnicity, time, and space. Such fluidity, I would argue, is necessary in generating a counterpublic to oppose Thatcherite ideology that privileges the enterprise logic of the middle classes and reduces state support for, among other things, the arts, enunciating a British public discourse in line with Matthew Arnold's philistine.

The Arnoldian project, if it can be put briefly, was to develop a moral attitude by which culture can be pursued, studied, and created. It was a critique of British social life, but as an early statement of the aestheticization of politics, it appeared conservative. The Bloomsbury Group, as one of the circles that inherited the project, radicalized an antiphilistine outlook by explicitly politicizing the domestic sphere of the educated, upper middle classes of Deep England. Such a project had its moments of publicity, as during the Grafton exhibitions of 1910 and 1912 and the running of the Omega Workshop.

Sammy and Rosie continues in this spirit by refusing to concede the uselessness of the intellectual and the aesthetic as it enforces links with the erotics of everyday life. It does so by elaborating the Bloomsburyite call for engaged enjoyment. Such a position is evoked in Alice's defense of "things we enjoy—Constable, Claridge, Chopin"—against the "proletarian and theocratic ideas you [Rafi] theoretically admire [that] run civilization into dust." The same position is also suggested in Sammy's description of why Rosie and he are together in solidarity as Londoners: Saturday walks in the park, lectures in semiotics at the Institute of Contemporary Art, attending shows of political satire. Hence, it is not that middle classness is scorned altogether, nor is privacy devalued in the name of public action. It is rather Thatcher's promulgation of them in their narrow technocratic and corporate forms that the film rejects.

Like Bloomsbury, what is being articulated is a fraction, perhaps a fringe of the educated classes—intellectual, civic, self-critical, antiphilistine, heterodox—who shun the parochialisms of Thatcher and Rani and the mainly moralist positions they occupy. Yet, in the late 1980s staging of *Sammy and Rosie*, an antiphilistine public culture seems not only elitist, but utopian. Therefore, if in Bloomsbury the movement was from the intimate sphere to an active public discourse where questions of sexuality and gender could be posed, in the mise-en-scène of *Sammy and Rosie*, we feel the retreat from the public sphere to an elaborate but essentially private intimate sphere. In both cases, however, what is ignored is the unlikelihood of such a position's generalizability outside the dislocations and remappings of the British capital, and thus in the nation, at large or among the less privileged and educated (or even to other Westerners in comparable social positions elsewhere).

Furthermore, similar to the Bloomsbury group's inability to recognize "their own formations as individuals within society, of that specific social formation that made them explicitly a group and implicitly a fraction of a class" (Williams 1980: 165), Rosie, Sammy, Rani, and Alice are unable to realize how each of their own positions and forms of enjoyment imply a certain nonknowledge, an ignorance, of their own historical and ideological formations. Perhaps this is why Bloomsbury can only figure for Rosie and Sammy discontinuously, as icons, as imagined lovers: "Who would you rather have as a lover, Sammy, Virginia Woolf or George Eliot? For looks only, Virginia." It is why "the old British ideological subject of radicalism has become very indeterminate" (Spivak 1993: 245). As we see especially with Rosie in the heated dispute on ethics with Rafi in the restaurant, "[t]he repetition of [her] tenets then in turn becomes more and more *ideological"* (Williams 1980: 165; emphasis mine).

ANIMATING AGENCY IN THE SPACES OF THE GLOBAL CITY

In the concluding pages of his review article on kinship, James Faubion frames renewed anthropological interest in European kinship as part of a larger "problematization of belonging" (1996: 89). Citing such ongoing concerns as the rights debates around the new reproductive technologies, the displacement of colonial self-understandings by more contested postcolonial formations, and with reference to the fraught tones of the talk around the European Union, he writes that "[t]he practical dilemmas of both cultural disintegration and the exercise of sovereignty have grown especially monstrous" (90).

While Faubion evokes the difficulties of belonging as an emergent but still hazy problematic in the anthropology of kinship, I have staged a London-based discussion of it through the relationships of affect, at once aesthetic and political, formed within the "space-time" (Massey 1995: 186) of the house. This discourse of modernity and urbanity has a reuniting effect on older kinship ties, such that, through the sharing of social space *outside the family* home, new "fictive" kinship relations can be formed.

This is instrumental in Bloomsbury. For its members, the house became the first place of critique and transformation, away from the Victorian, imperial domesticity of the West End intellectual family, to newer, less consanguineous and affinal, but still class-based, ways of organizing the domestic sphere in London's Bloomsbury district. Indeed, it is only with their brusque departure from the West End and its pleasantries that the Bloomsbury quarter can become an overdetermined space of freedom, creativity, and individuality. The district becomes an archetype of a new form of urbanity, with re-formed ethical commitments to aesthetic, gender, and sexual politics, where the licenses of individuality were pivotal.

The legacies of the Bloomsbury Group are activated in the assemblage of acts in *Sammy and Rosie Get Laid*. Sammy, abandoned as a child by his father, raised in England, forms an interracial common-law marriage with Rosie, a classmate at university. Rosie's family is never in the picture. On display instead are their alliances with friends and lovers, an ethos of solidarity and critical agency against Thatcherism knotting them together. Similar to Bloomsbury, this knotting is done through the domestic scenes of bathrooms, dining and living rooms, Rosie's study, walks, and rituals of tea. Whether these private scenes weave a commitment to a public discourse that escapes the imperial nostalgias of Thatcherism and its courting of conservative, suburban England is the lingering problem of the film.

Tripping along the uneven footpaths between solidarity and belonging is the migrant who wants to inhabit the national subject (Spivak 1993: 145). As one myself, I am curious of the metropolitan, critical agencies of the Bloomsbury Group and the actors in *Sammy and Rosie*. The solidarities attempted in the film, between Sammy and Rosie, Rani and Vinia, Alice and Rosie's friends, for example, refigure the moral terrain of both familial kinship and Thatcherite domesticity by activating the space of the house to achieve sociality (cf. Strathern 1992: 208 n. 13). Beyond the disdain and disaffection for philistine self- and national understandings, through which Thatcherism effectively repeats and is reminiscent of the Victorian period, are the crises of affect. These center both Faubion's questioning of belonging as they do my tracing of how the house plays a pivotal role in defining a politics of intimacy.

Among the Bloomsbury Group, due to its initial complicity with the discourse of Deep England, we see the possibility of a politics of a private sphere coming into public discourse. In a Habermasian frame, the Bloomsbury Group transformed the bourgeois self-communicated subjectivity of the English "patriarchal conjugal family" into an aesthetic-literary public shaped around an everyday politics of intimacy (see Habermas 1989: 43–56). By contrast, in the London of *Sammy and Rosie*, we see the failure of civic politics in the form of the demolished squatter community as we feel a nostalgic or utopian urge for such politics to thrive. In the film, this feeling is spurred on by the triumphal hymn, "I Vow to Thee My Country," that plays as the caravan of buses leaves the embattled site. Nonetheless, this momentary utopianism is tempered by the film's argument that the intimate sphere must be politicized first before there can be a rapprochement with the public sphere.

This leads me to read *Sammy and Rosie* alongside Holston's notion of "insurgent spaces of citizenship." Insurgent citizenship points to a notion of citizenship that differs from that legitimated by the state and seeks to unravel the "estrangement" with the social through the spatialized practices of new identities—elite, subaltern, racial, cultural, and sexual (1996: 54, 59 n. 12). He argues that such insurgent spaces respond not only to the rejection of modernism's redemptive power, but from "the more general dissolution of the idea of the social itself [and] . . . the inability of the professions of planning and architecture to . . . develop a new activist social imagination" (1996: 54).

Holston, along with new work in geography (see Massey 1993; May 1996; Soja and Hooper 1993) and architectural history (Boyer 1994; Hayden 1995), observes how spatial forms and practices configure new formations of identities, agencies, and solidarities in the city. One spatial form, the house, is not only the emblem of new domestic relationships, but as both Bloomsbury and *Sammy and Rosie* illustrate, the spatialization of an ethics of affect, where affect encompasses aesthetic, intellectual, and erotic politics.

Hence, the house, rather than the strict interiority of the "home," as in Habermas's intimate sphere (1989: 28–29, 43–51), reanimates ongoing work on social relationships, which includes both kinship and citizenship. For, if we remodel our notion of citizenship outside those legitimated by civil law, as Holston argues, can we think of kinship as the remodeling of the intimate sphere, including relations that exceed such legitimation as well? Both are changing "as new members emerge to advance their claims, expanding [their realms], and as new forms of segregation and violence counter these advances, eroding [them]" (Holston 1996: 57).

This returns us to my opening remarks. For it is precisely the expanding and sites of kinship and citizenship and a Bloomsbury-inspired ethics of affect that have led me to redefine my own terrain of engagement. As a Canadian and British citizen whose largest kinship ties remain in western India, this has resulted in a shift in my ethnographic field, from colonial discourse in India to the predicament of agency in the global city.[17] For me and my relationship to anthropology, it means recognizing that the majority of my psychic, political, and intellectual production has been as a Westerner. This admission has drawn me to understand this social fact beyond an ethnicist allegiance to migrant identity politics or multiculturalism—although that stage in itself was crucial. It has also allowed me to begin rethinking myself in a position akin to the Bloomsburyites and the *Sammy and Rosie* troupe. As such, the contradictions and fault lines I occupy become less and less objects of migrant or postcolonial guilt. More and more, they present themselves to be potentially rich vistas for a still underexplored urban anthropology of London.

NOTES

Earlier and partial versions of this chapter appeared as "An Anthropology of Old Bloomsbury," given at the Kinship and Cosmopolitan conference held at Rice University March 28–29, 1997; and as "Kinship and the Scripting of the Bloomsbury Fraction," at the American Ethnological Society meetings in Seattle, March 6–9, 1997. For their comments and staunch support, I would like to thank my major papers' committee, James Faubion, George Marcus, and Kathryn Milun.

1. Although few South Asians would claim a close kinship with other people from the subcontinent and are divided by linguistic, ethnic, caste, regional, and religious identities that are carefully maintained, the politics of multiculturalism and anti-racism and often vaguely expressed notions of shared heritage and immigrant experience make notions of the South Asian Canadian, South Asian American, and the British Asian viable and, potentially, politically expedient. In Canada, for example, the ascription "South Asian Canadian" shares discursive space with older names such as "Indo-Canadian" and "East Indian." In the United States, the Census Bureau maintains the category "Asian Indian." For those unfamiliar with Britain, I should note that "Asian" in that context is equivalent to South Asian and is used by Britons of South Asian descent and by the British press, the government, social service agencies, and community activist groups.

2. The publication of critical essays, biographies, and the like on the prominent members of the Bloomsbury Group, especially Virginia Woolf, who had a lasting effect on English literary modernism, is a cottage industry. The art of Vanessa Bell, Duncan Grant, Roger Fry, and other colleagues goes more unnoticed. An exception is the exhibition at the Tate Gallery in London during the fall of 1999, "The Art of Bloomsbury." The exhibition traveled to the Huntington Art Gallery in San Marino, California, during the spring of 2000 and spent the summer at the Yale Center for British Art.

3. Leslie and Julie Stephen, having married each other after the death of their first spouses, lived in Hyde Park Gate with their four children, Vanessa, Thoby, Virginia, and Adrian Stephen, the three children Julie had from her first marriage with Herbert Duckworth, George, Gerald, and Stella Duckworth, and Leslie's daughter, Laura, who was committed to an asylum at an early age.

4. The Resident was the representative of the colonial administration of each of the three presidencies of British India (Bombay, Bengal, and Madras) stationed in regional cities across each of the presidencies. Poona (Pune) was in Bombay Presidency, the second largest city after Bombay (Mumbai), much of what is the western part of the present Indian state of Maharashtra. He shared this appointment with none other than James Mill. The Resident's office would have been possible for selecting civil servants from the pool of largely Cambridge and Oxford graduates who applied.

5. I have used anthropology's convention of specifying kinship relations in abbreviated form. Each initial stands for a particular relation, to be read in the respective order that it is written. They are F (father), M (mother), S (son), D (daughter), B (brother), Z (sister), and H (husband).

6. Douglas Blair Turnbaugh (1987) has written a biography of Duncan Grant. For Duncan's family history see 17–23; for Holroyd's collaborative evidence, see Holroyd 1967: 16.

7. In an annotation to Strachey (1971), Holroyd writes: "Though the shell of 69 Lancaster Gate remains the same today, the interior has been merged with the houses on either side and is unrecognizable. Since May 1959 the Stracheys' old home has been part of Douglas House, the large American Forces Club which now occupies Nos. 66–71 Lancaster Gate" (15).

8. Letter to Violet Dickinson, 30 October 1904; no. 156 in V. Woolf (1975: 147).

9. Spalding has taken the passage from Vanessa Bell, Memoir III, then in possession of her daughter, Angelica Garnett.

10. Thoby Stephen occupied the study until his death from typhoid in November 1906.

11. John Singer Sargent was an artist and teacher at the Royal Academy where Vanessa was an art student. Charles Furse was another artist who influenced her early work and whose portrait of her was hung in the New English Art Club in 1902. The Club was founded in 1886 as an alternative to the Royal Academy. See Spalding (1983: 34–37).

12. Interestingly, among the Bloomsbury Group, philistinism reaches its height in the entrepreneurial families of Clive Bell, the eldest son of a nouveau-riche coal mine–owning family in Wiltshire, and Roger Fry of Fry's chocolates and cocoa, both of whom go on to become major art critics of their time. In fact, Spalding describes Cleeve House, the Bell family home, as "a Victorian pile masquerading as a Jacobean baronial mansion" (1983: 67). Rosenbaum (1995) notes that the Omega Workshops were established in 1913 "with the help of an inheritance from [Roger's] chocolate-making uncle" (316).

13. Letter to Roger Fry from Vanessa Bell, no specific date, spring 1912, in Spalding (1983: 108).

14. Letter to Violet Dickinson from Virginia Woolf, Sunday 27 November 1910; No. 502 in V. Woolf (1975: 437, 440).

15. Letter to Vanessa Bell from Virginia Woolf. Written at Little Talland House, Firle, Lewes Sussex, 1911; No. 581 in V. Woolf (1975: 475–76).

16. In one of the last letters Virginia wrote to Leonard Woolf, she says, "But I know that I shall never get over this: and I am wasting your life. It is this madness. Nothing anyone says can persuade me" (Letter 3710 in V. Woolf 1980: 486–87). There is controversy regarding the dating of Virginia's last letters (see 489–91), but for comparison see (Bell 1972: 226).

17. I reiterate the importance of the Bloomsbury Group and *Sammy and Rosie Get Laid* in giving me an ethnographic object in the global city in Nityanand Deckha, Repackaging the Inner City: Historic Preservation, Community Development and the Emergent Cultural Quarter in London (Ph.D. dissertation., Department of Anthropology, Rice University, April 2000).

BIBLIOGRAPHY

Annan, N. G. 1955. The Intellectual Aristocracy. In *Studies in Social History; A Tribute to G. M. Trevelyan*. Ed. J. H. Plumb. London: Longmans Green, pp. 241–87.

Arnold, Matthew. [1869] 1994. *Culture and Anarchy*. Ed. S. Lipman. New Haven, Conn.: Yale University Press.

Bell, Clive. 1957. *Old Friends: Personal Recollections*. New York: Harcourt, Brace.

Bell, Quentin. 1972. *Virginia Woolf: A Bibliography*. 2 Vols. London: Hogarth Press.

Boyer, M. Christine. 1994. *The City of Collective Memory: Its Historical Imagery and Architectural Entertainments*. Cambridge, Mass.: MIT Press.

Byrne, Andrew. 1990. *Bedford Square: An Architectural Study*. London: Athlone Press.

Carsten, Janet, and Stephen Hugh-Jones, eds. 1995. *About the House: Lévi-Strauss and Beyond*. Cambridge: Cambridge University Press.

Chambers, Iain. 1993. Narratives of Nationalism: Being "British." In *Theories of Identity and Location*. Ed. E. Carter et al. London: Lawrence and Wishart, pp. 145–64.

Collins, Judith. 1984. *The Omega Workshops*. Chicago: University of Chicago Press.

Elliott, Michael. 1986. *Heartbeat London*. London: Firethorn Books.

Faubion, James D. 1996. Kinship Is Dead: Long Live Kinship. A Review Article. *Comparative Studies in Society and History* 38 (1): 67–91.

Frears, Stephen, and Hanif Kureishi. 1988. *Sammy and Rosie Get Laid*. 35 mm. London: Film Four.

Habermas, Jürgen. 1989. *The Structural Transformation of the Bourgeois Public Sphere*. Trans. T. Burger. Cambridge, Mass.: MIT Press.

Hayden, Dolores. 1995. *The Power of Place: Urban Landscapes as Public History*. Cambridge, Mass.: MIT Press.

Holroyd, Michael. 1967. *Lytton Strachey: A Critical Biography*. Vol. 1: *The Unknown Years (1880–1910)*. New York: Holt, Rinehart, and Winston.

Holston, James. 1996. Spaces of Insurgent Citizenship. *Architectural Design* 66 (Nov.–Dec.): 54–59.

Lancaster, Osbert. 1948. *Home Sweet Homes*. London: J. Murray.

Lévi-Strauss, Claude. 1987. *Anthropology and Myth: Lectures 1951–1982*. Oxford: Blackwell.

——. 1991. Maison. In *Dictionnaire de l'ethnologie et de l'anthropologie*. Ed. P. Bonte and M. Izard. Paris: Presses Universitaires de France, pp. 434–36.

Massey, Doreen. 1993. Power-Geometry and a Progressive Sense of Place. In *Mapping the Futures: Local Cultures, Global Change*. Ed. J. Bird, B. Curtis, T. Putnam, and G. Robertson. London: Routledge, pp. 59–69.

——. 1995. Places and Their Pasts. *History Workshop Journal* 39 (Spring): 182–92.

May, Jon. 1996. Globalization and the Politics of Place: Place and Identity in an Inner London Neighbourhood. *Transactions of the Institute of British Geographers* 21 (1): 194–215.

Morgan, David. 1982. Cultural Work and Friendship Work: The Case of "Bloomsbury." *Media, Culture and Society* 4: 19–32.

Olsen, Donald J. 1986. *The City as a Work of Art: London, Paris, Vienna*. New Haven, Conn.: Yale University Press.

Rosenbaum, S. P., ed. 1995. *The Bloomsbury Group: A Collection of Memoirs and Commentary*. Toronto: University of Toronto Press.

Soja, Edward, and Barbara Hooper. 1993. The Spaces that Difference Makes: Some Notes on the Geographical Margins of the New Cultural Politics. In *Place and the Politics of Identity*. Ed. M. Keith and S. Pile. London: Routledge, pp. 183–205.

Spalding, Frances. 1983. *Vanessa Bell.* New Haven and New York: Ticknor and Fields.

Spivak, Gayatri Chakravorty. 1993. *Outside in the Teaching Machine.* New York: Routledge.

Strachey, Lytton. 1971. Lancaster Gate. In *Lytton Strachey by Himself: A Self-Portrait.* Ed. M. Holroyd. London: Heinemann, pp. 16–28.

Stephen, Sir Leslie. 1977. *Sir Leslie Stephen's Mausoleum Book.* Oxford: Clarendon Press.

Strathern, Marilyn. 1992. *After Nature: English Kinship in the Late Twentieth Century.* Cambridge: Cambridge University Press.

Turnbaugh, Douglas Blair. 1987. *Duncan Grant and the Bloomsbury Group.* Secaucus, N.J.: L. Stuart.

Warner, Michael. 1993. The Mass Public and the Mass Subject. In *The Phantom Public Sphere.* Ed. B. Robbins. Minneapolis: University of Minnesota Press.

Williams, Raymond. 1980. The Bloomsbury Fraction. In *Problems in Materialism and Culture: Selected Essays.* London: Verso, pp. 148–69.

Wolff, Janet. 1996. The Failure of a Hand Sponge: Class, Ethnicity and the Art of Mark Gertler. *New Formations* 28 (Spring): 46–64.

Woolf, Leonard. 1960. *Sowing: An Autobiography of the Years 1880 to 1904.* New York: Harcourt, Brace.

———. 1964. *Beginning Again: An Autobiography of the Years 1911 to 1918.* New York: Harcourt, Brace, World.

Woolf, Virginia. 1975. *The Flight of the Mind: The Letters of Virginia Woolf,* Vol. 1: *1888–1912.* Ed. N. Nicholson. London: Hogarth Press.

———. 1980. *Leave the Letters Till We're Dead: The Letters of Virginia Woolf,* Vol. 6: *1936–1941.* Ed. N. Nicolson. London: Hogarth Press.

———. 1985. *Moments of Being.* Ed. J. Schulkind. New York: Harcourt, Brace, Jovanovich.

Wright, Patrick. 1985. *On Living in an Old Country: The "National Past" in Contemporary Britain.* London: Verso.

Žižek, Slavoj. 1989. *The Sublime Object of Ideology.* London: Verso.

7

This Week the Blue Room: Locating Kinship in a Split-Level House

Susan Ossman

THE FAMILY

Edward Thomas Ossman Jr., 1934
Camille Joan, née Radzicki, 1939
Susan Marie, 1959
Linda Camille, 1960
Mary Ellen, 1961
Laura Ann, 1964
Kathleen Ann, 1964
Julie Elizabeth, 1966

Brother is flying out of the family room again. "There he goes," cries Kathy as her twin sister Laura rushes to catch him. Laura manages to capture him and tries to pet him. She puckers her lips and coos with birdlike sounds as he moves toward her, kissing her with his firm parakeet beak. In return he bites her and flies off when she exclaims with anger. "Time to get back in the cage, Brother," she cries. Kathy watches as she captures him in a dish towel and gives him a pat on his behind. "Bad boy, Brother, bad boy."

Whether Brother was indeed a male budgie was never actually clear. But, in the home that my father shared with seven women and a female dog, the choice of the bird's name met with no resistance. When the family members had gathered after dinner to propose suggestions for the bird's name and cast their votes, no other name was seriously entertained as a possibility. "Brother" was thus christened as a living symbol of what we perceived to be missing in our family. As our Brother grew, we often allowed him to fly freely about the family room where we played, watched television, or stud-

178

ied. He liked to flutter into the adjoining kitchen. However, if he slipped through the door into the formal living and dining rooms of the house, a hot pursuit immediately followed. All of us kids knew that those parts of the house were off-limits for play. But how could one teach a bird that, while I was required to enter this space to play the same songs each and every day in preparation for my weekly piano lesson, his consistently original melodies were unwelcome in this part of the house? The living room and dining room were associated with Sunday shoes and dresses, ties and holiday customs. Much as Brother was admonished for crossing into these sacrosanct spaces, so, too, were we chastised for transporting inappropriate clothing or activities into them. Playing the baby grand in hopes of mastering Chopin's more arduous arpeggios was about the only *pratique quotidienne* deemed appropriate in this part of the house.

Nonetheless, it was through this carefully decorated and arranged formal landscape that we had to go to reach the upper floor of our home. Unlike earlier versions of American homes, the plan of this 1960s split-level dwelling was based on an open floor plan. No back stairs, attics, or rooms set in turrets or towers could cut up the even flow of air, light, and sound throughout the house. On the ground story of the house, the power of this new house plan was challenged by a single door set between the dining and kitchen areas. But even this door was, of necessity, often left ajar. For it was only by crossing this space that we could reach our second-story bedrooms. This movement through the living room toward the stairs tended to calm us; transforming the downstairs playfulness and instituting an upstairs order and calm were de rigueur. Brother was barred from this part of the house. We also understood that our friends were to be entertained downstairs or outside. The bedrooms were to be kept free of dirt and noise, that is, of certain childhood activities that would apparently disturb them. The architects had designated one of the rooms as the "master" bedroom. Of all of the rooms of the house this is the only one that I cannot bring to mind today. I remember standing at the door, waiting to be admitted. I do know that it was slightly larger than the other rooms and had its own bathroom. Of the upstairs hallway, on the other hand, I can still form a clear image. That was where there was a shelf for our books—there I would sit during the hours when we children were supposed to be asleep, and before my parents came up to bed, poring over whatever volumes I might find there. Like the basement of the house, where I often went to paint, this space was coveted by no one but me. The hallway was white, colorless because it seems not to have been considered as built space at all.

The bedrooms, on the other hand, were generally unavailable as spaces for flights of imagination, because they in fact came to symbolize what was most curious and apparently creative about our family. While the downstairs rooms were carefully planned out according to their purposes, with only

halls and basements left to the imagination, the rooms upstairs were endowed with personalities of their own. While the downstairs areas were decorated in coordinated colors and according to styles reminiscent of sets for
The Brady Bunch, or photos in *Better Homes and Gardens,* the bedrooms
were painted and upholstered and curtained and carpeted regularly and in
tune to the more upbeat or "cool" fashions of the time. Each room was regularly redecorated as our tastes evolved. As my mother notes, all of the girls
discussed these changes that gave the rooms "personality."[1] Thus, from rus-
tic French provincial with white lace, the "peach" room turned electric orange in 1970. Zebra striped bedspreads appeared on the beds in the freshly
painted lime green room while the "blue" room became violet. Unlike our
later, teenage rooms, there were no musical accompaniments to the visual
movement of the decor, no posters of rock idols pinned to the walls. Yet,
when I think of these rooms today I associate them with their "theme" songs
of the era. The blue/violet room is my father's favorite, "The Boxer" by
Simon and Garfunkel. The green room makes me think of a sickly sweet
mixture of the Tom Jones and Engelbert Humperdinck tunes my mother and
her friends often listened to. And the orange room still brings to mind Jim
Morrison imploring, "Come On Baby Light My Fire."

The very fact that these rooms clearly mark our memories seems to indicate that their decoration was in some way a success. Yet, perhaps even
more than the formality of the downstairs rooms, the "personalities" we gave
these rooms seemed also to overwhelm any identification between them and
their inhabitants. The environments they created might remind us of an
epoch, but apart from the identification of the master bedroom with the parents, the other rooms remind us of no one in particular. What then was going
on in this careful and comfortable creation of lived environments? Can we
look back and read these rooms as icons of a specifically American middle-
class popular culture that is alienated from place and obsessed with making
life resemble magazine images? Indeed, as portrayed by the super-8 film my
father shot during this period, the rooms of our split-level home appear to be
organized according to the same codes as those of most of our neighbors in
this new suburban area of Chicago inhabited by the grandchildren and great-
grandchildren of immigrants from Southern and Central Europe. Formality
downstairs, privacy upstairs. Indeed, our house and our mother resembled
others in the neighborhood, but somehow, just a little more so. As Girl Scout
mother and PTA president, my mother seems to have been a local "personality" at a young age (see Truxell 1968). My father, although certainly not
wealthy, was nonetheless the only university professor in our neighborhood.
Apparently, this was worth some "cultural capital." But these minor differences aside, our house resembled those of our neighbors. With only two
basic models from which to choose in the housing development, this was
not surprising.

What really distinguished the Ossmans from the Wisners, the Bronders, or the Scalzos were not their "style" but rather their covey of six perfectly dressed and absolutely courteous little girls. Indeed, it was not only the number and sex of their children that most marked off my parents from their neighbors, but their apparent ability to keep us "disciplined." Unlike the homes of many of the larger families in the area, our house was never in disarray. Although we did hand down clothes, family photographs show how well groomed and fashionable we always appeared. Was this a mere reflection of a taste for fashion, or did a more insidious bent for organization and social engineering inform such an overwhelmingly organized approach to family life?

I remember how my maternal grandmother used to pore over women's journals always in the pursuit of more nutritious diets and home improvements. Each object in her house inhabited its own special place and contributed to an overall style. But, unlike our house, the basic tone of Grandma's house never changed. I maintain a very clear memory of the colors and arrangements of each chair, each crystal vase, or souvenir she kept. Even in 1998 in her nursing home studio, some of the furniture she bought at the time of her wedding in 1934 still surrounded her.[2] Our house was as carefully arranged as Grandma's, but it was constantly altered. While Grandma seemed to want to learn about decoration or style in order to get things "right," my mother's constant refurbishing, revarnishing, wallpapering, and sewing, like her desire to select always appropriate attire for given social occasions, emphasized the fleeting nature of "rightness" as embodied in objects or people. Personal and domestic decoration required many hours of shopping and debates about style and decorum. There was an aesthetic training involved in this activity. But it was a training in how identifiable styles could relate to a variety of social questions. We used decor to play on color and form, but also to clearly distinguish and coordinate a variety of domestic routines. Even today, in talking about the house on Kathleen Drive, my mother does not dwell on attachments of special spaces, or on the precise ways in which she adorned walls or floors, but rather on the relationship of space to household organization. While Grandma dwelled in place, in her house, well anchored in a Polish American Chicago community bounded by name, lineage, language, and religious practice, my mother's approach might be seen as a move toward integration, Americanization, or a postmodern sense of space.[3]

Thinking of changing decor reminds me of how my mother used to complain that her name was not "American" enough. She told us how her relatives were scandalized when she married someone who was not only not a Pole, but had a German name. But such a willingness to engage in becoming less "ethnic" and more "American" would perhaps be too general an explanation for some of the very particular ways in which my mother came to organize her own and her children's movements through space. If, as I mentioned, each bedroom of our split-level house was "given a personality," the ways we were to use these spaces had to do more with creating a sense of social continuity that hoped to defy or deny or make use of space for its own ends. Or at least, this is how my mother explains one of her most unique inventions: the room changing scheme we came to call "the lottery."

THE LOTTERY

The story began in the spring of 1965 when my parents found out that they were soon to have a sixth child. Our small ranch-style, three-bedroom house in Des Plaines was clearly not big enough to hold us all, and so by the summer we moved to the new house in a housing development in the same town. In this house, as I noted, the architect had clearly indicated the location of the parents' master bedroom, but the three other bedrooms had to be assigned to the children. Obviously, the kind of alternative "boys' room/girls' room" arrangement adopted in many large families was impossible. This fact also seemed to make social divisions among us more my mother's than my father's concern. Initially, she divided up the rooms according to age groups. I, the oldest, and my sister Linda, my junior by one year, were given the blue room to share. This was simple enough. But problems become apparent when we consider the arrangement for the next in line. Mary, one year younger than Linda, slept alone, but knew that she was to be set up with the new baby, who was not yet named Julie, and who would arrive at the beginning of 1966. Laura and Kathleen, fraternal twins, were to share the remaining room.

This schema seems to have functioned smoothly until the spring of 1966 when the baby moved from my parents' room to sleep with Mary. According to Linda, Mary began to complain about having to share a room with an infant, in spite of the development in family discourse of two triads, the "big kids" and the "little kids." Here was Mary, a "big kid," having to share a room with the smallest of the "little kids." She complained of crying at night, of the odor of diapers. But in fact, the issue was primarily one of status. As the youngest of the "big kids" she could at least expect to share a room with one of the older "little kids." This might have been the most logical solution, especially since one of the twins, Laura, was more robust, taller, and generally closer to Mary than the other. However, due to my parents' desire to demonstrate the twins' equality, this possibility was never seriously considered. While the age-group arrangement seemed to work out for most of us, the existence of the twins, and my parents' attitude to their relationship, was inherently disruptive of the age order. Age hierarchies, that, being the eldest, I fully endorsed, were progressively delegitimated by the impossibility of their total application. As a result of the difficulty of classification according to age groups in the context in which the "little kids" included a set of twins, we were all soon to be literally disembedded (Giddens 1991).

My mother devised a solution to the bedroom dilemma. Rather than perceiving each room as a site of special identification and affection attached to a specific individual or group, why not conceive of the "bedroom space" as continuous, in spite of the walls that the masons had set up to confound our correct thinking about this space? Why not reinterpret this divided but identical space for sleeping to illustrate social relations in ways that would blend the daughters into a single class, rather than emphasizing social distinctions of age or pointing up the very apparent differences between the twins? In 1970, when the youngest daughter was three and able to sleep in a regular bed, my mother must have been implicitly thinking along these lines when she devised a new system of managing the private parts of the home. We called it the lottery.

This is how it worked. Every other Saturday night each of our names was put in a hat. The names of two of the girls would be pulled and set down on a chart to indicate that they would be "roommates" for the following two weeks. Since each bedroom was identified by its decor, order would proceed from these stylistic distinctions. Roommates would rotate between the rooms. Sheets would be changed, favorite teddy bears moved, and life would go on. Thus each room would be considered as stable, but its occupants varied. At first, all of our possessions followed us to the new rooms. But, as my mother notes, this was impracticable. So our "original" bedrooms were assigned to us as "homerooms," serving as sites to store our clothes and special belongings.

Although this system quickly became a habit, it remains an object of discussion within the family. Indeed, when I was asked to write a paper on my own experience of "kinship" and "cosmopolitanism" for the conference on which this book is based, instead of my individual experiences of living in several countries as a "cosmopolitan" it was to this specific "solution" to sleeping that my mind turned. When I conducted interviews with family members about the lottery, I found that they, too, had always perceived it as a very odd practice that nonetheless defined our family. Apart from my father, who simply said that the system was something my mother devised, and my sister Julie, who says she can't remember anything about it since she was too young, other family members were happy to share their memories and opinions about this method of organizing space and family relations. One sister writes:

> I do not know why we started the lottery—I think it may have been that we were getting so many children in the family that they didn't know whom to put with whom so they just kept mixing us up. Maybe so we would get to know everyone.

Indeed, our mother says that the system was instituted to "keep things fair because the girls complained that they didn't like the sister that they had to share with." She also notes that two of the three rooms had bunk beds and most of the girls didn't like to sleep on top. She writes, "The parents wanted to teach the girls that they can't always get what they want. They had to share and get to see that knowing other personalities was important for their growth." They also had to learn "teamwork." But, as Linda remarks, the system also forced us constantly to think simply about where we were. "Sometimes we got confused. I remember that Kathy used to sleepwalk. She'd forget which bed she was supposed to be sleeping in and she'd get in on top of you in the middle of the night." Kathy writes:

> The room rotation system was mostly interesting. I can't say that it was good—it may have actually been bad in some ways and good in a few ways. I found myself confused where I was sleeping. Especially right after a room change, getting up at night to go to the bathroom I would always walk the wrong direction. Or before going to bed I would try to remember what room I was in. This took thought for me. Or I often lay awake in my bed trying to concentrate to remember what room I was in.

This way of organizing family life not only discarded age hierarchies as a recognized system of differences, but also dissolved the special relationship of the twins. While a strict age grading system would have put Laura, two minutes older than Kathy, with a "big kid," and presented Kathy as somehow inadequate by joining her to a child two years her junior, this new system set us all up as equals. Kathy continues:

> I also remember wanting to like every possible sister I would roommate with. I never wanted to like one more than the next. I also remember thinking as I was in a room with a sister, "I wonder how many more nights we will stay here together?" This would make me sad. Or sometimes we would change rooms, and I would have a new sister and I would realize just how different she was than the last one. It was always interesting. I quickly learned how to be accommodating, because I didn't want any of my sisters to dislike me. I also remember when we were picking names how everyone would yell out, "No I don't want to sleep with so and so; they're a baby, or they're a bully, or they are stubborn, or they talk all night in their sleep." This would sometimes create tension and sadness, and certain parts made us laugh. I also remember contemplating which room I liked most. I usually went with the green room or the purple room. The room option was also a debated issue and open for discussion. I also remember being afraid of starting a new night with a new sister: Would I know what to say, would I know how to act? Also, some sisters could make me behave differently. One would create a reaction in me of being silly (Linda or Julie), the next to talking intelligently (Susan), the next to complaining or trying to figure something in life out (Laura), or simply being a bit quiet (Mary).

In spite of the stated goals of this system there were favorites as roommates. The lottery did not eliminate special ties or make us less aware of the rift between the big kids and the little kids. Rather, it led us to develop a more subjective, perhaps reflexive, relationship to these categories. Much as during family decisions made by election, "party" platforms emerged. Individuals were judged according to their propensity to snore, their talkativeness before bed, whether they hid flashlights under their covers to be able to read at night and bother their roommate. As "beings in a territory," the territory of my mother's styled spaces, we appeared equal, unattached, delocalized, uprooted, dislocated. In the name of equality, our dreams were to move with us, following us from room to room, nomads traversing the varied landscapes of our own house. Could this imagination be related to the kind of modernist dream described in literature on colonialization or globalization (cf. Rabinow 1989)? Can domestic space and family relationships be reconsidered in terms of these apparently impersonal processes, or is a specific family history responsible for the adoption of what appeared to one reader of this work as evidence of the dissolution not only of age-based difference, but of the very idea of family?

In a sense, our peregrinations could be seen as a reflection of family experiences of movement over the last and upcoming generations. On each side of the family, immigrating was the norm rather than the exception. Our nuclear family moved from an apartment in Chicago to a townhouse in the suburbs, then to a larger house, then to the San Francisco Bay Area. These moves, however, resembled those of other families. Yet, I have never met anyone whose family engaged in anything like our room lottery arrangement. Did it relate to the way we assured fairness at Christmas, clearly indicating that each child would receive a gift of exactly the same value? The way in which we held family elections to decide on issues of common concern?

My mother makes a point of noting that each of us had a small, indeed tiny, space to call our own, our "original" room. Each of the dressers that occupied the three children's rooms was used to store our clothing. However, we did not simply attribute a dresser to a specific individual. Rather, the dressers were assigned to the "original" inhabitants of each of the rooms. Then, for each pair, the drawers were identified by their contents: an underwear drawer, a sock drawer, a t-shirt drawer, and so on. Each sister was, however, given a specific drawer, usually the top drawer of a dresser, where she could keep her personal possessions. Within this treasure store, the organization of each inch followed the general family pattern. To each sector of the inside of the drawer was carefully ascribed a specific function: to store jewelry, to keep a special box, or to keep the old vitamin bottle that each of us was given to "save" our baby teeth after the tooth fairy had repaid us for them. Birthday cards, diaries, shiny rocks, photographs from summer camp, or cameras: all of the various valuables of childhood were organized around the space of the drawer. My mother says that we each had a 30-by-20-inch box in the closet to keep "private things, art, school work, and photos." I don't remember this, but it might explain why, years later when I began to watch Moroccan film in the context of research for my doctorate, I was particularly struck by *Wechma*. The film is about a young boy who stashes a secret box in the hills, far from the eyes of his strict stepfather. In the film, the father discovers the secret, and the boy is humiliated. In our case, it was our mother who so obligingly provided the "secret" place. Was this any less problematic? Invoking the immigrant experience once more, this designation of personal spaces might be equated with the setting up of a festival in the "home" village to which to occasionally return, a setting of nostalgia (Appadurai 1996; cf. also Seremetakis 1996). Referring to the organization of identity of "beings in territory" evoked earlier, permission to set up a special space might be understood as recognition of the residue of modernizing, abstracting ways. In the course of fashioning a fully autonomous self these are essential, but they, like other remainders, must also be managed and controlled (Ossman 1998).

Even today, in discussing family issues, there is a rift between those who accepted this preestablished place as their own, and those who instituted alternative places to keep their things. When a group of us got an astrology reading together at the 1997 Danville, California, village fair, this contrast came to the surface as the astrologist discussed the role of our mother in our lives. "Those guys just never had conflicts with her since they wanted to do as she told them, unlike me," exclaimed Linda. Indeed, some of the sisters seemed at ease with the empty box of privacy they were offered. Others, like Linda, reacted by making their own boxes elsewhere. Other sisters adopted friends' rooms in other houses. Later, Kathy would move into the office of a horse stable. As for me, the space became imaginary. As I set up my easel in the basement, it became my space. When I practiced scales in the living room, I made the house move to my touch. I consistently adopted the spaces of self provided by my mother, as well as colonizing other spaces, setting them up as places (Harvey 1996).

My mother says that the "system was good because it was fair and it encouraged the children to learn to work with other people. The younger girls were taught by their elders about rules and family expectations" and "they talked about what they like, their friends, and the parties they went to." As the eldest, I inevitably felt cheated by the system. Who would teach me? I remember reading my mother's old high-school yearbooks for clues about older kids. I envied my friend Cynthia who had *three older brothers*! I tended to make friends with children who were older than I was. I still remember reading with approval about how older siblings in places such as China not only had responsibility for their younger sisters and brothers, but also could expect a special position and respect in turn. I continued to dream of having a "real" room. Of not having to explain to my friends why my space moved about every two weeks. I maintained a strong attachment for the "purple room" (that became the blue room) that had been the place I shared with Linda before the lottery was devised. To my relief, in this room at least, the lace curtains, antique desk, and black and white etchings we had inherited from one of my father's relatives were maintained. Even if the color changed it remained pastel. Since this had been my first room in this house, I still thought of it as mine. It was there that my clothes filled the French modern drawers and there that the closet held my favorite dress from Bonwit Teller and my jewelry box that, thank God, had no little dancing ballerina inside of it to make music.

MOVING OUT

My father loves to drive anywhere out of the city—just away. On Sundays we would take long drives to see the countryside, and, if possible, to please my mother by visiting the "model homes" of any new subdivisions in the region. We also drove to take vacations. When I was very young we simply spent August at a lakeside cabin in Michigan or Wisconsin. Then, we began to take cross-country car trips in our station wagon. Of all the places we visited we liked the San Francisco Bay area the best. Several friends and colleagues of my parents had moved there in the 1960s, and we decided that we, too, would like to leave the bitter Chicago winters for the California sun. In 1973 my father was offered a job at California State University, Hayward, and the family voted unanimously to move. My parents bought a new split-level house in Danville, California. There, the lottery system was abandoned.

One of the bedrooms in the new house was exceptionally large, and we called it the "dorm." There was quite enough room for the three "little kids" to share this space. The other two "big kids," Mary and Linda, shared the other room. I was overjoyed. I acquired my own room. In the haste of my parents' house-buying trip to the Bay Area I was given no choice of the color or location of what would become my space. But the aesthetics of the room held little interest for me. I was to sleep alone, have my own closet, and glimpse the golden view of the La Trampas hills from my western window.

Areas of potential conflict shifted. As we grew older, and our collection of hair dryers, curling irons, and makeup assumed truly astounding dimensions, the upstairs bathroom became a site of constant movement and potential hazards. My mother remembers that this new situation was determined in terms of thinking about the future: "There was the idea that they (the girls) would all eventually be in their own rooms as the older girls moved out or went to college." Unsurprisingly, it was now the second sister, Linda, who felt cheated, for she would have had her own room but for one apparently significant year. (I obliged the system by moving out as quickly as possible, just after my seventeenth birthday.)

Today, my mother is quick to note that the move to California did not entail any disorganization. While we no longer changed rooms, a rotating system was devised to divvy up household chores. Linda graphically represented her rotation in a rotating wheel posted in the kitchen. "It was decided that the wheels should be moved one turn each period. If you did not like the job you got you could trade it, but both parties had to agree." Since my mother returned to full-time work soon after our move, the smooth working of the household did indeed rely on the kind of "teamwork" and "fairness" that she perceives as essential to the family's functioning. Besides the shared tasks, we each participated in the elaboration of the shopping by listing what we needed and wanted on a notepad in the kitchen. My father subsequently went to the store. On a second yellow legal pad we checked in and out, providing information on our whereabouts so our parents could reach us at all times. What might we make of this series of interwoven decisions about spatial and family organization? What idea of the family and, specifically, relations between siblings does it propose? Would it indeed be possible to find answers to these questions in terms of reflections on families, or kinship, or would it be necessary to speak not only of "family values" but also of social organization more generally?

The lottery system was, indeed, unique. No family members know of any other family that has used such a system. One of my sisters even writes, "I never heard of such a thing. Maybe one of the hundreds of American Indian tribes thought of it." At first I thought that she was using the idea of the "Indian" to signify the most absolute difference. What she explained to me was that she was thinking about the vast number of distinct North American cultures, each of which had its own language and customs. She said that it was this variety she was trying to get across: she used the reference to "Indians" rather like old-time anthropologists sifting through lists of culture traits in field notes gathered throughout the world.

To me, the words we used to describe the room moving recall a tale that was also distant from our own family history. It reminds me of a story I read in high school called "The Lottery" (Jackson 1992). In that tale, set in a New England town, a lottery is periodically organized by the townspeople to designate a sacrificial victim. Family members of the chosen person are expected to reaffirm their belonging to the community by stoning their loved one, like us, treating their own feelings about specific people as either to be ignored or altered in order that harmony be maintained within the larger community. In both cases, it is a "system" that determines whether to select a victim or designate roommates. While leaders or parents might regulate the smooth working of the rules once they are set up, their role becomes one of surveillance and of coordination, certainly not one of decision in terms of selecting individuals for specific fates. For our family the fate of a single individual is not perceived as the point of the system, unlike in the story or in the state lotteries that allow certain randomly associated numbers to bring instant wealth to individuals. Were this the case, it would be easy enough, for example, to read my mother's organizational strategy as a reflection of an ideology of risk and luck, and to relate it to a penchant for gambling and attending horse racing that does indeed seem to be passed from one generation to the next in my father's family. In gambling situations, one's chances are the same as anyone else's—but in the case of the room lottery there are no winners. But no one was supposed to be sacrificed, either. That was just the point.

This decided dismissal of preference, or singularity, calls to mind the abstract, ideally commensurate world maps that seem to spring from a secular, modern vision of the world. To refer to this "modern" space, Anthony Giddens, for one, writes of the "disembedding" mechanisms of modern social life, a turn of phrase that aptly describes the way the lottery system works (Giddens 1991: 2). The lottery system could be read as evidence of how modern modes of spatial organization have been effectively brought even to family life. But there is clearly more to this story than a uniformization of space and time. First, the lottery limited the scope of the application of the modern ideal. It defined the family against the background of the general social world. The "girls" were perhaps interchangeable among themselves, but they were clearly identified as a part of the Ossman family. The rooms, too, while not identified with reference to any individual, offered clearly differentiated landscapes. In a sense it was the domestication of global trends, and not the desacralization of some fundamental tradition that seems to have been at work here. Moving through the dioramas that were our rooms was also an experience of stylistic difference and play—one that resonates as we walk through the period sets of a museum, the specialized boutiques of the shopping mall, or the neighborhoods of contemporary cities (Silverstone 1998; Zukin 1991). Second, the lottery was adopted only when distinctions of age or gender failed to "work." The fact that it was abandoned and that the floor plan of the new house in California proved to offer a "solution" shows that in spite of the fact that my mother thought the lottery to be successful, my parents continued to perceive it as anomalous. What did persist, however, was a sense of the household space as essentially flexible and changing over time. The individual bedroom here is not presented as a given, but still as something desirable.

Family identity was not linked to property or place but instead to the "values" that my mother expected the lottery to help to instill in us. These "values" were not the kinds that have come to pervade discussions about families in America since the 1990s. In our case, each was equal before the draw. The reasons given for starting the system in the first place had much to do with attempting to canalize perceived differences between the sisters in the absence of an adequate system of classification. Thinking back again to my mother's high-school yearbooks, I wonder whether her lottery project was not in part inspired by her experiences at school. One might relate the arrangement to those that are common in American secondary schools where each student has a "homeroom" and a "locker" to keep his or her possessions, but moves from classroom to classroom, teacher to teacher, each hour. Our moves through the house were not hourly, but they did entail the kinds of shifts of people and place one experiences in following the schedule of an American high-school student. In a very different way than Laurel George's chapter in this volume describes the importance of schools as family, perhaps the school and the office played a role in shaping our family as a family.

Thinking about the lottery and its possible sources of inspiration makes me doubt some ideas about how individuality is linked to spatially delimited privacy, in turn a corollary to notions of modernity for many anthropologists or architects (cf. Rybczynski 1986). It has also made me wary of writings that would see nomadism as a solitary enterprise or propose that it implies disorder, or that it requires long treks over the face of the earth. Just as Stanford Carpenter's chapter in this volume shows how his family draws up a map of America through family card games, it seems that our family was attempting to use space in ways that helped us to move while maintaining connection. Is it significant that one of the cities where Mr. Carpenter lived was also the Chicago suburb where the lottery took place? While his story involves being middle class and black in places such as Des Plaines where racial integration was resisted, it might be interesting to remember that many of the white people living in suburbs like that did not necessarily perceive themselves as fully "American"—perhaps they were on the way to that "Americanness," but in the 1960s and 1970s they were not yet "there."[4] That "there" was related to ideas of nation, but it was also a place, it seems to me, that was not conceivable simply in terms of "passing" in the world of Anglo-Saxon Protestantism. Indeed, unlike blacks, these white ethnics could easily change their names and convert to any of the many protestant churches. But the idea of space opening up, of moving though diorama-like landscapes while keeping together, seems to me to be one that might offer a promise of a logic that moves beyond such a model. This logic works with certain processes involved in economic and educational institutions and plays with passing contents. This might lead us to notice how processes that often have been associated with exiles or diasporas involving complex relations to home, place, and nation might be at work at the heart of what is often seen as the heartland of "family values."

CHICAGO 1994

In 1994, in the middle of our usual summer visit to my parents in California, my father, my son Nathanael and I took a trip to Chicago to see members of our extended family. As a part of that visit, we took a drive by all of the houses in which we had lived in the area. As we drove by a townhouse, the small three-bedroom, and the "house on Kathleen Drive," my father and I told Nathanael stories about each place, and it was in these stories, recounted with reference to the circumstances of these little moves, and consistently referring to the subtext of the big moves to California and the subsequent inclusion of France and North Africa into our paths, that the family story seemed easiest to piece together. Indeed, although my own attitude toward the lottery was apparently among the most "conservative" of the family, I am certainly the family member who has most contributed to enriching the wealth of the family's moving stories since that time. One could read my own use of domestic space as profoundly marked by the experience of mobility and the conceptions of self and community that the lottery implied. Indeed, from the point of view of my son, one could say that I have expanded on some of the core ideas of the project to include not only serial changes, but also contemporaneous investments in several rooms. Nathanael, like me, considers one of the rooms in my parent's California house as his own. He has a room at my apartment in Paris and another at his father's apartment, three blocks away. His father's old bedroom at his paternal grandmother's home is also full of his old toys. While I was working in Casablanca and Rabat for several years he also had a room in my apartments there.

Even amid such a plethora of "private" spaces, deciding how to create "boxes" for one's valuables continues to require self-reflection. Which things should always be on hand even *between* the rooms? And how do the rooms relate to one another? This is perhaps the real question. For it encourages us to see that a sense of self and of private space issues not simply from identifying oneself by a name or place, but by creating the meaning of names and places by how one constitutes them through movement. Choreographies of connection take us down paths that are not just anywhere; as broad or narrow as they might be, they remain bordered and regulated, controlled and surveyed, or stylishly decorated to ensure a likely outcome to the journeys they allow (Ossman 2001). Kinship and talk of family values might be perceived as one means we use to define and limit these paths, at least, if we conceive of family and culture and the educative process as grounded in some easily identifiable habitus. But they might also be conceived in terms of other ways of thinking about what holds kin or cultures together. In many cases today kinship could be seen as a collective effort in overcoming space. This includes practical, collective experiments in how to rework maps, organize air travel, design family Web sites, and decorate prefabricated homes so as to focus on family ties and give value to particular notions of equality, age, or authority.

The lottery might be seen as an education and as a maintaining of identities in a mobile world. It acts as a reminder of the ways in that such a world is profoundly social in spite of what some accounts of the abstraction of modernity might lead us to believe. The landscapes of the rooms, blue, green, or orange, were not open to anyone. Not even Brother was allowed to flutter between them. The lottery did not preclude alternative arrangements or even bargaining among sisters regarding the roommates they might draw. It did not alter the ritual "kiss goodnight" procession of my parents who, following evening prayers, nightly traveled from room to room to talk with each of us about our day, the books we read, how time evolves, or how people interact. This, wherever we might be sleeping.

NOTES

In memory of Bernice Radzicki, 1908–1998.

1. To prepare this work I interviewed all the family members. Some people in the family had few memories of the lottery system (for instance, Julie, who was quite young). Others had a lot to say about it—following my explanation that I was writing this work, and again, subsequent to my circulating a rough draft of it, a couple of family members wrote me very long letters about their perception of the lottery system.

2. My grandmother, Bernice Wrobel Radzicki, died in November 1998. Since then the family has become aware of her extensive collection of copies of her letters, journals, and photographs. The way she arranged her archives seems to have been inspired by her own secretarial training. She typed all of her correspondence and made carbon copies of each letter. These letters and her journal are so precisely detailed that they make one think that she was preparing field notes on the note and queries model. Perhaps the involvement of models of organization from the office in the life of the family actually started before my mother came of age, but all I can hope to do is provide an account of what seems to me to be one of the more exotic practices that such arrangements produced.

3. My grandmother's parents came from a part of Poland under Austro-Hungarian control, while my grandfather's ancestors were bilingual Polish- and German-speaking Poles from the Smolna region. (Barbara Sabel has recently retraced the Radzicki family tree for this "Prussian" branch of the family.) They were thus not precisely a part of the group that William I. Thomas and Florian Znaniecki studied for their *Polish Peasant in Europe and America*, being that the authors of that classic study focused on immigrants from the parts of Poland then controlled by Russia. However, my relatives were very much a part of the Polish American community that developed in Chicago, as described by Thomas and Znaniecki.

4. The relation between the ethnic groups in the Chicago area is not my focus. A lively account of one racial conflict at the beginning of the twentieth century is presented by William M. Tuttle, Jr. (1970).

BIBLIOGRAPHY

Appadurai, Arjun. 1996. *Modernity at Large: Cultural Dimensions of Globalization.* Minneapolis: University of Minnesota Press.

Giddens, Anthony. 1991. *Modernity and Self-Identity.* Stanford, Calif.: Stanford University Press.

Harvey, David. 1996. *Justice, Nature and the Geography of Difference.* Oxford: Blackwell.

Jackson, Shirley. 1992. *The Lottery and Other Stories.* New York: Noonday Press.

Ossman, Susan. 1994. *Picturing Casablanca. Portraits of Power in a Modern City.* Berkeley: University of California Press.

———. 1998. Introduction. In *Miroirs Maghrébins: Itinéraires de soi et paysages de rencontre.* Ed. S. Ossman. Paris: CNRS Editions.

———. 2001. *Three Faces of Beauty, Casablanca, Paris, Cairo.* Durham: Duke University Press.

Rabinow, Paul. 1989. *French Modern: Norms and Forms of the Social Environment.* Cambridge, Mass.: MIT Press.

Rybczynski, Withold. 1986. *Home: A Short History of an Idea.* New York: Viking.

Seremetakis, Nadia C. 1996. The Memory of the Senses, Part I: Marks of the Transitory. In *The Senses Still.* Ed. N. C. Seremetakis. Chicago: University of Chicago Press, 1–18.

Silverstone, Roger. 1998. Les espaces de la performance: musées, sciences et rhétoriques de l'objet. *Hérmès 22: Mimesis. Imiter, représenter, circuler,* 175–88.

Truxell, Leland Ellis. 1968. Personality of the Week. *Des Plaines Suburban Times,* 17 October: n.p.

Tuttle, William M., Jr. 1970. *Race Riot: Chicago in the Red Summer of 1919.* New York: Atheneum.

Woolf, Virginia. 1990. *A Room of One's Own.* New York: Harcourt and Brace.

Zukin, Sharon. 1991. *Landscapes of Power: From Detroit to Disney World.* Berkeley: University of California Press.

8

What We Bring to the Table: The Means of Imagination in an African American Family

Stanford W. Carpenter

SETTING THE TABLE

I am not alone. I have a sister, a father, and a mother. My parents have been married for more than thirty years. They have been homeowners for twenty-five. We have had two pets—a dog and a cat. As is the case with most pets, they have died before us. Our race aside, we fit the image of the standard American nuclear family. Brother, Sister, Father, Mother . . . definitive kinship terms that obscure our ambiguous biological relatedness.

In the summer of 1992 my sister and I, taking advantage of our "reckless youth," drove across the United States. During the fall of 1995 a friend and I followed Cleo Fields as he attempted to become Louisiana's first African American governor. During the summer of 1997 I went to Africa. These accounts come together to form a passage of sorts, beginning on the west coast of Africa, continuing through Louisiana, and ending in the midwestern United States, highlighting the tensions inherent in being African and American as well as black and of the suburban middle class.

During the holidays my extended family and a few close family friends come together to swap stories and play cards. The card game that I describe never happened. It is an assemblage of games past, played in many locales, each game being a partial reenactment of games past. It is an attempt to capture the lived quality of tales retold and memories inspired by privileged spaces. What follows are a series of stories, memories really, and a game of Dirty Hearts that, once woven together, form a narrative of kin relationships in a middle-class African American family. The narrative makes sense of my family's ambiguous biological relatedness and addresses many of the tensions inherent in being a suburban middle-class African American male.

I end my tales on a lonely stretch of road somewhere East of Kansas City, Kansas, during a road trip that took place several years before my trip to Africa. This switch reconfigures this narrative, making it an allegory of the entry of many African Americans into the Americas. The events in between these two trips (a game of cards, memories of kin, and most important, the remaking of kin) serve as the middle passage between an imagined Africa and an unsettling American landscape.

HINTERLANDS

I remember visiting the Cape Coast Monument in Ghana, Africa. It was my first trip to Africa—the "motherland"—a phrase, a clue, an indicator of my identity. I watched, barely concealing my own emotion, as the tour group gathered in the courtyard. On the podium was a banner stating "One Africa." A Jamaican played drums, two African American men talked (a Jew and a Gentile), and then an African American woman spoke (the leader of the group). They spoke of repatriation, as the tour group of African Americans looked on. "Look how far we have come that a few of us can make this journey—the journey home." Libations were poured, a reenactment of the Middle Passage was performed, and the African American tour group lit candles and slowly walked into the dungeons that housed the slaves so many years ago. It was a reenactment of the event that ripped a people out of sync with their African forebears, transforming any memory of this "dark" continent into that of an imagined golden age, the fall of which was the prelude to a well-documented American nightmare. They became their own ghosts as they entered this space of previous erasures. The candles faded, snuffed by the darkness. They were dead to us.

"Look what those African Americans do," said my African host, as if my lack of participation in this strange ceremony defined me as something other than African American.

A song by Arrested Development entitled "Tennessee" played over and over in my head: "Take me to another place, take me to another land, help me forget all that hurts me, let me understand your plan." Like any self-respecting ghost, they/I/we always come back "as we walk the walk our forefathers walked, talk the talk our forefathers talked." The Ghanaians watched from the edge of the courtyard, releasing an occasional laugh or smirk to vent the discomfort that they could barely contain. The Europeans lined the stairs descending into the courtyard, a confused silence. White Americans lined the stony balcony, backs pressed against the wall. They looked nervous—or were they feeling guilty . . . or afraid?

I was amazed at the extent to which the story of African Americans seemed to reconfigure the space of its reenactment. At first, everybody watched. By the time that the African American tour group began to participate in the reenactment of "their story," the Ghanaians, Europeans, and white Americans had segregated themselves into the groups that corresponded to the factions represented in this story of the Middle Passage. And in a strange way African American identity never made more sense to me than it did at this moment.

Above the courtyard was the Cape Coast Museum. In it were housed the images, artifacts, and narratives meant to reveal the tale of this ancient castle. It was a rather schizophrenic display. On the one hand, it was the story of a castle, a bit player in the history of Ghana. On the other hand, it struggled to accommodate the castle's place in the lives of African Americans, for whom it was the beginning of a recorded past—the line between history and myth. One wall explained the slave trade in economic terms. Slaves were sold to the Americas to gather raw materials for the creation of goods in Europe. Another wall explained, for African consumption, the notion of an African diaspora. The text struggled to make sense of the people bearing the prefix "African" who are so different from the Africans born and raised in African countries:

> Though some African peoples probably reached the shores of the Americas before Christopher Columbus, the African Diaspora began [afterward]. . . . Over the following four centuries, European-Americans brought millions of Africans across the Atlantic as unwilling immigrants. Throughout these years a much smaller number of Africans came as free people to explore both the Americas and Western Europe. This dispersal or "Diaspora" distributed African peoples throughout the Americas.
>
> This massive movement helped construct American society from its earliest days. Blending their culture with those of Native Americans ("Indians") and Europeans, peoples of African descent created new American cultures. Through contact, conflict, and occasional cooperation with others, African peoples forged new lives creating new religions, family structures, food ways, and music genres. . . . Due to the separations and dislocations created by the Atlantic slave trade, more people of African descent in the Americas have lost contact with their families in Africa. Most Americans do not know from which ethnic group or from which nation their ancestors were taken. In contrast to most Africans who know their family trees for seven or more generations, many Americans of all ethnicities do not know much about their extended families or their ancestors.
>
> Some families, however, have been concerned about keeping up family ties. In the United States these families generally kept in touch through annual family reunions. There are a number of black genealogists who specialize in researching the African, Native American, and European ancestors of present-day black families. In the last twenty years, since the publication of Alex Haley's book *Roots*, more and more families have begun to document their histories.

As the African Americans used this space to look back to an origin point, the Ghanaian, European, and white American onlookers were forced to reconcile a counternarrative to their stories . . . their histories. I was left with memories to reconcile.

In October 1995, in New Orleans, Louisiana, we had come to this particular black church in connection with my friend's work. She was a reporter covering the gubernatorial race. This church was having a banquet to raise funds and help get out the vote. As we waited for Cleo Fields, the African American candidate for governor, to arrive, we introduced ourselves to the organizer.

"Oh, it's so wonderful that you are pursuing your education," she said to me. She assumed that I was an undergraduate and gave me a speech about how important it is that young black men don't end up in jail. "You are an endangered species," she told me just before decrying the plight of the "broken" African American family. "When you are finished with your bachelor's you should think of getting your master's." It seemed to burst her bubble when it came out that I was from a stable home and working on my Ph.D. She shifted gears and introduced my friend to a young "at-risk" African American man who is trying to raise money to go to college. Cleo Fields arrived.

It was an African American woman who had assumed that my home was "broken." She saw me, a young black man, and immediately identified me as "at risk." This was in keeping with media images of the time, images that I would argue have changed very little. During the next two weeks, we would follow the Fields campaign across the state of Louisiana. The "endangered young black male" and the "broken black family" were the topics of conversations and questions at almost every stop. As is the case with many political campaigns, Fields's role as a family man was central. However, being a good husband and father did not give him the image of "mainstream America" so much as it marked him as being exceptional.

As Fields moved his way across the state of Louisiana, one million black men marched on Washington D.C. From the intense news coverage I got the sense that many were waiting, almost hoping, for something else. David J. Dent was there as a participant. In his account of the march he called it the day in which "the competing and popular images of black men—as predators, vagrants, and troubled people more likely to be in jail than college if between 18 and 24—disintegrated" (1996: 59). Most of the attendees of the march were family men, and—contrary to popular belief—most were middle class (Dent 2000). For some African American men it was an act of "atonement" for having let their people down; for others it was "spiritual release" (Dent 1996). For Fields the march was a potential liability: "Let one person get their wallet stolen and they [the voters] will hold me responsible at the debate tonight." Political campaigns are very much about public perception, public perceptions that find their ground in stories. The public expected that something bad would happen. The Million Man March fell short of public expectation.

RULES OF THE GAME

In *There Ain't No Black in the Union Jack*, Paul Gilroy argues that "racism rests on the ability to contain blacks in the present, to repress and to deny the past" (Gilroy 1987: 12). Although the rhetoric of kinship employs many biological referents, it is a constructed category. Kinship narratives serve as both a primary matrix for contextualizing the self and resistance to the repression of the past. Kinship narratives do this by placing the self within events and time, thereby transforming history into a family story.

In "Narrating the Self," Elinor Ochs and Lisa Capps argue that "the power to interface self and society renders narrative a medium of socialization par excellence. Through narrative we come to know what it means to be a human being" (1996: 31). For Toni Morrison, "narrative is radical, creating us at the very moment it is being created" (1993: 22; cited in Ochs and Capps 1996: 22).

Kinship narratives play an important role in situating the self within history. As the present slips away it can only be recovered in the form of traces left by the past that can only stand for or represent it (Ricoeur 1984: 2). This runs counter to the idea that history exists within a structure of homogeneous, empty time; rather, in accordance with Walter Benjamin's "Theses of the Philosophy of History," "[t]ime [must be] filled with the presence of the now" (1968: 261). Within this context, memory becomes a material resource for political action. In Marxist terms, memory becomes "the means of imagination" (Boyarin 1994: 24).

In "Can You Be Black and Look at This?" (1995), Elizabeth Alexander argues that at the core of African American identity is a "group memory" based on "witnessing" through the circulation of stories, rumors, and images. Alexander uses slave narratives, newspaper articles, videos, and memoirs to demonstrate how "experience can be taken into the body via witnessing and recorded in memory as knowledge [creating a sense that] 'it could be my turn next'" (1995: 87). Boyarin also comments on Alexander and observes that like Benjamin, she, too, "reminds us of the demands of our ancestors who died unjustly; their death is, in a powerful sense, not 'past,' but subject to the meaning it is given through action in the present" (Boyarin 1994: 11).

Although my trip to Africa is the most recent of the events recounted, it is also, depending on your point of view, the beginning—a crucial beginning that has a transformative effect on the reading of the rest of the tales. Africa, the "motherland" as many African Americans describe it, is a symbolic point of departure for the African diaspora. Jacqueline Nassy Brown argues that diasporas are "completely defined by their longings for home . . . for a past rooted in someplace else" (1998: 293). Kinship narratives, however, collapse the notion of home and family such that the longing for a "past rooted in someplace else" becomes the longing for a past rooted in someone elsewhere.

This is why I believe that Alexander's description of Middle Passage as the "originary rupture"—the moment African Americans use to organize memories—is so appropriate when applied to kinship narratives. Alexander argues that vicarious witnessing is marshaled in the effort to give name to "the ghostly or ancestral aspect of memory that vitalizes everyday life" (Alexander 1995: 82). Not only does Alexander's notion of witnessing link the story of that act or this occurrence to the story of someone's sister, father, mother, or—as I will discuss later—"moms," it also links these relations to places. Maps of places become maps of stories, memories, and desires.

I opened this section with Gilroy's argument that "racism rests on the ability to contain blacks in the present, to repress and to deny the past" (1987: 12). So far I have argued that kinship narratives situate the self and reintroduce the past. My experiences in Louisiana, however, highlight what it means to be "contained in the present," to live in the face of rather grim societal expectations. This is the inherent dilemma of being African American and middle class.

Public debates that invariably link African Americans to poor urban settings, crime, social pathologies, and uproar over the production of objectionable gangsta rap music cast a long shadow, obscuring the black and middle class from public view (Coontz 1992; Dent 2000; Lott 1999; Pattillo-McKoy 1999). While Coontz (1992) and Lott (1999) make similar arguments, both of which forge a virtual link between the African American middle class and their poorer counterparts, Pattillo-McKoy (1999) argues that the link is spatial. Essentially, Coontz and Lott critique the appropriation of Daniel Patrick Moynihan's writings by both liberals and neoconservatives to argue that the problem of race can be traced back to pathologies within the black family (cf. Moynihan 1965a, 1965b). These two articles document the flow of Moynihan's ideas from an academic text to such popular media as newspapers, magazines, and television, as well as to the floor debates in Congress. Pattillo-McCoy (1999: 2–4) argues that the vast majority of the African American middle class lives in "black belts" that serve as buffers between their poor urban counterparts and the white suburban middle class. While she acknowledges her obvious omission of those middle-class African Americans living in mostly white suburban and rural settings—such as my family—she develops an argument that middle-class African Americans living in urban black belts are deeply affected by the social pathologies of their poor urban counterparts by virtue of their physical proximity (1999: 30).

While Dent (2000) would likely agree with the arguments of Coontz, Lott, and Pattillo-McKoy, he addresses the middle-class African American from a slightly different perspective. Dent argues that "the black middle class—vastly diverse and complex—is one of the most frequently 'discovered' groups in the nation's history, yet one of the most misunderstood, too, and it often remains all but invisible between its periodic discoveries" (18). Dent goes on to cite a *New York Times* article on the thriving but hidden black middle class published in 1895! Dent's book is an exploration of an African American middle class that inhabits small towns, suburbia, and rural America. In addition he makes an important observation. He argues that media attention intent on shedding light on the black middle class often falls prey to what Dent identifies as a complementary "latent" form of contemporary racism "that tags everything that is good and black as new, rare, and worthy of praise" (16–17). He goes on to argue that "the real story of black achievement in America is the story of transcending societal expectations, not race" (20).

I would argue that regardless of physical locale African American middle-class kinship narratives are stories of black achievement that transcend societal expectations. Kinship narratives "reintroduce history" (Gilroy 1987: 12), thereby exposing the suppression and denial of the past while avoiding the pitfalls of being identified as rare, unique, and, ultimately, alone.

CHEATING IS LEGAL

San Ramon, California: The house sits on a hill overlooking Route I-880. A shrill voice disrupts the relative calm.

"Hey! Anyone who's playing better get their butts over here!"

"Ah, c'mon Crawford," interrupts Leslie, Jr., "we can hear you."

"Just gett'n everyone's attention. Hey! Stanford! Get your rusty-dusty down here! You were the one who whined that time we started without you . . . so hurry up!"

"Nobody wanted to play an hour ago when I wanted to. You can wait a few more seconds!"

Thanksgiving, Christmas, and our biannual family reunions are the only times that bring so many of us together. The exact roll call is altered slightly from gathering to gathering. We are a scattered bunch, living in such cities as San Ramon, Santa Cruz, Ventura, Los Angeles, Kansas City, Atlanta, Chicago, Oak Park, Bollingbrook, Mt. Prospect, Washington D.C., Houston. Every year cities drop off the list and new ones are added as professional obligations spur relocation after relocation. We "hear" about one another second-hand through the odd phone call or the family reunion newsletter. At times we drop out of sight. We don't question our existence—an African American family scattered throughout the United States with the resources, if but for a few days out of the year, to transcend the distances that separate us. We just do it. We show up in one of the cities and catch up with one another over a meal, around a fire, or at the table over a game of Dirty Hearts.

As I scurry into the kitchen my Uncle Leslie is sitting at the table with a glass of wine. My cousin Jamal is putting a CD in the boom box. Aunt Phyllis and Granddad each shuffle one of the two decks of cards. Dad is washing the dishes. "Hey, Dad, I thought we were starting—"

Crawford: Well if it hadn't taken you so long—

Granddad: Will both of you stop bickering, come to the table, and play.

Leslie, Jr.: Alright, so whose deal is it anyway?

Phyllis: This deck's ready. I'll do it. (She begins to deal the cards.)

Stanford: So where're we passing?

Phyllis: I don't know—

Leslie, Sr.: Good. It'll be an honest game. No pass.

Phyllis: It's dealer's choice, two to the right.

Granddad grumbles. Stanford cheers. Jamal calmly scans his cards. Leslie Jr. and Crawford look at each other and smirk. There is a moment of silence.

Stanford: You always were my favorite Aunt.

Phyllis: Right.

The first time I remember playing Dirty Hearts as a family was Christmas in the early 1980s. We were living in Blue Ash, Ohio. My grandparents and an assortment of aunts and uncles from both sides of the family had come to visit. We had just christened the newly remodeled basement. With nothing else to do that could include all three of the generations present, we decided to play hearts. Granddad taught us the rules. Several hands later he was caught cheating—"re-nigging," a word with uncomfortable double meaning in our household. After much deliberation, no penalty was assessed. Someone at the table said sarcastically, "Well, why don't we just make cheating legal?" I guess we did. Since then, his attempts at cheating have become the stuff of legend—like the time that granddad was caught looking at our cards in the reflections off the silver or when he conspired to get us all, especially the young ones, drunk. In every instance there was an uproar followed by threats of sanctions and jokes about there being a "re-nigger" at the table. As if the ribbing and that word are punishment enough, the game goes on, the only sanctions being social. Over time these incidents have become fewer and farther between. Cheating is legal. Yet, except for the occasional accidental misdeal, nobody does it anymore.

The game itself is rather simple. The cards are evenly distributed among the players, with the remainders forming a kitty. All hearts are worth one point, the ten of diamonds is worth ten points, the queen of spades is worth thirteen points. The first person to score points also gets whatever is in the kitty. The first person to score 125 points loses. Anyone who acquires all the points in one hand gets zero points, while all the other players receive thirty-six points. This is commonly referred to as shooting the moon. We call it running a Boston. When someone tries and fails to run a Boston, we call it an Austin. Aside from our "unique perspective" on cheating and changes in terminology, our game of hearts has an additional twist. Like most card players we alternate being the dealer. In our game, however, the dealer has the option to declare alterations to the rules. Usually these changes center around one of two things. The first change centers around having the players pass cards to one another. We call this either passing trouble up- or downstream. In the second instance the size or content of the kitty is manipulated. We call this poisoning the kitty. While one deck of cards is dealt another is shuffled in preparation for the next hand. Of late, we have been using the cards that feature paintings of black folk sitting at a table playing cards.

Only so many people can be playing cards at the same time, and still we have never been able to sustain more than one table at a single location. When too many people want in we play rise and fly. In this format the losers give up their space at the table for others to play. It is considered unsporting for the winner to leave the table. A perfect game ends when the losers give up.

IT'S ALWAYS THE DEALER'S CHOICE

The first hand ends. Crawford picks up a legal pad and a pencil. Feigning regret as he writes our initials and scores on the legal pad: "Well, let's do the scores. PEB?"

Phyllis: Ten.

Crawford: Let's see . . . JGB?

Jamal: Four.

Crawford: LEB2?

Leslie, Jr.: Thirteen.

Stanford (feigning surprise): Damn. What an unlucky number.

Crawford: Yep, and we have two for CTC! That makes him the big winner followed by LEB1, SWC, JGB, PEB, and the BIG LOSER . . . LEB2!

Leslie, Jr.: Big loser? We just started!

Crawford: Hey, I'm just a scorekeeper—

Phyllis: So who were the big losers last time?

Crawford is suddenly silent as he shifts his glance from the other players to his cards. Stanford looks up at the ceiling and whistles. "It's awful quiet at the other end of the table," remarks Leslie, Jr.

Although there is nothing particularly special about the paper or pen we use to keep score, the scorecard does map out a series of relations. The long vertical columns used to keep track of the scores do not bear the players' names. Instead we use our initials. Our naming system has become more than just an efficient way of keeping score. From the start of the game, players routinely slip between calling one another by initials and by name. This is an erasure of sorts in which the distinctiveness and the personality of a name are displaced in the coding of a more visible relatedness. We become our initials. I am always SWC. My father is CTC. You can see our relatedness in the "C" that marks us as Carpenters, while the "B" in PEB (my maternal aunt), LEB1 (my maternal grandfather), LEB2 (my maternal uncle), and JGB (my maternal cousin) marks them as Beckers. Coincidentally, this system also delineates the "fictive kin" and guests. Some are friends who happen to be in town for this or that holiday. Others, through years of participation, have become a part of the family. In the case in which two people share the same initials, the oldest is "1" and so forth. For example, my grandfather on my mother's side is LEB1, and my uncle is LEB2. Our code is inextricably tied up in the de facto patronymics dictated to us by the America in which we reside.

DON'T FORGET THE RULE ABOUT CHEATING

My sister, NRC, enters the room. "So, who's winning?"

> *PEB:* It's too early to tell.
>
> *CTC:* No it isn't—
>
> *LEB1:* We just finished the first hand.

NRC walks by, scanning our hands. Her initials mark her a Carpenter, yet her personal history reveals a much more complicated and ambiguous relationship to the players at the table. This story, her story, is important not just for the events but for the possibilities with which it confronts the family. Our stories are dependent on her story.

Like many of my contemporaries, my memories largely begin in the 1970s. In one I am sitting in a dentist's chair, waiting—no, dreading—his return. In moments the good doctor would enter the room, tools in hand, ready to extract two of my teeth. My sister was in the adjoining room, in a similar chair, awaiting the same procedure—the removal of the same teeth. This was the case with most of our dental appointments. This time, however, he entered the room shuffling through a pair of folders containing our records.

"When is your birthday?" he asked.

"September sixteenth," I replied.

"What year?"

"1968."

"Your sister just told me that she was born on November tenth of the same year. Are you sure you were born in 1968?"

"Yes," I replied.

"How is this possible? Your dental records are almost identical, and you are so close in age!"

My sister and I are fifty-five days apart. We are blood relatives who share neither biological mother nor father. She is adopted. I am older yet, we were so close in age that it was inevitable that we would be raised as twins. She is my sister. She could have been my cousin. She was almost my aunt. If not for some intense family politics and some slick legal maneuvering, she would have been no relation to me at all. Her biological father is LEB2. She could have been NRB (my cousin) or NRM (unacknowledged). She is Jamal's cousin . . . and his half sister. Ironically, the only person at this table to whom she isn't related by blood is CTC, the man she calls her father. She was adopted, the papers signed before she breathed her first breath, into the Carpenter household. Through the manipulation of the legal system her designation is NRC.

This is one of my family's many private stories. It is a personal narrative, obscured by a paper trail of documents ranging from tax returns, to school records, to census reports, a veritable avalanche of public information, responsible for the maintenance of the public image of this American nuclear family. But the law (and the public image that it creates) has little bearing on what transpires at this gathering. What seems to matter most is what she calls us. CTC is her father. LEB2 is her uncle. LEB1 is her maternal grandfather. PEB is her maternal aunt. I am her brother.

BOAST! THERE ARE NO GOOD WINNERS

Although the players would like to see themselves as center stage, the game is always played at the margins of other activities: at a table, in the kitchen or in the dining room. Meanwhile, the others huddle by the fire in the living room watching movies or participating in what the table lacks—discussion. There is plenty of table talk but it consists primarily of one-liners, jokes, monologic comments, ribbing, declarations, and boasting. It is so loud at times that it intrudes upon the other activities. So loud are the players in the margins that it begs a response from the center. My mother, TEC, once commented, "We don't have to sit at the table; we'll just keep track from the living room." It never fails. CTC, the anal one, washes dishes between hands while LEB1 or 2 picks up the phone and calls another "B" in another state. Inevitably, somebody calls us. The phone gets passed around the table. We take turns putting music in the boom box. Good choices are praised, bad choices are ridiculed. But the ribbing doesn't end with musical choice as the conversation vacillates from one topic to the next. As one player ribs another, someone else claims his or her connections and rushes to defend his or her kin.

LEB1: Gi-od! You actually listen to this, Jamal?

LEB2: Now just give it a chance, Dad!

(LEB2 continues with a two-minute monologue relating JGB's hip-hop music to some of LEB1's favorite Jazz artists.)

JGB (LEB2's son) responds defensively: Hey man, if you don' like it I can turn it off.

CTC: C'mon. Let's hear it out. Besides, you better pay attention to the game. Don't let LEB2 pull ahead.

The song changes. LEB1 starts bobbing his head: Now that one's not so bad. I was beginning to worry about you.

SWC (looking over at the score sheet): Isn't CTC in the lead?

LEB2: So Stanford, why haven't you said anything about this new woman I heard about?

SWC scolds CTC. CTC rolls his eyes toward the ceiling and smirks.

CTC: I don't know noth'n bout noth'n.

LEB2: So when are we going to meet her?

SWC: You know, Dad has gotten all the books so far . . . somebody has got to sacrifice soon or he'll run a Boston.

CTC: All right now, roy, you should be paying attention. It's your deal.

As much as this is space where almost anything can be said and the hierarchies of who is related to whom shifts with every sentence, there are some words that are definitely off-limits. One of them is "boy." I honestly can't remember when or how it got started, but at the table we substitute the word "roy" for "boy." It has become the way to assert oneself in a way that mocks the racist use of the word "boy." It always accompanies a request or a demand, usually one that, because of circumstance, can't or won't be refused. The few white members of the family rarely use the word "roy."

GB: So Crawford, why is your son changing the subject?

CTC: I don't know. You'll have to ask him.

My mother, TEC, enters the room. Biologically she is a Becker. Legally she is a Carpenter. "So who's winning?" she asks.

CTC (picking up the score sheet): I don't know. But the big loser is LEB1 followed by JGB.

SWC: I see they're keeping it in the family.

CTC: Well you know those Becker genes, they always were a bit iffy.

LEB1: You know Jamal, Stanford still hasn't answered the question. I wonder why that is?

LEB2 (looking at LEB1 and then moving his eyes to CTC): I don't know, but if he were my son I'd know who she is and what she brings to the table.

Not only is "what someone brings to the table" the first question asked of significant others introduced to the family, it is also the yardstick by which family members are judged. This yardstick is not a measure of material achievement but refers directly to level of education, ambition, and a sense of purpose in life. It is the answer to the question, "Why would we be interested in putting our time into you?"

CTC (looking at SWC) says, "You know, we don't waste our time with just anybody. Definitely not with any 'dees,' 'dose,' and 'dems' people."

The table is an apt metaphor precisely because we play Dirty Hearts at family gatherings and because these games occur simultaneously in different states. The table is a privileged space in which norms are routinely violated. It is a function of the game that we at once give up our identities and negotiate our individuality within a framework of monologues and cheap shots. We are judged by what we bring to the table, be it education, music, a set of genes, or our taste in significant others, experiences that can be shared at the table but never taken away. I would argue that this sharing of experiences through stories told at the table (and other privileged spaces) brings us into the kin structure, while a lack of access defines the outsiders.

AVOID AUSTIN

There is no such thing as a Boston that the entire house doesn't hear about. But it doesn't stop there. This card game frequently transcends space altogether, as family members in other cities and states play as well. Although the game was started in Blue Ash, Ohio, it was during Christmas of 1987 in Kansas City, Kansas that it became a multisited event. I remember the time that CTC ran a Boston in San Ramon, California, and called LEB2 in Kansas City at that moment (2 A.M.) to inform his father-in-law of "this important victory." The next day we received a call from SWC2 (my younger cousin on my father's side) in Chicago. He ran two Bostons. CTC replied, "You must be mistaken." Within hours SWC2 faxed the score sheets to CTC, along with the signatures of the losers.

Kansas City has always occupied a unique place in the lives of my parents, my sister, and me. My father's job moved us from state to state about every four years. Every other move was back to the western suburbs of Chicago. I consider suburban Chicago "home." In spite of all the moving, in my mind's eye there is little difference between the places we grew up. They were all predominately white; we were the only black family on our block. Wherever we lived we were that mythical black "friend" or "family" that some white person evoked to prove his or her "open-mindedness." In these environs, to be black was to be a Carpenter. The world around us was "other." Many of "them" were friends, and some were closer still, but we were always overcoming "their" preconceived notions.

When I was growing up, Kansas City was the only black community that I knew. My sister and I spent every other summer there with my mother's parents. It offered an entirely different set of possibilities, an alternative configuration of the world in which being "black" was more than a synonym for Carpenter, and the idea of family was much broader. In white suburbia the picket fence marked the space of each nuclear family. In Kansas the boundaries were less defined.

In Kansas my family circle grew, bending the rigid biological notions of kin so common to a suburban white middle-class existence. All the people were black, like me, creating a sense of family and safety all around. It was one of those neighborhoods where all the "older" people played the role of parent, aunt, uncle, or older sibling. I spent much of my time across the street at the Jones's house. Dr. Jones had a private medical practice with my grandfather. His son Dwayne was several years older than I. Dwayne looked out for me, and more important—he read comics! Mrs. Jones spoiled me. Even when Dwayne wasn't home I would still go over to the Jones's and eat their food, swim in their pool, and play with their dogs. They were part of the extended family.

I was not a perfect child. One day I crossed Mrs. Jones. She said, "No," and I figured—well, she was pissed. She grabbed me by the arm and raised her hand. I was about to get a spanking. I knew I deserved it, but my parents had sat my sister and me down years before and told us, "Just like you, we have rules, too. One of them is that it is wrong for us to hit you."

"You can't hit me," I said as I tried to squirm out from her grasp.

"Oh, really . . . why's that!?!"

Good question: as long as Mom wasn't around she was mom. What would Captain Marvel do in a situation like this? I thought to myself. I stopped squirming, looked her in the eye, and said, "Because I have the power!"

Her jaw dropped, and her grip loosened. I pulled away from her and ran as fast as I could. When I got to Grandma's I hid under the bed. Over and over I kept saying to myself, "SHAZAM!"

Grandma and Mrs. Jones both love retelling this story. Although I didn't get spanked, from that day forward "no" meant no. As with the "re-nigger" at the card table, the price of getting away with a wrong act is to be forever in its shadow.

In addition to summers, my sister and I also journeyed back to Kansas City along with Mom and Dad for many Christmases. It was during one of these visits that Granddad tried to get us drunk and later looked at our cards in the reflection of the silver in order to gain the upper hand in Dirty Hearts. Kansas City was also the site of the prelude to what is now a biannual tradition, the Becker–Occomy–Slaton family reunion.

It was Christmas 1987. That year my mother's father's sister and brother decided to come out for the holidays. So did their children. This was the first time that I ever saw Grandfather, Grandaunt Nelly, and Granduncle Adolf together in the same place. The card game grew. Toward the end of their stay Aunt Nelly suggested that we do this more often, as a family reunion. This wasn't a surprise. Nell conducts genealogical research as a hobby. The first family reunion took place in Chicago the following summer and is hosted by a different set of family members in different states every other year.

It could be said that during Christmas 1987 we became "the African American family" described on the museum wall at Cape Coast Castle, concerned about keeping up family ties in the shadow of their destruction. In the wake of "the separations and dislocations created by the Atlantic slave trade, [having] lost contact with their families in Africa, [not knowing] from which ethnic group or from which nation their ancestors were taken," we would keep in touch through family reunions. But how does one reconcile this statement with the obvious alternative that America offers—the nuclear family snuggled safely behind a white picket fence. I agree that African Americans have had to build not only family but also identity and personhood in the shadow of their very destruction. I would add, however, that for African Americans kin has become a refuge, that the emphasis on fictive kin as well as ongoing concerns over black community and identity address anxieties over safety in the here and now. The separations and dislocations of the past are not the problem so much as the still-present threat that what has been built could be taken away. America is not safe. A biological notion of kinship is not flexible enough to address this concern.

Constructing kin in its absence not only provides refuge, but it reconfigures "home" as a physical space giving way to an imagined counterpart. To borrow a cliché, home can literally be where the heart is. I found this to be the case in Ghana. During my first full day in Ghana, I needed to get a visa extension. My guide, Bossman, drove me. We arrived, walked down a narrow corridor, and entered the room. It was full of expatriates of varying persuasions. Two older women (YW and OW), both retirees, caught my eye. One was much older than the other. Wrinkles aside, their relation was evident. I began to eavesdrop on their conversation.

The younger woman spoke firm and lovingly: "Now stop talking and fill out these forms!"

Two young black men (BM1 and BM2) entered, wearing jeans and T-shirts with an "African" design on them. They swaggered in all too familiar fashion. Both wore big hats to hold in their dreadlocks. They scanned the room. Each of them asked the other where he thought they should go. Finally, one of them pointed at the two women. "Let's ask them," he said.

They approached the two women, and from a distance I observed as they introduced themselves to one another. The younger woman asked the young men where they had been. "We've been traveling from country to country for a while now," one of the young men replied.

"Yeah, we just got to Ghana, but we've been away for a while. We're kind of ready to head home," interjected the other young man.

BM1: It's like . . . being here is great, you know, back to the motherland and all. . . .

OW: But you're so young, we had to wait till retirement to come here.

BM1: I know, but still, you get this far away and it's not home so much as Mom's.

BM2: It's so great talking to the two of you—

BM1: Yeah, kinda like home.

OW: So where's home?

BM2: Chicago.

YW: No! We're from Chicago, too!

BM1 & 2: Aw, man!

BM2: Like Mom's here!

OW: So tell us more about your trip.

As they continued speaking, I walked over and waited for a break in the conversation. I introduced myself. "So where are you from?" asked the older woman.

I replied, "Just outside of Chicago, West . . . Wheaton."

This is always an uncertain moment for me. Although they are close geographically, growing up in Wheaton is a stark contrast to Chicago. While Chicago is urban and diverse, Wheaton is a largely white suburb that views the city as either a dangerous space or a playground. And the Chicagoans know it. My coming from Wheaton is a marker of sorts; it makes me "safe" to most whites while compelling other African Americans to question my "blackness."

The younger woman, picking up on my discomfort: "I got some cousins near there—"

Her older companion interrupted: "Oh, you're from Chicago like the rest of us." The conversation continued with little pause. We described our routes, and traded cautionary tales. And missing home, missing "Moms," kept coming up.

"Have you been to Cape Coast?" asked the young man.

YW: Not yet . . . but we're not leavin' till we see where it all started.

BM2: It's so good to talk to you.

BM1: Yeah man, Mom's here!

YW: You know she's thinking of you. Come here and let Mom give you a hug.

They approached her, and she smothered them in the way that only a mother can. She turned to me and did the same.

BOSTON!

The game continues. Each of us continues our quest for that elusive "Boston" and all the bragging rights that come with it.

PEB: Somebody better sacrifice or Les is gonna get a Boston.

CTC: Austin maybe. . . . but Boston? (He looks over at SWC).

CTC and *SWC:* Nahhhh.

SWC: You know, Granddad, I think it's exceedingly noble of you that you are willing to sacrifice for the good of us all. Especially since the only point LEB2 doesn't have is the ten of diamonds!

SWC smiles. It is the second to last hand. Stanford leads a four of diamonds. CTC follows with an eight of diamonds. LEB1 puts down a jack of diamonds.

LEB1: It appears that someone is willing to sacrifice! You can surrender that ten of diamonds now.

PEB: Some sacrifice. The king hasn't been played.

LEB1: Well I guess you'll have to make the sacrifice. I had the best of intentions.

CTC: OOOOOHHHHH. . . .

SWC (looking at CTC): To his own daughter!

PEB (slides a six of clubs across the table): I'm all out of diamonds.

LEB2 (smiles as he gently pushes a king of diamonds to the center of the table, pulls the pile of cards toward himself, pauses . . . and slams the ten of diamonds onto the table). "This is the last diamond—"
A stunned silence overtakes the table.

LEB2: Where's all the noise?

CTC (trying to change the subject): Hey PEB, you done with your wine? Why don't I refill it for—

LEB2: Wait a second. Isn't there a word for this? Hmm . . . what is that term? I know! Could it be . . . a Boston?

The gloating begins. LEB2 picks up the phone to make a few calls. The rest of us stand up to stretch and replenish our drinks. I look out the sliding glass door. The fog is clearing. At the bottom of the hill is I-880. I remember when that particular road was much less familiar. We were running on empty. Neely and I had been driving for twenty-six hours straight. It was the tail end of a cross-country road trip.

Several years ago, my sister and I decided to go on a cross-country road trip. We planned our trip over the phone, each of us rattling off stops along the way as we put dots on our respective maps. I was in Pittsburgh, Pennsylvania. She was in Berkeley, California. She had recently (and quite by accident) discovered that her biological mother was living outside of Des Moines, Iowa. Des Moines would be one of our stops.

NRC met me in Chicago, where our journey together would begin. We continued with stops in Des Moines, Kansas City, and San Ramon, California—a cross-country road trip, a mythic, uniquely American joy ride along the highways and byways. As we put dots on the map to mark our route, an interesting picture emerged. We had created a map of relations. At each of these stops were kin of many sorts: aunts and uncles, grandparents, parents, people with whom we share a deep kin connection. The dots coincided with the many locales of previous card games. Although we didn't play Dirty Hearts during this journey, we did sit at the tables and mingle with the echoes—the memories—of games past. We broke bread with the players and spectators.

We met my sister's biological mother—a contributor to my sister's genetic code, or should I say story—which Neely and I do not share. We had both heard the story as early as kindergarten of the sexual union between LEB2 and Sue M.: a child born out of wedlock to two college students, one black, the other white, my uncle and, until this trip, a stranger. A man who sits beside me at the card table telling his tales and a woman known to me primarily through her biological function. She gave birth to my sister. Her letters, written before Neely was born, made my sister cry. I hated her for that.

My sister and I separated for a while in Iowa City. I stayed with a friend while she went to Des Moines where she would meet Sue M. in person for the first time. Hours later my friend would drive me to Des Moines. And for the first time I heard Sue M.'s story. She left college to have Neely. She wondered what I would be like—would I be raised as her big brother or her twin, would I even know about her? Her comments continually begged the question, "What must you think of me?"

"Only the stories that have been told to me," I think to myself, simultaneously realizing that these stories were not about Sue M. These stories were always told by someone else or about someone else, in which Sue M. provided a biological placeholder, served as an object of desire, needed to be rescued from the fate of being a single white mother to a half-black child. She was a device to create, spur, maintain or justify the social relations or the actions within the story. These stories were told to me by the people who occupied the privileged spaces at the table—be it the card table, the dinner table, or any other space where almost anything can be said, the space where histories are consummated, ties bound, and trajectories set.

If it is true that "the struggle of man against power is the struggle of memory against forgetting" (Kundera 1981: 3; cited in Ochs and Capps 1996: 21), we must look not only to the stories that are told but also to the spaces that facilitate the passage of the stories through the generations. In the case of my African American family a card table serves this function. Dirty Hearts exists outside of "homogeneous, empty time." It is like the calendar allowing the same day to reoccur in the guise of "days of remembrance" (Benjamin 1968: 261). Although stories are rarely told at the table, it is the table that brings the traces of our individual experiences together.

Ricoeur argues that the paradox of the trace is that it "becomes a trace of the past only when its pastness is abolished by the intemporal act of rethinking the event as thought from the outside" (1984: 11). When we come together to play Dirty Hearts, the game itself is very much the reenactment of the games that have been played before. While the winners, losers, scores, and locations may change, the players consist of family members coming together—resolving the paradox of the trace in terms of our identification as "family."

Our middle-class status gives us access to those "technologies of transportation and communication" that, as Jonathan Boyarin argues, "have profoundly altered our sense of time and space" (1994: 3). The fact that our family is dispersed geographically means that the card table must not only move from place to place but also exist in multiple spaces. It is a point of reference, a space that comes into being in the presence of family. Boyarin argues that "the only place in the universe where we might feel at home is with the realization that we are not home" (4). In our case, as the family members become increasingly dispersed it is the distance that we must travel that underscores the importance of family. The game itself links family in Chicago to family in San Ramon not just in its play but via phone and fax. Family reconfigures the sense of home.

HINTERLANDS REVISITED

The road trip continues. After several hours of conversation, Neely and I proceeded on to our next stop, Kansas City. At first we talked about our meeting with Sue M., and then there was a long pause. When the conversation resumed we found ourselves talking about all the things that concerned us about this trip. We had started our journey shortly after the Rodney King verdict and the subsequent riots. Out in the hinterlands, the places between the dots on our map of relations, things were still tense. The riots dominated the talk radio stations that are all too common the farther one travels from the major cities. Over and over we would hear about how the riots had started in Los Angeles and seemed to spread to other cities. The image was of angry black mobs along with their mostly brown and a few white sympathizers bent on the destruction of anything, even if it was their own things.

It was against this backdrop that we would stop in the hinterlands, looking for gas, a meal, maybe lodging. With few exceptions, we were the only people of color, always under suspicion, our presence bringing conversations to a halt or a whisper. We never did find lodging. Although we weren't turned away, we didn't feel comfortable about staying the night in the hinterlands, even when it meant driving twenty-six hours straight. We would joke constantly, as the wheat, corn, and desert whizzed by our windows, where no one will hear you scream and they would never find the body!

The notion of a road trip across America is tied to the idea of rugged individualism so ingrained in its western regions. In this land we make ourselves, and on a trip like this Neely and I get to see what this "we" of American myth makes of itself firsthand. I wonder what this trip would have been like without our road map of relations. Our trip across the United States emerged from a long held and deeply shared American fantasy, a story, a myth in which the young and adventurous, the truly American, strike out on the open road with neither worry nor care. In spite of this myth, we started with a map of places that quickly became a map of relations.

It seems to me that self-construction without a matrix, like a cross-country trip without a map, is a risky venture. Neely and I traveled from familiar to familiar place with long periods in the hinterlands between. How appealing, how palatable, would this trip have been had it been outside the refuge of family relations? I find it hard to imagine life out in the hinterlands for an undetermined period of time with no destination in particular—nowhere to go, no one to hear you scream, little hope of finding the body, and no one to have any inclination to look or care. We always found the energy to drive a few more hours to the marks of relation on our map . . . to a place at the table.

BIBLIOGRAPHY

Alexander, Elizabeth. 1995. "Can You Be Black and Look at This?": Reading The Rodney King Videos. In *The Black Public Sphere: A Public Culture Book*. Ed. Black Public Sphere Collective. Chicago: University of Chicago Press, pp. 89–98.

Benjamin, Walter. 1968. Theses of the Philosophy of History. In *Illuminations*. Ed. H. Arendt. New York: Shocken Books, pp. 253–64.

Boyarin, Jonathan. 1994. Space, Time, and the Politics of Memory. In *Remapping Memory*. Ed. J. Boyarin. Minneapolis: University of Minnesota Press, pp. 1–39.

Brown, Jacqueline Nassy. 1998. Black Liverpool, Black America, and the Gendering of Diasporic Space. *Cultural Anthropology* 13 (3): 291–325.

Coontz, Stephanie. 1992. *The Way We Never Were: American Families, and the Nostalgia Trap.* New York: HarperCollins.

Dent, David. 1996. Million Man March: Whose Reality? *Black Renaissance Noir* (Fall edition): 58–70.

———. 2000. *In Search of Black America: Discovering the African American Dream.* New York: Simon and Schuster.

Gilroy, Paul. 1987. *There Ain't No Black in the Union Jack.* London: Hutchinson.

Kundera, M. 1981. *The Book of Laughter and Forgetting.* Harmondsworth, U.K.: Penguin.

Lott, Tommy L. 1999. *The Invention of Race: Black Culture and the Politics of Representation.* Oxford: Blackwell Publishers.

Morrison, Toni. 1993. *The Nobel in Literature.* New York: Knopf.

Moynihan, Daniel Patrick. 1965a. Employment, Income, and the Ordeal of the Black Family. In *The Negro American.* Ed. T. Parsons and K. Clark. Boston: Beacon, pp. 134-59.

———. 1965b. *The Negro Family: The Case for National Action.* Washington, D.C.: Government Printing Office.

Ochs, Elinor, and Lisa Capps. 1996. Narrating the Self. *Annual Review of Anthropology* 25. Palo Alto: Annual Reviews Inc., pp. 19–43.

Pattillo-McCoy, Mary. 1999. *Black Picket Fences: Privilege and Peril among the Black Middle Class.* Chicago: University of Chicago Press.

Ricoeur, Paul. 1984. *The Reality of the Historical Past.* Milwaukee: Marquette University Press.

9

"Like Family to Me": Families of Origin, Families of Choice, and Class Mobility

Laurel George

Among the themes that surface in this story of chosen families and class mobility are the following: the powerful and conflicted drive to do better than one's parents, a characteristically North American variant of the myth of progress; the construction of identity through and against family; families of choice and the role of "fostering"; the legacy of class identity as it seeps into these new relationships; and the persistence of family as a category of meaning even as one's experiences diverge from those of one's family of origin.

As I look back over the last fifteen years, a span that represents both half of my life and the amount of time I have been largely out of contact with my biological family, I realize that the stories of my choices and of my families, not surprisingly, extend back well into those first fifteen years. That is, the choices I made about whom to forge and maintain family-like connections with as well as where I found those new families had much to do with the hopes, desires, and fears of my family of origin.

The hopes, dreams, and fears of my biological family—a working-class family in which no one in the generation before mine had attended college, and many in the generation before that had left school after the eighth grade to help support their family—evolved around material security and class mobility. In this mix, education and, more precisely, schools took on great symbolic and practical significance for all of my family, and for me especially. I want to explore how the schools I attended acted as both institutional stand-ins for families and as conduits for new "fictive kin" relationships. The related and interconnected themes as a whole, then, are institutions and their mediating influence of kin; class mobility and family tensions; families of choice, and the role of "fostering"; the construction of identity through and against family; and the persistence of family as a category even as one reshapes one's identity through experiences foreign to one's family of origin. A recent addition to the anthropological literature on kinship is Kath Weston's *Families We Choose* (1991), an ethnography of lesbian and gay kinship in the United States. Weston's title seemed to promise an anthropological framework for my experiences of nonbiological families. As Weston underscores in *Families We Choose*, both family and choice are dense and complicated concepts that are highly resonant in the contemporary United States, especially in white middle-class culture (110).

Rather than try to define these terms, I attempt to sketch out some of their boundaries by showing how they operated and were put to service in the unfolding and understanding of my own life trajectory. This trajectory has taken me through the experiences of an outlying region of the middle class, that is, the lower-middle or working class, to those of another, the upper-middle class (albeit a segment of it, academia, richer in cultural and intellectual capital than in purely economic capital). I describe key moments such as "choosing" between biological family and school, and forging a long-term relationship with a particular family. I hope the events and stories I relate will show that a sense of family extends beyond biological ties and comprises emotional, social, and economic ties. Similarly, these stories illustrate that that which gets constructed as free choice in any one person's life is also the product of chance, and even sometimes of coercion. Although this coercion may take the form of the class aspirations and expectations of one's biological family or of the subtle but powerful pressure to conform to one's surroundings, it is important to retain the notion of coercion as a counterpoint to that of choice.

ALMA MATER—THE WILLIAMS STORY

The institution that first bridged experiences of class, families of choice, and my family of origin in a significant and sustained way was the Williams School. Williams was the college-preparatory day school in New London, Connecticut, that I attended for all four years of high school. This school was the first institution to link me with people outside my family whom I would come to see as family and with whom I would actually live. At the time, Williams also represented a way out of my class situation and, therefore, out of my family to such a degree that, at times, the institution itself took over the role and function of family.

My mother decided to enroll me in Williams because she and my teachers believed I wasn't being sufficiently "challenged" at my small-town junior high school. Williams had a reputation as a rigorous but nurturing college-prep school that was more affordable and probably less daunting than the more prestigious boarding schools throughout Connecticut. As I prepared to start there in the ninth grade, both my mother and I were nervous about whether I would "fit in" and channeled our anxieties into the dress code. Williams itself had a bit of an identity crisis. The school was an odd mix of the bohemian and the old-fashioned: we had modern dance and African drumming classes, but also Latin and Greek instruction; we were required to stand whenever an adult entered the room, but also called our young arts teachers by their first names. The quirkiness of the school somehow made me feel at home, while the elitism, dated traditions, and the preciousness of the physical plant with portraits of former headmistresses made me feel secure.

In an odd way, the unconventionality of Williams resonated with the facts of my current home life, and the security was an antidote to the tumultuousness of that home life marked by divorce, custody disputes, frequent moves, and financial insecurity. In the middle of high school, when I was fifteen, my mother and her soon-to-be husband, a Cuban ballet dancer who had come to the United States as part of the Mariel boat lift, moved to Miami. I stayed behind and began to work in return for room and board as a babysitter for the three grandchildren of our landlords, who lived a few houses down. That arrangement lasted only a few months, until Thanksgiving of my eleventh-grade year, at which time the Williams School's dance teacher invited me to live with her family, where I remained until graduation. Although I had already begun to experience Williams as the primary caretaking force in my life, this was the time when the school really started taking over from the family. Neither of these early living arrangements nor any of those that would follow after high school and into college would ever be formalized legally, say by adoption or the naming of these families as foster families. This partly accounts for my experience of Williams and the relationships with friends and teachers there as familial, and for my experience of Williams as a true "alma mater" (fostering mother). (Interestingly, one of the antiquated traditions of the school that carried over into the 1980s was the frequent singing of the alma mater.) The school-as-foster-parent relationship was symbolically secured, upon my mother's move to Miami, by my father's agreement with the headmaster to send his court-ordered child support payments directly to the school.

It was also my father who years earlier had set into motion a shift in allegiances from family to school. After I began school at Williams in ninth grade, he said, and would reiterate, "You think you're better than the other kids because you go to that stuck-up, fancy private school." (My brother and sister had ended up with him after the divorce, and I had stayed with my mother, so he was also impugning her child-rearing decisions.) Perhaps, with an adolescent's logic, I believed him and believed that one had to choose between one's family and one's school, and all that it represented.

But I was receiving mixed messages about class from within my biological family. While my father transmitted a sense of class identity as something to be embraced, my mother's words and actions continually transmitted a sense of class aspiration. So, at the same time that I was fulfilling my mother's class aspirations, I was betraying my father's class identity. The conflict between not being ashamed of one's class standing, occupation, habits, associates, school, and all the other elements of life that flow from it, on the one hand, and working all the time to change one's class standing, on the other hand, was not only an external conflict emerging, for example, through my father's accusation that my mother's placing me in a private school would make me stuck-up, but was also an internal one. In other words, each working-class person who buys into the American dream in its many manifestations takes on this conflict as one to be worked out within him- or herself. My betrayal of my class origins enacted through becoming increasingly identified with not only certain elite institutions but also with the members of those classes associated with those institutions was thus simultaneously a betrayal and a fulfillment of a certain class identity. In fulfilling the class aspirations of my mother by choosing increasingly to associate and identify with those individuals I met at Williams, I also fulfilled the narrative of American class mobility.

This "choice" between family and school was not only psychologically loaded, but also ideologically loaded. My experiences of choosing family and constructing belonging show how the categories of class and of family work to alternately reinforce or challenge each other. In the contemporary United States, family is something that we think exists as a concrete entity but really doesn't, while class is something that we think doesn't exist, but really does. Rayna Rapp (1982) does much to explore the relationship between family and class in the contemporary United States. Although many of her insights into both categories as "processes" are relevant, I want to turn to her discussion of family and class mobility in rethinking that statement of my father's: "You think you're better than us because you go to a private school."

Rapp discusses the problems of upward mobility for one person within a working-class family, which mine was and had been for several generations. Rapp's view of these problems relies on her view of the family (or more precisely household) as a unit in which resources are pooled. In such a system, for one person to "get out" often means that his or her resources, especially labor power, become unavailable to being recycled into the economic system of the family:

> No one gets ahead because individual upward mobility can be bought only at the price of cutting off the very people who have contributed to one's survival. Upward mobility becomes a terribly scarring experience under these circumstances. To get out, a person must stop sharing, which is unfamilial, unfriendly and quite dangerous. It also requires exceptional circumstances. Gans speaks of the pain working-class children face if they attempt to use school as a means to

achieve mobility, for they run the chance of being cut off from their peer group. The chance for mobility may occur only once or twice in a lifetime—for example, at specific moments in a school career or in marriage. (1982: 179)

In my case, the loss that Gans cites as a disincentive to children using school as a means to achieve mobility, that is, the risk of being cut off, actually happened between my family of origin and me. The betrayal in my case lay not in my refusal to "stop sharing" economic resources, as I was not a viable wage earner. Even a perceived future betrayal of the economic well-being of my biological family seems insufficient cause for the vituperativeness of my father's comment about fancy private schools. My father *also* perceived me as failing to share a set of common experiences and assumptions, habits, and tastes. For all of my splintered biological family, then, including me, Williams represented more than just a chance for a good education. It also represented access to what Pierre Bourdieu (1977) would call cultural capital and also social capital, in the form of the kinds of people and networks to which I gained access. No matter that I have yet to convert those into economic capital and that my brother the carpenter and my sister the nurse probably make as much as I will at least as a junior faculty member.

Although a purely economic interpretation of problems of class mobility and family cannot be sustained for the reasons mentioned above, I did and still do see education as a way out of the financial strain I had come to know through living with a single mother who had two or three jobs at once—as secretary, donut-shop waitress, cook, and nursing-home attendant. While my father resented my perceived shift in allegiances to Williams and what it stood for, my mother encouraged it. Her own hard work seemed aimed partly at ensuring that her dashed hopes of becoming a dancer or going to college and her often unsatisfying and demeaning jobs were not passed on to me. The fact that class and class mobility are not at all strictly economic matters was not lost on my mother.

At the time I entered Williams, my mother was the secretary to the dean of an academic department at Yale. This job choice and how she negotiated her relationship to her employer now seems meaningful to her own experience of the complicated character of class. With her secretarial skills, she could have earned considerably more in a corporate setting. But I remember that Yale symbolized for her a way to be around what she called "interesting" people, and a way to bring herself up. In *Landscape for a Good Woman: A Story of Two Lives,* Carolyn Steedman discusses the intricacies and specificity of class distinctions, even within certain seemingly fixed class categories. Steedman says of her own mother:

> The point of being a Lancashire weaver's daughter, as my mother was, was that it was *classy*; what my mother knew was that if you were going to be working class, then you might as well be the best that's going, and for

women, Lancashire weaving provided that elegance, that edge of difference and distinction. (1987: 23)

For my own mother, it was working at Yale that symbolized "that edge of difference and distinction." Furthermore, I believe she unconsciously strove to convey to me the significance of that "edge of distinction." When I was ten and eleven, she would take me to work with her during summers and school vacations, and I would help with filing and other tasks. Bringing me into that environment was a way to introduce me to a world outside of our own. But the access to education as a way out soon became more concrete through her association with Yale. When I was accepted at Williams, and it became clear that even with her second job and my scholarship, it would be a huge strain for me to go, my mother's boss, the dean, stepped in and gave her a check to subsidize my tuition. In retrospect, it seems that many hands were involved in pushing me out of one class bracket and pulling me into another.

Recently when I was back at Yale as a research fellow, I mentioned the "dean episode" to a friend and fellow graduate student who had been involved in the recent labor disputes there. He remarked that the dean's actions amounted to nothing more than a token gesture, and had clearly done nothing to ameliorate the underlying problem of clerical workers' severe underpayment. His comment stung. Of course he was absolutely right, but his analysis detracted from the cozy feeling that I had a benefactor eager to reward my industriousness and promise. As I unravel that act of noblesse oblige yet further, I realize that the dean's giving my mother that "bonus" check both validated her work and invalidated her occupation, by recognizing that pains should be taken to avoid having me "end up" like her. The symbolic significance of this action, which had always marked a pivotal moment in a personal version of a Horatio Alger narrative, has changed but not diminished. Now the dean's largesse seems to point most clearly to the complicated relationship between families and class, and the alliances and betrayals that are put into action when family members are driven apart by class differences—internal and external to the family itself.

ALLIANCES AND AFFINITIES, BELONGING AND BETRAYALS, CHOICE AND CHANCE—THE MAKING OF A CHOSEN FAMILY

As I said, I wish I could say that I remembered my first day at the Williams School. I don't. In fact, the first two years are telescoped into a few key images. One of them is of a goofy, floppy kid who had obviously just started an adolescent growth spurt bounding up the stairs from the science room to the catwalk of the school. He was wearing bright green pants with whales embroidered on them, and a long knitted scarf in all colors of the rainbow. I was drawn to him; he was vibrant, funny, and a little outrageous. About fifteen years later this person would give me away at my wedding, after many years of shared Thanksgivings, three years at the same high school and four at the same university, many disagreements, shared projects, tears, uproarious laughter, and even going to my junior prom together. Fifteen years after leaping up those high-school stairs Stephen would take my arm and walk me down another set of stairs and down the aisle to stand just feet away from me as I got married. On that day, his father set up the sound equipment, his mother zipped me into my wedding dress, his sister wrote out the place cards, and his partner read a poem for the ceremony.

When I speak of the Schwartzes, and sometimes even to them, I say, "They are like family to me" or "Stephen, he's like a brother." And I wonder what is contained in that word "like." How does it indicate both a whole constellation of similarities and affinities, likenesses and kinship, while also indicating distance and difference? Along what lines do the similarities and differences exist? Beyond my great affection for each of them and for them as a family, what does it mean to say that they are "like family" to me? What does it mean about the choices we made in choosing each other?

No life situation can be seen as the product of choice alone, surrogate families notwithstanding. Indeed, any new connections that are forged, whether with institutions who stand in for family or with "actual" families, are at least partly shaped by experiences with our families of origin. Paradoxically, choice is not only a limited term when it comes to describing how families are constructed and experienced, it is also a uniquely *loaded* term.[1] Choice is, in many ways, *the* central and defining concept of middle-class existence in the United States today, from family and financial planning to the overwhelming number of so-called lifestyle choices we are daily called upon to make. Consumerism has combined with an older American ideal of free will and self-determination to create an imperative of continual self-construction dependent upon an endless series of apparent choices. But if our lives and our associates, especially the people and institutions who function as fictive or surrogate kin, are not solely determined by choice, what are the forces that *do* determine the trajectories of lives and relationships? To answer this question, it will be useful to consider what choice is *not*. Choice does not account for chance, does not recognize constraints, and choice does not admit the implicit coercion of narratives of normal families.

In her ethnography of chosen families, Kath Weston briefly interrogates the implications and assumptions that inhere in the use of the term *choice* to describe the lives and families of the people she studies. She points to the ideological weight of this term as she contends that "[c]hoice is an individualistic and, if you will, bourgeois notion that focuses on the subjective power of an 'I' to formulate relationships to people and things, untrammeled by worldly constraints" (1991: 110). In her more recent *Long Slow Burn*, Weston extends her critique of the category of choice by pointing to the gap between the rhetoric of free choice and real-life constraints involved in the formation and recognition of chosen families. She argues that while chosen families may appear endlessly customizable or "made to order," they are in fact shaped by social pressures and normative ideas about what counts as family. That is (and here Weston makes a play on words), chosen families are constructed ("made") as a way of bringing a certain kind of cultural and social sense ("order") to relationships that exceed or simply escape available categories (1998: 84–85). Finally, it is impossible to analyze the rhetoric of choice without taking into account its consumerist connotations. It is impossible to ignore the resonances of Weston's explanation of the ways in which chosen families are "tailored and constrained" by larger cultural narratives and norms, personal history, and economic and practical contingencies (84) with contemporary understandings of the external forces that shape "individual" and even self-making consumerist desires. In the stories that follow, I explore the *un*chosen circumstances and elements, the constraints and unarticulated cultural narratives and norms that helped to structure my own "choices" of surrogate kin and of schools as surrogate kin.

Of all the families that I moved in and out of as a quasi-member—most if not all of them associated with school and the friends and teachers I encountered there—Stephen's family has been the most constant. It has, for example, become rare to not spend Thanksgiving with them. They have also participated in other kinds of ritual moments, particularly rites of passage such as receiving my first real job out of college—they helped me with moving expenses—and of course, the wedding, giving me an engagement party. And I have also been with them through many of their life passages—birthdays as well as deaths—watching as Stephen lost three grandparents and remaining in the house as the Schwartzes sat shivah for his maternal grandmother, Giggi, during a summer I lived with them.

It was at moments like this, moments of great change, weddings and funerals, that the tension between belongingness and not-belongingness surfaced. I remember feeling like an intruder during the time that Stephen's grandmother was being mourned, and even suggested to Myrna that it might be best if I went to stay elsewhere while they sat shivah. Myrna insisted that I stay, saying that they could use my help, that her mother would have wanted it that way, and, after all, I was living there, so why would I go anywhere else? Her reaction to my crisis of feeling like I didn't belong, especially because of the religious nature of the mourning ritual, showed me several things: (1) that my personal anxiety and discomfort was secondary to the larger crisis occurring around me; (2) that the bonds of caring can and must be stronger than the bonds of religion or biology, and finally (3) that there are circumstances, such as death, that even the most stable families don't choose, but that must nonetheless be endured. It was instructive to see how the family I chose coped with a tragic circumstance that they did *not* choose.

Despite my current understanding of the Schwartzes as fictive kin or "surrogate family," and about how we chose and continue to choose one another, I have occasionally felt a bit at sea in this new family structure. In my effort to make sense of how I felt like I both belonged and didn't belong, I made the Schwartzes' ethnicity a repository of significance. In some kind of calculus of affect, I made the equation that Jewish people were *like* Italian people (i.e., where I came from). Judaism, or more precisely, Jewish traditions, quickly became familiar as I allowed what I encountered to resonate with my childhood experience of the combined religious and ethnic celebrations of my Italian and Greek Catholic relatives. These likenesses, although superficial and born of my mother's ethnic stereotyping ("Your Italian relatives are warm and kind and love to cook for you kids. Your English Protestant relatives are cold and give you leftovers"), nevertheless provided a sense of familiarity and therefore access to a new family and its traditions.

But even more than this concatenation of ethnic similarities, the Schwartzes' specific class standing had significance for me. When I first met them they seemed, in comparison to the families of other high-school friends, solidly middle class. In retrospect, I realize that they are and were upper-middle class, and that many of my other friends were slightly more upper upper-middle class. I continued to think of the Schwartzes as middle class until very recently, when I was asked to describe the material conditions of life at the Schwartzes, and was told that they didn't *sound* middle class but rather that their income and assets put them in the economic top one or two percent of American households.

As I have found from my own experience, though, class habits and class identity don't settle into one's being in a matter of years or even within one generation. Maybe the Schwartzes' *own* class backgrounds made them a bit more fluid in terms of sharing their lives and resources. Their recent experiences of working their way up and of being ethnic outsiders made them perhaps more sympathetic and more approachable than other classmates' families. While their surface middle-classness appealed to me as *different* and as more secure, perhaps their candor about the newness of this economic security for *them* also made them feel less alien to me. For example, they could talk about being on the board of the local country club where they were avid golfers, but also about how they couldn't join until a couple of decades ago.

I have recently begun to think that the Schwartzes' recent family history as working class, even "working poor," affects how they currently inhabit their upper middle-classness and, in turn, how I read their class standing. The Schwartzes' family room is covered with pictures of immediate and extended kin. A multigenerational collage of photos including baby pictures, prom pictures, and the like dominates one wall. Arranged in a loose family tree configuration, each upper corner features a picture of Stephen's grandparents as newlyweds. The photograph of Stephen's paternal grandparents shows them stylishly dressed in the fashions of the late 1930s; his grandmother poses leaning against a fence in the middle of a grassy field, and his grandfather stands behind her looking dapper and relaxed. The overall impression of the photograph is one of leisure and freedom from worry. Stephen's maternal grandparents in the other corner of the collage seem almost to stoop forward and to be carrying something. I can't quite remember if they are *actually* carrying luggage in this photo, but that's the impression I remember. Dressed in heavy and somewhat worn overcoats, they look travel-weary yet expectant, as if caught between leaving somewhere and going somewhere else. Their status as immigrants comes through with an immediacy absent from the other picture. At the time these pictures were taken, Stephen's father Bob's parents were successful merchants in a family furniture business, and Myrna's father was selling automobile parts out of a van. Bob's parents, likewise, were part of Jewish society in southeastern Connecticut, while Myrna's father was a Socialist. In the course of two or three decades, fortunes were to shift. Not long after these pictures were taken, a family feud caused Bob's father to be pushed out of the family business. When Bob reached adulthood, he took his in-laws' auto parts business and built it up into what Stephen and his friends jokingly called "Bob's auto parts empire." The palpable constructedness of the Schwartzes' class standing, which comes through in their visual and oral narration of their family history, appealed to me and drew me to them. This, of course, is not the only factor, and there are other bonds just as significant, such as my affinity for Stephen, a sense of similar ethnic backgrounds and positioning, and, above all, the Schwartzes' ethos of inclusion and welcome.

In addition to the Schwartzes' ethnicity and class history, it was perhaps Stephen's being gay that was one of the initial attractions to him as a friend and to his family as a surrogate family. Within the upper-middle-class environment of Williams, an environment that I initially saw as the "inside track" to a more secure future, Stephen was enough of an outsider to not feel foreign to me. In fact, most of my closest friends during that time and those who remain close friends were outsiders in one way or another—either ethnically, or in terms of sexual orientation, or because of their own family secrets.

In order to do full justice to the complexity of my relationship with this surrogate family, I want briefly to revisit the question of what is contained in the word *like*; especially as used in the formulation "like family to me." Specifically, I want to entertain the possibility that along with the perceived similarities to my family of origin, the very ways in which I perceive the Schwartzes to be *different* drew me to them as a foster or surrogate family. In other words, the ways in which the Schwartzes initially represented an ideal, middle-class family in contradistinction to my less-than-ideal, dispersed, and working-class biological family accounted in part for their attractiveness to me as surrogate kin.

WALKING THROUGH WESLEYAN:
CLASS CODES, CULTURAL COMPETENCE, AND CULTIVATION

> She wanted to find out about this hazardous business of "passing," this breaking away from all that was familiar and friendly to take one's chance in another environment, not entirely strange, perhaps, but not entirely friendly. What, for example, one did about background, how one accounted for oneself.
>
> —Nella Larsen, *Passing*

> The family and the school function as sites in which the competencies deemed necessary at a given time are constituted by usage itself, and simultaneously, as sites in which the *price* of those competencies is determined, i.e., as markets, which, by their positive or negative sanctions, evaluate performance, reinforcing what is acceptable, discouraging what is not, condemning valueless dispositions to extinction.
>
> —Pierre Bourdieu, *Distinction*

When I think about my chosen families, I cannot help but think of schools as families. The Williams School, for example, was not only a connection to the long-lasting and continually evolving surrogate families like the Schwartzes, but it also functioned as family in and of itself. Each of my alma maters has in its own way acted as both a symbolic and a literal fostering mother. When I moved out from my mother's household at the age of fifteen, my father met with the headmaster of Williams and arranged to send his required child support payments not to me or to my mother, but rather to the school itself in order to subsidize my tuition scholarship. Similarly, when I entered college at Wesleyan and had no permanent home address, my dormitory became my home and my scholarships a way not only to pay the tuition, but also to ensure food and shelter for at least nine months out of the year. In this way, my relationships to schools and the intellectual work I had to do to stay enrolled there became highly charged—if I were to fail my classes, I would not only lose my connection to the school, but would also have no home.

In fact, what allowed me to stay in college as much as my intellectual labor was my physical labor: I paid my family's estimated contribution with wages and tips from waitressing during the school year and in the summertime. In retrospect, I think the friends I made waitressing, some of whom I still see, were a reassuring link to my working-class past as much as my new wealthy friends seemed a reassuring bridge to a more financially secure future. Although waiting tables was tiring and took far too much time from my studies, I can't imagine my college years without it. Being able to commiserate with fellow workers about Wesleyan students' narcissistic sense of entitlement (we called it the "world-is-my-living-room" mentality) offset how out of place I could sometimes feel among those very students when I walked back uphill after work and became one of them again.

The symbolism of the literal downtown/uptown split was not lost on a favorite coworker, Jean, who called Wesleyan that "big rock candy mountain." Beyond the social connection to a working-class past, waitressing also provided me with a link to a more secure way of surviving than maintaining the grades that would allow me to keep my scholarship. Waitressing provided the psychological security that if all of this (that is, the scholarship and the connection to this elite environment with rich friends) were somehow to evaporate, then I would still be able to walk a few blocks to the neighborhood restaurant, work hard, and come home with fifty dollars in cash in my pocket. As much as I still occasionally fear that waitressing is what I will "end up" doing, I also miss the clarity and security of waitressing, of exchanging hard physical labor for hard currency. Carolyn Steedman's relationship to her own labor, as she describes it in *Landscape for a Good Woman*, strikes a chord. Despite a successful career as an academic, Steedman's childhood experiences continue to shape her basic feelings about the value of her labor. Steedman finds the legacy of manual labor as passed down from both of her parents not entirely disempowering, and she relates that "I sometimes find myself thinking that if the worst comes to the worst, I can always earn a living by my hands; I can scrub, clean, cook and sew: all you have in the end is your labour" (1987: 43).

The contrast of the security of waitressing with the insecurity I felt about my place at college reveals that I rarely experienced these alma maters, these fostering mothers of schools-as-kin, as consistently dependable nurturers. Their institutionality and impersonality was a double-edged sword. On the one hand, they couldn't dismiss or reject me on a whim, but neither could they offer unconditional affection or security. Nevertheless, the conditions attached to their nurturance and shelter were always pretty clear-cut: "Continue to perform at a certain level, and we will continue to house and feed you." And that, perhaps, is not so unlike the implicit contract of many biological families after all.

As I moved physically between the downtown restaurant where I waitressed and the campus of Wesleyan, I also passed affectively and psychologically between two places in which I felt at least intermittently "at home." On my way from the dormitory to work, I walked past the classrooms in which my professors taught by example the rewards of that other kind of hard work, intellectual labor. Many of these teachers, by communicating a deep love of learning, enabled me momentarily to forget that class distinctions are an integral part of attending an elite institution such as Wesleyan. A few of them, those who would become special mentors and friends, introduced me to the complicated lesson that elite universities themselves produce and reproduce not only pure knowledge but also class inequalities.[2] Certainly what made Wesleyan a stand-in for family was not only its promise of institutional security, but the fact that it, like Williams, was peopled with kindred individuals such as these special professors.

My waitressing experiences are significant not only for the contrast they provided to those as a student at Wesleyan, but also because they symbolize a more complicated process of moving between two worlds. The symbolics of space and place in the making of a life are richly explored in Nella Larsen's novel *Passing* (1929). In Larsen's novel, two childhood friends who had both grown up African American encounter each other in a segregated, whites-only rooftop cafe. During the years that have elapsed, one of them, Clare, has broken ties with her past and begun to live exclusively in white society. The other, Irene, lives the life of an upper-middle-class African American woman. As the two friends tentatively reconnect, Clare inquires of Irene, "You know 'Rene, I've often wondered why more colored girls, girls like you and Margaret Hammer and Esther Dawson and—oh, lots of others—never 'passed' over. It's such a frightfully easy thing to do. If one's the type, all that's needed is a little nerve" (Larsen: 187). Clare's phrasing highlights the fact that reshaping one's identity involves not only forgetting or concealing but also an active move into another world, another kind of space with new rules and habits. This meaning of passing, then, connotes not passing *for* that which one is not, but as Clare says, passing *over* into a new domain. The brilliance and richness of Larsen's novel derives from the fact that her characters experience passing as both things, often simultaneously.

For all of the differences in the specifics of my situation and that of Larsen's characters, the characters' struggle with the duality of passing speaks to my situation at Wesleyan in a way that no other writing has. The duality hinges on an uncanny feeling of being an impostor in a certain milieu—passing *for*—as well as being a rightful new member of that previously off-limits community—passing *over*. This latter view of passing as passing over resonates with my experience of self-remaking and self-cultivation that occurred at Wesleyan. Passing over to a world of material and intellectual privilege didn't involve the active concealing of origins that Larsen's characters grapple with, but nonetheless entailed a kind of daily distancing from and forgetting the people and experiences that inhabited my past.

But, as much as that walk downtown to work took me through the spaces of an increasingly familiar new life, it also took me through parts of that recent past rapidly becoming unfamiliar. As I walked toward the edge of campus, away from College Row and toward Main Street, I also approached past memories and associations. I grew up not far from Wesleyan and as a child would drive by its campus with my mother. I remember how she often admired the old buildings on the edge of campus, particularly a Victorian house she called the "Gingerbread House." I was surprised to discover later that this house is indeed known on campus as the Gingerbread House; it was not just a whimsical saying of my mother's. I also remember my mother's remark about the Wesleyan students we passed by one day: "For such privileged kids, they sure could dress neater."

As I reached Main Street, with its Italian grocers and restaurants, my walk to work also took me through a landscape full of class and ethnic memories and associations. My biological family's strongest ethnic identification was with the Italian and Greek backgrounds of my maternal grandparents, who kept alive those linguistic, culinary, and religious traditions. Not only the storekeepers and residents of Middletown but also many of my fellow waitresses reminded me of that past as they spoke with the southern Italian cadences and colloquialisms that my family had also used. Entering back into the somewhat familiar territory of Italian American working-class life was perhaps a way to remember that past and to keep my passing over from being a complete and irreversible act.

Speech patterns, clothing, and food are just a few of the indicators that class standing and mobility as well as identification with a certain community have distinct bodily dimensions. It follows, then, that moving into a new social and class milieu involves corporeal adjustments. Through these adjustments one accommodates to one's surroundings until an appropriate and comfortable identity settles into one's body through speech patterns, gestures, and postures. Pierre Bourdieu (1984) talks about this process of accommodation as the acquisition of cultural competence, which he says is enacted and read through the body. Bourdieu suggests that both school and home combine to create cultural competence, but we must ask, What happens when the messages from home clash with those received at school? What happens, for example, when one receives approbation and recognition for certain speech practices in school, but criticism for the very same practices, such as using "big words," in the family?

Inasmuch as school was the place where I received approbation and recognition for academic and other accomplishments, Williams and later Wesleyan ended up supplementing if not fully supplanting the biological family in the making of identity. The directors of the Williams School, for example, self-consciously and explicitly sought to convey to its students what is now known as moral values or character building. Being a good Williams student entailed not merely the assimilation of information, but rather involved becoming an educated person. Williams, then, valued a process of cultivation and all that implies—nourishment and tending, but also refinement and improvement.

My education at Williams, with its unreflectively elitist stance, prepared me to experience Wesleyan as not just an opportunity to improve my lot through professionalization, but also as a key site for the continuation of my intellectual, personal, and social cultivation. This view of education as cultivation rather than information accretion is a decidedly elite one, and the mechanisms by which such elite privileges are extended to particular people are complex but not random. Gender partly determines who is absorbed from the ranks of a subordinate social and economic class into a higher social class. If becoming a model Williams or Wesleyan student got played out, as it most certainly did, through the surface of one's body, through one's clothing, gestures, speech patterns, postures, and bearing, then girls and women have more room to negotiate class mobility through both conscious and unconscious adjustments in such embodied habits. If the body is a fluid site in which class habits can be partly remade, it is also an especially vulnerable one because corporeal, linguistic, and sartorial actions have serious effects. Among these effects are the "positive and negative sanctions" that Bourdieu argues are imposed primarily by family and school. These sanctions, he argues, ultimately shape one's actions and relative degree of competence in the cultural codes of a given milieu (1984: 85).

The process of the cultivation of a person though negative and positive attention is, according to Bourdieu, the process by which class habitus is transmitted and reinforced. His notion of habitus, which is glossed as a "system of dispositions" (1977: 86), is closely linked to that of embodiment, or more specifically of "body *hexis.*" Body hexis is the system of bodily techniques through which class habitus is inhabited, perpetuated, and read. Bourdieu explains the connection between body hexis and class:

> Body hexis speaks directly to the motor function, in the form of a pattern of postures that is both individual and systematic, because linked to a whole system of techniques involving the body and tools, and charged with a host of social meanings and values. (1977: 87)

Although Bourdieu insists on the tenacity and self-perpetuating quality of class habitus, notions such as body hexis as well as cultural and intellectual capital strongly suggest not only the possibility of class mobility, but also the means by which it might be achieved. But such bodily habits are neither superficial nor completely under one's own control, a fact that renders comprehensible the often visceral quality of anxieties that come along with finding oneself in a class milieu different from that in which one was raised.

In her own story of class and family, Carolyn Steedman underscores the *gendered* dimensions of class mobility by describing how her mother communicated her desires for certain material comforts, such as the desire for a full-skirted New Look dress. She also says of her mother's transmission of class aspirations:

> What we learned . . . was how the goods of that world of privilege might be ap-
> propriated, with the cut and fall of a skirt, a good winter coat, with leather
> shoes, a certain voice; but above all with clothes, the best boundary between
> you and a cold world. (1987: 38)

Steedman weaves such family narratives with descriptions of class within British academia, and she notes that class operates very differently for women and for men in this milieu. She argues that the narrative framework of men's working-class escape stories is "ignorant of the material stepping stones of our escape: clothes, shoes, make-up" (1987: 15), and she suggests that admission into elite classes for women relies heavily on the ability to enact and perform convincingly. Steedman's story underscores how class aspirations get inscribed on and played out across bodily surfaces. Her specific emphasis on how she read and fulfilled her mother's class aspirations indicates that such desires and our struggles to fulfill them are often fueled by the unconscious. Indeed, the remaking of oneself would have to become unconscious, even naturalized, because continual scrutiny and policing of one's own actions and bearing would be impossible to maintain. Thus, the "choice" to identify with and participate in a particular social and cultural milieu, like the "choice" of a new family, is not really a choice at all, but rather the result of internalized expectations and external sanctions that combine to spark a process of accommodation to one's surroundings.

Such a process of accommodation achieved through continual and repeated acts of self-styling calls to mind Judith Butler's understanding of the enactment of gender identity. For example, discussing gender performativity, Butler suggests that "gender is the repeated stylization of the body, a set of repeated acts within a highly rigid regulatory frame that congeal over time to produce the appearance of . . . a natural sort of being" (1990a: 33). This point seems especially relevant to the process of bodily consolidation of a certain set of class codes—elements of one's self-presentation such as habits, tastes, and speech patterns—that begin to feel comfortable and even "natural" through repetition and individual modification.

It is precisely the personalization of class codes that enables them to settle into one's body and not simply to be like a garment to be donned and shed as one chooses. The internalization of class codes explains how I gradually began to feel more "at home" in school than I did with my biological family. The unconscious dimension of the internalization surfaced in a series of misrecognitions that happened to me at Wesleyan, incidents that pointed up the fact that a specific variety of an upper-middle-class bearing had seeped into my being deeper than I myself knew. These misrecognitions happened as early as the first week of my first year at Wesleyan. A hallmate who remains a close friend revealed years later, after she knew my background, that she had originally assumed, because of my interests and the way I presented myself, that I was from an upper-middle-class Jewish family, probably from the Upper West Side of Manhattan. We laughed not only at the inaccuracy of her assumption, but also at its specificity; she had pinned me down (albeit inaccurately) to a neighborhood! In my second year of college, a professor made a similar assumption about where and how I had grown up when I told him I wanted to do a research paper on the experimental choreographer Meredith Monk. He asked which of her pieces I'd seen in New York, to which I replied with chagrin, "None, I've just read about her in books." What I didn't tell him was that I had never seen *any* dance performances in New York. Both of these college incidents still puzzle me somewhat. I still wonder precisely what I was doing and how I was acting to make people think things about me that were so far from the truth.

Perhaps the only real answer to that question lies in admitting that there is no *one* truth about one's "real" family or one's "real" class identity. Furthermore, as illustrated in examples from my own experience as well as those of Carolyn Steedman and of Nella Larsen's characters, the relationships between one's families and one's shifting identities (class and otherwise) are multifaceted and multidimensional. Further, these relationships between past associations and present identities continually make themselves known and call for attention in everyday life. The real truth about families we choose, whether comprised of people or represented by institutions like the Williams School and Wesleyan, lies between total self-determination and total predetermination. Interestingly, both Butler's notion of performativity and Weston's discussion of chosen families seem at first glance to err on the side of individual freedom of choice and self-determination, while Bourdieu's notion of habitus can be read as excessively determinative.

I have attempted to show the ways in which our experiences of families of origin continually beg to be revisited and renegotiated as one forms new family-like arrangements. Similarly, one's early and internalized experiences of class identity and class aspirations instilled within that family of origin continually resurface in the form not only of class anxieties, but also as unexpected and positive sources of pride and connection to others. One example of this unexpected resurfacing of class identity is the deepening of my connection to the Schwartzes once I fully appreciated the history of class mobility, both upward and downward, in their family. The identifications we start out with continue throughout life to affect how we make sense of and build lives and connections. At the same time, there is an undeniable reality and solidity to the new associations, new families, and new tastes and habits we acquire, even though, or perhaps *because*, those bonds and associations have been cultivated.

In order to fully appreciate the significance and potential of new families, it is necessary to turn away from the sense of cultivation as refinement and betterment and to understand cultivation as an ongoing process of tending. But what does this understanding of cultivation as tending, as nurturing growth, mean for the difficult question of class mobility? After all, the notion of cultivation first arose here in my discussion of the class mobility made possible by my assimilation into elite educational institutions such as Williams and Wesleyan. It's important to remember what attracted me to these places and what kept me there. On a most basic and concrete level, these institutions offered a way to survive and exist in the world by providing, first, access to surrogate families (the Williams School) and, then, actual shelter (the dormitory at Wesleyan). The schools also offered, although not consistently, sustenance through their recognition of hard work and intellectual questioning.

That these were wealthy, elite, and private institutions that stepped in to meet these very basic needs and rights is deeply troubling, for it implies that material security and good schooling are the birthright only of the already secure and educated. In such a system, only occasional acts of noblesse oblige, like the Yale dean's subsidy of my secondary education, momentarily open the door to admit someone from the working classes. To see the story I've just told as a celebration of the dean's action or even as a story of personal triumph over adversity would be to miss the point. The point is, rather, that the kinds of affective and intellectual relationships others have cultivated with me and I with them need to be fostered both within biological families *and* chosen families, both within public educational institutions *and* private ones, and, finally, within all socioeconomic classes. Most important, to strengthen emotional connections that exist within any one of these domains should not be seen as a betrayal of the affective bonds that exist within any other domain. Then chosen families could be seen as complements, not threats, to biological families, and education as a way to understand and remedy, rather than perpetuate, class inequalities.

NOTES

I wish first of all to thank James Faubion for inviting me to contribute to this volume and also to thank the participants and discussants who attended the Kinship and Cosmopolitanism Conference at Rice University in March 1997. I am deeply grateful to those who encouraged this project and read drafts along the way, including Ravit Avni-Singer, James Faubion, Kim Fortun, Laura Helper, Janet Jakobsen, Stephen Schwartz, Ann-Louise Shapiro, Julie Taylor, Michael Trask, and Dar Williams. There would be no story to tell without *all* of the families, friends, and teachers mentioned herein, but I wish especially to acknowledge the Schwartzes. Finally, I thank whatever force allowed me to choose Erik and him me.

1. I am grateful to Michael Trask for pointing out the loadedness of the term *choice* in the United States today, and especially for bringing my attention to its centrality in the building of middle-class lives and families.

2. Indeed, an ironic dimension of my experience at Wesleyan was that my education there furnished me with the tools with which to critique my precarious place and my position within that elite institution. In *Cultural Capital: The Problem of Literary Canon Formation* (1993), John Guillory makes a similar point as he discusses the role of the school in the reproduction of class and of social stratification, and he also points out that "adversarial pedagogies are largely restricted to elite institutions" (58).

BIBLIOGRAPHY

Butler, Judith. 1990a. *Gender Trouble: Feminism and the Subversion of Identity*. New York: Routledge.

———. 1990b. Performative Acts and Gender Constitution: An Essay in Phenomenology and Feminist Theory. In *Performing Feminisms: Feminist Critical Theory and Theatre*. Ed. S. E. Case. Baltimore: Johns Hopkins University Press, pp. 270–82.

Bourdieu, Pierre. 1977. *Outline of a Theory of Practice*. Trans. R. Nice. Cambridge: Cambridge University Press.

———. 1984. *Distinction: A Social Critique of the Judgement of Taste*. Trans. R. Nice. Cambridge, Mass.: Harvard University Press.

Guillory, John. 1993. *Cultural Capital: The Problem of Literary Canon Formation*. Chicago: University of Chicago Press.

Larsen, Nella. [1929] 1992. *Passing*. In *An Intimation of Things Distant: The Collected Fiction of Nella Larsen*. Ed. C. R. Larson. New York: Doubleday.

Miller, Nancy K. 1996. *Bequest and Betrayal: Memoirs of a Parent's Death*. New York: Oxford University Press.

Panourgia, Neni. 1995. *Fragments of Death, Fables of Identity: An Athenian Anthropography*. Madison: University of Wisconsin Press.

Rapp, Rayna. 1982. Family and Class in Contemporary America: Notes toward an Understanding of Ideology. In *Rethinking the Family: Some Feminist Questions*. Ed. B. T. and M. Yalom. New York: Longman.

Rubin, Lillian B. 1994. *Families on the Fault Line: America's Working Class Speaks Out about the Family, the Economy, Race and Ethnicity*. New York: HarperPerennial.

Schneider, David M. 1968. *American Kinship: A Cultural Account*. Englewood Cliffs, N.J.: Prentice-Hall.

Stacey, Judith. 1991. *Brave New Families: Stories of Domestic Upheaval in Late Twentieth Century America*. New York: Basic.

———. 1996. *In the Name of the Family: Rethinking Family Values in the Postmodern Age*. Boston: Beacon.

Steedman, Carolyn Kay. 1987. *Landscape for a Good Woman: A Story of Two Lives*. New Brunswick, N.J.: Rutgers University Press.

Weston, Kath. 1991. *Families We Choose: Lesbians, Gays and Kinship*. New York: Columbia University Press.

———. 1998. *Long Slow Burn: Sexuality and Social Science*. New York: Routledge.

10

Be/longings

Kristin Peterson

Daisy Violet Ruth Roberts Flint lay in her casket in the same graceful way she used to adorn her chaise longue. In the state of sleep, she was intended to be seen as elegantly as her roots had constructed her. She was a proud descendant of Lord Thomas Fairfax, whose family occupied the entire northern neck of Virginia in the mid-1600s up until the Revolutionary War. The Fairfaxes, who schmoozed with the Washingtons in nearby Mt. Vernon, held slaves so that the art of respectable lounging could be practiced—a trait, no doubt, of inheritability, that Daisy, no doubt, perfected. Death became her.

Rita and I are hanging out in front of the McCallister building in San Francisco. We just finished a meeting upstairs with a local nonprofit organization and were thinking about the outcome of the day's events. I'm leaning up against the wall while Rita blows her smoke. We see someone we know pass by who's with a surly guy. We both snicker, and Rita says something really catty—not repeatable.

Rita and I have known each other for quite some time. We became close after a friend of mine was brutally murdered by the police. The very same cops beat my brother, Aaron, before they killed Jason. It took my parents a long time to convince Aaron to leave town, but their fears of him staying were warranted. Rita's son is a minister in my hometown where all this took place. Her son and grandchildren and my brother were heavy on our minds while members of the community organized to expose the brutalities. Our worries about family seem to strengthen our connection, and because of this I have a complete sense of comfort being with Rita. It's a comfort that I share with other close friends, but something I do not have with members of my family, even though their safety and health worries me more than anything or anyone else.

Just then I see a woman cross the street who is almost hit by a car. I instantly flash on my great-grandmother, Daisy, who *knew* how to handle San Francisco traffic, unlike the wimpish dodge that enabled this woman's bare escape. I ask Rita what time it is because I have to pick up Magdalena at work. I tell the ghost (Daisy) that I will talk to her later—maybe she can help me find the Fielding Hotel in what is now the Tenderloin district, where she and my grandmother lived. It was the place from which Daisy ventured out to read cards, tell fortunes, and massage the bodies of San Francisco's elite. Daisy has been rather uncooperative in this search—I've tried to find the old hotel, but not with any luck.

TWO

> When I was five years old, I remember she (grandmother or great-grandmother) became very ill and mother (Daisy) went up, and she took me with her, to take care of her mother. . . . And I can remember, she took me walking down the street, and she would walk like this (shows me)—just a little fellow . . . and she never looked to say move or anything, she just WALKED. And everybody got out of her way and that was my great-grandmother, or was it my grandmother? But she owned the world.
>
> —Joanne

These are the words of my grandmother, struggling to recall the details of her relationship to four generations. This is an extremely difficult task for her, because at the age of ninety, her memory of the past is committed to more pleasant histories, and at times, no history at all. She also is quite vain, or better, proud, as well as equally accustomed to being in control and always adored, something that all older women on this side of the family expect. As a consequence, the lack of recall sometimes results in embarrassment. Such a situation often shapes how she references the answers to my questions and certainly how she frames a verbal response to my curiosities that evolve into more inquiry.

I am inextricably linked, completely intertwined in recollections and stories such as this one. Like Marilyn Strathern (1992), who reminds me of reflection, I understand the continuity and change of familial relations from the hindsight of generations. My upbringing is marked by the reworking of history and family memories that linger from one generation to the next, much in the same way Sylvia Yanagisako (1985) understands present-day kinship relations as linked to the past. Old histories and memories are integral to family narratives and are intended for children such as me to embody a certain kind of respectable identity. On one side of the family, this identity is connected to nostalgia for long-lost imaginings of petty royal tastes, the emergence of which is about what it means to be American and white—something that was profoundly shaped in the late nineteenth to early twentieth centuries in my family history, not only by selected memories of the seventeenth century but also by the political and economic climate of different periods. Memories of kinship past may be crucial to understanding what it means to belong to a family, to history, or as John Borneman (1992) indicates, a nation. On another side of the family, the absence of memory is crucial because forgetting signifies a historical juncture when one could finally let go of "tainted" markings of immigration or native history and be entitled to a new kind of acceptance: color-coded Americaness.

So I always push my grandmother further, because I am looking for the details and the ghosts who may reveal silences, the unspoken, and forgetfulness. Like Avery Gordon (1997), who looks to ghosts to understand complex personhood, I too search for these ghosts because they not only help me to rethink history, but they function as reminders of my own family discourses of respectability and ways of being in the world. I look to them to give me other points of view, because I don't always count on my relatives to tell stories of the dead in ways that may elucidate complex family histories or subjectivities. At times they are nonpresence, they are silent, but they do not seem to be forgetful. Listening to them puts family narratives of nostalgia to rest and allows remembering/forgetting to take on other connotations. Listening to remembering/forgetting helps me find the moment when, and the reason why, it was easier to think of oneself never as poor; always as white and sometimes with aspirations.

Depending upon who is in the room, these ghosts appear and disappear with a single utterance, and sometimes in private, the lingering of a story may last for hours. But in the opening passage above, with my mother and grandfather present, I have just asked my grandmother to tell me about one of her grandparents, someone about whom I know very little. I want to understand the situations of different generations: names, various dates, occupations—the dry details that represent beginnings and give form to my inexperienced desire to talk to ghosts who only have meaning on my genealogical sketch. My grandmother is neither interested in my insistence on separating the generations into a linear comprehension, nor does she follow my need to understand a life history from beginning to end. What she gives me is not anything I ever ask for, and it appears that her answers provide much more than my questions could possibly demand. What I need to know in this response is that it does not matter which woman out of the four generations she was talking about in the above quotation. What does matter is that I understand that this woman, characteristic of the many women in the family, could walk into San Francisco traffic, put her hand up—a gesticular halt—to walk as she desired across the street, signifying that she owned the world. Indeed I am to believe this, and not be bothered by anything else. Even ghosts can be silent.

THREE

I'm gonna slap that fuckin' *pendeja* upside the head. Do you hear me? Fuck this non-violent shit. *¡Hijo de puta!* I did AIDS work at the Stanford Prison Experiment for God's sake, and what, that education doesn't count for nothing to start me out at a decent salary at a big-time service provider? *¡Pendeja!*

Magdalena is going off on the personnel woman who is making her life unhappy at the moment. We get out of the building, meet up with my friend Sarita, and the three of us walk to the bus to go home. I met Magdalena when she and Jesus were getting married—a marriage she described in a bar one night to Sarita and me, like this: she flexed her right arm and declared, "colonization!" flexed her left arm and declared, "heterosexual privilege!" then grabbed her crotch and "lifted it" to the declaration of "La Migra!" followed by a long loud grunt, indicating that her privileged status as a colonial subject of the United States and getting married were two of the better ways to tell the Immigration and Naturalization Services (INS) to "fuck off" especially after witnessing the pain and trauma that the INS causes people when forced to negotiate with its institutional complexities. Indeed both of Jesus' lovers were at the wedding in City Hall, and he was doing his best to pull off the greatest butch act of all time. My friends, Emma and Chantal, had boutonnieres wrapped for both of the guys who stood no chance of marrying Jesus so that he could dodge deportation. Magdalena's lover was there too, and anyone who needed to, was dressed to look as straight as possible.

The day before, I met my father at Mario's Italian restaurant for lunch. He got on the subject of Esme's (my roommate's) boyfriend—or rather the man standing in our living room who he assumed to be her boyfriend simply because he is male and she is female. I mistakenly opened a can of worms by indicating that she is not his "type." "Does that mean that Esme is gay, too?" (When questions like this arise, they typically include curiosity-filled anxieties. They always anticipate the hope that words or gestures will provide reassurances; and I am reminded that anxiety is not always simply anxiety). I took a long, long sip of my Chianti while mulling over some kind of clever response, as usual, in vain. But I was interrupted as Mario came to our table to deliver a flirtatious hello. In this one interaction with Mario, the entire conversation between my father and me was cued back into a comfortable heterosexual context.

At Jesus and Magdalena's wedding everyone cried, including the tourists walking through City Hall. For the moment we were complicit with heterosexuality and its institution, marriage, as they both seemingly sorted out any confusion over who belonged to which nation and to which men; and witnesses—a judge, tourists, and queers in drag—cleverly cleared up the messiness of crossing borders. Witnessing also meant that we understood and acknowledged that the performance of a particular master trope was needed in this moment for the state and the INS to confirm that this love was for real: heterosexual sex. We also knew that other performances around race and gender, around being newly American and without uncomplicated "border identities," in much the same way that Luibheid (1999) describes, were needed for later when the INS would come to visit them in their own domestic space that they would have to maintain long after the wedding. As witnesses, we soothed any essentialist and compulsive obsessions that the state, the INS, and a judge may have had about love. Magdelena and Jesus knew that love was about something far greater than the state could ever possibly imagine. But we remained silent for the sake of legitimacy, and any anxieties that day were thankfully alleviated.

Longings

Legitimacy seems to lie in the realm of extreme comfort. Love, its surveillance and its frequent meeting with institutional legitimacy, makes me really wonder about extreme comfort. As with acts of respectable longing, it seems to be forgotten that love and legitimacy have their own exclusionary histories. Many elites of past generations managed their comfort, their sense of love and legitimacy, through someone else's labor, enabling slavery and marriage (not to mention respectable longing) to simultaneously emerge as interdependent legitimate institutions. This history is forgotten, in the present among kin, even though it is talked about and reconfigured from one generation to the next, even though love must still find a sense of legitimacy whether or not it is comfortable. So generations later I tell stories of generations past. I pause when the gaps are too deep and wonder what love must be found out, beyond surveillance and legitimacy, beyond my imaginings. Unearthing stories of love and legitimacy must approach a critical point of accountability: that you can see yourself being shaped by the stories of the past and that you can find yourself in them; that you can imagine that love and legitimacy are a part of you as much as they were a part of slavery and acts of respectable longing; that you feel that you are precisely a product of this history. I am looking for a richer vocabulary to accomplish this, one that includes and transcends the boundaries of my lineage. I am looking to find a different kind of longing.

FOUR

My grandmother, Joanne, tells me that I must remember my history, not to forget that I came from a Fairfax line. And sometimes she tells me this without saying this. She talks of the house in Piedmont, occasionally of the one in Salinas, but utter silence on the tenement in Richmond. We drive by the house in Piedmont, say hello to the current residents, and recall how the stenciling and tile in the bathroom have not changed in fifty years. I have never heard her talk about Richmond. But I have heard her say—followed by a note on the Fairfaxes—that you should always live at the cheapest address in the best neighborhood.

She says, "He was the young man, a stable boy, who took care of the cattle and the horses and everything . . . and it was a romance with her [Fairfax daughter]. And when the [Fairfax] family heard about this and she was going to run off with him, they said, 'Never have we known of you and never will we know of you again.' And that was it."

I am linked to this memory, completely intertwined in recollections. In fact, my very use of "I" rarely exists in isolation. "I" simultaneously occupies "we," "they," "our" spaces, moving in and out of multiple subjectivities. I am "I" as informant, "I" as masquerade, as I choose what to remember, what to forget, and what to reveal about all of "us"—romantically, bitterly, or ambivalently. As "I" occupy multiple subjectivities, moment to moment linearity appears illusory. But this illusion seems to stabilize the ease in which one can access remembering/forgetting; memory and history are completely mobile, contended, and up-for-grabs.

With such mobility, I am always tempted to *re*tell my grandmother's stories as the generations before me have always done: Was it really the stable boy or was it the outcome of a fractured Revolutionary War that brought the downfall of the Fairfaxes and the subsequent beginnings of the ways in which future generations would come to rescue this family's memory? Both, really. Because they were upstanding royalists, the Fairfaxes were kindly asked to leave the five million acres they held in the name of the king over the last century and a half to the victors of this war. With the acquisition of land, the new Americans, that is, the enfranchised few, were drawing similar elite lines across race, class, and gender in the wake of the Fairfax departure. The remapping and retelling of this new America became embedded in the memory and utterances of future generations who compelled themselves to hold tightly to a legacy they could claim as their own.

Somehow this mythic stable boy supersedes the loss of land and wealth. He manages to catch the eye of a young Fairfax daughter, and off the two of them run to who knows where. I look for the three missing generations to provide evidence of the stable boy, to validate the meaning he has for the older generation, of which my grandmother is one of the last. If I were to guess and write my own narrative, the two young lovers ended up in the forests of Kentucky, far from the royal comforts of Virginia, the king, and his blessings. Maybe this is why the question, "What happened to the Fairfax daughter and the stable boy?" is one that has remained unanswered since I was a very young child. Venturing a guess seems to complicate the existence

of the story itself. It complicates my great-grandmother Daisy's peaceful position in death, the history of Richmond, and the reason why Piedmont is the
story that is told. I try not to ask anymore.

FIVE

Are you adopted? Are you sure?—a Bastard Nation motto. Are you white?
Are you sure?—Sarita's modification to the Bastard Nation motto.

She asks me: "Can you imagine if people got their records and found out
they're, um . . . not quite white? Hmmm . . . amended (falsified) birth certificates and miscegenation laws . . . go figure."

With the three of us on the bus, Sarita tells us of the current Bastard Nation
dynamics, a computer listserver for adults who were adopted and are seeking to implement adoption reform through the advocacy of one's right to
open records, perhaps the only adoption rights organization taking this approach. Yet opening records leaves consanguinity completely exposed and
vulnerable; and belonging both to parents and to listservers has muddled,
yet similar, confusions. Secrets are much easier, less messy. But navigating
secrets happens with too few tools in hand, as the Bastard Nation list (and
many others) tends to get antigovernment legislation mixed up with civil
rights rhetoric. Posting Ebonics jokes to the list, while at the same time declaring civil rights violations, and looking for consanguinity through the historical lens of civil rights, is apparently not a problem or seen as divisive.
Navigations and confusions also persist through heterosexual searches and
are often satisfied through single imaginings of the past and future as the
Bastard becomes a particular kind of Bastard in a particular kind of
Nation/alism. Secrets of sexuality and legacies of one-drop-of-blood-makes-
you-black rules may be blown open; kin may belong elsewhere, no longer
to parents or listservers.
   Sarita sums up the day's exchange:

So I said, "No one is going to throw coffee on you, spit on you, sic dogs on
you, lynch you, for this birth certificate thing. It's just you and a fucked-up
judge with a fucked-up attitude," and you know what? They thought I was
advocating civil disobedience! I should have just gone straight to the Fourteenth Amendment. I mean who actually argued the Fourteenth Amendment in court and won? You know who did? Southern Pacific Railroad.
Good old Mr. Stanford. (She winks wryly at Magdalena.) Wow. And two
years before *Plessy.* They argued that they were an entity comparable to
personhood, over what? Violation of property rights—all ties in with Manifest Destiny. In fact that's what Mr. Plessy tried to argue from the perspective of a black person riding on a train for God's sake and the Supreme

Court said "No, we're not violating a thing!" So the railroads have more rights than people! And apparently that's not a problem, and so apparently it won't work for us poor bastards to argue that our civil rights are being violated. . . . You know, it just occurred to me that if we argued that bastards are someone's property somewhere—that is, we're not persons, we're bastards—we might get somewhere arguing for our rights—as property.

There is always the fear that your presence in this world may not work out in the end. Belonging, not being sure, and manifested destinies affect how you fit into Americaness, how your family shifts and changes its remembering and forgetting. But still, you may not always feel quite right. What doesn't feel quite right about my inheritance of a mythic stable boy is the erasure of early Virginia history—the numerous uprisings of the poor against rich colonists, the frequent slave rebellions and the eventual liberation of tens of thousands of slaves intended to fight for the British, the complex maneuverings of the foreseeable disenfranchised, within and against elite colonials and British authority (Robinson 1997). These disenfranchised, who knew their fate, would one day in the future be caught in another matrix called Manifest Destiny. So when I cannot evade my curiosities, I continue to ask: Who was this stable boy? Did he long for and (so) belong to the Fairfax daughter, or did he belong to the Fairfax family, as most stable boys "working" for large landowners did? What details could possibly be missing? Stories of belonging and property can be very confusing; my attempts to reconstruct the fragments of oral history seem terribly out of reach, and there are times that I am not quite sure why I want to do it. Other times I feel my own sense of mortality pushing for answers, desiring to understand my situation in this history.

If an adoptee searches for birth parents, and "gets an identity" and understanding of his or her history, do the concepts of where and to whom to belong become any more reachable? When the unspeakable is finally enabled to speak, what is said of belonging?

SIX

On our last visit together, Joanne shows me a framed photocopy of the obituary of her great-grandfather, Colonel William Jennings Martin (supposedly a Fairfax descendant), born in Kentucky in the early 1800s. It says, in part:

Colonel Martin was a leading figure in all the early Indian Wars, and his name stands inscribed on the history of Oregon as one of those who helped to lay the foundations for the good government of which it boasts. In recognition of faithful services, the government allowed him a pension of $25 a month for wounds received at the battle of Lake Okachuba [*sic*], in the Seminole War, in Florida, when he was twenty-one years of age.

During that battle he was struck by four bullets and carried off the field for dead. During his last illness of three months he complained constantly of one of those wounds. He was a lifelong Southern Democrat, a man of strong convictions and a deep sense of right.

I have a copy of this obituary, as well as many others like it. They all celebrate the great heroes of the Seminole War, the shakedown of Chief Joseph, and the clearing of the Oregon Trail. These are histories that constitute a certain respectability that sit alongside the pictures and holiday mementos of my grandmother's household. Like the stable boy, they work as reconfigured narratives, meaning that they are living products, proof and assurances that one's family ended up on the respectable side of Manifest Destiny. If I am lucky, I will find other ancestors from another side of the family on the scrolls of Indian records. They are not cataloged through the birth, death, military, and marriage certificates that I seek, and their movements are barely traceable. I have few pictures, and there are no memorabilia to celebrate their existence.

My ninety-four-year-old great-aunt poured us both a shot of bourbon, and lit her second cigarette after telling me about the no-good son-of-a-bitch cousin of hers. Somehow we got on the subject of high school: "When I was a freshman, we were just treated terribly by the sophomores. . . . I have never been treated so badly in my life—girls and boys, too. . . . 'Oh you're just a freshman' (they'd say) like you just got out of kindergarten!. . . . 'You don't know anything!' Here, my god, I had worked in a confectionery and sporting goods store. I had worked in a long-distance telephone office. . . . I had. . . . (Laughs) I had danced with a movie star!

"It was Monty Bleu. MGM studio was making Told in the Hills, *and there's lots of Indians associated with it. And Monty Bleu used to come up to the long-distance office. I was only fourteen, and he would make a long-distance phone call almost every night, collect, to his wife in Hollywood. Monty Bleu played the part of the young Indian boy, and Eileen Percy was a white girl in the movie. I had to go through five exchanges: Nez Perce-Lewiston-Spokane-Seattle-Los Angeles, and then Hollywood. And this one Saturday night Eileen had gotten her call through [first], and Monty stayed on [waiting] and visited with me.*

"He asked me, 'What does a young person do in a small town like this to celebrate on Saturday nights?' (Laughs) Well, we go across over there to the theater, have a show, and then after the show, push the benches back. 'Push the benches back? What do you mean?' Well we have to push them back against the wall and then they clean it up and put talcum powder on the floor, and by that time the orchestra arrives and we dance. 'You mean you dance?' Yes. 'How long have you been dancing?' I've been dancing since I

was eight years old. Well, later he left and I locked up, and I went across the street to dance. It had already started . . . and I went over and sat down on the bench with my friend, and she gave me a nudge, 'Isn't that one of our movie stars?' And I looked over and here was Monty Bleu. He was looking over the crowd . . . you know, standing, watching. . . . The music stopped, and he came over and very formally asked, 'Miss Wann, may I have this dance?' We stepped down and we started dancing. . . . And you know I never missed a step!"

I still see these ghosts in the obituaries of other ancestors such as Colonel Martin. They make me wonder what exactly it is that counts as kinship, and what counts as respectable, speakable. I constantly go back to issues of representation and find myself wondering what it is that I am not supposed to know.

One-drop rules got hidden in a dance with a movie star, so that any ostracism from a community who had residents who could claim their fame, perhaps their only moments out of humdrumness (a method of alleviating poverty), as the heroes of occasional "official" and "clandestine" Indian raids. No one knew. (But how did it remain so well concealed? What was said of concealment?) She never missed a step.

Joanne gives me a tour of her house, one that I have visited infrequently over the last thirty years. She shows me all of her furniture, her paintings, pictures, knickknacks. Nothing is unfamiliar. All of it has a story, a history, and a deep sense of comfort for her. With each item she recalls a story, which is a productive task for her. I can see the joy it gives her to remember things, without too much difficulty. It is as if all the forgetting found some sort of mortality, as if imminent death had a need to search for memory, as if she realized that forgetfulness may not have served her as well as she wished. But nevertheless I am listening to her historicize her own experience—one from which my own subjectivity cannot escape. As the picture leads to a story of her second husband's proposal, the desk sparks remembrance of a friendship, the vase reminds her of a trip. Beyond these walls and objects, she is not entirely sure what street she lives on.

"Do you know who this is?" she asks me. "Yes, I do," I answer her. "Tell me the name again," she asks me. "It's William Jennings Martin, Joanne." "Oh yes, he is one of our great ancestors. What was . . . he led one of those . . . you know . . . across the . . ." "You mean the John Fremont expedition?" "Yes, that's it." She smiles. I see a picture of Daisy, her mother, near the Martin obituary. In the picture she is sitting on a chaise longue. I ask her to tell me about the picture. "Oh yes, that was my mother, "she says dryly. We move on to find more stories she can tell me.

Longings

Silence always gets too close to love. It's that unspeakability that so loudly circulates in families; it moves from one person to the next. Silence completely invigorates simultaneous disavowals and needs for love—and I always return to silence, never for right or wrong reasons. Silence always gets too close to love because each always reveals the other as if to cue a mirror facing me forever. That kind of vision always makes too much sense—it's a dangerous kind of sense-making, because you never know how long a mirror could sustain such imagined and unimagined images without cracking. It's not the fear of picking up the pieces after the mirror shatters, but it is the overwhelming sense of memory that causes it to break, especially memory that is tempted to recapture forgetfulness. But I do not need to be surrounded by mirrors. I can only recall very occasional blank stares coming from my grandparents, all of them, who at one time or another I caught sitting alone in the corner of a room. Clearly, they had transported themselves somewhere or reimagined the current set of relations in the house and got lost in a long moment. This look on their faces is always the same, always haunting, always completely silent. I never wonder what it is they must be thinking about because I am too busy sensing all the mirrors they must be fighting off. When those gentle eyes come back to the reality they move in and out of, I wonder if it is memory that is capable of separating silence from love—at least for long moments. Despite the blank stares in the corner of the room, and the histories that pull them away from this space, they return loving someone, and maybe that is precisely why they do return.

SEVEN

Magdalena, Sarita, and I walk into my apartment. Esme is there, and we begin to prepare a big dinner for friends coming over to visit. Just before I am expecting my friend Carl to arrive for dinner, I open up the oven door to light the gas, and as usual, I receive a visitation from my great-grandmother.

Before the turn of the century, her future husband, who had settled in the Northwest, sent a letter to her father asking to marry his eldest daughter. By the time the letter arrived, Edith was already married, so my great-grandmother, the second daughter, became the mail-order bride who married my great-grandfather, a man more than twice her age. Upon arriving in San Francisco, she passed Angel Island, where many Chinese women were incarcerated because raced-based exclusion kept them from husbands, future husbands, and perfect strangers with whom they intended to spend the rest of their lives. Ellen, however, did leave the ship; she stood on land in a long, white dress with wooden clogs, and a sign pinned to her chest, indicating where she was to be directed. She never learned to speak English, even though most of her life was spent away from her "home." I always wondered if the act of not speaking English was a result of alienation or an act of resistance, or both.

My father has a picture of his grandmother—a beautiful woman—and he romantically reminisces on her mail-order bride history. The picture and her beauty help to reconstruct memories of kinship through nostalgic representations of early American immigration stories, movement west, and fetishes of American heritage. Articulating stories of women who can actually step off a ship is when nostalgia commences in the telling of a family history. With stepping-off-the-ship nostalgia, joy may be part of some family histories, and bitterness may not be at all imagined for other histories. Nostalgia also seems to affect views on current immigration patterns to the United States, and is powerful in making clear who is entitled to legacies of Manifest Destinies, that is, who is entitled to belong to a family, to history/heritage, and to a nation. But if nostalgia allows you to feel like you belong, it equally provides a way for you to forget history. In my history and so many others, nostalgia enables you to forget that you emerged out of the woods, leaving outhouses and poverty behind with a defunct logging industry for a possible future of financial stability and success. Nostalgia lets you forget who may hate you if they knew about your shit-kickin' past. Recovering forgetfulness is not necessary. Indeed, fixations on heritage, on immigrations past and present, are much more pleasurable, easier to indulge.

One day, the oven exploded and Ellen burned to death. Every time I strike a match to light the oven, I think of her and nervously hope that my fate will not be the same. This day, the oven lights just as it always does and Ellen disappears. The doorbell rings. It's Carl.

EIGHT

Oh, and then there was the time [laughs] when Daisy married this man from England and they went on their honeymoon to London, where he was from. And then [laughs] when they come back through Canada, they won't let him through for one reason or another. And grandma [Daisy] crosses the border anyway and never sees him again [laughs more]. —An in-law

Carl comes in after a long overnight shift at a youth shelter. Magdalena, Sarita, Esme, and he hang out as I finish the final touches on homemade sangria. Carl's father recently died of cancer and had been visiting here quite a bit lately. When his father was dying, and it seems that AC Transit (for which he worked) speeded up his death sentence by denying the man his health insurance, I found myself at their house along with our friends, Emma and Chantal. Emma just went through the same with her own father and knew the drill quite well. We all have had our severe difficulties and exasperations with our blood ties, yet in times like this, something in us shifts, because responding to death doesn't seem to fly well without the presence of others—it offsets the various silences that are insisted upon, even in the afterlife. But there is no place for silence when grief and rage just take you over, and since silence is so often contained in our family units, looking to nonblood ties seems to give permission to let go of grief and rage, not through the lens of silence, but through something else that families often are unable to offer.

Carl asks me what I'm making. I ask him to try it, and then I proceed to tell everyone this story: I called my friends Manny and Nancy to see if they and their daughter, Maria (my goddaughter), wanted to come to dinner, and also to get the sangria recipe from Manny. Manny was just picked up by plain-clothes INS officials in broad daylight—not an unusual happening in the Mission District. They threw him into an unmarked car and refused to identify themselves. Because he could speak English and knew his rights, he managed not to get dumped god knows where. What "saved" him was the fact that he had his City-Hall wedding picture, and upon immediately recognizing that Nancy was white (conveying citizenship and ideas of who has rights and who doesn't; conveying ideas of who is entitled to contest clandestine state actions and who has no right to speak about such atrocities), the men who picked him up stopped the car and kicked him out. (Imaginings of marriage and whiteness seem to disrupt the agenda of state activities from time to time.) "Ho-ly shit! Get out, girl! Damn that's been happening way too much lately! Son of a bitch!" were the responses from the kitchen.

So when I called Manny, he was in good spirits, and the support from the community and friends kicked in. But before I could get the sangria recipe from him, I had to endure a quiz: So, at your party, do you want people to dance or do you want them to just hang out? Do you want them to stay up all night, or do you want them to go to bed early? Do you mind if people are loud, or do you want them to be more or less quiet, with the neighbors, and all? and on and on, and finally I got a recipe according to the answers I provided. Carl pours the sangria and dinner is almost ready.

Longings

There is something quite daring in leaving the unspeakable fixtures of gambling halls, tarot cards, and working-class whiteness behind for a free trip to London. The romance of it all! But then there was a specific kind of messiness to crossing borders once again. It was as if the border-line pointed to where and to whom you belonged, indicating exactly what you are to return to; as if you were required to walk past the line without any gesticular halts—just WALK across. It is as if this returning was completely desired—perhaps the path to the familiar is precisely what she wanted. But then again, what happened to the longing before the honeymoon even ended? What was said of love—was it even the right word? Perhaps speaking this word, "love," was completely out of reach. Maybe it could not cross borders with her, it could not soothe her. For the very utterance of "love" could reveal unfulfilled longings and suppressed tears of generations past, tears that could shatter patterns of silence for good. But silence suited her better. Love may or may not have ever been a part of the deal. She went home without him and not one tear followed her.

NINE

Daisy died six months before I was born. When she lay in her casket, one of my cousins slipped the ace of spades and a five-dollar poker chip in between her folded hands. As the congregation came forward individually to view the body, pay their respects, and say their good-byes, the crying slowly turned into suppressed laughter. Joanne was furious—this was not the history that was to be told. In front of her was a mockery of the Fairfax legacy, but poker chips and the ace of spades were a sure sign that it was beginning to waver. Trying to control the narrative of a heavily invested legacy can be haunting. It's haunting because there is the fear that a gag like this at a funeral could happen, or worse, that it was something that you never expected, and a clever public secret is suddenly made into spectacle. It's haunting, because just when you thought that silence made you feel like be/longing is real, you discover that ghosts are not always silent; neither are the living. It's haunting, because suddenly survival doesn't seem possible when things like deviance, pain, and shame are hopelessly revealed.

My sense of kinship, my reworking of it, is not unlike what the generations before me have always done. But the reworking of narratives may help to reconfigure the imagination that both sides of my family are descendants of great respectable American myths in which understandings of kinship are implicated in the realm of current political symbolism in American culture (Rapp 1987: 128). My desire is not simply to provide a critique of dominant American mythology, but to understand why it emerges, who and how it protects, and how beliefs of survival may be at stake in pursuing American dreams—how these dreams are imposed or revitalized from one generation to the next. Legacies of stable boys may still persist, but the pleasure I get from this particular legacy is that I know that there is always more to the story, more to my family, even though I may never know what it is. There are, after all, appropriate moments for silence.

TEN

Daisy came home, walked through the front door, took all her gambling money and threw it around the room, declaring that she won and put the likes of Dirty Shirt Harry under the table. The grandchildren rushed to grab it. Daisy stopped them with a very forceful reminder that it was hers—even though her son-in-law (Otis), a fellow gambler (and swindler), gave her part of that month's rent to try her luck. Joanne was not impressed. Her own husband and mother completely allied as he encouraged her to tell how she won. Daisy knew every hand, every play, every move of all the men at the surrounding tables, and she could sit up all night long and tell you about it.

This story was told to me in not at all mixed company, and I have retold it here as my imagination pictures the life of Daisy. There are certainly family members who would not approve of such disclosure, much less my reimagination of the story. The narratives of family behavioral politics are always competing. I, of course, have taken sides just as the generations before me have always done. I compete, using my own narratives, borrowing from older ones, and retelling new ones for the future, in order to show my understanding and my desire for a rearticulation of kinship; and as Pierre Bourdieu (1977) has written, I am not anything other than a specification of a collective history.

David Schneider (1968) was right to point out that kinship does not exist, certainly not as Claude Lévi-Strauss ([1949] 1969) or other structuralists imagined it, imposing upon it Western ideas of biological symbolism that naturalized its allegedly ultimate grounds. Kinship is something that is beyond the boundedness of consanguinity; although we do emerge in this world already marked by a history of kinship, we are inundated by its cartographies.

In thinking through nostalgia and history, in order to understand various cultural practices and "culture" itself, Kathleen Stewart writes:

> On one "level" there is no longer any place for *anyone* to stand and nostalgia takes on the generalized function to provide some kind (any kind) of cultural form. In positing a "once was" in relation to a "now" it creates a frame for meaning, a means for dramatizing aspects of an increasingly fluid and unnamed social life. . . . By resurrecting time and place, and a subject *in* time and place, it shatters the surface of an atemporal order and a prefab cultural landscape. To narrate is to place oneself in an event and a scene—to make an interpretive space—and to relate something to someone: to make an interpretive space that is relational and in which meanings have direct social referents. (Stewart 1988: 227)

Histories of narrative, and articulations of nostalgia found therein, have been curiously absent in most studies on kinship. But what has been overlooked is the generative force of oral history, particularly its expressive content which evokes structures of feeling, nostalgia, and modes of belonging, never in a fixed time, yet mostly in a reified place—these are the way stories situate and position us within kinship frameworks. Moreover, the intersections of those around us who do not "count" as relatives, and even the ghosts, weave a more complicated web of what may count as family. As Kath Weston (1991) points out, families are something that we may choose. *Retelling* stories, that is, the telling of ghost stories, can be a haunting experience. It is this very experience that moves beyond oral history to reveal how we are haunted or even moved by that which preceded us, by that which remains unspeakable, even if we follow necessary retreats into comfortable silences. But, within and beyond so-called bloodlines, the repetition of stories, the over-and-over-again, the gap that opens up to repeat that which remains in the realm of speakability: it is this repetition that may be more haunting than silence itself. Mostly it is the repeatability of stories about people whom I never knew or met that remains with me. For in speaking, ghosts are conjured up and something new may emerge. Silence may actually get brave and start saying something. Haunting may have its own tactics and agenda, and belonging may find new meanings.

BIBLIOGRAPHY

Borneman, John. 1992. *Belonging in the Two Berlins: Kin, State, Nation.* Cambridge: Cambridge University Press.

Bourdieu, Pierre. 1977. *Outline of a Theory of Practice.* Trans. R. Nice. Cambridge: Cambridge University Press.

Collier, Jane F., and Sylvia J. Yanagisako, eds. 1987. *Gender and Kinship: Essays toward a Unified Analysis.* Stanford, Calif.: Stanford University Press.

Gordon, Avery. 1997. *Ghostly Matters: Haunting and the Sociological Imagination.* Minneapolis: University of Minnesota Press.

Lévi-Strauss, Claude. 1969. *The Elementary Structures of Kinship.* Revised edition. Ed. R. Needham. Boston: Beacon.

Luibheid, Eithne. 1999. "Looking Like a Lesbian": The Organization of Sexual Monitoring at the United States-Mexican Border. *Journal of the History of Sexuality* 8 (3): 477–503.

Rapp, Rayna. 1987. Toward a Nuclear Freeze? The Gender Politics of Euro-American Kinship Analysis. In *Gender and Kinship: Essays toward a Unified Analysis.* Ed. J. Collier and S. Yanagisako. Stanford, Calif.: Stanford University Press, pp. 119–31.

Robinson, Cedric. 1997. *Black Movements in America.* New York: Routledge.

Schneider, David. 1968. *American Kinship: A Cultural Account.* Englewood Cliffs, N.J.: Prentice-Hall.

Stewart, Kathleen. 1988. Nostalgia—A Polemic. *Cultural Anthropology* 3 (3): 227–41.

Strathern, Marilyn. 1992. *After Nature: English Kinship in the Late Twentieth Century.* New York: Cambridge University Press.

Weston, Kath. 1991. *Families We Choose: Lesbian, Gays, Kinship.* New York: Columbia University Press.

Yanagisako, Sylvia J. 1985. *Transforming the Past: Tradition and Kinship among Japanese Americans.* Stanford, Calif.: Stanford University Press.

11

Family I Imagine

Carolyn Babula

Inevitably at Christmas, my parents and I have the same emotionally fraught discussion about the efforts I make for family members with whom I have little connection or relationship other than blood ties. Somewhere in the middle of an annual weeklong baking marathon and a similarly massive undertaking of gift wrapping, I reach a melting point and bitterly wonder aloud why I make the extraneous efforts I do. My family, the majority of whom dwell in and around New York City (about thirty individuals), are part of a very expensive and extensive gift exchange. I find myself having to be extraordinarily creative in finding affordable gifts for everyone, because I am obliged to give gifts to these people to whom I am related but really do not care about that much. There are people in my family, in fact, from whom I would just as soon disengage myself altogether. Although in recent years I have decided to make this creative process more fun for me and a mere coincidence that I give all my creations away wrapped with red and green paper and bows, it is still a harrowing process, because some members of my family do not seem to understand my financial constraints or appreciate my efforts to make up for this fact. Yet every year I bring them platters of cookies and buy or make and wrap gifts for them. This is not only because they are related to me by blood or because of the enormous guilt instilled in me by my parents, but because of the guilt I impose upon myself—the need to continue this gift exchange is so deeply ingrained. What is most frustrating, however, is the knowledge that since my time and energies are frittered away on family members to whom I have such obligations, I am unable to indulge people I care about most. The illogical nature of this situation, the fact that I can not seem to get myself out of it, and the very real emotional and financial burden have made this a most discombobulating holiday.

It becomes clear in these annual moments of rupture that "family" is a problematic category for me in many respects. This is partly because of the way in which it traditionally has been defined and normalized with regard to consanguinity, not only in my family, but in society in general. Anthropologists, too, have contributed to normalizing conceptualizations of kinship in their attempts to find means of dealing with the ways in which humans claim they belong together. More often than not, their analyses adhere closely to bloodlines, that, in my case as in others, results in many unwanted burdens and obligations.

I like to imagine instead what it would be like to have a family that includes only the people who figure prominently in my life in an affective and positive manner. Indeed, this does include certain members of my biological family and certain individuals whom I call "aunt" and "uncle" although their only relation to me is because they are my parents' close friends, neighbors, and/or fellow parishioners at their Catholic church. My godparents are included here as well, chosen because they were dear friends of my parents who were "good Catholics," and whose children I have always referred to as my cousins although there is absolutely no shared ancestry. Furthermore, there are people who have entered my life at various stages and mostly in my "formative years" who I believe are also a part of my family—the family I imagine.

Hopes of what my family might be seem to confound staid anthropological notions of kinship while they simultaneously maintain some of the most central features of traditional kinship structures. These include the use of normalized kinship terminologies as in classificatory kinship systems and an adherance to blood ties. In laying out a brief summary of anthropological kinship theory, I hope to bring to the fore issues pertaining to how I position myself in relation to my family related by blood and family that is beyond the normative domain of kinship as defined and contested in recent anthropological writings. I then detail what it is like for me to be part of my family through a narration of my Christmas experiences that will bring to light my seemingly inexplicable penchant to attend to what I perceive as my familial obligatory duties. Questions about what family is for me compared with what I imagine family should or might be are illuminated in my memories of and thoughts about the Christmas season. I propose that perhaps it is the ethnically marked extended family that is still acted out in these exchanges that explains why my experiences and my feelings about family seem to diverge from "normative" family patterns. Specifically, I want to question my persistence in maintaining relationships with people for whom I have but a modicum of care and concern, and more of a feeling of duty and obligation.

I argue that although recent developments in anthropological kinship theory suggest a paradigm for the family I imagine, in my case, it would be practically impossible to remove myself from my biological family. This would require, in essence, a rewriting of myself. The more I consider my family's history and the relationship I have with the members of my family for whom I care a great deal, I find that I am inextricably tied to my family and, therefore, emotionally incapable of letting go of my familial obligations.

A BRIEF OVERVIEW OF ANTHROPOLOGICAL KINSHIP THEORY

An article on the front page of the *New York Times* remarks on a recent dilemma faced by teachers of a private school in New York City and in many schools throughout the country. Students were assigned to create a family tree in order to make a connection with their ancestors and construct family histories. This is an assignment that has been given to elementary school students in the United States since the 1950s. Recently, however, it was creating confusion and taking an emotional toll on children who came from "nontraditional" families, such as children of international adoption, children of gay parents, children with foster parents, or children conceived through advanced reproductive technologies (Holloway 1999: A1–A51). Rather than put children in the awkward position of having to decide between their biological lineage and their "nontraditional" family, the assignment has been revised in many instances so that the children create a family tree that includes the people important to the children. Yet, children, confronted with the assignment and coming home from school with a glossy and colorful form to fill out, tend to think that there is something wrong with their family—not that something is wrong with the assignment when all the blanks cannot be filled in accordingly. While some schools promote creating a family "orchard" or a "wheel" instead of a tree, other teachers stand by the importance of traditional genealogical research and will not permit children to include even stepparents. For example, one teacher from Wisconsin states, "No matter how much they love a person, they are not a part of a child's ancestry," and he requires that the children support the information on their charts with birth and marriage certificates (A51).

This chapter provides a poignant example of how shifting definitions and understandings of kinship affect everyday life even in the most mundane of classroom activities. Clearly, technological advances and shifts in how people construct their families have altered perceptions of family at a fundamental level. While some people recognize these shifts and are flexible in their definitions of family, others maintain staid notions that harken back to an era that simply does not address the issues of the end of the twentieth century. These shifts have been duly noted in anthropological literature on kinship for the duration of the history of the discipline and take into account the shifting paradigms for what comprises a family.

For example, in *Development of the Family and Marriage in Europe* (1983), Jack Goody effectively argues that kinship structures are manipulable and subject to change at different historical moments. The import of such a theme is evident in later theoretical work in anthropology where kinship systems are described as nonstatic and mutable, as opposed to being strictly defined and unchanging over time, from one generation to the next, and so forth. Indeed, these malleable structures are taken as givens in later analyses of kinship. Although they are entangled with other institutions, these structures often defy conventional wisdom.

Clifford Geertz offers a useful analysis of kinship structures in "The Integrative Revolution" (1973) that charts out modalities of belonging. He accepts Talcott Parsons's understanding of culture as a structuration of moods, symbols, rules, and practices used in a public context that people share although they may have no other connection to each other. Such notions still have currency in discussions about nation-state formation and ethnicity. Too, they bring us back to discussions of kinship as one kind of attachment that is particularly enduring but that deviates from normalized anthropological notions of kinship rooted in consanguinity. Important here is the emerging idea that families are yet another cultural construction, but the rhetoric of the family that signifies particular kinds of attachment with particular kinds of concerns remains.

The development of Geertz's ideas is especially useful in understanding my own family. As mentioned before, my family is comprised of people who are outside of my bloodline, although I still refer to them with standardized kinship names, such as "aunt" or "cousin." Recalling Geertz, I find myself defaulting to a model of a "traditional" family for conceptualizing my imagined family. Moreover, I understand my relationship to my family through a shared history—the stories of my ancestors' arrival to this country, the hardships they endured, and the ways in which they supported each other to ensure survival. Clearly this is not a universal history or one shared outside this kin group, which supports Geertz's conception that kinship is particular in character.

David Schneider's important and influential *Critique of the Study of Kinship* (1984) examines understandings of kinship that escape a strict adherence to biological bonds. He asserts that anthropological definitions of kinship that seem only coincidentally tied to the "natural" or that seem to escape biologism have actually failed to do so in the end. He criticizes the American tradition of kinship studies, which prioritizes Western kinship categories when describing non-Western cultures; he questions the very existence of kinship as a valid category outside the West. Unfortunately, his critique is fundamentally negative. For example, while putting forth his methodology for understanding kinship relations in non-Western cultures, he provisionally accepts Ward Goodenough's postulate that the fundamental kin relationship is between mother and child—but in the end, he does not offer an alternative or solution to the questions he raises. Nevertheless, Schneider seems to have opened the door to new focuses of research for anthropologists, particularly those that investigate kinship relationships in gay/lesbian communities, that are not frequently defined by bloodlines.

Kath Weston's ethnography, *Families We Choose: Lesbians, Gays, Kinship* (1990), is another effort to revamp American kinship theory. The work obtains much of its power from anthropologists such as Goody, Geertz, and Schneider. In addition, the decades of the 1970s and 1980s contextualize and influence Weston's work and mark a particular historical moment in which the personal became political, including kinship and family formations. For Weston, kinship is not a thing to be studied so much as it is an analytical code used to approach people claiming to be part of a community with like minds and interests. Late capitalism is marked by new modes of interaction and new ways of cohabiting, affected primarily by increasing pressures of urban density, the skyrocketing prices of urban real estate, and increasing mobility. Here, the cultural becomes a new topic of contestation with the emergence of the idea of "alternative family."

Though they do raise interesting questions about new conceptions of the family that are not rooted in an insistence on or assumption of procreation, Weston's theses are in many respects not revolutionary. Indeed, the marriage relationship itself, for instance, has long been conceived of in the West as a "choice" by which one partner consents to marry another because of mutual affection and commitment. Moreover, some vignettes in Weston's work—particularly those relating to the Christmas holidays—indicate that blood ties still linger as one of the most powerful and defining characteristics of kinship. In this way, Weston risks exaggerating the potency of choice as an alternative to family blood ties, although it is clear that choice and biologism still depend on each other for meaning. I argue below in my own Christmas narratives that the power of blood ties in my conceptualization of family is extraordinary and in many ways outweighs my ability to choose who is and who is not a part of my family. Regardless of how much I do not want to include certain blood relatives in my kinship network, they somehow still manage to occupy a very significant portion of the people I consider to be family.

One might extrapolate from both Weston's ethnography and the work of John Borneman (in this volume) that kinship structure is fundamentally "normative care." This can be conceived of as a set of rules that determine to whom a person has inalienable rights and duties. In their respective ethnographic investigations, however, they enlarge the domain of kinship beyond the inalienable duties of care for those to whom one is blood-related to those significant individuals in one's life who are not so related. If we accept kinship as a set of rules that define duties to others, it seems counterintuitive to want to take on more duties and responsibilities for persons outside of bloodline in addition to the obligations that one might already have to one's biological family. This would simply result in enlarging the kin group to include persons not related by blood or not part of the normatively defined family structure. In any event, such was my initial reaction—and it reveals my conflict with my own family, that I may or may not have in common with the general populace. Indeed, I agree with Weston and Borneman: it is quite possible for one to expand one's kinship group to include only those for whom one cares and eliminate those for whom there is no affect or love, including, and perhaps especially, those in one's biological family. For me, however, this is beyond the realm of possibility and exists only in the imaginary.

Notions of care are particularly crucial to Borneman's theorization of recently reconceptualized and legalized kinship relations, particularly for gays/lesbians. Yet, his understanding of care indicates a far more sentimental and nurturing relationship than one that would consist primarily of rights and duties. I find this concept of care especially appealing when imagining who would comprise my ideal family, free of unnecessary tensions and unkind people, and obligations and duties that inspire nothing in the way of negative affect. Furthermore, "care" becomes particularly seductive as the fundamental component of familial relations when it is extended to romantic relationships. Here, it seems obvious (to this modern American) that emotion and affect should be the preeminent bond between two people proposing to make a lifelong commitment—as opposed to inalienable obligations—as they should for any sort of emotionally committed relationship, kinship or otherwise.

Micaela di Leonardo's ethnography *The Varieties of Ethnic Experience: Kinship, Class, and Gender among California Italian-Americans* (1984) analyzes kinship studies as they relate to ethnic identity and construction in American communities. She pays particular attention to women's work (child care, housework, cooking, and so forth) and to the seminal role of women in what she calls the "work of kinship." Here, the maintenance of family relations, care of the elderly, and the organizing of family gatherings are the responsibility and the "field of expertise" for women. Such responsibilities are most apparent during the holidays, especially Christmas, where women are expected to write Christmas cards, cook the holiday meal, bake traditional cookies, shop for gifts, and invite and prepare for guests. For di Leonardo, "holidays, besides serving as material and symbolic markers of family conflict and consensus, serve for women as foci of kinship power—*or as a series of unwanted obligations*" (1984: 218; emphasis mine). The narratives that di Leonardo includes in her monograph are eerily analogous to my experiences with my Polish/Italian/Irish family at Christmas, during which women figure prominently as officiants in the organization of family gatherings. It is clear to me that however unique my own experiences seem, the similarities between them and those told in di Leonardo's work cannot be merely coincidental. I support di Leonardo's claim that the rationale for many seemingly commonsensical actions and notions of proper behavior are rooted in a shared European Catholic immigrant ancestry—a mélange of ethnic groups, kinship groups, and religious ideologies. Following are some anecdotes that I hope will illuminate the conflicts of thinking of family and kinship in ways that deviate from traditional anthropological kinship theory. I expect at the very least that they will illustrate the ways in which my family's religious, cultural, and physically and cognitively peripatetic history profoundly affects how I perceive my relation to them.

TALES OF CHRISTMAS PAST

Long Island

Adherence to traditional notions of family can make for some rather bizarre relationships and make people (like me) engage in irrational activities, all in the name of respect and maintenance of the bloodline. I was raised in a devout Catholic family and have been informally educated about the lives of my ancestors and indoctrinated into family traditions that have been handed down for generations. Christmas has always been a big family-gathering holiday, particularly on my mother's side of the family, which is comprised of Irish Catholics and Italian Catholics interspersed with non-practicing Jewish men (who frequently dressed as Santa on Christmas Day). My maternal grandmother was acutely agoraphobic, only leaving the house for special occasions and only if accompanied by my grandfather. Her fear was so severe that she could not even step out on her front stoop without getting dizzy with panic and falling (which she once did, breaking several ribs and her arm). In order to enjoy the holidays and spend time with her sisters and nieces and nephews whom she otherwise would not see, she usually hosted the whole extended family in their tenement apartment in Brooklyn and later in their house in Queens. As my grandmother aged and was no longer able to prepare the house and the food, my mother took over and prepared two houses for the holidays—my house for the traditional Polish Christmas Eve festivities (Vigilia) for my father's side of the family, and my grandmother's house (that was just around the corner from mine) for an Italian feast on Christmas day.

My mother's cooking skills, which she learned from her Irish mother, who in turn learned hers from her non-English-speaking Italian mother-in-law, are renowned throughout the family. Christmas became a culinary treat—fresh antipasto, big vats of homemade sauce, lasagna, ziti, manicotti, ravioli, meatballs, sausage, crusty semolina bread, and so on. She also made an impression with her many varieties of elaborately decorated and decadent cookies. As I grew older, my responsibilities increased in order to take pressure off of my mother—in part, the inheritance of the cookie-baking marathon.

My grandmother's health steadily declined, starting in 1986 when she began to suffer from dementia. She was so weak that she had to have a portable commode next to her bed. Her bed was located in the dining room because she could not walk to the bathroom a mere fifteen feet away. My grandfather, who still had tenacious control of his faculties, became more and more uncomfortable at having to shoo twenty relatives into the adjoining living room on Christmas day every year. Nevertheless, my grandmother was still in full view of her guests as she maneuvered to the commode in the middle of opening gifts or having dessert—as luck would have it, there always seemed to be a toilet-related emergency at the most inopportune times. There were many occasions, in fact, when my mother had to change my grandmother's soiled bed linens in the middle of the festivities as well. After ten years of attempting to continue the Christmas tradition, my mother finally had to tell my aunt, who is the self-appointed matriarch of the family and my mother's first cousin, that the tradition would have to end in order to alleviate my grandfather's embarrassment and anxiety. That year, my aunt held Christmas at her house, instead. My parents and I were unable to attend, having to care for my grandmother because her full-time caretaker had the holiday off.

There were other Christmases that my parents and I sat by ourselves caring for my grandmother, the most memorable and most dreadful being the year my grandfather passed away less than a month before Christmas. That year, my mother called my aunt and invited her and the rest of the family to my grandmother's house, being that my grandfather was not present to be uncomfortable. In this way, she hoped to resume or at least partake in the family's Christmas tradition. Moreover, she hoped we might avoid sitting by ourselves next to my grandmother's hospital bed in her dining room. I should say that the death of my grandfather was a huge blow to my mother, as she, too, is an only child and wanted to be around family—particularly this aunt, whom she grew up calling "sister." Nevertheless, my aunt flatly declined the invitation, saying that she would prefer to celebrate the holiday with "her family" in her home.

Another year passed, and again my parents were responsible for my grandmother's care. I had finally obtained my driver's license by that time and drove to Long Island by myself to represent our part of the family and bring a platter of cookies and their gifts. At some point in the evening, my aunt approached me in the kitchen and told me what a selfish woman my mother was because she ruined the family's time-honored Christmas tradition by not having it at my grandmother's house two years before. I was flabbergasted and could do little but stare at her and cry. I eventually escaped to the bathroom to rinse my red face and eyes so that I would not be conspicuously upset during dinner.

At the risk of being unkind, I must say that my aunt is not a talented cook. In an apparent attempt to re-create my mother's traditional feast, she served Ragu meat sauce over ziti, iceberg lettuce salad, and flavorless sandwich rolls. In fact, there is usually very little for me to eat, anyway, because I am vegetarian. Everything served has meat, including the salad, into which chunks of greasy salami are usually tossed. My younger cousins, being too young to remember the history of my grandmother's/mother's Christmas preparations, made a brownie mix and baked the kind of chocolate chip cookies that come as preprepared dough in a tube. As I stood in the kitchen that Christmas, still trying to recover after my aunt's harangue against my mother, I watched as the family dove into the brownies and chocolate chip cookies, leaving my platter of meticulously decorated confections untouched. For me, this was the seminal moment where I could no longer justify the efforts I made for Christmas for these people, who clearly had no appreciation for what my parents and I were going through, and no appreciation for our efforts to maintain the tradition throughout the years that my grandmother was so ill. To be sure, we still go out to my aunt's house to eat her attempt at a Christmas meal, and I still stand silently by as they ignore my cookie platter that I continue to arrange.

My aunt (or actually, Mrs. Claus-for-the-day, because she wears a red fuzzy hat topped with a white pom-pom) occupies herself for the whole year buying Christmas gifts. Indeed, it is a huge disappointment to her if her children can manage to fit their presents in their respective sports utility vehicles. If they have to leave some packages at my aunt's house, at least she is assured that they will be by soon for another visit to collect the remaining gifts. This is why we are not "allowed" to pick out a name from a hat and purchase only one family member a gift per year, as is the custom for many large families I know. It would simply ruin my aunt's holiday if she were not able to spend literally thousands of dollars at the local shopping mall to buy, for example, Winnie the Pooh shirts and other Disney paraphernalia for both her two thirty-something children and her spoiled and unappreciative grandchildren.

In truth, my parents and I have become somewhat marginalized, known as the "city folk" who travel to the "country" for the day, and sit and watch wide-eyed while a gluttonous gift exchange takes place of which we are really not a part. This is partially due to the fact that I have grown out of the "cute" stage. My cousins are all either fifteen years older than I, or fifteen to twenty years younger. They think me strange for still being in school (since few have gone beyond high school) and are incredulous that I left New York for college, thereby "deserting" my family. Moreover, if they do remember that I study anthropology, they are convinced, no matter how many times I tell them otherwise, that I am bound for Egypt to dig up pharaohs' tombs or some other equally exotic Indiana Jones-esque archaeological adventure. So, they typically ask the perfunctory questions regarding what I have excavated recently, and I ask about their children's sports teams, and soon our polite obligatory exchange is over. Thus, although surrounded by family in the middle of my aunt's living room, my parents and I still sit alone, making it seem remarkably and uncomfortably similar to the years that we sat alone in my grandmother's house on Christmas day. Regardless, it would be simply unthinkable not to continue to participate, however superficially, in these holiday festivities.

Poland

Indubitably and somewhat inexplicably, I have a powerful sense of connection with people who share with me a particular ancestry. In 1991, while living and going to school in France, I was advised most vociferously by my parents, grandparents, aunts, uncles, and cousins from both sides of the family (and even my aunt from Long Island) that I should not spend the holiday "alone," or in other words, "without family," although this meant leaving my roommate literally "alone" in Paris for several weeks. Nevertheless, I decided to go to Poland to a small town south of Krakow to visit my father's side of the family before backpacking for a month in Eastern Europe. There, I would partake of the traditional Vigilia meal for Christmas Eve, see the village where my paternal grandparents grew up, visit with my grandfather's brother on his apple orchard, and visit my grandmother's stepsister, who lives on a farm with a few chickens and pigs and a dog. I would also visit a cemetery brimming with ancestors I never knew I had and the neighboring church in which all these relatives were baptized and married and where they were buried.

Thus, I traveled twenty-seven hours by train to visit my family for Christmas. By all standards, they were perfect strangers. When I disembarked the train it took a long time for my blond-haired, blue-eyed, pale-skinned relatives to realize that I, an olive-skinned brunette with brown eyes, was indeed their kin. I was greeted like a prodigal child, complete with tears of joy and embraces that knocked the wind out of me. Not being able to speak much Polish aside from some pleasantries and necessary requests, I basically communicated through my thirteen-year-old cousin who was learning English in school, and through a fair amount of ad hoc sign language.

My Polish aunts in New Jersey were beside themselves with delight as well because someone from my generation had made the harrowing trek "home." They telephoned Poland every day as if in disbelief that I was really there. I suspect that they also wanted to make sure that I was not too much of a burden—financially or otherwise—on their favorite nephew, with whom I was staying. These same aunts also warned my Polish relatives ahead of time that I did not eat meat. Such inroads were deemed necessary because my Polish relatives apparently needed time to process the idea. They were, in fact, completely horrified that I did not eat meat. For them, it was criminal for a "rich American" not to eat meat. Indeed, they thought that my aunts were lying when they explained the situation and assumed that because my aunts knew about their precarious financial situation I was told not to eat meat so that they would not go out of their way to slaughter one of their pigs to feed me.

Vigilia, the Polish Christmas Eve meal, is traditionally a meatless meal as a religious observance, which makes it one of my favorite family traditions. This is one holiday where I have no eating inhibitions and can therefore participate fully. My Polish grandmother had wistfully regaled me with stories of her

Vigilia meals in Poland as a little girl, where her stepmother and father would lay straw on the living room floor to make their home like a manger for the Christ child, and of the feast that consisted of upwards of seven courses. It seemed to me that the holiday was taken very seriously indeed and would be a great experience to compare with the Americanized version of the same event. My cousins and I spent at least two days cooking for the meal, although preparations had been under way for this meal well before I had arrived in the country. After all this preparation and anticipation on my part, the whole meal took about twenty minutes to eat. All of the courses were consumed in silence, and the group only became animated after the dessert dishes were cleared from the table, a bottle of vodka was introduced, and we turned on the television to watch dubbed versions of "Dynasty" and "Gone With the Wind."

The visit to my grandmother's stepsister on Christmas Day was one of the more bizarre events of the trip. The stepmother of Cinderella fame might very well have been modeled on my grandmother's own stepmother. It was for this reason that at the age of sixteen my grandmother left her family behind in Poland and came to the United States. Because of the guilt my grandmother apparently feels for leaving her stepsister with the responsibility of caring for their father and her stepmother in their final years, my grandmother now dotes upon this stepsister with care packages from America. Otherwise, she has no relationship with her stepsister other than a self-imposed moral obligation. My grandmother made a pointed plea that I visit this woman on Christmas day while visiting her brother-in-law and his family who live less than five minutes away from the stepsister on a neighboring farm. The visit was short and awkward. The relatives with whom I was visiting wanted nothing to do with the aunt who seemed a little dotty. (Who wouldn't lack certain social graces if they lived alone on a farm in the middle of Poland with no one to talk to except some pigs and chickens and a mangy dog?) She excitedly greeted us with lard-shortened cookies of which she was clearly quite proud. We had little to say since my chauffeurs were not keen on translating for me. Nevertheless, my grandmother was thrilled that I had made the effort, and her stepsister was ecstatic to have the only company she would have on Christmas day.

All in all, I spent ten very long days in my uncle's home, or rather his kitchen, going from one meal to another, as eating was the focus of every day's activities. Interestingly enough, it became for me the melding of two Christmas traditions. My uncle indicated that when he visited the United States when I was an infant, my mother had made spaghetti and meatballs and wondered if I could make that for dinner one night. I agreed to make the spaghetti, but declined on making the meatballs. After scouring the closest village for the ingredients in a recently democratized Poland and spending $13—which my relatives considered to be a fortune for just one meal—I spent the day producing a large pot of my mother's pasta sauce and garlic bread, and had found the perfect opportunity to introduce the Beaujolais that I had smuggled into Poland from Paris. There were fifteen for dinner that night, whom I was instructed to teach how to eat spaghetti by twirling it on a fork. It seemed to me that the guests, aside from my uncle and his immediate family, were relatively unimpressed with the novelty of this meal, which did not even have meat . . . the essential part of any substantive meal. Rather, they were astounded, perhaps even appalled, that I had made so much.

When planning my itinerary, I had made further plans to travel north to Warsaw from my relative's village to visit one of the women who had cared for my mother's mother for several of the years that she was ill. She had since returned to Poland to resume her career as an ophthalmologist. Lest I travel alone, my uncle insisted upon taking the train with me to make sure that I arrived safely. This seemed unnecessary, but I could not argue. He explained that if something were to happen to me, he would be responsible, and my Polish aunts who had helped to facilitate my journey and, of course, my parents would never forgive him. In retrospect, however, I would have had a much better memory of that Christmas with this part of the family had he not accompanied me on the trip.

Arriving in Warsaw and en route to my hotel, my uncle stopped at every magazine kiosk we passed in order to browse through the pornography, purchased a liter-sized beer on the street, which he drank out of a paper bag, and gawked at women passing by. He then revealed to me in broken English that he kept a mistress, intended to spend his night in Warsaw with a prostitute, and could not stand being home with his wife and children. He found his wife unattractive because she had aged and gained weight, and thought little of his daughter's appearance because she was not svelte, either. This man—who had been touted as a wonderful and kind family man, and was the pride and joy of the family because he had attended the University of Krakow and earned a degree in engineering—was really just a balding overweight lecher whom my aunts in the States showered with gifts and money because they felt guilty for their comparatively wild financial success in America. Regardless of his prestigious degree, my uncle was never employed as an engineer, but worked instead as a taxi driver. Of course, this afforded him the opportunity to keep odd hours, which in turn accommodated his extramarital affair.

After being silent for several years thereafter and listening to my father and my aunts praise this uncle for his hard work and dedication to his family and for his generosity in hosting me, I finally told my father the truth about his so-called wonderful cousin's exploits in Poland. This happened not coincidentally with the immanent arrival of his daughter to the United States. It was anticipated that I take his daughter under my wing in America to reciprocate his having hosted me in Poland. I met her at the airport with flowers to welcome her to America. Her first comment to me in the terminal was that New York was disgusting because of all the "brown, red, yellow, and black people" around us. I have neither seen nor been in contact with her since. Fortunately for me, it was arranged that she stay with her aunt, who cleaned houses in the New York area. She turned out to be an enormous burden on that family, refusing to work or help in the house. When she did accompany her aunt to work and begrudgingly cleaned a room or two, she expected and, in fact, demanded, half her aunt's wages even though she otherwise contributed nothing to the household.

In recounting the story about my ungrateful and selfish cousin, I am surprised that the quasi-sordid details of her stay in the United States managed to trickle down to me through my aforementioned great-aunts. It seems clear that my Polish relatives in New Jersey and the woman who hosted my cousin were operating under the code of obligatory behavior and inalienable duties that are unspoken but quite recognizable among many members of my family, both maternal and paternal. In retrospect, I took advantage of my Polish relative's obligation to me, although at the time it was discussed as a sacrifice I was making to pay tribute to my family heritage. The rhetoric altered slightly after my trip was complete and acknowledged the efforts and generosity of my uncle. However, after my cousin's disappointing stay in America, about which no one was happy or satisfied (including the girl herself), the duty and obligation-laden aspects of the relationships were brought to light. Talk revolved around responsibilities and appropriate and inappropriate expectations of her, of her father, and of the aunt with whom she had stayed. Although I would be surprised to discover that there is but the most minimal affection between these relatives with whom she was so close while they still lived in Poland, the bitterness regarding their obligation to each other cannot be denied.

These family members, who were strangers although related by blood, and who had taken me into their home precisely on that obligatory basis, turned out to be as objectionable as my aunt and the rest of my maternal family from Long Island. Indeed, my paternal family became another source of duties that I do not want and feel little inducement to oblige, but I still feel the need to include them as part of my family.

IN SPITE OF IT ALL

Perhaps the most illogical conclusion to these Christmas vignettes is that regardless of how much I dislike many of the people in my family or how they have hurt or disappointed me in the past, they still comprise the vast majority of those individuals whom I consider to be family and are in fact the central figures. I know that their "privileged" position in terms of kinship relations has little or nothing to do with "care" and more to do with duty and obligation. As mentioned before, there are members of my blood family for whom I care very much, but they are few and far between, and sprinkled sporadically through generations on both sides of my family. Interestingly, the people for whom I care the most and who are most important in my life are marginalized on what would be my "family tree," or kinship chart. They have no clear connection to me other than through experiences that cannot be formally indicated on a standard anthropological kinship chart. Indeed, they would need thorough verbal explanation for why they are included in the utopian family I imagine. In sum, the family I imagine does not include the people I do not care for, most especially when the relationship is obligatory and absent of an affective kind of care. Thus, I find it difficult to come up with a plausible explanation for why, after being so clearly alienated by my family, I still participate so readily in these family-oriented activities.

The one thread that runs through my narratives is a harking back to my ethnically marked heritage, Catholic upbringing, and primary socialization. With this in mind, I realize that I am not the only person in my family who feels obligated to maintain familial relationships, either in my own generation or those that came before. To be honest, I am not certain that those other family members share my disdain for the maintenance of what are, for me, loveless relationships. Perhaps for them, the relationships are emotionally fulfilling. It is simply inappropriate for me to ask such questions, because they would be too revealing of my own feelings on the subject and would surely subject me to greater alienation. It seems that I have a desire to want a family or I want to need a family, conflated with ideas of being independent. Upon further reflection, this is in keeping with my ancestor's own life experiences.

My Polish grandmother, for example, had a fairy-tale-like wicked stepmother who favored her own children over the offspring of her husband and his deceased first wife—my grandmother's biological mother. The stepmother would not give my grandmother and her younger brother and sister as much food as her biological daughters and was cruel in general. As a result, my grandmother spent a great deal of time with the family on the neighboring farm, where she would play with the children, be fed properly, and be told stories by the farmwife such as the account of the grandeur and tragedy of the *Titanic*. I would argue that my grandmother regarded this family as her own because she and her biological siblings were so alienated by her own family.

When she turned sixteen years of age, she asked permission from her father to accompany yet another neighbor to Gdansk, where she could board a ship to America. He reluctantly conceded, knowing that she would have more opportunities in the United States than in Poland. She was actually born in the United States, but when her mother died, her father returned to Poland in order to find a wife to care for his children. Thus, her U.S. citizenship made her proposition much more reasonable.

When she arrived in New Jersey, she lived with some of her cousins. Eventually, she was well enough established and self-sufficient to send for the daughters of the farm neighbors—to come to stay with her. Soon thereafter, their brother came as well. This man soon became her husband and was my grandfather; his sisters were the same aunts who helped make possible my journey to Poland.

Understanding the history of my grandmother's childhood and relationship with her family clarifies why my grandmother's sense of obligation to her stepsister is so odd. They spent their youths together under the same roof and ostensibly in the same family, yet were estranged from each other because they had different biological mothers. My grandmother's stepsisters were privileged in the family because their mother was still alive. Because they alienated my grandmother, she left for America. Yet, years later, my grandmother somehow feels guilty about how much better her life turned out to be in contrast with her remaining stepsibling and feels the need to compensate for her comparatively unhappy life in Poland. Perhaps my grandmother's precedent helps to explain my own nonsensical sense of duty to maintain superficial relationships with family members. However, this is not the only prelude to my own illogical behavior.

My maternal grandmother's mother, an Irish immigrant, was hit by a taxi in New York City and died from internal injuries when my grandmother, the middle child of five, was only about nine years old. She and her sisters spent a good deal of their childhood in an orphanage run by nuns in Brooklyn while her brother was sent to live with an uncle in upstate New York, where his progeny still live today. As a result, my grandmother became instant caretaker of two younger siblings at an extremely young age.

My maternal grandfather was a muscle-bound amateur boxer, who was born in what is now called Soho in Manhattan. His Italian immigrant father died when my grandfather was eleven months old, leaving his non-English-speaking wife with two sons. She quickly remarried another Italian man who owned a cork factory in Brooklyn. Although my grandfather was accepted to Stuyvesant High School—a prestigious and competitive science-oriented public school in Manhattan—he was told by his stepfather that he could only attend provided he still worked at the factory forty hours per week. Seeing the impossibility of this situation, my grandfather spent his adolescence and, in fact, the rest of his life—until he retired at the age of seventy-four—in factories while he watched his stepbrother go to medical school and his stepsister go to college and vacation in Paris with her college friends.

Thus, my maternal grandparents, like my paternal grandparents, were no strangers to traumatic childhood experiences and familial obligations that called for immense self-sacrifice. The stories of their dedication to their families, especially in times of hardship, were impressed upon me in my youth perhaps more than I ever realized. More than this, however, is the importance of family in their lives and how dramatically it affected their own lives, often in spite of their own personal desires. Maintaining familial bonds and fulfilling familial obligations were never questioned but rather were always presumed, in their generation as in my own. My parents, too, have made enormous sacrifices for their families despite their own wants and their own happiness. No doubt they imagined that their families were different and that they were not as alienated from them as they were. If they did, their actions as reported to me indicate nothing of what I consider to be a selfish desire to free myself of my own "inalienable duties" to people in my biological family.

Disassociating myself from the people who make up my biological family is absolutely incomprehensible on a practical level, despite the theoretical possibilities proposed by anthropologists in the last twenty years. I believe that my experiences and my relationship with my family point to the limits of kinship constructivism, and the inextricability of the self and one's kin group. I think the specifics (ethnically or idiosyncratically) of my family history and the narratives shared in this essay are not as important as the shared history of ancestral struggle and survival by bonding together in hard times. This shared history provides an arena for a certain kind of familial tradition of gratitude that has defined my family's culture and that made and makes me the person I am. In attempting to turn my back on this history and create a new narrative based on my utopian imaginings I would in effect have to rewrite myself and my place in the world. I believe that I can say this without being overly dramatic precisely because of the inexplicable sense of belonging and/or obligation I have toward these individuals who make up my family despite the lack of genuine (positive) affect that I have for them. As a result, I foresee myself continuing to bake cookies at Christmas for family members who would rather eat Betty Crocker's cookies and continuing to nod in agreement as my Polish aunts praise my lascivious uncle in Poland. I will also continue to imagine wistfully what it must be like to have a family comprised only of the people for whom I care and who care for and respect me in return.

BIBLIOGRAPHY

di Leonardo, Micaela. 1984. *The Varieties of Ethnic Experience: Kinship, Class, and Gender among California Italian-Americans.* Ithaca, N.Y.: Cornell University Press.

Geertz, Clifford. 1973. "The Integrative Revolution: Primordial Sentiments and Civil Politics in the New States." In *The Interpretation of Cultures.* New York: Basic, pp. 255–310.

Goody, Jack. 1983. *The Development of the Family and Marriage in Europe.* Cambridge: Cambridge University Press.

Holloway, Lynette. 1999. In Schools, Family Tree Bends with Times. *New York Times* (Feb. 2): A1–A51.

Schneider, David. 1984. *A Critique of the Study of Kinship.* Ann Arbor: University of Michigan Press.

Weston, Kath. 1990. *Families We Choose: Lesbians, Gays, Kinship.* New York: Columbia University Press.

Index

About the Contributors

Carolyn Babula is a doctoral candidate at Rice University in the Department of Anthropology. She is currently conducting her field research in New York City on vintage clothing, public and private collections of clothing, and seasonal collections of clothing, as tangible invocations of the past at the end of the millennium.

Jamila Bargach teaches anthropology and social science at the National School of Architecture in Rabat, Morocco. She is the author of *Nothing above Family* (2001).

John Borneman, professor of anthropology at Princeton University, received his Ph.D. in 1989 from Harvard University, and he has done fieldwork in Germany, Central Europe, and Lebanon. His current research focuses on the symbolic forms of political identification and authority, and on issues of accountability, justice, and violence. From 1991 to 2001 he taught at Cornell University, and he has been guest professor at the University of California, Berkeley, Stockholm University (Sweden), Bergen University (Norway), and Senior Fulbright Professor at Humboldt Universitaet zu Berlin (Germany). He has written widely on issues of kinship, sexuality, nationality, justice, and political form. His publications include *Belonging in the Two Berlins: Kin, State, Nation* (1992), *Settling Accounts: Violence, Justice, and Accountability in Postsocialist States* (1997), and *Subversions of International Order: Studies in the Political Anthropology of Culture* (1998).

Stanford W. Carpenter is a doctoral candidate in the Department of Anthropology at Rice University. He is currently working on a dissertation examining the personal experiences and the source materials of comic creators that affect the representation of race, gender, and ethnicity in comic books. Carpenter is a researcher at the Friends Research Institute and an associate at the Smithsonian Institution Center for Folklife and Cultural Heritage

Nityanand Deckha received his Ph.D. in Anthropology from Rice University in 2000. His current writing focuses on contemporary urban life and space, including "Repackaging London: Spatial Politics in the Global City," based on his doctoral dissertation. Most recently, he has worked as a professional anthropologist in advertising in New York.

James D. Faubion is associate professor of anthropology at Rice University. He is the author of *Modern Greek Lessons: A Primer in Historical Constructivism* (1993) and of the forthcoming *Shadows and Lights of Waco: Millennialism Today*. His edited volumes include *Rethinking the Subject: An Anthology of Contemporary European Social Thought* (1995), *Essential Works of Michel Foucault, Volume 2: Aesthetics, Method, Epistemology* (1998), and *Essential Works of Michel Foucault, Volume 3: Power* (2000).

Laurel George is a doctoral candidate in anthropology at Rice University. Her research addresses the patterning of the funding of contemporary U.S. choreography, a topic on which she published in the volume *Corporate Futures* (1998) and in the journal *Terrain* (1999).

Lamia Karim is a graduate student in anthropology at Rice University. Her research interests include women in South Asia, immigration, anthropology of NGOs and development, and the study of alternative political processes in a globalized world order.

Susan Ossman is the author of *Picturing Casablanca, Portraits of Power in a Modern City* (1994) and *Three Faces of Beauty: Casablanca, Paris, Cairo* (2001), and editor of *Miroirs Maghrébins, Itinéraires de soi et paysages de rencontre* (1998). She teaches at the American University of Paris.

Kristin Peterson is a doctoral candidate in the Department of Anthropology at Rice University. She is currently conducting dissertation research on global trade, biotechnology, and access to essential medicines in Africa.

Deepa S. Reddy graduated from the Department of Anthropology at Rice University with a thesis on Hindu ethnicism and women's activism in India. She teaches anthropology at the University of Houston, Clear Lake.

Denise Youngblood is a doctoral candidate in anthropology at Rice University. A native of Trinidad, Youngblood is a former consultant on culture and multiculturalism to the government of Canada, and to several NGOs on international policy analysis and global education. She also functioned as an intercultural specialist for corporations such as Prudential International. In recent years, she moved from the position of managing editor for a strategic intelligence Internet publishing company, CountryWatch.com, to become vice president of research and development.